Frampton could be described as a storyteller. H‹ the profession of architecture to bring work aliv simultaneously aware of the intellectual–philoso and its physical realities. By employing his deep u1 of designing and crafting buildings, Frampton peel ing to reveal its meaning, to understand its relevai ... ...ιραct. He inhabits the world between thinking and doing, observing what is being done, capturing with incisive clarity the inner workings of projects, charting their equally possible outcomes. Just in case we might forget in this busy, digital world, Frampton reminds us that people's experience of architecture is of highest cultural importance.

YVONNE FARRELL AND SHELLY MCNAMARA, Grafton Architects, Dublin

Well-argued, well-grounded, well-written these texts based on architectural practice, critique and history reach beyond the particular discipline of architecture and the built environment. They touch all design professions that strive to make artifacts compatible with daily life practice in a fragile environment. Design having become increasingly vaporous in recent years, needs a (re-)linking to the social-political domain confronting the "conflict between power and reason".

GUI BONSIEPE, author of *The Disobedience of Design*

To those who have read him, and even to those who have not, the name Kenneth Frampton suggests an intellectual and ethical beacon in architecture. And like a beacon, Frampton has continued to cast light on some of the enduring and critical topics of our times. Perhaps similar to Rilke's letters to the young poet, Frampton's writings have alerted generations of architects, young and not so young, across the world, to abide by the cultural ethic of architecture, and compelled them to contemplate on what they *do*.

KAZI KHALEED ASHRAF, architect, architectural critic, director of the Bengal Institute

Architecture and the Public World

RADICAL THINKERS IN DESIGN

Not the least of the sins of the obsession with the "research" in the contemporary university is that it unreflectively privileges the appearance of the new. Failing to see the extent to which its own thinking is thereby hobbled and limited, understanding turns in even narrower circles of concern. Design is not immune to this condition. Expansion in practice and the global increase in numbers of those with design education or who study design has not necessarily brought with it increased understanding of design. On the contrary, despite real attempts to counter these impulses, reduced to the crudest understanding of vocation, depth of thought disappears, crises remain untouched, genuinely new practices and conceptions struggle to be comprehended.

Radical Thinkers in Design, a moment of the wider project *Designing in Dark Times* seeks in a small way to try to address this situation. The project is to bring back into circulation, as provocations and aids to thinking, some key texts in contemporary thinking on designing.

As acting in the world descends ever deeper towards instrumentalism these books offer a counter view. In what they open towards, what they explore and present, above all in what they *anticipate*, they point to the concrete possibilities, as well as to the necessity, of paradigm-shifts in our conceptions of what designing today can and should be. They offer approaches, concepts, modes of thinking and models of practice that can help not only in thinking how design can be re-thought and re-positioned in its internal momentum, but how it offers an integral mode and capacity of acting in the world. By showing how, at base, designing contains irreplaceable critical and affirmative moments, they point us towards ways of reversing some of the negative and destructive tendencies threatening to engulf the world.

Wild Things: The Material Culture of Everyday Life, by Judy Attfield
Defuturing: A New Design Philosophy, by Tony Fry
Designing Designing, by John Chris Jones
Design Noir: The Secret Life of Electronic Objects, by Anthony Dunne and Fiona Raby
The Disobedience of Design, by Gui Bonsiepe
Architecture and the Public World, by Kenneth Frampton

Clive Dilnot
Eduardo Staszowski

Architecture and the Public World

Kenneth Frampton

Edited by Miodrag Mitrašinović

For Ivan
yet another book
Best Wishes
Kenneth
21/c/24
London.

BLOOMSBURY VISUAL ARTS
LONDON · NEW YORK · OXFORD · NEW DELHI · SYDNEY

BLOOMSBURY VISUAL ARTS
Bloomsbury Publishing Plc
50 Bedford Square, London, WC1B 3DP, UK
1385 Broadway, New York, NY 10018, USA
29 Earlsfort Terrace, Dublin 2, Ireland

BLOOMSBURY, BLOOMSBURY VISUAL ARTS and the Diana logo
are trademarks of Bloomsbury Publishing Plc

First published in Great Britain 2024

Copyright © Kenneth Frampton and Miodrag Mitrašinović, 2024

Kenneth Frampton and Miodrag Mitrašinović have asserted their right
under the Copyright, Designs and Patents Act, 1988, to be identified as
the Author and Editor of this work.

For legal purposes the Acknowledgments on pp. xvii–xviii constitute
an extension of this copyright page.

Cover design by Andrew LeClair and Chris Wu of Wkshps

All rights reserved. No part of this publication may be reproduced or
transmitted in any form or by any means, electronic or mechanical,
including photocopying, recording, or any information storage or
retrieval system, without prior permission in writing from the publishers.

Bloomsbury Publishing Plc does not have any control over, or responsibility
for, any third-party websites referred to or in this book. All internet addresses
given in this book were correct at the time of going to press. The author
and publisher regret any inconvenience caused if addresses have changed or
sites have ceased to exist, but can accept no responsibility for any such changes.

A catalogue record for this book is available from the British Library.

A catalog record for this book is available from the Library of Congress.

ISBN: HB: 978-1-3501-8379-7
        PB: 978-1-3501-8378-0
        ePDF: 978-1-3501-8381-0
        eBook: 978-1-3501-8380-3

Series: Radical Thinkers in Design

Typeset by Integra Software Services Pvt. Ltd.
Printed and bound in India

To find out more about our authors and books visit www.bloomsbury.com
and sign up for our newsletters.

To Maya and Maxim

That even in the darkest of times we have the right to expect some illumination, and that such illumination may well come less from theories and concepts than from the uncertain, flickering, and often weak light that some men and women, in their lives and their works will kindle under almost all circumstances and shed over the time span that was given them on earth [. . .] Eyes so used to darkness as ours will hardly be able to tell whether their light was the light of a candle or that of a blazing sun. But such objective evaluation seems to me a matter of secondary importance which can be safely left to posterity.

Hannah Arendt, *Men in Dark Times* (New York: Harcourt Brace & World, Inc., 1955), ix–x.

Contents

List of Figures xi
Acknowledgments xvii
Editorial Notes xix
Kenneth Frampton: A Biographical Sketch xxi

Introduction 1

Kenneth Frampton in Conversation with Miodrag Mitrašinović 11

The Human Condition and the Critical Present

1 Introduction to Section 1 31
2 The Status of Man and the Status of His Objects: A Reading of *The Human Condition* 37
3 Industrialization and the Crises in Architecture 53
4 Apropos Ulm: Curriculum and Critical Theory 67
5 *Modern Architecture: A Critical History*, Introduction to the 1st Edition 81
6 Towards an Ontological Architecture: A Philosophical Excursus 85

Urban Landscape and the Eclipse of the Public Realm

7 Introduction to Section 2 93
8 America 1960–1970: Notes on Urban Images and Theory 101
9 The Generic Street as a Continuous Built Form 111
10 Technology, Place & Architecture 123
11 Civic Form 131

12 The Legacy of Alvar Aalto: Evolution and Influence 139
13 Toward an Urban Landscape 157
14 Megaform as Urban Landscape 167
15 Land Settlement, Architecture, and the Eclipse of the Public Realm 177

Cross-Cultural Trajectories, Place Creation, and the Politics of Counter Form

16 Introduction to Section 3 185
17 On Reading Heidegger 193
18 Towards a Critical Regionalism: Six Points for an Architecture of Resistance 199
19 Tadao Ando's Critical Modernism 211
20 Place-Form and Cultural Identity 219
21 Modernization and Local Culture 231
22 The Predicament of the Place-Form: Notes from New York 239
23 Plan Form and Topography in the Work of Kashef Chowdhury 247
24 2018 Society of Architectural Historians Plenary Talk 251

The Predicament of Architecture in the New Millennium

25 Introduction to Section 4 259
26 Architecture, Philosophy, and the Education of Architects 265
27 Reflections on the Autonomy of Architecture: A Critique of Contemporary Production 271
28 Seven Points for the Millennium: An Untimely Manifesto 281
29 Typology and Participation: The Architecture of Álvaro Siza 289
30 Towards an Agonistic Architecture 295
31 The Unfinished Project at the End of Modernity: Tectonic Form and the Space of Public Appearance 305

Afterword: "The Criticism of Architecture is Worth More Than Architecture," by Clive Dilnot 317

Bibliographic Sources 344
Biographies 348
Index 350

List of Figures

1 Unified Education Center in Jambeiro em Guaianases, São Paulo, Brazil (2001–04). Centros Educacionais Unificados (CEU) were developed by architects Alexandre Delijaicov, André Takyia, and Wanderley Ariza as a network of 21 community and learning centers in the city's poor areas during the administration of Mayor Marta Suplicy. Photo © Henrique Boney, licensed under the Creative Commons Attribution-Share Alike 4.0 license. Source: Wikimedia Commons 16
2 Corringham Building in Bayswater, London. Kenneth Frampton with Douglas Stephen and Partners (1960–1962). Photo © No Swan So Fine licensed under the Creative Commons Attribution-Share Alike 4.0 International license. Source: Wikimedia Commons 20
3 Corringham Building in Bayswater, London. Kenneth Frampton with Douglas Stephen and Partners (1960–1962). Illustration courtesy of Kenneth Frampton 21
4 Corringham Building in Bayswater, London. Kenneth Frampton with Douglas Stephen and Partners (1960–1962). Sections and plans. Illustrations courtesy of Kenneth Frampton. Illustration courtesy of Kenneth Frampton 21
5 Public courtyard in the Marcus Garvey Park Village, built in Brownsville, Brooklyn, New York. Kenneth Frampton, Arthur Baker, Anthony Pangaro, and Michael Kirkland (1973–1976). Drawing by Craig Hodgetts, 1973. Source: *Another Chance for Housing*, MOMA exhibition catalog, June 12–August 19, 1973: 20 27
6 "The Aurora Room," in Thomas Hope's Duchess Street house, London, 1807. Source: "The Aurora Room," Plate 7, "Household Furniture & Interior Decoration," by Thomas Hope, London, 1807. NAL Pressmark 57.Q.1. Courtesy of Victoria and Albert Museum 39
7 The Ringstrasse plan, Vienna. Camillo Sitte, 1889. Source: Camillo Sitte, *Städtebau*, 1889 39

LIST OF FIGURES

8 Miletus, Greek Hippodamia city, 5th Century BC. "The gradual growth of three sequential public realms or 'agoras' linked to each other by Stoa: the harbour agora, the market agora, and the civic agora. The 'sacred' public realm is removed from this sequence to one side." Source: Kenneth Frampton, "Labor, Work & Architecture," in *Meaning in Architecture*, eds. Charles Jencks and George Baird (New York: George Braziller, 1969), 153. Drawing by Sara Dević 42

9 *Augusta Raurica*, 44 B.C. "The Roman Ideogram of the town as reflected in the street is rotated through 36° from the cardinal north so that on the summer and winter equinoxes respectively the sun shines down the streets on rising and setting. In contrast, the land division, the sub-urban area surrounding the town was divided to correspond with the cardinal points." Source: Kenneth Frampton, "Labor, Work & Architecture," in *Meaning in Architecture*, eds. Charles Jencks and George Baird (New York: George Braziller, 1969), 156. Drawing by Sara Dević 42

10 "Karl Gruber's reconstruction of a typical walled medieval city. Note the standardisation of the urban vernacular construction of the new colony or *faubourg* being added to the initial foundation and the protection afforded by the castle keep etc." Source: Karl Gruber, *Die Gestalt der Deutschen Stadt* (Berlin: Bibliographisches Institut, 1937). Drawing by Sara Dević 42

11 *La Cittá Nuova, casa a gradinate con ascensori esterni.* Antonio Sant'Elia, 1914. Illustration @ Sailko under the Creative Commons Attribution 3.0 Unported license, Wikimedia commons 48

12 New Babylon Paris. Constant Nieuwenhuys, 1963. Collection of Haags Gemeentemuseum, The Hague 48

13 Crystal Palace, London, United Kingdom. Joseph Paxton (with Fox and Henderson), 1851. Construction details. Source: P. Berlyn and C. Fowler Jr. *The Crystal Palace: Its Architectural History and Constructive Marvels* (London: J. Gilbert, 1851) 54

14 Crystal Palace, London, United Kingdom. Joseph Paxton (with Fox and Henderson), 1851. The "Glazing Waggon." Source: P. Berlyn and C. Fowler Jr. *The Crystal Palace: Its Architectural History and Constructive Marvels* (London: J. Gilbert, 1851) 54

15 "Cathedral of the Future," woodcut, cover for Bauhaus program. Lyonel Feininger, April 1919. In the collections of The Museum of Modern Art, New York, and Harvard Art Museum, Busch-Reisinger Museum 59

16 The 3rd Battle of Ypres Salient, 1917. In the collection of the Imperial War Museum, London 59

17 Pravda newspaper building, Leningrad (St. Petersburg), Russia. Leonid, Viktor, and Alexander Vesnin, 1924 63

18 Master plan for Stalingrad, Russia, N.B. Miliutin, 1928 63

19 Hochschule für Gestaltung Ulm, Germany. Max Bill, 1952–1955. Axonometric drawing based on the original Max Bill's drawing. Drawing by Eddy Voltaire 68

20 Hochschule für Gestaltung Ulm, Germany. Max Bill, 1952–1955. A view of the building in 1955. Photo © Florian Aicher, Rotis; HfG-Archiv/Museum Ulm. Inv. Nr. HfG Ar Sti F 55.0001 68

LIST OF FIGURES

xiii

21 Kenneth Frampton, *Modern Architecture: A Critical History*, cover of the first Thames & Hudson edition, 1980. Cover of Kenneth Frampton's personal copy. Courtesy of Thames & Hudson 80
22 A "three-strand" Linear City Proposal for linked townships in Central Lancashire, UK. J.R. James for the British Ministry of Housing and Local Government, 1967 105
23 Analysis of the ground surfaces in downtown Los Angeles, California. Konstantinos Doxiades, 1968. Drawing by Sara Dević, based on the original drawing 105
24 Bochum University competition entry. Candilis, Josic and Woods, 1962. Source: Joedicke, J. (Ed) (1970) *Candilis, Josic, Woods. A Decade of Architecture and Urban Design*. London: Alec Tiranti Publishers 117
25 Student Housing Union Building (HUB), University of Alberta, Edmonton, Canada. A. J. Diamond and Barton Myers, 1973. The linear arcade. Photo @ Ken Eckert licensed under the Creative Commons Attribution-Share Alike 4.0 International license. Source: Wikimedia Commons 117
26 Frankfurt-Römerberg Center competition entry, Frankfurt-am-Main, Germany. Shadrach Woods and Manfried Schiedhelm of Candilis, Josic and Woods, 1963. Model. Source: Joedicke, J. (Ed) (1970) *Candilis, Josic, Woods. A Decade of Architecture and Urban Design*. London: Alec Tiranti Publishers 118
27 Brunswick Center, London, United Kingdom. Patrick Hodgkinson, 1973. Section. Drawing by Sara Dević, based on the original drawing 118
28 The Centraal Beheergebouw insurance company office building, Apeldoorn, The Netherlands. Herman Hertzberger, 1965–1972. Plan and section. Drawings by Eddy Voltaire, based on the original drawings 128
29 The Centraal Beheergebouw insurance company office building, Apeldoorn, The Netherlands. Herman Hertzberger, 1965–1972. Photo @ Willem Diepraam. Courtesy of Herman Hertzberger 128
30 The British Library, London, United Kingdom. Colin St John Wilson and Mary Jay Long, 1963–1997. Panoramic view of the library. Photo @ Patche99z licensed under the Creative Commons CC BY-SA 3.0 license. Source: Wikimedia Commons 133
31 The Stavros Niarchos Foundation Cultural Center, Athens, Greece. Renzo Piano Building Workshop with Betaplan, 2008–2016. Longitudinal section. Drawing by Sara Dević, based on the original drawings 135
32 The Stavros Niarchos Foundation Cultural Center, Athens, Greece. Renzo Piano Building Workshop with Betaplan, 2008–2016. Photo by Nikos Karanikolas. Courtesy of the Stavros Niarchos Foundation Cultural Center 135
33 National Pensions Institute, Helsinki, Finland. Alvar Aalto, 1952–1956. Aerial view of the Institute. Photo @ Suomen Ilmakuva Oy. Courtesy of Suomen Ilmakuva Oy 141

34 National Pensions Institute, Helsinki, Finland. Alvar Aalto, 1952–1956. Construction detail drawing of the skylights. Drawing by Eddy Voltaire, based on the original drawings 141
35 National Pensions Institute, Helsinki, Finland. Alvar Aalto, 1952–1956. Interior of the customer service facilities. Photo @ Richard Peters. Courtesy of the Alvar Aalto Foundation 141
36 The Säynätsalo Town Hall, Säynätsalo, Finland. Alvar Aalto, 1949–1951. Section through the courtyard. Drawing by Eddy Voltaire, based on the original drawing 147
37 The Säynätsalo Town Hall, Säynätsalo, Finland. Alvar Aalto, 1949–1951. Plan. Drawing by Sara Dević, based on the original drawings 147
38 The Säynätsalo Town Hall, Säynätsalo, Finland. Alvar Aalto, 1949–1951. Radiating trusses of the Council Chamber hall ceiling. Photo by Kenneth Frampton. Courtesy of Kenneth Frampton 147
39 Kenneth Frampton in front of the Säynätsalo Town Hall, 1980s. Source: Canadian Centre for Architecture (CCA), Kenneth Frampton fond. Courtesy of CCA 148
40 Alvar Aalto's Structural Map of the General Town Plan of Imatra, Finland. Dated 1 August 1951. Source: *Imatra. Kauppalan yleisasemakaava.* Courtesy of the Alvar Aalto Foundation 152
41 Robson Square, Vancouver, Canada. Arthur Erickson and Cornelia Hahn Oberlander, 1979–1983. Section through the complex. Drawing by Sara Dević, based on the original drawing 169
42 Robson Square, Vancouver, Canada. Arthur Erickson and Cornelia Hahn Oberlander, 1979–1983. A panoramic view of Robson Square and the Law Courts complex (1986). City of Vancouver Archives, image # COV-S544-: CVA 784-115. Photo by Vancouver (B.C.) Social Planning Department. Courtesy of the City of Vancouver Archives 169
43 The Berlin Philharmonie, Berlin, Germany. Hans Scharoun, 1960–1963. Section. Drawing by Sara Dević, based on the original drawing 172
44 The Berlin Philharmonie, Berlin, Germany. Hans Scharoun, 1960–1963. Plan. Drawing by Sara Dević, based on the original drawing 172
45 Igualada Cemetery, Barcelona, Spain. Enric Miralles and Carme Pinós, 1984–1994. Site plan. Courtesy of Carme Pinós 174
46 Bagsværd Church, Bagsværd, Denmark. Jørn Utzon, 1968–1976. Section and plan. Drawing by Sara Dević, based on the original drawings 205
47 Bagsværd Church, Bagsværd, Denmark. Jørn Utzon, 1968–1976. View of the main chamber. Photo @ seier + seier licensed under the Creative Commons Attribution 2.0 Generic license. Source: Wikimedia Commons 205
48 Koshino House, Ashiya, Kobe, Japan. Tadao Ando, 1980–1984. Plans and axonometric. Drawing by Sara Dević, based on the original drawings 214
49 Koshino House, Ashiya, Kobe, Japan. Tadao Ando, 1980–1984. Section. Drawing by Sara Dević, based on the original drawing 214

LIST OF FIGURES

50 Kahere Eila Poultry Farming School, Koliagbe, Guinea. Heikkinen-Komonen Architects, 1997–2000. Site plan. Drawing by Eddy Voltaire, based on the original drawing 236

51 Kahere Eila Poultry Farming School, Koliagbe, Guinea. Heikkinen-Komonen Architects, 1997–2000. Plan of the school complex. Drawing by Eddy Voltaire, based on the original drawing 236

52 Serge Chermayeff and Christopher Alexander, *Community and Privacy: Toward a New Architecture of Humanism*. Anatomy of urban realms: areas of responsibility. Source: Serge Chermayeff and Christopher Alexander, *Community and Privacy: Toward a New Architecture of Humanism* (New York: Anchor Books, 1963), 206. Diagrams by Sara Dević, based on the original drawing 241

53 Serge Chermayeff and Christopher Alexander, *Community and Privacy: Toward a New Architecture of Humanism*. Urban clusters incorporated into a linear superblock. Source: Serge Chermayeff and Christopher Alexander, *Community and Privacy: Toward a New Architecture of Humanism* (New York: Anchor Books, 1963), 211. Diagrams by Sara Dević, based on the original drawing 241

54 First phase of the low-rise, high-density housing plan for the Garden City Puchenau, Austria. Roland Reiner, 1965–67. Source: Frampton, K. (2020) *Modern Architecture: A Critical History*. London: Thames & Hudson: 587. Drawing by Sara Dević, based on the original drawing 242

55 Siedlung Halen, Bern, Switzerland. Atelier 5, 1955–1961. Cross-section through the Siedlung Halen housing estate. Drawing by Sara Dević, based on the original drawing 242

56 Siedlung Halen, Bern, Switzerland. Atelier 5, 1955–1961. Site plan. Drawing by Sara Dević, based on the original drawing 242

57 Belapur Incremental Housing scheme, Navi Mumbai, India. Charles Correa, 1983–1986. Schematic diagrams of the basic housing configuration composed of nine units with a courtyard (9×9 meters), is grouped into a larger housing configuration (21×21 meters) with a shared space at the heart of this artist village. Drawing by Sara Dević, based on the original drawing 243

58 The Asian Games Village, New Delhi, India. Raj Rewal Associates, 1980–1982. Photo @ Raj Rewal Associates. Courtesy of Raj Rewal Associates 243

59 The Friendship Centre, Gaibandha, Bangladesh. Kashef Mahboob Chowdhury, 2012. Section. Drawing by Sara Dević, based on the original drawing 249

60 The Friendship Centre, Gaibandha, Bangladesh. Kashef Mahboob Chowdhury, 2012. Panoramic view of the complex. Photo @ Iwan Baan. Courtesy of Iwan Baan 249

61 Montessori School Delft, The Netherlands. Herman Hertzberger, 1960–1966. Overall plan. Drawing by Sara Dević, based on the original drawings 273

62 Montessori School Delft, The Netherlands. Herman Hertzberger, 1960–1966. Planned extensions between 1960–2009. Drawing by Sara Dević, based on the original drawings 273
63 Montessori School Delft, The Netherlands. Herman Hertzberger, 1960–1966. Exterior view. Photo @ Herman Hertzberger. Courtesy of Herman Hertzberger 273
64 Bouça housing settlement, Porto, Portugal. Álvaro Siza, 1974–1977. Site plan. Drawing by Sara Dević, based on the original drawing 292
65 Bouça housing settlement, Porto, Portugal. Álvaro Siza, 1974–1977. Forecourt between the housing blocks. Photo @ António Amen licensed under the Creative Commons Attribution-Share Alike Unported 3.0 license. Source: Wikimedia Commons 292
66 Seabird Island School, Agassiz, British Columbia, Canada. John and Patricia Patkau, 1988–1991. Plan and section. Drawings courtesy of Patkau Architects 301
67 Seabird Island School, Agassiz, British Columbia, Canada. John and Patricia Patkau, 1988–1991. East exterior view. Photo @ James Dow/ Patkau Architects. Courtesy of Patkau Architects 301
68 The Philopappou Hill pathways approaching the Acropolis, Athens, Greece. Dimitris Pikionis, 1954–1957. Site plan. Drawing by Sara Dević, based on the original drawings 308
69 The Philopappou Hill pathways approaching the Acropolis, Athens, Greece. Dimitris Pikionis, 1954–1957. Photo @ Miodrag Mitrašinović 308
70 Madrid-Barajas Airport Terminal 4, Madrid, Spain. Rogers Stirk Harbour + Partners with Estudio Lamela, 2005. Photo @ Diego Delso licensed under the Creative Commons Attribution ShareAlike 4.0 International (CC BY-SA 4.0). Source: Wikimedia Commons 311
71 Luigi Bocconi University, Milan, Italy. Grafton Architects, 2008. View of the auditorium under the new public square. Photo @ Paolo Tonato/ Camera Work. Courtesy of Paolo Tonato and Grafton Architects 311
72 Fuglsang Art Museum, Lolland, Denmark. Tony Fretton Architects, 2008. Building plans and sections. Drawings by Sara Dević, based on the original drawings 314
73 Fuglsang Art Museum, Lolland, Denmark. Tony Fretton Architects, 2008. East facing panoramic window, Fuglsang Kunstmuseum. Photo @ Grey Geezer licensed under the Creative Commons Attribution-Share Alike Unported 3.0 license. Source: Wikimedia Commons 314

Acknowledgments

My first encounter with Kenneth Frampton's *Modern Architecture: A Critical History* was as an undergraduate student of architecture at the University of Belgrade in 1987, reading it over many months with the book in one hand and an English–Serbo-Croatian dictionary in the other. I met Kenneth Frampton in 1992 at the Berlage Institute in Amsterdam, the Netherlands, where I began my graduate studies and where Frampton taught theory and history of architecture in coordination with Max Risselada. As I recall, the first time I truly understood the entanglements of design, culture, society, and politics explicitly vis-à-vis the public realm was through Frampton's weeklong opening lectures at the Institute. Our annual theme was *The New Public Realm*, and Frampton wrote an introduction to our annual publication with the same title. Frampton's erudition—displaying a plethora of examples from around the world, explained in incredible detail with such rigor, and argued with a contagious passion for the subject matter—was simply awe-inspiring. Conversations with him in Amsterdam between 1992 through 1994, whether during his lectures and follow-up discussions or over informal dinners at which Frampton generously and enthusiastically joined our peer group, were the most formative learning experiences of my lifetime. Ever since, his criticism of my work has always been direct and constructive, and it gave me ground to stand on even when we disagreed. Over these many years, he has always been there, a phone call or an email away, to offer advice, write a recommendation letter, or simply enjoy chatting about mutual friends and their successes.

First and foremost, I would like to thank Kenneth Frampton for his generous support in the process of making "our book," and for his kind and equally critical help in putting it together. Contentwise, the book is solely his; the Bloomsbury co-editors and I were merely facilitators in its becoming. On the other hand, as the editor, I take full responsibility for it.

Sincere appreciation also goes to Silvia Kolbowski, whose guidance and advice in the making of the book have been perpetually caring, thoughtful, and instrumental. I am also grateful to Jilly Traganou for maintaining that an in-depth interview with Frampton should be the cornerstone of this volume. Her contributions to the book are manifold, and her critique at every stage of the process was essential.

Likewise, I extend my appreciation to the editors of Bloomsbury's book series Radical Thinkers in Design, Clive Dilnot and Eduardo Staszowski, whose hard work laid the ground for this book. Special gratitude goes to Clive for his guidance, insight, and inspiration in developing the book. His long-standing conviction that Kenneth Frampton's work ought to find its way to broad design audiences as well as to those across the social sciences and humanities supplied the true vigor behind making this book a reality. At our favorite coffee and pub tables in Brooklyn and Manhattan, and through passionate and productive conversations about both Frampton's work and design more broadly, we indeed made it through one more project together.

In addition, a very special thank-you goes to Sara Dević who meticulously redrew the illustrations in this book, transcribed the original texts, and prepared them all for publication. Sincere thanks also go to Jennifer Simonton and Nicholas Arvanitis for transcribing Frampton's public talks and interviews from online videos, to Eddy Voltaire for redrawing some of the illustrations in this book, and to Roberta Werthein for preparing the illustrations for print.

My appreciation also goes to Amy Dorta McIlwaine, who has one more time delivered outstanding copy editing on the introductory chapter and introductions to each section.

And special appreciation goes to Kelly Shannon, Robert McCarter, Vedran Mimica, and Benoît Moritz for supporting this book, providing critical feedback, and kindly helping with grant applications.

This book was made possible in part by funding from The New School Provost's Office and Parsons' School of Design Strategies; both generously supported the making of this book through multiple grants between 2019 and 2022.

Editorial Notes

When in spring 2019 Clive Dilnot, co-editor of Bloomsbury's book series Radical Thinkers in Design/Designing in the Dark Times asked me to consider editing a volume on the work of Kenneth Frampton I was puzzled and quickly became worried. *Editing a book of Kenneth Frampton's publications? No one has ever done that.* Frampton has long been in full command of his publications and had edited the only volume of his selected essays still in circulation—*Labour, Work and Architecture: Collected Essays on Architecture and Design* (Phaidon 2002)—with the possible exceptions of John Cava's editorial role in *Studies in Tectonic Culture: The Poetics of Construction in Nineteenth and Twentieth Century Architecture* (MIT Press, 1995), and more recently Ashley Simone's in *A Genealogy of Modern Architecture: Comparative Critical Analysis of Built Form* (Lars Müller Publishers, 2015).

Dilnot's editorial request was that the book be accessible to broad design audiences, including architects but not limited to them, and that it be focused on the multivalent relationships between architecture and culture via (broadly speaking) the apparatus of criticism. The argument has been that Frampton's *oeuvre*, originally intended to address primarily architectural audiences, ought to be read outside of that context, where it would find wider resonance. This perspective has been based on the belief that Frampton's radical (re)thinking of architecture contains lessons for young and emerging design practitioners and theorists across design fields and disciplines.

We agreed that the book should tackle the most underdiscussed aspect of Frampton's work: namely, his "left-of-centre" political impulse, which certainly goes back to his early reading of Marxist theory, Hannah Arendt, and the Frankfurt School, although it was equally propelled by his move to the United States in the mid-1960s. This explicit political dimension of Frampton's work is particularly evident in his discussion of the relationship between architecture and the public realm, and in his commitment to Arendt's political philosophy. This emphasis guides the present book's unique angle and its organizing logic.

It seems essential to note that Kenneth Frampton's work has an incredible intellectual consistency that often results in the persistence of key themes and topics, and that also reveals Frampton's intellectual commitment to the Arendtian thesis. In that respect, the most difficult part of the editing work was reducing the size of Frampton's original texts, partly in order to stay away from duplication while maintaining the book's own internal consistency, and partly to make the book feasible. When parts of the essays were redacted due to repetition, indications of reductions and cross-references appear in footnotes inserted into the original texts by the editor of this volume.

Many of the essays herein have not been reprinted earlier, and for the first time reappear as part of a collection. This book is complemented by a few brief excerpts and quotes from Frampton's public talks, intended to highlight additional dimensions of Frampton's discourse, his personality, and his unwavering conviction. While Frampton is an elegant and prolific writer, he is also a passionate and erudite speaker, and an intense debater. The excerpts attempt to capture some of the captivating atmosphere known to those who attended Frampton's lectures and debates.

The interview with Kenneth Frampton was conducted on 14 June 2021, in Frampton's and Silvia Kolbowski's house in Athens, New York, as part of an unforgettable eight-hour-long visit that included lively conversations with Kolbowski and Jilly Traganou as well. The editing process and additional questions and responses were completed between July and December of the same year. The interview was envisioned as a way to bring to light the intentions behind Frampton's work: both the emotive and logical dimensions of his reasoning, and also anecdotal aspects of his lifetime living in and through architecture.

The book is illustrated with drawings and photographs of the buildings Frampton discusses in its chapters. As noted in the List of Figures, some of the illustrations appeared alongside the original essays, and some were redrawn, but most were selected for this volume and had not appeared in Frampton's earlier publications.

Kenneth Frampton: A Biographical Sketch

Kenneth B. Frampton (born 1930) is one of the most widely published and cited, critically acclaimed, and awarded architectural theorists, historians, critics, and educators. Frampton practiced as a professional architect in the United Kingdom, Israel, and the United States. His most notable buildings include the Corringham Building (1960–1962) in Bayswater, London (Figures 2, 3 and 4), designed while he worked with Douglas Stephen and Partners; and the Marcus Garvey Village built in Brooklyn, New York (1973–1976), a highly acclaimed design (in collaboration with Arthur Baker, Anthony Pangaro, and Michael Kirkland) seen at that time as a model for low-rise, high-density urban housing in the United States (Figure 5).

Frampton is the author of over twenty books, many in multiple editions and translated into several languages, and over 120 scholarly articles. They include the seminal *Modern Architecture: A Critical History* (Thames & Hudson, 1980), "Towards a Critical Regionalism: Six Points for an Architecture of Resistance" (1983), *Studies in Tectonic Culture: The Poetics of Construction in Nineteenth and Twentieth Century Architecture* (MIT Press, 1995), and the forthcoming *The Other Modern Movement: Architecture, 1920–1970* (Yale University Press, 2022).

Awarded, highly admired, and treasured as an educator, Frampton taught at Princeton University from 1966 to 1972, and at Columbia University from 1972 until his retirement in 2020. He also held visiting professorships in over thirty schools of architecture across the world, including the Royal College of Art in London, United Kingdom; the Berlage Institute in Amsterdam/Rotterdam, the Netherlands; and École Polytechnique Fédérale de Lausanne, Accademia di Architettura di Mendrisio (AAM), and the Eidgenössische Technische Hochschule (ETH) Zürich, in Switzerland.

Introduction

The past decade has seen a noteworthy increase of worldwide interest in Kenneth Frampton's work. A *festschrift*[1] for Frampton, who is now ninety-one years old, has just been published, in addition to edited volumes, monographs, dissertations, critical essays, interviews, documentary films, countless new and old public lectures uploaded to online platforms, and social media posts and blogs, all concerned with Frampton's critical historical and theoretical work. In 2020, his *Modern Architecture: A Critical History* of 1980 was reprinted as an enlarged fifth edition.[2] The same year, Patteeuw and Szacka's article—"Critical Regionalism for our Time"[3]—which revisits, re-evaluates and celebrates Frampton's 1983 essay "Towards a Critical Regionalism: Six Points for an Architecture of Resistance"[4] became *The Architectural Review*'s most read story of the year.[5] Why such a growing interest in Kenneth Frampton and his ideas today?

Kenneth Frampton stands without peer as a true public intellectual and the most influential scholar of modern and contemporary architecture. In 2018, Frampton was awarded the Golden Lion for Lifetime Achievement by La Biennale di Venezia. Yvonne Farrell and Shelley McNamara, the curators of the

---

[1] Karla Cavarra Britton and Robert McCarter, eds., *Modern Architecture and the Lifeworld: Essays in Honor of Kenneth Frampton* (London: Thames & Hudson, 2020).

[2] Kenneth Frampton, *Modern Architecture: A Critical History* (London: Thames & Hudson, 1980). The fifth edition, published in 2020, contains a new part IV (pp. 367–616) titled "World Architecture and the Modern Movement."

[3] Véronique Patteeuw and Léa-Catherine Szacka, "Critical Regionalism for our Time," *Architectural Review*, No.1466 (November 2019), 92–98.

[4] Kenneth Frampton, "Towards a Critical Regionalism: Six Points for an Architecture of Resistance," in *The Anti-Aesthetic: Essays in Postmodern Culture*, ed. Hal Foster (Port Townsend, Washington: Bay Press, 1983), 16–30.

[5] Stylianos Giamarelos, *Resisting Postmodern Architecture: Critical Regionalism Before Globalisation* (London: UCL Press, 2022), 135. See also AR Editors, "AR Reading List 040: Most Read Archive Stories," *Architectural Review* No.18 (December 2020), http://www.architectural-review.com/archive/reading-lists/ar-reading-list-040-most-read-archive-stories.

16th International Architecture Exhibition who selected the awardee, wrote the following:

> Through his work, Kenneth Frampton occupies a position of extraordinary insight and intelligence combined with a unique sense of integrity... His humanistic philosophy in relation to architecture is embedded in his writing... His experience as a practicing architect has given him a deep understanding of the process of designing and crafting buildings. This makes him both more sympathetic and more critical of the various forms of the practice of architecture. His consistent values in relation to the impact of architecture on society, together with his intellectual generosity, position him as a uniquely important presence in the world of architecture.[6]

Frampton has been a key figure in the evolution of the discipline of architecture over the past sixty years. One of the key reasons Frampton has occupied such a prominent position not only in architecture but also, importantly, beyond its strict boundaries is that he never perceived architecture as a singularly materialistic, formalistic, or technical enterprise. For him, architecture is an extraordinarily broad human activity that relies equally on the most complex philosophical and theoretical ideas and on its connections to place, culture, and landscape, and to the most grounded tactile and cognitive experiences, articulated by the fact that it is ultimately constructed as a material presence in the world. In his words, the full potential of a building "stems from its capacity to articulate both the poetic and the cognitive aspects of its substance"[7] while simultaneously revealing the entanglements of the human condition with politics and ethics. Ultimately, for Frampton, buildings are designed as multifaceted human artifacts whose purpose is to secure the existence of the public realm. When asked in 2014 about the meaning of architecture, Frampton quickly responded, "Architecture guarantees the public realm... Architecture ultimately is about 'the space of public appearance.'"[8]

The quadripartite configuration of architecture–place–culture–public realm has been at the core of Frampton's perceptive critical assessment of some of the deepest problems and perplexities, and the most dangerous tendencies

---

[6] Frampton was awarded the Golden Lion on 26 May 2018. In the award announcement (https://www.labiennale.org/en/news/kenneth-frampton-golden-lion-lifetime-achievement, accessed 15 November 2021), the curators also wrote the following: "His seminal [works] include 'Towards a Critical Regionalism,' which was a leader in the influencing of architects to re-value context, place and culture. His *Studies in Tectonic Culture* was a key work in highlighting the connection between the language of construction and language of architecture. In *A Genealogy of Modern Architecture: Comparative Critical Analysis of Built Form*, he captures with incisive clarity the inner workings of projects, de-coding them to make them legible for us all."

[7] Kenneth Frampton, Studies in Tectonic Culture: The Poetics of Construction in Nineteenth and Twentieth Century Architecture (Cambridge, MA: MIT Press, 1995), 26.

[8] Kenneth Frampton, "What Is Architecture?" *Arch Daily* Interviews, 14 July 2014, YouTube video, https://www.youtube.com/watch?v=OsqH6D64LkI.

in modern life and culture, as well as their political consequences—which, particularly today, take on a sense of real urgency. Many of these concerns that Frampton began to write about more than fifty years ago have not disappeared; on the contrary, they have become more intense and more threatening lately. Particularly salient have been his keen observations on the erosion of the public realm and the suppression of participatory democracy, two critical conditions that have been amplified by the dual working of conformism and mannerism in mainstream architectural practice and theory at the beginning of the new millennium. His "left-of-centre" political ideas, and his explicit politicization of architectural history, criticism, and practice, have returned to prominence because they illuminate the possibility of thinking and acting ethically and politically through and by means of architecture. In addition, his ongoing effort to move the scholarship of modern architecture beyond its Eurocentric focus, and to discuss both the beginnings of the modern movement and its continuation in the recent past outside of Europe and the United States, has been groundbreaking.[9] In our "dark times," to borrow Hannah Arendt's memorable phrase, Frampton's radically critical work has offered a uniquely relevant *designing-based perspective* on our current political and environmental impasse. Frampton himself put it thusly when interviewed for this book:

> In retrospect, it seems to me that the ultimate value of my career as an historian *manqué* is that all of my texts have been written with the mind of an architect, obsessed with the vision of a liberative future that now seems unattainably utopian—particularly at this historical moment, as nature in the form of unmanageable climate change begins to exact its ruthless revenge on the Promethean hubris of the constructivist technician.

Frampton often evokes Gramsci's slogan "Pessimism of the intellect, optimism of the will,"[10] which in many ways epitomizes his own lifelong work. The pessimism of the intellect reveals a critical analysis of the evolving human condition, and the changing social, cultural, and political dynamics of the past half century, through the "critical history" as well as the "critical present." Optimism of the will is revealed in his radical propositions for very specific and concrete forms of action through designing: his critical (re)reading of the genealogy of modern architecture, his theory of resistant architecture, and his critical theory of building. Frampton's legacy in this respect is not only in the recovery of the Arendtian "common public world," but in the construction of a different public world: a world for which Frampton repositions architecture—its theory, professional

---

[9] See particularly Part IV, "World Architecture and the Modern Movement" (pp. 367–616), in the 5th edition of Frampton's *Modern Architecture: A Critical History*.

[10] In his 1947 *Prison Notebooks*, Antonio Gramsci develops a "pessimistic" analysis of the authoritarian trends of the 1930s while simultaneously offering an "optimistic" commitment to the potential for socialist transformation through effective strategies of the workers' movement. See Antonio Gramsci, *Prison Notebooks*, trans. Joseph A. Buttigieg (New York: Columbia University Press, 2011).

practice, history, criticism, and education—as an ethically grounded and politically defined praxis. In that respect, his lifework offers precious illuminations, sometimes as "the light of a candle" (in Arendt's words) and sometimes as "that of a blazing sun."[11]

ARCHITECTURE AND THE PUBLIC WORLD

While Frampton's political impulse can certainly be dated back to his early reading of Marxist theory and fascination with Soviet revolutionary art and architecture, he has maintained that his politicization is undoubtedly due to his nearly simultaneous reading of Hannah Arendt[12] and the Frankfurt School,[13] as well as his move to the United States in the mid-1960s. The explicit political dimension of Frampton's work, particularly his understanding of the interdependencies of architecture and the public realm, gives it a singular perspective—one that this book is set to explore. As Frampton himself habitually reveals, his scholarly work is deeply indebted to Arendt's 1958 book *The Human Condition*,[14] which to this day remains a formative influence: Frampton often observed that he "shall never recover from" this book that has shaped his "entire outlook on architecture."[15] In his own words:

> On reading Arendt's book in 1965, I realized how these discriminations [between "labour" and "work"] were able to illuminate the time-honoured but invariably confusing distinction between building (process) and architecture (stasis), with architecture having as its primary charge the creation of the public realm—within which her third term, namely *action*, plays itself out, testifying, as she puts it, to the fact that men, plural, inhabit the world. For Arendt this plurality was the precondition of all political life. It is this specifically politicized view of culture which launched my writing on its left-of-centre trajectory, which is paradoxical given the conservative dimensions of Arendt's thought—dimensions which are, in my view, redeemed by her

---

[11] Hannah Arendt, *Men in Dark Times* (New York: Harcourt, Brace & World, Inc., 1955), ix–x.

[12] Hannah Arendt (1906–1975) was one of the most important political philosophers of the twentieth century, and her work continues to receive significant scholarly attention. For reference, See R.J. Bernstein, *Why Read Hannah Arendt Now* (Cambridge, MA: Polity Press, 2018).

[13] The Institute for Social Research (*Institute für Sozialforschung*) at the University of Frankfurt, Germany, now a part of the Goethe University Frankfurt.

[14] Hannah Arendt, *The Human Condition* (Chicago: University of Chicago Press, 1958) [New York: Doubleday Anchor Book, 1958].

[15] Frampton often uses this line; see, e.g., Kenneth Frampton, Plenary Talk at the 71st Annual International Conference of the Society of Architectural Historians (SAH), 20 April 2018, Saint Paul, MN, transcript by SAH (in Section 2 of this book).

insistence on the *polis* as the physical and institutional prerequisite for the continual enactment of democracy.[16]

Discovering his intellectual approach and political resolve in Arendt's book—and syncretizing it with other key influences, including Frankfurt School philosophers such as Herbert Marcuse and Theodor Adorno—Frampton has been preoccupied with the question "How does the public realm come into being?"[17] He developed his attitude toward the entanglements of architecture and the public realm first via the critique of late-capitalist society and the emerging universal (technological) civilization, and then through the demand for radical action (praxis) in order to organize meaningful forms of resistance through design as a means of overcoming their overwhelmingly destructive effects. Namely, what has been lost through instrumental modernization and capitalist development, he has argued, is the Arendtian "common public world" that holds people together and enables them to act "in concert." His commitment to the recovery of the public world, and his tenacious quest to define architecture's role in its edification and stewardship, singularly distinguishes Frampton's *oeuvre* from all his contemporaries'. By bringing together an edited selection of Frampton's publications and public talks from 1969 to the present day, this book explores Frampton's enduring inquiry into the complex relationships between architecture and the public realm, and his exploration of architecture as an important means through which the "common public world" acquires its transcendental dimension.

As chapters in this book will demonstrate, Frampton's reading of Arendt's concepts—the "public realm," the "space of appearance," and the "public world," together with her distinction between labor, work, and action—contain an omnipresent urgency with which Frampton discusses architecture as a cultural discourse and political resource in the twentieth and twenty-first centuries alike. Although Frampton is not, strictly speaking, an Arendtian scholar, and his interest in Arendt's philosophy is focused nearly myopically on its application to architecture, his theoretical work follows deeper analogies to Arendt's scholarship in at least two important aspects. First, in an essay titled "Introduction into Politics," Arendt asks, What is the meaning of politics? The answer, she writes, "is so simple and so conclusive that one might think all other answers are utterly beside the point. The answer is: The meaning of politics is freedom."[18] Extending Arendt's thought, one could argue that the meaning of architecture in Frampton's work is to configure and articulate the condition of "freedom" by means of building.

---

[16] Kenneth Frampton, Labour, Work and Architecture: Collected Essays on Architecture and Design (London: Phaidon, 2002), 7.

[17] Kenneth Frampton, "Megaform as Urban Landscape," Senior Loeb Scholar Lecture, Harvard University Graduate School of Design, 25 October 2017, YouTube video, https://www.youtube.com/watch?v=USRaFhH7jIw.

[18] This text was written in 1958–1959 as part of a book proposal titled "Introduction into Politics," abandoned as a book project in 1960. See Hannah Arendt, *The Promise of Politics*, ed. Jerome Kohn (New York: Schocken Books, 2005), xvii, 108.

In his work, the Arendtian notion of "freedom" by means of politics has been expressed in shorthand through the concepts of self-consciousness, autonomy, sovereignty, and liberty—all identified as key objectives of the "architecture of resistance." Second, although Frampton's work suggests normative goals for resistant architecture, as a nonformalist he stays away from prescribing a new type of architectural practice. Instead, his work offers to *reclaim the capacity for action* by means of architecture. These two dimensions place Frampton squarely at the core of Arendtian thesis, set him far apart from his contemporaries, and render his critical contributions truly inimitable.

ORGANIZATION OF THE BOOK

The book is organized into four sections that group Frampton's essays around the themes central to his work and also reflect his employment of Arendt. Each section is prefaced by brief introductory essays, particularly aimed at readers who are not already familiar with Frampton's work. The individual essays that follow are arranged to reveal the genealogy of Frampton's ideas and the main themes in his work.[19]

Section 1—"*The Human Condition* and the Critical Present"—is conceived as an introduction to the main theoretical and philosophical underpinnings of Frampton's lifework. It opens with "The Status of Man and the Status of His Objects,"[20] which remains a key reference regarding Frampton's reading of Arendt's *The Human Condition* by initiating his career-long effort to ground theory and criticism of architecture in Arendt's work. Frampton employs Arendt's distinction between labor, work, and action in discussing the advent of industrialization since the mid-eighteenth century, and then, in "Apropos Ulm," provides a critical evaluation of design culture which emerged at the intersection of industrialization and the rise of consumer cultures. Here, Frampton employs the dialectic critical method of the Frankfurt School of social theory and critical philosophy. The introduction to *Modern Architecture: A Critical History* clearly outlines his critical historical method, while "A Philosophical Excursus" delivers insights into his uniquely syncretic work in constructing a theoretical apparatus for the interpretation and evaluation of a broadly envisioned design culture by bringing together references from across ontological and phenomenological philosophy. This opening section gives us a distinct understanding

---

[19] Organizing the book this way is an attempt to depart from more conventional categories such as "theory," "history," and "criticism" (as employed, for example, in *Labour, Work and Architecture*), because Frampton's work effortlessly spans across these three domains. This approach also sidesteps the common tactic of clustering around chronological concepts focused on Frampton's key theoretical contributions, such as "Critical Regionalism" in the 1980s or "Tectonic Culture" in the 1990s.

[20] In her work, Arendt employs masculine nouns and pronouns to refer to human beings, and Frampton follows this trend when discussing Arendt's work and making references to her concepts.

of how Frampton employs the critical dialectical method not only in creating a critical genealogy of modern architecture, but equally in interpreting its present, and in suggesting courses of action toward its transformation.

Section 2—"Urban Landscape and the Eclipse of the Public Realm"—provides a closer look into the consistency with which Frampton has engaged in studying the disastrous effects of capitalism largely by means of "unending urbanization." These effects are further exemplified by the propagation of megalopolitan conditions, the capitalist predicament regarding private property and the proliferation of free-standing built forms, land expropriation and landscape degradation, resource extraction and environmental destruction, uneven development and the asymmetrical distribution of wealth and public resources, as well as by the erosion of the public realm and of democracy itself. This section examines how Frampton establishes direct antagonisms between urbanization and the city (*polis*), and the agonistic potential of architecture embedded in public and civic forms. He initiates this discourse forcefully in 1971's "America 1960–1970: Notes on Urban Images and Theory" by delivering a fierce critique of the North American cultural, political, and architectural tendencies toward mass culture, populism, kitsch, and capitalist land-settlement patterns. In the essays that follow, Frampton identifies theoretical and methodological anchors for the recovery of the public realm amid rapidly expanding megalopolitan conditions by way of reclaiming the potentialities of existing urban and architectural forms in "public mode" such as the generic street, the atrium, and the civic form. Starting in the mid-1990s, Frampton more assertively addressed questions of urban and landscape form vis-à-vis the challenge of creating true spaces of appearance within megalopolitan development regimes. In the section's closing essays, he develops concepts of "remedial landscape" and the "megaform" as critical counter forms to the ongoing destructive commodification of the human artifice and the public world.

Section 3—"Cross-Cultural Trajectories, Place Creation, and the Politics of Counter Form"—opens with Frampton's astute reading of Martin Heidegger, inflected by Arendt, and provides us with the phenomenological-hermeneutical basis for Frampton's own distinction between place and production, and for his later critical theory of building as situated between the infrastructural and superstructural domains of human activity. Frampton's seminal "Towards a Critical Regionalism" essay puts forth the idea that architecture which emerges through a consciously cultivated culture of place can deliberately evolve in direct opposition to the domination of hegemonic power, as a form of resistance to the cumulative and totalizing working of universal technology, commodification, and environmental destruction. Frampton's treatment of these issues is exquisitely exemplified in his 1984 essay on Tadao Ando featured in this section. Furthermore, in "Place-Form and Cultural Identity," Frampton advances his general theory of resistant architecture by positing that the political emerges precisely in the confrontation between universal civilization and rooted culture, while reminding us that its application is every bit as salient in the so-called "developed world" as it is in the "periphery." This line of inquiry is evoked further in a set of essays that address the "liberative promise" of the resistant "architecture of the periphery" in rooted cultures of places where "the degree zero of building culture" prevails, such as India, Bangladesh, and Guinea. In each of these instances, Frampton discusses the conditions under which human artifice is capable of opposing, withstanding, and resisting the pressure of universal civilization, and how such resistance is mediated through the design of public forms. The section closes with the 2018 Society of Architectural Historians Plenary Talk, which offers an adroit snapshot of Frampton's persistent exploration of the basis upon which a responsible culture of architecture can be pursued.

The final section—"The Predicament of Architecture in the New Millennium"—features Frampton's recurring theme of "predicament," which he has frequently employed in order to "to determine limits in order to do work of quality" and which, in that sense, serves as his rhetorical device to first identify and then transgress such limits. Frampton recognizes and often unearths the limits in a set of pressing themes addressed in this section, including his frequent focus on the relative autonomy of architecture; the necessity for philosophical reflection; environmental education and the urgency of assuming an ecologically minded practice; the debate around participation; the urgent need to invent incremental urban strategies and to reassign significance to landscape; the demand for reassessment of the center-periphery dialectic; and the agonistic political future of architecture, of participatory democracy, and of the public realm. This section also addresses Frampton's conviction that the unfinished project of modernity still carries a unique emancipatory potential capable of improving the lives of ordinary people through modern design, but also his recognition that the new millennium brings contemporary problems that cannot be addressed by courses of action prescribed by the avant-garde modernism of the twentieth century. Hence, Frampton suggests, if we are to recreate the public world, we urgently need new political and cultural imagination.

The afterword—"Criticism of Architecture Is Worth More Than Architecture" by Clive Dilnot—employs a deliberately polemical title whose origin lies in the Comte de Lautréamont (aka Isidore Lucien Ducasse) aphorism: "*Les jugements sur la poésie ont plus de valeur que la poésie*" ("Judgments on poetry are worth more than poetry").[21] Dilnot's essay probes the value of historical criticism for architecture but crucially also for designing as a whole. It looks at Frampton's architectural critique (both critical *and* affirmative) as an essential form of political and social reflection.

As Farrell and McNamara indicated in 2018, Frampton's work continues to exert its significant influence today, arguably more than ever. Their tribute to Frampton reaffirms the extent to which his legacy has been formative for generations of contemporary practicing architects, both emerging young designers and the most awarded and accomplished ones.[22] In addition, the belief

---

[21] Comte de Lautréamont, *Maldoror and Poems*, trans. Paul Knight (New York: Penguin, 1978). Originally published as *Poésies II* (Paris: Librairie Gabrie, Balitout, Questroy et Cie, 1870).

[22] Farrell and McNamara are themselves highly accomplished architects who were awarded the Pritzker Architecture Prize in 2020, an annual international award often referred to as architecture's Nobel Prize. For reference, see https://www.pritzkerprize.com/about.

that Bloomsbury editors and I share is that Frampton's work ought to find its way also to non-architectural audiences, where it will find even wider critical resonance. His rethinking of how architecture is interlaced with the human condition, his conviction that architecture is both a cultural discourse and a frame for life, his highly syncretic scholarly work, and his passionate belief in the power of designing as a radically ethical pursuit—such vision offers irreplaceable illumination to "eyes so used to darkness as ours."[23]

How ought one to close the Introduction to a selection of essays which epitomize Frampton's matchlessly aspirational pursuit? Perhaps by quoting one of his favorite authors, Antoine de Saint-Exupéry: "If you want to build a ship, don't drum up the men to gather wood, divide the work, and give orders. Instead, teach them to yearn for the vast and endless sea."[24]

---

[23] Hannah Arendt, *Men in Dark Times* (New York: Harcourt, Brace & World, Inc., 1955), ix–x.

[24] Antoine de Saint Exupéry, *The Little Prince* (New York: Reynal & Hitchcock, 1943).

Kenneth Frampton in Conversation with Miodrag Mitrašinović

MM: This book includes your essays published between 1969 and 2021, and in many ways it chronicles your lifelong propensity for employing Hannah Arendt's political philosophy to polemicize the relationship between architecture and the public realm. You have talked and written extensively about how you encountered the work of Arendt and about the influence *The Human Condition* has had on your "total attitude to architecture and to life in general." Is it true that you attended Arendt's lecture at The New School in the early 1970s?

KF: Unfortunately, I did not attend her lectures, however I did meet her briefly in 1972 in a symposium dedicated to her work in York University in Canada when I presented the argument which I had first advanced in my essay "Labour Work & Architecture" which was published in Charles Jencks' and George Baird's *Meaning in Architecture* in 1969. Arendt encouragingly remarked after my presentation that my application of her categories of labor and work to architecture was convincing. It was just a short encounter, in passing, which was regrettably the only exchange between us.

MM: In the 1991 ACSA/AIA award address, you mentioned Hannah Arendt and the "aphoristic Tomás Maldonado" as key influences. Elsewhere, you have claimed that Maldonado had a strong influence on your "politicization." How influential was Maldonado on your thinking about design?

KF: I find it difficult to specify exactly how Maldonado influenced me. What is certain is that he introduced both Alan Colquhoun and myself to the Frankfurt School and above all to Herbert Marcuse's *Eros & Civilization*. My main contact with Maldonado was at Princeton where we both taught in 1968–69. His *Design, Nature & Revolution* was given as a series of lectures in Princeton which I attended. His overall contribution to my critical awareness of the predicament of our epoch was perhaps never more forcefully expressed than in his memorable aphorism, "While one cannot make anything without waste, this is distinguishable from an ideology of waste."

MM: Maldonado taught at the Hochschule für Gestaltung in Ulm between 1954 and 1966, and also served as its rector. What, in your mind, was so critically important about Ulm?

KF: I visited the Hochschule für Gestaltung in Ulm in 1963 when I was technical editor of the British magazine, *Architectural Design*. I met both Maldonado and the Swiss architect Claude Schnaidt on this occasion. Together, they made up the core of a Neo-Marxist circle in Ulm, as did Gui Bonsiepe who played a leading role in the communications department of the school. Bonsiepe was the author of one of the small *Uppercase* booklets edited by my predecessor at AD, Theo Crosby; it was a critique of graphic design as a rhetoric of advertising.

MM: As you have indicated, you were introduced to *The Human Condition* just before leaving for the United States in 1965, by the architect-polymath of the London architectural scene, Thomas Stevens. You arrived in the US as a "high modernist kid" (as you characterized yourself recently) and begin to employ Arendt's work to frame your critique of the emerging commodity culture and the inability of American architects to resist it—in particular, the Las Vegas kitsch and Venturi and Scott Brown's celebration of populism, as well as Melvin Webber's coinage of the concept of "non-place urban realm." Nonetheless, were you somewhat encouraged by Christopher Alexander's and Serge Chermayeff's *Community and Privacy: Toward a New Architecture of Humanism* of 1963?

KF: Apart from Arendt's *The Human Condition* which I read on the eve, so to speak, of my coming to the States, I was exposed at this time to many influences, not the least of which was the achievement of Siedlung Halen, outside Bern, in Switzerland in 1960. This remains in my view, even now, the most compelling example of low-rise, high-density housing realized in the second half of the 20th century. The thesis of Chermayeff and Alexander's *Community and Privacy* pales by comparison, not only because nothing was built but also because they were unable to resolve, even theoretically, a workable relationship between parking and housing, something which Atelier 5 handled in Bern through the provision of a large collective garage and through covered walkways between this garage and the individual units; the one provision Chermayeff and Alexander's compromised vision of an "alternative suburbia" could not even imagine.

MM: You have often said that you were politically naïve when you arrived in the United States, and that your politicization occurred here.

KF: I came to the United States initially for a weekend conference at the behest of Peter Eisenman who organized a meeting of young architects in Princeton. It was the beginning of the so-called CASE meetings, i.e. the Committee of Architects for the Study of the Environment. This was the occasion when, in the Lowrie House in Princeton, I first met all the "young turk" academic-architects of the East Coast who were already established in Ivy League schools with the singular exception of the GSD Harvard which was somewhat oddly not represented. In order to catch my Sunday evening transatlantic flight back to London, I was driven up the New Jersey Turnpike to Newark Airport where I boarded a helicopter to Kennedy. It was twilight and looking down from the helicopter at a Piranesian consumption of energy at an industrial scale—that is at the pinnacles of brightly lit skyscrapers and the ceaseless movement of innumerable cars on the serpentine expressways beneath—presented to my eyes an overwhelming panorama of the consumption of gasoline and electrical power of a dimension I had never seen before, and this left an indelible impression on me. This was the beginning of my politicization which was metaphorically underlined later when a British colleague of mine Michael Glickman remarked, "You have to understand, in England the claws are hidden, while in America you see them." Further to this, I recall that when I first came to Princeton in the company of James Gowan, James Stirling's partner, he looked around at surrounding suburbia and remarked in his broad Scottish accent: "It looks as though it could all be blown away tomorrow." I still think that this is an accurate perception of the endless suburban proliferation, and how insubstantial it all feels. In this respect, my politicization was a kind of osmosis, gradually arrived at through personal and phenomenological experience.

MM: In going through your writing, interviews, and lectures, I found only one brief reference to the 1968 student protests. I am curious to hear more about your experience of the events of 1968, and your thinking, at that very moment, of the possible influence the global student movement could have had on architecture.

KF: Since I was not in Columbia University in 1968, I totally missed the infamous Columbia "bust" when the student "take-over" was ended abruptly and violently by the police. However, I did participate in October 1967 in the protest against the Vietnam War in Washington D.C., as documented in Norman Mailer's *The Armies of the Night* (1968). I recall being with students facing a line of American soldiers with fixed bayonets, protecting the perimeter of the Pentagon while above looking down on us were Robert McNamara and others. However, equally shocking after this was the fact that the Students for a Democratic Society—the SDS which had so vigorously protested the Vietnam War—ceased to exist virtually overnight after the Nixon government discontinued the draft.

MM: In a recent interview, you were asked a simple question: What is architecture? You responded by saying, "Architecture guarantees the public realm … and is ultimately about the space of public appearance." To me this implies—significantly for this historical moment as well—that "while architecture … cannot act politically," as you have suggested, it is indeed intrinsically connected to the political.

KF: Exactly, and a prime example of this for me would be the program of a high school rendered as a community center as was the case when Marta Suplicy, a member of Lula's Worker's Party, became mayor of São Paulo and under her administration managed to build over 40 schools as community/learning centers in the favelas of the city (Figure 1). These schools were open as community centers in evenings and at weekends. They clearly functioned as spaces of public appearance, that is as social cores in the midst of spontaneously aggregated self-built housing.

MM: In a contribution to the book (Section 3), you describe Alvar Aalto's work as particularly important in relation to your conceptualization of the space of appearance—how he articulates it by organizing the entry sequence extending from the street to the inner core of the building, often in the form of an atrium. On this occasion you remarked, "I think that the human subject experiences the environment phenomenologically, and I think this phenomenological, existential condition has political implications." In what way is the phenomenological experience of space and architecture, and of the material form, related to the political?

KF: The phenomenological experience of built form only becomes political by virtue of the experiential potential of a given space sequence, as I attempted to make clear in the introduction to my 1995 book *Studies in Tectonic Culture*, where I allude to the approach to the first-floor council chamber in Aalto's Säynätsalo Town Hall of 1949 as being a phenomenological *promenade architecturale*. A similar example for me is Hans Scharoun's Philharmonie Berlin of 1963 where the audience ascends by a series of stairs and lounge spaces into the "terraced" vineyard seating of the auditorium, only subsequently to reverse this movement in the intervals, where the concert goers congregate on the lounge spaces suspended beneath the seating.

I suppose my position is that the value we accord to a space is consummated by our mutual interaction within that space. All of this, in my view, is inherent in Arendt's concept of the "space of public appearance." With her commitment to participatory social democracy, the ultimate sites of political agency for Arendt were the worker's councils that were spontaneously formed immediately after the Russian Revolution, the original Soviets that is, which were then duly suppressed by the Bolsheviks. Somewhere she writes in this regard that power will remain with people as long as they live closely together.

MM: In your essay "Typology and Participation: The Architecture of Álvaro Siza," you describe Siza's design for SAAL housing settlements São Victor and Bouça in Porto, and his later housing project for Quinta da Malagueira realized outside of Évora. Would you agree that your discussion of participation in these projects further elaborates Arendt's concept of "action" (in addition to "work" and "labor") as enabled not only by a completed building but through the conceptualization and making of architecture as well?

KF: The first two housing schemes were realized in Porto at the time of the so-called Portuguese Spring in April 1974 when they were the result of the SAAL system of participatory design established by the short-lived revolutionary councils controlling the discourse between architects and their working-class clients. In this regard one needs to read Siza's cautionary remarks to the effect that, "Certainly the architect has to learn from the people, but the people also have to learn from the architect, but they are ill-informed and this makes for an abrasive situation." At the same time, despite these reservations he was able to design and develop the extensive low-rise, high-density housing of the Quinta da Malagueira over a twenty-year period, largely because of the Communist government of Évora continued to build this housing in defiance of the power center in Lisbon.

MM: This relationship between typology and action/participation brings me to another dimension of your work in relation to Hannah Arendt. Namely, how do you see the difference today between "public" and "social"? Arendt made very clear distinctions between them.

KF: What she has to say about the rise of the social in relation to the private, the public, and above all intimacy is complex, brilliant and audacious. She writes: "The astonishing flowering of poetry and music from the middle of the 18th century ... accompanied by the rise of the novel, the only entirely social art form, coinciding with a no less striking decline of all the public arts, especially architecture." In other words, the social *in se* undermines the political potential of the public realm. However, for me, the "space of appearance" is more than just the political, it is the "space-form" through which the community reorganizes and represents itself to itself.

MM: You recently claimed that the decline of architecture in our age is experienced in parallel with the decline of the public realm and of the trust in the democratic system itself. However, you often invoke Gramsci's slogan "Pessimism of the intellect, optimism of the will." To me that indicates both your radical criticism of the role of architecture in the "dark times" and yet also a clear commitment to the exploration of the possibilities for political and social transformation through architecture and design. After all, both your critical theory of building and your theory of resistant architecture emerge out of this dialectic, don't they? What potential does architecture have to transform social reality in the West today? What kind of autonomy does architecture need in order to perform as intended? What do you see today as preconditions for the re-emergence of the "public common world" through architecture?

FIGURE 1 Unified Education Center in Jambeiro em Guaianases, São Paulo, Brazil (2001–04). Centros Educacionais Unificados (CEU) were developed by architects Alexandre Delijaicov, André Takyia, and Wanderley Ariza as a network of 21 community and learning centers in the city's poor areas during the administration of Mayor Marta Suplicy.

KF: Although they are related, these are two separate questions. On the one hand, since architecture is a quintessentially material culture, it can only aspire to a relative autonomy, for while space, light and form have a direct phenomenological impact on the subject, architecture's essential poesis resides in the poetics of construction, which is the thesis I developed in my book *Studies in Tectonic Culture* of 1995. At the same time, architecture is a microcosmogonic art form that is unable to create Arendt's "space of human appearance" without the wish and the will of the society. As Álvaro Siza once put it to me, in a letter congratulating him on his many new commissions, "Yes, I have many projects, but I am not happy. How can one be happy when Europe has no project?"

In the last analysis, the practice of architecture is unable to transcend rudimentary functionalism without the desire of the client for creating an environment that is infused with deeper values.

MM: What you have keenly worked on since the early 1970s, and particularly since the mid-1990s, has been the potentialities of architecture vis-à-vis the "unending processes of urbanization." In a conversation with Rem Koolhaas at The Berlage Institute back in 1998, Koolhaas characterized your work as "anti-urban" and "apocalyptic," arguing that you had attempted to delineate the field of architecture as distinct from the field of urbanism. How would you respond to such an assertion today?

KF: In the 5th edition of my *Modern Architecture: A Critical History* which came out in 2020, I cite at the beginning of the section dealing with contemporary developments in China (p. 488), a text that Rem Koolhaas published in 2001 in relation to a studio he gave at the GSD Harvard on the planning of the Pearl River Delta in which he wrote: "Maybe Team X and Archigram were, in the 60's, the last real movements in urbanism, the last to propose with conviction new ideas and concepts for the organization of urban life ..." This passage ends with the words "The field is abandoned to 'events' ... There is nothing left between chaos and celebration." It is an ironic fate that Rem Koolhaas' career has largely consisted of designing and realizing qiagantic "events" of which his CCTV in Beijing is one of the most spectacular. A decade prior to his despairing text at the Millennium, I gave a lecture entitled "Megaform as Urban Landscape" in which I attempted to present the way in which the universal chaos of the Megalopolis may still be structured and redeemed by large continuous horizontal, multi-storey building forms such as the 800-metre long L'Illa block in Barcelona built to the designs of Manuel de Sola Morales and Rafael Moneo in 1992. A constant reference for me in this regard was the long-standing German tradition of "big building form" pre-dating CIAM, let alone Team X and Archigram.

MM: In this same "Megaform" essay, you also clearly indicate that you "have attempted to trace the recurrence of the megaform as a unifying environmental trope in twentieth century architecture and civic design so as to suggest that it may be one of the only programmatic strategies that remains available for the realistic mediation of the random megalopolis as an iterated form." You are one of the first architects to write about and insist on the significance of turning our critical attention to what you called "remedial landscape" more than 30 years ago. How do you see the relationship between architecture and landscape with regard to the public realm as it evolves in the next few decades?

KF: Given the challenge of the megalopolis—the British landscape architect Geoffrey Jellicoe's motopia—one may imagine a mandatory reforestation of the environment not only to mitigate climate change but also to reunify, piece-by-piece, our endless proliferation of totally unrelated free-standing objects strewn across the urbanized regions of the world. As a result of the world-wide mass production and ownership of the automobile, the concomitant world-wide construction of limited access autoroutes, and the industrialization of agriculture, we have lost out former spontaneous capacity for ecological land settlement. Hence the pathetic *non sequitur* of urban planning as fictive academic discipline in postmodern society. As Jerzy Soltan once said to me in the GSD Harvard in the 1960s, "What would become of surgery if it were never practiced?" To this one can add Alison and Peter Smithson's aphoristic observation that "above the 6th floor one loses contact with the ground." If this phenomenological limit were respected, we would once again be able to generate horizontal forms of residential development that were simultaneously micro-landscapes in themselves. I have in mind the low-rise, high-density housing of Atelier 5 and Roland Rainer. My "Megaform as Urban Landscape" of 1999 is referential to this.

MM: Part IV in the fifth edition of *Modern Architecture* is titled "World Architecture and the Modern Movement." In it, as in your lectures and essays, one of your foci is the study of modern architecture "on the periphery," in all its manifold manifestations. Elsewhere, you talked about Milan Kundera's employment of Goethe's concept of "world literature" and how instrumental it was in your approach to "world architecture." In this volume, we include your essays on resistant architecture in India, Bangladesh, Japan, and Guinea, where you discuss conditions under which architecture is capable of opposing, withstanding, and resisting the pressure of universal civilization, and how such resistance is mediated through form by articulating spaces of appearance and "micro public realms." In 2013, you wrote, "For me, a liberative promise for the future resides in an agonistic architecture of the periphery as opposed to the subtle nonjudgmental conformism of ruling taste emanating from the centre." Why is it important for you to establish and maintain the center-periphery dialectic, and what is its significance for the concept of world architecture today?

KF: In as much as the "city-state" still exists either as a reality or as an idea, the center versus periphery dialectic still has some significance for me.

When working as Technical Editor of the British magazine *Architectural Design* in the early 1960s, I had the idea that unlike their British counterparts, certain European architects seem to be working quite consciously in relation to the city-state. I had in mind in this regard such figures as Gino Valle practicing in Udine, O.M. Ungers in Cologne, and Ernst Gisel in Zürich. In retrospect, this is now linked in my mind to the workers' Soviets which spontaneously came into being after the Russian Revolution—Arendt's ideal of "participatory democracy"—and the nation-wide social democracy which came to power in Sweden in 1931. More recently, this idea is connected for me with Chantal Mouffe's "agonistic" political future. That is to say, "agonistic" rather than "antagonistic." This brings one to the Italian philosopher Massimo Cacciari, who was twice mayor of Venice, and to his idea of "federation from the bottom" which is antithetical to the current European Union. One recalls at this juncture the neoliberal "market-driven" policies of the EU which have had an important influence on the regional welfare-state culture of the European periphery. I have in mind in particular the weakening of the Colegios di Arquitectos in Spain after 1992.

MM: It is of great interest to me that going back over many years, when asked whether you are a critic or a historian, you have always claimed that you are first and foremost an architectural educator and a writer. It seems to me however that this has also been your—

KF: Way out!

MM: Yes, your way out—but your work has been admired for elegantly and effectively integrating theory, history, criticism, philosophy, and practice, in writing as well as in teaching of architecture. Your work serves as a model for critical architectural scholarship and education. Thus, the "way out" indicates to me the omnipresence of an uneasiness with theory, history, and philosophy on the part of the broader design community, and especially its latent tendency to push aside anything that isn't practical and applied, i.e., vocational and technical. If these issues are not urgently addressed, where does this leave the future of architectural scholarship and education?

KF: Well, this trend is increasingly detectable today in the tendency of governmental and corporate power to emphasize thorough maximizing of "cost-benefit" analyses and to subsidize technological research rather than any other kind of value; quantity finally rather than quality much to the detriment of the humanist university. It is this same trend that accounts for the recent closure of the prestigious history/theory doctoral program in the School of Architecture, Cambridge University. Ideologically speaking this is related to the erstwhile Design Methods approach advocated by the German Mathematician Horst Rittel, who also taught in the HfG Ulm. In the Anglo-American world, this approach was favored in the late 1960s as a way of legitimizing the architectural profession as a kind of applied

FIGURE 2 Corringham Building in Bayswater, London. Kenneth Frampton with Douglas Stephen and Partners (1960–1962).

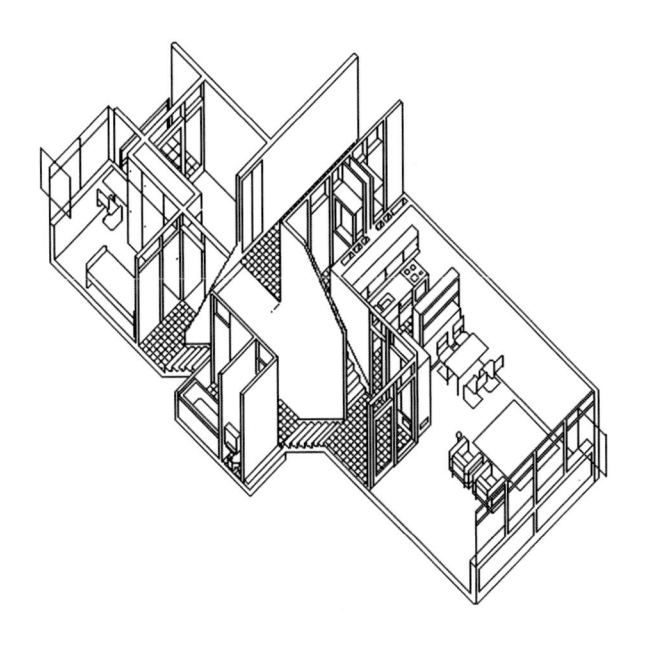

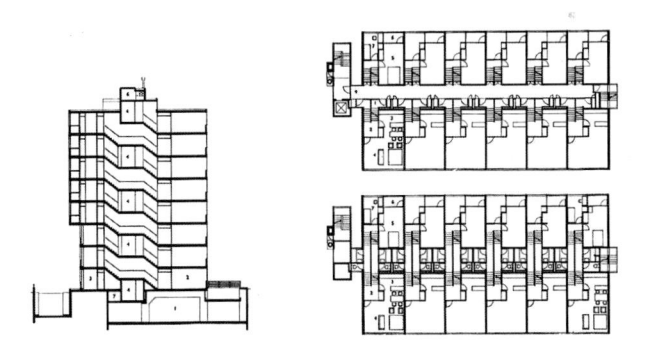

FIGURES 3 AND 4 Corringham Building in Bayswater, London. Kenneth Frampton with Douglas Stephen and Partners (1960–1962). Axonometric of an apartment unit (top), and section and plans (below).

technology; an approach which was sharply criticized by Alan Colquhoun in his seminal essay of 1967, "Typology and Design Method." In my view, Colquhoun's emphasis on typology as a point of departure is inadvertently echoed by Christopher Alexander's retreat from the "mathematization" of design, implicit in his repudiation of his own initial approach—in such essays as "City is not a Tree"— to his subsequent pragmatic "populist" embrace of a hypothetical "time-honored" American domestic vernacular as this seems to be embodied in his latter day "pattern language" concept of late 1970s.

Despite the fact that architecture is a material culture dependent for its realization on a wide range of techniques, it remains in the last analysis a microcosmic craft culture dedicated to the everyday accommodation of the human subject. In this sense one needs to resist the tendency towards science-based instrumentality on the part of the modern university. We also need to recognize that architecture is ultimately a craft discipline that in this regard involves the process of "learning through doing." This explains why the field has always sat somewhat uncomfortably within the confines of university, irrespective of whether the focus of the institution is humanist or technical. At the same time, it is obvious that one cannot apply a discourse of history/theory of architecture directly to some kind of design synthesis. However, the formation of the architect as a well-rounded critical intellectual is desirable in order to cultivate a sophisticated, critical *intentionality* on part of the designer prior to his or her involvement in the act of design. It is clear that the "unfinished modern project," to coin the felicitous phrase of Jürgen Habermas, will never be finished, particularly in view of the current escalating maldistribution of wealth in our Neoliberal world.

MM: You recently spoke about the necessity of revising architectural curricula to include subjects such as philosophy but also industrial design. What kind of learning environment would you create to recontextualize architectural education and integrate it together in some configuration with the humanities and with industrial design?

KF: As to the potential place of philosophy in architectural education surely Gianni Vattimo, after his teacher Hans-Georg Gadamer, would already have the last word, when he wrote: "If therefore, in architecture, as also in philosophy … we renounce any metaphysical, superior, transcendent legitimation … all that is left is to understand legitimation as a form of the creation of horizons of validity through dialogue, a dialogue both with the traditions to which we belong and with others."

In terms of what would be the pedagogical methods, one that is presently missing is to combine the teaching of history with the teaching of philosophy. I think that history and philosophy should somehow be overlaid one in relation to the other, so that a course inside the school of architecture, coming under the rubric of "history and theory," could also have a more philosophical dimension. For example, the emergence of phenomenology in relation to the evolution of the idea of modernity could be taught in this context. It is, of course, very demanding for any teacher to do this but an effort should be made to bring philosophy and history together inside the school of architecture. The book by Emilio Ambasz titled *The Universitas Project*, recently published by the Museum of Modern Art, is predicated on the possibility of basing a university on the challenge of design. It would have a humanist dimension and it would be connected presumably to some idea of a liberative modern project.

MM: And this would also include industrial design and design culture more broadly?

KF: Well, this issue takes us back to the HfG Ulm and at the same time the Stockholm exhibition of 1930, where Gunnar Asplund and Gregor Paulsson, together with others, issued a pamphlet titled *acceptera* for their projects of creating a normative middle-class environmental culture. This is linked to Ulm in the sense that the project of evolving a modern Scandinavian design manner throughout the 1930s and 1940s represented an attempt at the wholesale modernization of Swedish middle-class society. In the fifth edition of *Modern Architecture: A Critical History* of 2020 the importance of the Stockholm exhibition of 1930 is finally recognized. It is also important to note that Swedish Social Democratic party goes to power immediately after the Stockholm 1930 exhibition and remains in power for the next fifty five years until the assassination of Olof Palme in 1986.

There is a surely a moment in the 1950s when high-quality industrial design was the "classical" norm in Europe with designers like Otto Aicher and Nick Roerich. What fascinates me about industrial design was that it was an overcoming of the bourgeois *fin de siècle* idea of the redeeming total work of art by recasting it as part of universal well being, inseparable from life. However, a latent contradiction remains latent in the HfG Ulm, despite its radical aspirations, for its aim was ultimately inseparable from consumerism.

MM: It's a contradiction that you beautifully express in the Ulm essay—

KF: And consumerism is by definition preoccupied with the idea of "next," making durability incompatible with consumerism. Thus the post-war German economic miracle, of which Ulm was so obviously a part, involved commodification. It's a fascinating and complex issue, that's why I returned to Stockholm 1930 because if one still believes in the modern project, one has to remain impressed by the way in which Paulsson and Asplund sought to fuse modernity with a kind of popular accessibility which was once the touchstone of the vernacular.

MM: Your *Modern Architecture: A Critical History* was published in 1980, the same year Manfredo Tafuri's *Theories and History of Architecture* was translated and published in English. In his review of *Modern Architecture*—published in 1982 in *Modern Architecture and the Critical Present*, your edited volume published by Architectural Design—Tafuri calls it an "excellent book." Even though Tafuri himself doesn't mention "operative criticism" in relation to you, some architectural critics have suggested that Tafuri's critique of operative criticism applies directly to your work. Can you shed some light on your relationship with Tafuri and his work, and specifically on the notion of operative criticism? Did you know Tafuri personally?

KF: I can't say I knew Tafuri, although I met him on two occasions, once in the Institute for Architecture & Urban Studies in New York and once in Vincenza. I always found him somewhat aloof. I also feel that from his standpoint my position was seen as "operative" to the extent that I advocated a certain line, or a series of approaches to the design of the environment. However, it is equally clear that it was not operative in the same sense as Bruno Zevi's advocacy of organicism.

MM: In the 1980 introduction to *Modern Architecture: A Critical History*, you write, "Of the courses of action opened to contemporary architecture ... only two offer a possibility of significant outcome." What do you perceive as possible courses of action available to architecture today?

KF: One currently crucial factor as far as the future of the profession is concerned is the urgent necessity of doing something about the evident *mediatic malaise* that is eroding architectural education particularly in the Anglo-American world. This is evident from the mediatization of architectural education at many levels, most notably perhaps in the glossy, over-designed, annual publications, featuring each successive year's work being issued by leading architectural schools in the Unites States and elsewhere. These publications are not only unnecessarily verbose but also symptomatic of the extent to which the facility and complexity of digital drafting has had the paradoxical effect of blurring the ideational substance of any given project; to such extent that what we are left with spectacular, electronically produced graphic illusion which seems to promise unprecedented architectonic works, one after another, and often remains nothing more than a digital mirage, a manifestation of Guy Debord's *The Society of the Spectacle*. Hence these expensive publications have become rhetorical 'flip-books' lacking at any level of resolution. Unfortunately, this same *malaise* is evident in the work of many leading "star architects" in which the building, often at astronomical expense, is simultaneously both "there" as an object, but not there in terms of the phenomenological experience. It is surely evident that this spectacular *malaise* is inseparable from branding and that, both within and without schools, architects are losing their capacity to represent and critically assess what it is exactly that they think they are envisaging, and more importantly, why? Such is the price of "screen time" that young architects are losing their innate capacity to sketch a spatial idea or constructional joint as it first emerges in the mind. They are losing "head-hand" connection, that is the product of drawing and physically making, that is they are losing what Siza calls "drawing as the instrument of intuition." None of this is written in stone. As Renzo Piano has observed, "In my studio, every project has to pass constantly and continuously through three points of a triangle in its development: hand drawing, digital rendering, and model-making."

MM: I know you are an architect and scholar of strong convictions—that point comes through your work unambiguously. For this interview, however, I am also interested in the uncertainties, doubts, questions, and journeys that possibly didn't yield expected or satisfactory results—the "break points" in your thinking, as you once put it. Our mutual acquaintance, Gregory L. Ulmer, introduced me to the seventeenth-century Japanese poet Matsuo Bashō and the haiku, "Do not follow in the footsteps of the old masters, but seek what they sought." Younger scholars inspired by your work will not miss your footsteps, but they will indeed be concerned with the questions that have driven your work. What kinds of questions have you inherited from previous generations? How did they evolve? Are there questions that have recently emerged to which you have no answers?

KF: In many respects I find this the most penetrating question to date for it raises the issue as to what has motivated my activity over this long time and it compels me to acknowledge in retrospect what is the one significant architectural achievement of my life, namely, the design and realization of an eight-storey block of duplex apartments in the center of London in 1962, at the age of thirty-two. This work was obviously influenced by the ethical/aesthetic vision of the Russian Constructivists, and in the end it was naïvely inspired by their slogan, "Down with religion, religion is a lie; down with art, art is a lie; long live the constructivist technician." This vision was the ethos inspiring this work, and in the last analysis this also accounts for the overall character and substance of the first edition of *Modern Architecture: A Critical History* of 1980 and hence its "operative" manifesto-like character. This also accounts for the way in which it was influenced by Reyner Banham's *Theory & Design in the First Machine Age* although he would favor in the end a totally different "constructivist technician," namely Buckminster Fuller. Like the Italian Futurists that he so admired, Banham surely believed in the manifest destiny of technology under capitalism. Perhaps this difference between Banham and myself also accounts for Colin Rowe's deprecatory assessment of me at our first meeting in 1964 when he accused me of being a Marxist *manqué*, not that he was an admirer of Banham either.

Irrespective of these ideological affinities and associations, one thing is for sure—namely, everything I have been written has been written with the mind of an architect, one who has been obsessed with the vision of a liberative future that now seems unattainably utopian.

And this is another sort of autobiographic fragment ... from my own divided self between nostalgia for practicing architecture and the living reality of mostly teaching in studio, and in history and theory. This is a little interlude. It's a work that dates from 1972—the same as a project gets to be built ... Drawn by the illustrious Craig Hodges, who I think is still somewhere here in LA, a beautiful drawing. There's a touch of Peter Max about this, and it's a key illustration in the catalog produced by the Museum of Modern Art for an exhibition stage in the MoMA, which I curated, as well as participating in the design of this housing sponsored by the Institute of Architecture and Urban Studies. This extraordinary moment, pretty much created by Peter Eisenman, and the extraordinary institution that is Urban Development Corporation. It was this kind of shotgun marriage between the Urban Development Corporation and the Institute of Architecture and Urban Studies that was facilitated, so to speak, by the MoMA. And, well, finally this would get built and rebuilt and occupied in Brownsville in Brooklyn. The date of the exhibition and this project is 1972. The same date as Milton Keynes, the same date as Roland Rainer's *Livable Environments*. Actually, this book of Rainer's makes a very comprehensive argument for land settlement in terms of low-rise, high-density housing. Well, his book should be mandatory reading, in my opinion, in all architectural schools.

Kenneth Frampton, "The Predicament of Architecture: Seven Points in Retrospect," University of California at Berkeley, 28 April 2021, online lecture, https://ced.berkeley.edu/events-media/events/reflections-on-the-predicament-of-architecture-7-points-in-retrospect-with-kenneth-frampton.

FIGURE 5 Public courtyard in the Marcus Garvey Park Village, built in Brownsville, Brooklyn, New York. Kenneth Frampton, Arthur Baker, Anthony Pangaro, and Michael Kirkland (1973–1976).

SECTION 1
The Human Condition and the Critical Present

1 Introduction to Section 1

Conceived as a short introduction to the main philosophical, theoretical, and methodological foundations of Frampton's work, this section opens with Frampton's 1979 essay "The Status of Man and the Status of His Objects,"[1] which remains a key reference regarding his reading of Hannah Arendt's *The Human Condition*[2] and, together with the "Industrialization and the Crises in Architecture,"[3] presents his most systematic attempt to make Arendt's work relevant to architecture. One should also perceive the two essays as foundational for Frampton's longtime use of Arendt's political philosophy as a foundation for theory and criticism of architecture.[4]

---

[1] Kenneth Frampton, "The Status of Man and the Status of his Objects: A Reading of *The Human Condition*," in *Hannah Arendt: The Recovery of the Public World*, ed. Melvin Hill (New York: St. Martin's Press, 1979), 101–30. Somewhat reworked, it was also published in Kenneth Frampton, ed., *Modern Architecture and the Critical Present* (London: Architectural Design, 1982), 6–19. Both versions are a reworking of Frampton's original 1969 essay "Labour, Work & Architecture," in *Meaning in Architecture*, eds. Charles Jencks and George Baird (New York: George Braziller, 1969), 151–68. In her work, Hannah Arendt employs masculine nouns and pronouns to refer to human beings, and Frampton follows this trend when discussing Arendt's work and making references to her concepts.

[2] Hannah Arendt, *The Human Condition* (Chicago: University of Chicago Press, 1958) [New York: Doubleday Anchor Book, 1959]. As Margaret Canovan writes in her introduction (p. xii) to the 1998 edition of *The Human Condition*: "The book grew from the Charles R. Walgreen Foundation lectures which Arendt gave at the University of Chicago in April 1956, themselves an outgrowth of a much larger project on 'Totalitarian Elements in Marxism.'" Arendt's *The Human Condition* has been influential among architectural and design theorists but never so consistently as in the work of Kenneth Frampton. For examples, see George Baird, *Public Space* (Amsterdam: SUN Publishers, 2011); G. Baird, *The Space of Appearance* (Cambridge, MA: MIT Press, 1995); Pier Vittorio Aurelli, *The Possibility of an Absolute Architecture* (Cambridge, MA: MIT Press, 2011); and Virginia Tassinari and Eduardo Staszowski, eds., *Designing in Dark Times: An Arendtian Lexicon* (London: Bloomsbury Publishing, 2020).

[3] Kenneth Frampton, "Industrialization and the Crises in Architecture," *Oppositions*, 1 (1973): 57–82.

[4] In fact, the two essays have the same origin: Frampton's 1969 essay "Labour, Work & Architecture."

The first essay situates Frampton's reading of Arendt's distinction between "labor," "work," and "action,"—and of her concepts of the "public realm," the "space of appearance," and the "public world"—in relation to his search for foundation underpinning the theory and critique of architecture, at the very moment when his own generation of post–World War II architects had found themselves "without a plausible and operative theoretical basis" for their work.[5] In Frampton's view, Arendt's thesis of the transcendental worldliness of the public realm, which must be constructed by the "hands and minds" of people living closely together, provides the ethical imperative for architecture to assume a significant responsibility for its edification and stewardship. Frampton's aim has been to explore how *The Human Condition* reasserts politics as a fundamental realm of human action—*praxis*—and how architecture could acquire its capacity to configure the public realm in which politics takes place.

For Frampton, Arendt's conception of "public" sits at the intersection of her two closely related observations: first, that our feeling for and understanding of reality depends on appearances and thus on the existence of a public worldly realm into which we and our "objects" can appear; and second, that the term "public" signifies "the common world" as a human artifact fabricated by human hands and through human affairs.[6] The "space of appearance" is, for Arendt, directly related to her definition of the *polis* not as a physical or geographical location, but as the organization of people that arises out of acting and speaking together. As such, the *polis* precedes and is independent from the various forms of institutionalization through which the public realm comes into being.[7] And

---

[5] For more on this, see Frampton's "Place-Form and Cultural Identity" in Section 2 of this book.

[6] Arendt writes: "Only the existence of a public realm and the world's subsequent transformation into a community of things which gathers men together and relates them to each other depends entirely on permanence. If the world is to contain a public space, it cannot be erected for one generation and planned for the living only; it must transcend the life-span of mortal men. Without this transcendence into a potential earthly immortality, no politics, strictly speaking, no common world and no public realm, is possible." Arendt, *The Human Condition*, 55.

[7] Whereas, for Arendt, law and architecture precede politics, and are thus to be considered "pre-political," they are nevertheless preceded by the existence of the space of appearance. Arendt writes: "The space of appearance comes into being wherever men are together in the manner of speech and action, and therefore predates and precedes all formal constitution of the public realm and the various forms of government, that is, the various forms in which the public realm can be organized. Its peculiarity is that unlike the spaces which are the work of our hands, it does not survive the actuality of the movement which brought it into being but disappears not only with the dispersal of men . . . but with the disappearance or arrest of the activities themselves. Wherever people gather together, it is potentially there, but only potentially, not necessarily and not forever." Arendt, *The Human Condition*, 199. This is one of the core perplexing issues to which Frampton frequently returns in his thinking about the relationship between architecture and "action," and in this respect he has adhered closely to Arendt's thesis. Through the interview and the positioning of essays in this volume, I have attempted to suggest that architecture has indeed been positioned by Frampton, explicitly or not,

the key precondition for this, as Frampton points out, is people living together so that possibilities for action and deliberation are always imminent. Only when the power to act rests with the people will they be capable of establishing *the city* as the material precondition for permanence and for the continual enactment of democracy.[8] While the faculty of action is for Arendt ontological, the power to act "in concert" is always based on "the force of mutual promise," a commitment to "an agreed purpose for which alone the promises are valid and binding."[9]

Frampton follows Arendt's suggestion that architecture is an act of transfiguration—that is, "reification and materialization"[10]—and that as such it transgresses between thought, speech, action, and material artifice in order to edify and represent the realm of collectivization: the common world. The "sovereignty"[11] produced by the power of people acting together in speech and deed is indispensable, in Frampton's view, for the constitution of regional cultures that have enough political strength and identity to resist the onslaught of the "utilitarian instrumentalism"[12] of modernization and of "universal civilization";[13] this is one of the key tenets of Frampton's critical theory of the architecture of resistance (i.e., Critical Regionalism).

The content of "Industrialization and the Crises in Architecture" was first presented in 1972 at York University in Toronto, Canada, at a conference dedicated to the work of Hannah Arendt and organized by the Toronto Society for the Study of Social and Political Thought.[14] Somewhat reworked, this talk was published

---

into transgressing the domains of work and action; hence, for example, the inclusion of Frampton's 2013 essay on Siza (see Section 4) and his discussion of Soviet revolutionary art and architecture (in this section). Although Frampton's stance is that "architecture... cannot act politically" (see "Towards an Agonistic Architecture" in Section 4), this does not imply that architects should avoid acting politically in their respective capacities as citizens, public intellectuals, activists, community members, and the like—just as Siza, or for that matter the Soviet constructivists, have done. For an informative discussion of architecture as political and/or pre-political in both Arendt's and Frampton's work, see Hans Teerds, *At Home in the World: Architecture, the Public and the Writings of Hannah Arendt* (Delft: TU Delft Open, 2017), https://doi.org/10.4233/uuid:f0ab3483-7932-43e5-8557-7253cd2d58af.

[8] Arendt, *The Human Condition*, 201–4.

[9] Arendt, *The Human Condition*, 245.

[10] Arendt, *The Human Condition*, 169.

[11] Arendt, *The Human Condition*, 245.

[12] Arendt, *The Human Condition*, 174.

[13] Paul Ricoeur, "Universal Civilization and National Cultures" (1961), in *History and Truth*, trans. Charles A. Kelbley (Evanston, IL: Northwestern University Press, 1965), 271–86.

[14] Frampton met Arendt only once, on 25 November 1972 at the York University conference. As he suggests in the interview in this book, Arendt remarked that his "application of her [terminology] to architecture was convincing." Melvin Hill's edited volume (see note 1 above) represents a collection of papers read at the 1972 conference in Toronto.

in the first issue of the architectural journal *Oppositions*, in September 1973.[15] The essay discusses three paradigmatic moments or "crises"—of 1747, 1851, and 1918—vis-à-vis the historically evolving relationship between architecture, technology, and industrialization. The first crisis was caused by the separation of the profession of engineering from that of architecture thanks to the founding of the École Nationale des Ponts et Chaussées; Frampton argues that this schism has undermined "the object of architecture" ever since. He employs Arendt's distinction between labor (as related to the metabolic processes of life itself) and work (as related to the "unnaturalness of human existence") in order to differentiate between "building" and "architecture": whereas the former is process-oriented and dynamic, private, and impermanent, the latter is static, public, and permanent. The process of building, now largely relegated to the engineering know-how, is thus akin to biological labor, while the resulting task of architecture is *to edify*, thereby rendering the static edifice as a permanent space of public appearance.

The crisis of 1851 is exemplified by Joseph Paxton's Crystal Palace in London, constructed to house the Great Exhibition of the Works of Industry of All Nations. With this building, Frampton writes (paraphrasing Arendt), the question of *how* began at a public level to take precedence over the issue of *what*. Frampton contends that the emergence of a mass society committed to kitsch, wholesale commodification, and the focus on individual objects—and ultimately, to the separation of building from its emancipatory public character—caused "the fact that the world between [people had] lost its power to gather them together, to relate and to separate them."[16] The third crisis of 1918 was caused by the indiscriminate obliteration of industrial production capacities during World War I. The resulting "objectless world" suddenly created a new cultural space within which the German and Russian avant-garde speculated on alternatives. As Frampton suggests, unlike in prewar times, art, architecture, and engineering found new calls for unity in response to the "world of objects in action," in which buildings were "aggregations of elements in the process of being enacted." This "action" is evident in the work of Russian constructivists where architecture is fully contingent on the fabrication and preservation of a political realm of purposeful action—in fact "architecture reflexively depends on" this realm in order to save itself and the public world from the totalitarianism of universal technique.

In "Apropos Ulm: Curriculum and Critical Theory"[17] (1974), Frampton discusses the philosophy and curriculum of the Hochschule für Gestaltung Ulm—namely, the split between promoters of the Frankfurt School's social

---

[15] Frampton, "Industrialization and the Crises in Architecture," 57–82. In issues 1 through 4 of the journal, each of its three founding editors—Kenneth Frampton, Mario Gandelsonas, and Peter Eisenman—wrote a positional essay as an editorial, with the intention of establishing an intellectual agenda for subsequent issues.

[16] Frampton, "Industrialization and the Crises in Architecture," 36.

[17] Kenneth Frampton, "Apropos Ulm: Curriculum and Critical Theory," *Oppositions*, 3 (May 1974): 17–36.

and critical theory and advocates of the school's orientation toward neocapitalism and design in service of the global marketplace—through the voices of the main protagonists: Konrad Wachsmann, Max Bill, Tomás Maldonado, Otl Aicher, Hanno Kesting, Claude Schnaidt, and Gui Bonsiepe. For the first time in his published work, and notably under the influence of Tomás Maldonado's 1967–1970 Princeton lectures (published in 1972 as a collection of essays titled *Design, Nature, and Revolution: Towards a Critical Ecology*) and of their frequent conversations at Princeton in the mid-1960s, Frampton employs the adjective "critical."[18] In the Ulm essay, Frampton also discusses the impasse that design education faced between its commitment to serving social needs and articulating the public world on the one hand, and its practical dependence on land use, on the speculative world of development and construction, and on universal technology on the other. Ultimately, this impasse led to the demise of the school in Ulm.

In his introduction to the first edition of *Modern Architecture: A Critical History*, published in 1980—after ten years of work, having been originally commissioned by Robin Middleton of Thames & Hudson in 1970—Frampton establishes his method as distant from and yet influenced by Marxist analysis, and simultaneously reveals his affinity for the Frankfurt School[19] of social theory and critical philosophy concerning "the dark side of the Enlightenment." Elsewhere in his published writing, Frampton also revealed the influence of historian Edward H. Carr on his historical method: Carr believed that history is fundamentally a cultural activity and that the role of a historian is to interpret the relationship of interdependence of facts and values. Consequently, Frampton suggests (following Carr), each age writes its own history. The introduction to *Modern Architecture* also comes back to Frampton's earlier arguments about the split between architecture and urbanization, positing that the city had lost its capacity to establish spaces of assembly and collectivization, thus leaving architecture without its core subject: the *polis*.

Most important, this introductory essay outlines two courses of action available to contemporary architecture that "seem to offer the possibility of a significant outcome." The first is a nonrhetorical functionalist approach concerned with techno-scientific, rationalist optimization of production focused solely on the production of "silent," freestanding industrial objects. The second relies on the Heideggerian notion of "bounded domain," within which architecture attempts to reestablish a community of people reconnected with nature, in order to resist both the force of Enlightenment-related "progress" and also the processual flux of the megalopolitan reality outside its borders. "The sole hope

---

[18] For Frampton's use of the term "critical," see an illuminating discussion in Mary McLeod, "Kenneth Frampton's Idea of the 'Critical,'" in Karla Cavarra Britton and Robert McCarter, eds., *Modern Architecture and the Lifeworld: Essays in Honor of Kenneth Frampton* (London: Thames & Hudson, 2020), 20–42. Regarding Maldonado's influence, see the Frampton interview in this book.

[19] The Institute for Social Research (*Institute für Sozialforschung*) at the University of Frankfurt, Germany, now a part of the Goethe University Frankfurt, Germany.

for a significant discourse in the immediate future lies," Frampton wrote in 1980, "in a creative contact between these two extreme points of view." One of the questions in the opening interview in this book takes this salient observation as its point of departure.

The concept of the "critical present" was first established in Frampton's *Modern Architecture and the Critical Present* in 1982.[20] It marked a clear transfer of focus from employing critical theory in rewriting the history of modern architecture through political, cultural, and social paradigmatic shifts to an ongoing critical analysis of the urgencies of the present time. This section closes with an excerpt from Frampton's 2015 volume *A Genealogy of Modern Architecture: Comparative Critical Analysis of Built Form*:[21] a chapter titled "Towards an Ontological Architecture: A Philosophical Excursus," in which Frampton weaves together his reading of Hannah Arendt and Martin Heidegger with the work of Hans Georg Gadamer, Edmund Husserl, Herbert Marcuse, Jean-Paul Sartre, Maurice Merleau-Ponty, and Gianni Vattimo—intellectual approaches that are certainly not mutually exclusive, but nonetheless an uneasy marriage of ontological and phenomenological philosophy with the Frankfurt School. As Frampton argues in this essay, it is important to acknowledge that architecture is as much a presentation as much as a representation, and "body-being" cannot but encounter both aspects simultaneously. He employs the term "ontological architecture" here to delineate an architecture in which "the corporeal potential of the subject is envisaged as being realized both individually and collectively through the referential experience and articulation of the built-form." This is, to date, the only text wherein Frampton systematically and somewhat didactically elucidates his long-term commitment to Arendt while simultaneously interpreting it in the context of other leading phenomenological philosophers—and also reaffirming critical theory as a social critique of architecture—all in order to make his ultimate point: that the task of architecture is to influence social change and realize intellectual and cultural emancipation of all members of society.

---

[20] Frampton, *Modern Architecture and the Critical Present*.

[21] Kenneth Frampton, *A Genealogy of Modern Architecture: Comparative Critical Analysis of Built Form*, ed. Ashley Simone (Zürich: Lars Müller Publishers, 2015), 8–27.

2 The Status of Man and the Status of His Objects: A Reading of *The Human Condition* (1979)

THE ARCHITECTURAL COROLLARIES OF LABOR AND WORK

In her book *The Human Condition*, significantly subtitled "a study of the central dilemmas facing modern man," Arendt designated three activities—*labor, work,* and *action*—as being fundamental to the *vita activa*. She established at the beginning of her argument the particular meaning that she would consistently assign to each of these terms. Of *labor* she wrote: "Labor is the activity which corresponds to the biological process of the human body, whose spontaneous growth, metabolism, and eventual decay are bound to the vital necessities produced and fed into the life process by labor. The human condition of labor is life itself."[1]

Of *work* she wrote: "Work is the activity which corresponds to the un-naturalness of human existence, which is not embedded in, and whose mortality is not compensated by the species' ever-recurring life-cycle. Work provides an artificial world of things distinctly different from all natural surroundings. Within its borders each individual life is housed while this world itself is meant to outlast and transcend them all. The human condition of work is worldliness."[2] In her definition of the public and private attributes of the *vita activa*—the former having a dependency on the latter—Arendt amplified further her unusual distinction between *work* and *labor*. She argued that labor by being a constantly transforming but repetitive procedure—akin to the cycle of biological survival—is inherently *processal, private,* and *impermanent*, whereas work, by virtue of

---

Source: Kenneth Frampton, "The Status of Man and the Status of his Objects: A Reading of *The Human Condition*," in Melvin Hill, ed., *Hannah Arendt: The Recovery of the Public World* (New York: St. Martin's Press, 1979), 101–30.

[1] Hannah Arendt, *The Human Condition* (Chicago: University of Chicago Press, 1958), p. 7.
[2] *Ibid.*

being the precondition for the reification of the world as the space of human appearance, is by definition *static, public,* and *permanent.*

An architect could hardly fail to remark on the correspondence between these distinctions and the fundamental ambiguity of the term "architecture;" an ambiguity that finds reflection in the *Oxford English Dictionary* in two significantly different definitions—first, "the art or science of constructing edifices for human use" and second, "the action and process of building."[3] These definitions with their potential hierarchy latent even in the etymology of the Greek term *architektōn*—meaning chief constructor—proffer themselves as paralleling the distinction that Arendt draws between work and labor.[4]

The designation "for human use" imparts a specifically human, if not humanist, connotation to the whole of the first definition, alluding to the creation of a specifically human world, whereas the phrase "the action and process of building" in the second definition clearly implies a continuous act of building forever incomplete, comparable to the unending process of biological labor. The fact that the dictionary asserts that the word "edifice" may be used to refer to "a large and stately building such as a church, a palace, or a fortress" serves to support the work connotation of the first definition, since these building types, as the "representations" of spiritual and temporal power, have always been, at least until recent times, both public and permanent. Furthermore, the word "edifice" relates directly to the verb "to edify," which not only carries within itself the meaning "to build" but also "to educate," "to strengthen," and "to instruct"—connotations that allude directly to the political restraint of the public realm. Again, the Latin root of this verb—*aedificare,* from *aedes,* a "building," or, even more originally, a "hearth;" and *ficare,* "to make"—has latent within it the public connotation of the hearth as the aboriginal "public" space of appearance. This aspect persists even today in the domestic realm, where surely no place is more of a forum in the contemporary home than the hearth or its surrogate, the television set, which as an illusory public substitute tends to inhibit or usurp the spontaneous emergence of "public" discourse within the private domain.

Within the corpus of modern architectural theory, no text is more aware of the respective *stati* of architecture and building than Adolf Loos's essay "Architecture 1910," wherein he characterizes the eminently biological, innate, and repetitive nature of vernacular construction [...] Loos was aware that, like

---

[3] *The Shorter Oxford English Dictionary*, 3rd ed., rev. (Oxford: The Clarendon Press, 1947).

[4] Arendt provides the following etymological footnote on p. 136 of *The Human Condition* (the comment is referential to Chapter IV, footnote 1). The Latin word *faber*, probably related to *facere* ("to make something" in the sense of production), originally designated the fabricator and artist who works upon hard material, such as stone and wood; it also was used as translation for the Greek work *tekton*, which has the same connotations.

FIGURES 6 AND 7 "The Aurora Room," in Thomas Hope's Duchess Street house, London, 1807 (top); Ringstrasse plan, Vienna, *Städtebau*. Camillo Sitte, 1889 (below).

the pure instrumentality of engineering, this rooted vernacular had nothing whatsoever to do with the traditionally representative role of architecture.[5]

[...]

THE PUBLIC REALM AND THE HUMAN ARTIFICE

While the representative scope of architecture had already become severely curtailed by the turn of the [20th] century, the space of public appearance could still serve not only to house the public realm, but also to represent its reality. Where in the nineteenth century the public institution was exploited as an occasion on which to reify the permanent values of the society, the disintegration of such values in the twentieth century has had the effect of atomizing the public building into a network of abstract institutions. This dissipation of the *agora* reflects that mass society whose alienating force stems not from the number of people but from "the fact that the world between has lost its power to gather them together, to relate and to separate them."[6]

While the political life of the Greek *polis* did not directly stem from the physical presence and representation of the city-state, Arendt emphasizes, in contrast to our present proliferation of urban sprawl, the spontaneous "cantonal" attributes of concentration:

> The only indispensable material factor in the generation of power is the living together of people. Only where men live so close together that the potentialities for action are always present will power remain with them and the foundation of cities, which as city states have remained paradigmatic for all Western political organization, is therefore indeed the most important material prerequisite for power.[7]

Nothing could be further from this than our present generation of motopia and our evident incapacity to create new cities that are physically and politically identifiable as such. By the same token, nothing could be more removed from the political essence of the city-state than the exclusively economic categories of rationalistic planning theory; that theory espoused by planners

---

[5] Adolf Loos, "Architecture 1910," in Tim and Charlotte Benton, eds., *An International Anthology of Original Articles in Architecture and Design, 1890–1939* (New York: Watson Gupthill, 1975), pp. 41–45. In her essay "Thinking and Moral Considerations" Arendt directly relates representation with thought in her footnote on Augustine: "The image, the representation of something absent, is stored in memory and becomes a thought object, a 'vision of thought' as soon as it is willfully remembered." See *Social Research*, Vol. XXXVIII, no. 3 (Autumn 1971), p. 424.

[6] Arendt, *The Human Condition*, p. 53.

[7] *Ibid.*, p. 201.

such as Melvin Webber, whose ideological conceptions of *community without propinquity* and the *non-place urban realm* are nothing if not slogans devised to rationalize the absence of any adequate realm of public appearance within modern suburbia.[8]

The manipulative and "apolitical" bias of such ideologies has never been more openly expressed than in Robert Venturi's *Complexity and Contradiction in Architecture*, wherein the author asserts that the Americans don't need piazzas, since they should be at home watching television.[9] These and similar reactionary modes of beholding seem to emphasize the impotence of an urbanized populace who have paradoxically lost the object of their urbanization. That their power grew initially out of the city finds corroboration in Arendt's conception of the relations obtaining between politics and built form:

> Power preserves the public realm and the space of appearance, and as such it is also the life blood of the human artifice, which, unless it is the scene of action and speech, of the web of human affairs and relationships and the stories engendered by them, lacks its ultimate *raison d'être*. Without being talked about by men and without housing them, the world would not be a human artifice but a heap of unrelated things to which each isolated individual was at liberty to add one more object; without the human artifice to house them, human affairs would be as floating, as futile and vain as the wandering of nomadic tribes.[10]

It was a similar realization that the monuments of the Ringstrasse, built around Vienna during the second half of the nineteenth century, were nothing but a sequence of "unrelated things," that caused Camillo Sitte to demonstrate that each of these isolated public structures could be restored to being a

---

[8] See Melvin Webber, *Explorations into Urban Structure* (Philadelphia: University of Pennsylvania, 1964). See also his article in Wingo Lowdon, Jr., ed., *Cities and Space: The Future Use of Urban Land* (Baltimore: Johns Hopkins Press, 1963).

[9] Robert Venturi, *Complexity and Contradiction in Architecture*, MoMA Papers no. 7 (New York: Museum of Modern Art, 1966), p. 133.

[10] Arendt, *The Human Condition*, p. 204. See also her "Thinking and Moral Considerations," pp. 430, 341. In this text Arendt opposes the house to the nomadic tent. "We can use the word *house* for a great number of objects—for the mud hut of a tribe, the palace of a king, the country home of a city dweller, the cottage in the village, or the apartment house in town—but we can hardly use it for the tents of some nomads. The house, in and by itself, *auto kath'auto*, that which makes us use the word for all these particular and very different buildings, is never seen, neither by the eyes of the body, nor by the eyes of the mind; . . . the point here is that it implies something considerably less tangible than the structure perceived by our eyes. It implies 'housing somebody' and being 'dwelt in' as no tent could house or serve as a dwelling place which is put up today and taken down tomorrow." This recognition of the house as a *place of dwelling* is fundamentally Heideggerian and as such relates to the "darkness" of the *megaron*. As in Martin Heidegger's *Building, Dwelling, and Thinking* the argument implicitly links "house-building" to agriculture and to rootedness.

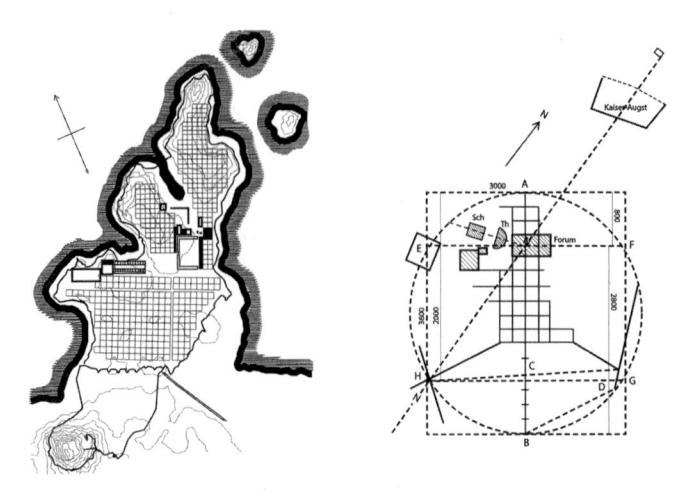

FIGURES 8 AND 9 Miletus, Greek Hippodamia city, 5th Century BC. "The gradual growth of three sequential public realms or 'agoras' linked to each other by Stoa: the harbour agora, the market agora, and the civic agora. The 'sacred' public realm is removed from this sequence to one side" (top left); *Augusta Raurica*, 44 B.C. "The Roman Ideogram of the town as reflected in the street is rotated through 36° from the cardinal north so that on the summer and winter equinoxes respectively the sun shines down the streets on rising and setting. In contrast, the land division, the sub-urban area surrounding the town was divided to correspond with the cardinal points" (top right).

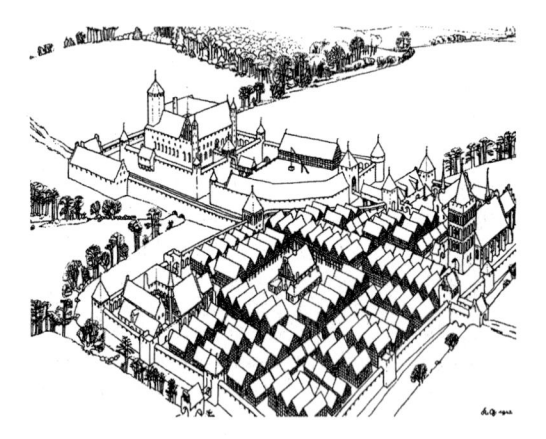

FIGURE 10 "Karl Gruber's reconstruction of a typical walled medieval city. Note the standardisation of the urban vernacular construction of the new colony or *faubourg* being added to the initial foundation and the protection afforded by the castle keep etc. From Gruber's *Die Gestalt der Deutschen Stadt*, 1937."

res publica in itself. In his *City Planning According to Artistic Principles* (1889), he revealed how the fabric of the medieval town had had the capacity of enclosing as a single "political" entity both the monument and its civic piazza.[11]

THE PRIVATE REALM AND THE RISE OF THE SOCIAL

While Arendt acknowledges that the rise of modern intimacy and individualism has largely eliminated the aspect of privation from the term "privacy," she nonetheless remains aware that a life excluded from the public realm is still "deprived" by virtue of its being confined to the shadowy domestic interior of the *megaron*—that traditional single-cell volume of the Greek peninsular, whose very etymology reveals the household as the domain of darkness.[12] Unlike the Greeks, who despised the individual domain or *idion* as the province of idiocy,[13] but like the Romans, who valued the interdependence of both realms, Arendt conceives of the private as the essential "darker" ground that not only nourishes the public realm but also establishes its experiential depth. At the same time, she recognizes that the rise of the social—to which the intimate is of course related—has had the ultimate effect of impoverishing both the public and private spheres and with this the mediatory capacity of built form to articulate one from the other. Arendt argues that the flowering of the social art form, the novel, after 1750 effectively coincided with the progressive decline of all the public arts, especially architecture.[14] The ultimate triumph of the social in collectivized life has, as Arendt puts it, given rise to a "... mass society [that] not only destroys the public realm but the private as well, [and] deprives men not only of their place in the world but of their private home, where they once felt sheltered against the world and where, at any rate, even those excluded from the world could find a substitute in the warmth of the hearth and the limited reality of family life."[15]

[...]

---

[11] Camillo Sitte, *City Planning According to Artistic Principles*, George R. Collins and Christiane Craseman Collins, trs., Columbia University Studies in Art History and Archaeology No. 2 (New York: Random House, 1965). As the translators point out, Sitte made pointed use of the term *platz* ("place") rather than the word "square" which has geometrical connotations antipathetic to Sitte's urban principles. Sitte's work was polemically against the normative gridded city as advocated by Reinhard Baumeister.

[12] Arendt provides the following etymological footnote on p. 71 of *The Human Condition:* "The Greek and Latin words for the interior of the house, *megaron* and *atrium*, have a strong connotation of darkness and blackness." She cites Mommsen, *Römische Geschichte*, 5th ed., Book I, pp. 22, 236.

[13] *Ibid.*, p. 38.

[14] *Ibid.*, p. 39.

[15] *Ibid.*, p. 59.

THE DUALITY OF THE *HOMO FABER*: ARTIFICE *VERSUS* INSTRUMENTALITY

The dependency of the human artifice on the work of *homo faber* stems from the intrinsic durability of objects and their capacity to withstand (*Gegenstand*) both the erosions of nature and the processes of use. As Arendt has written:

> The man-made world of things, the human artifice erected by *homo faber*, becomes a home for mortal men, whose stability will endure and outlast the ever-changing movement of their lives and actions, only insomuch as it transcends both the sheer functionalism of things produced for consumption and the sheer utility of objects produced for use. Life in its non-biological sense, the span of time each man has between birth and death, manifests itself in action and speech, both of which share with life its essential futility ... If the *animal laborans* needs the help of *homo faber* to ease his labor and to remove his pain, and if mortals need the help of *homo faber* in his highest capacity that is the help of the artists, of poets and historiographers, the monument builders or writers, because without them, the only product of their activity, the story that they enact and tell would not survive at all. In order to be what the world is meant to be, a home for men during their life on earth, the human artifice must be a place fit for action and speech, for activities not entirely useless for the necessities of life but of an entirely different nature from the manifold activities of fabrication by which itself and all things in it are produced.[16]

No other passage in *The Human Condition* formulates the essential duality of the *homo faber* so succinctly as this—man as the maker split between the fabrication of useless things, such as works of art, which are ends in themselves, and the invention and production of useful objects, which serve as various predetermined means to a given set of ends. For Arendt, *homo faber* is at once both artificer and tool-maker; the builder of the world and the maker of the instruments with which it is built. Where the one addresses itself to the "what" of representation and reification—that is to say, to that object of commemoration which Loos was to consign to the province of art—the other concerns itself with the "how" of utility and process, in which tools tend, at least in the modern world, to be the sole things to survive the occasion of their use. Nothing reveals this second condition of production more than the machine fabrication of goods for consumption, nor the first than the cyclical history of built monuments which, from inception to demolition, testify to a continual transference of value from the past into the future.

The ambiguity of architecture—its status as "edification" or as "building" and often as different aspects within the same physical entity—reflects the parallel ambiguity of the *homo faber*, who is neither pure artist nor pure technician. In a similar manner, representation and commemoration can never be

---

[16] *Ibid.*, pp. 173, 174.

entirely prized apart and the present embodiment of past value already assures its availability for the future. All signification in built form thus embodies a sense of immortality. This much Arendt attempts to make clear in her discussion of art.[17] [. . .]

While fabrication invariably terminated in the ancient world in either an instrument of use or an art object, it came with the emergence of empirical science to insinuate its process into the methodology of research and, with this deviation, to remove itself from the traditional teleology of artifice in favor of achieving the abstract instruments of cognition. The Renaissance, split between the liberal and the mechanical arts—already anticipatory of the industrial division of labor—led to the rise of the *homo faber* as a man of invention and speculation; of which the architect and *uomo universale*, Filippo Brunelleschi, was one of the earliest examples. As G.C. Argan has shown,[18] this rise of the *homo faber* as architect resulted in widening the incipient division between invention and fabrication and led to the degradation of the traditional craftsmen into the status of the *animal laborans* [. . .] This willful creation of distance between conceiving and building pervades the entire Renaissance. It was as much present in Brunelleschi's invention of perspective or in his machines for the building of the cupola over Santa Maria del Fiore in Florence in 1420, as it was in Galileo Galilei's invention of the telescope in 1610, with which men first established the proof of the Copernican universe. The effective split of appearance and being that was the consequence of this proof, served to institute Cartesian doubt as the fundamental basis of the new scientific perspective[19]

[. . .]

This shift from the "what" to the "how" found its reflection in the division of engineering from architecture during the Enlightenment; first in Colbert's categorically anti-guild creation of the various royal academies for the arts and sciences including the *Academie Royale d'Architecture* (1677), whose "architectural" graduates were to dedicate themselves solely to the "what," that is, to the reification of public structures commissioned by the State; and then in 1747, with Perronet's creation of the *École des Ponts et Chaussées*, whose "engineering" graduates were to concern themselves largely with the "how," namely, with the processal means of gaining permanent access to the realm. That these two aspects of the *homo faber* had already become professionally

---

[17] "In this permanence, the very stability of the human artifice which being inhabited and used by mortals can never be absolute, achieves a representation of its own. Nowhere else does the sheer durability of the world of things appear in such purity and clarity, nowhere else therefore does this thing-world reveal itself so spectacularly as the non-mortal home for mortal beings. It is as though worldly stability had become transparent in the permanence of art, so that a premonition of immortality, not the immortality of the soul or life but of something immortal achieved by mortal hands, has become tangibly present to shine and be seen, to sound and be heard, to speak and to be read." Ibid., pp. 167, 168 [Quote moved to footnote by the editor].

[18] G.C. Argan, *The Renaissance City* (New York: Braziller, 1969), pp. 25–6.

[19] Arendt, *The Human Condition*, pp. 282, 283.

divided over the defense and siege of the walled city may be gauged from the fact that according to Michel Parent and Jacques Verroust: "In the sixteenth century the defense of towns and castles was the work of *architects*. The word *engineer* remained reserved for those who not only built the siege machines but also handled them."[20] The progressive invasion of the city of artifice by the machine—first the siege engine and later the locomotive, and then of course the electric tram and the automobile—accompanied the ultimate dissolution of the walled city in the middle of the nineteenth century. Aside from its monumental rhetoric and its simultaneous reduction of honorific built-form to the status of being a rentable commodity, the Ringstrasse that came to replace Vienna's fortification in the second half of the century was coincidentally the initial proving ground for the horse-drawn tram.[21]

[. . .]

THE *ANIMAL LABORANS* AND THE FUNGIBILITY OF THE WORLD

[. . .]

The fundamental worldlessness of the *animal laborans* that manifested itself in the eighteenth century with the "blind" mechanical production of the workhouse and the mill was paralleled in the twentieth century by the equally blind processes of mass consumption.[22]

[. . .]

That the *animal laborans* cannot construct a human world out of its own values is borne out by the accelerating tendency of mass production and consumption to undermine not only the durability of the world but also the possibility of establishing a permanent place within it. The science fiction forms projected by the utopian urbanists of the twentieth century have arisen out of either elitist or populist attempts to reify industrial process as though it were some "ideal" manifestation of a new nature. From the futurist architect Antonio Sant'Elia's *Città Nuova* (1914), of which, to quote from the *Manifesto of Futurist Architecture*, he stated that "our houses will last less time than we do and every generation will have to make its own,"[23] to Constant Nieuwenhuys'

---

[20] Michel Parent and Jacques Verroust, *Vauban* (Paris: Editions Jacques Freal, 1971), p. 60.

[21] The horse-drawn tram of the Ringstrasse gave way to the electric tram in the early 1890s. In his *Teoría General de Urbanización* (1867), Ildefonso Cerda, the planner of modern Barcelona and inventor of the term *urbanización*, argues that "the form of the city is, or must be, derived from the necessities of locomotion." From this date onwards the city becomes inundated by mechanized movement.

[22] Arendt, *The Human Condition*, pp. 125, 126.

[23] See Reyner Banham, *Theory and Design* in *The First Machine Age* (New York: Praeger, 1960), p. 135.

spontaneously dynamic "New Babylon" (1960), where urban change would be so accelerated as to render it pointless to return home—in each instance we are presented with equally kinetic images that project through prophetic exaggeration the fundamental placeless tendency of our present urban reality[24] [...]

From the point of view of machine or rationalized production, architecture has been as much affected as urbanism by the substitution of productive or processal norms, for the more traditional criteria of worldliness and use. Increasingly buildings come to be designed in response to the mechanics of their erection or, alternatively, processal elements such as tower cranes, elevators, escalators, stairs, refuse chutes, gangways, service cores, and automobiles determine the configuration of built form to a far greater extent than the hierarchic and more public criteria of *place*. And while the space of public appearance comes to be increasingly over-run by circulation or inundated at the urban scale by restricted high-speed access, the free-standing, high-rise megaliths of the modern city maintain their potential status as "consumer goods" by virtue of their isolated form. At the same time the prefabricated elements from which such forms are increasingly assembled guarantee the optimization of their production and consumption within the overall industrial economy.

[...]

The consequence of all this for contemporary architecture is as distressing as it is universal. Elevated on freeways or pedestrian decks or alternatively sequestered behind security fences, we are caused to traverse large areas of abstract, inaccessible urban space that can be neither appropriated nor adequately maintained. In a similar way we are confronted by piazzas whose hypothetical public status is vitiated by the vacuousness of the context or alternatively we are conducted down streets evacuated of all public life by the circulatory demands of traffic. We pass across thresholds whose public-representative nature has been suppressed or we enter foyers which have been arranged or lit in such a manner as to defeat the act of public promenade. Alternatively we are caused to depart from airports whose processal function defies the ritual of leave-taking. In each instance our value-free commodity culture engenders an equivalency wherein museums are rendered as oil refineries and laboratories acquire a monumental form. By a similar token public restaurants come to be rudely incarcerated in basements, while schools find themselves arbitrarily

---

[24] Nieuwenhuys wrote: "There would be no question of any fixed life pattern since life itself would be as creative material... In New Babylon people would be constantly travelling. There would be no need for them to return to their point of departure as this in any case would be transformed. Therefore each sector would contain private rooms (a hotel) where people would spend the night and rest for a while." For the complete text see Constant Nieuwenhuys, "New Babylon," *Architectural Design* (June 1964), pp. 304, 305 [quote moved to footnote by the editor].

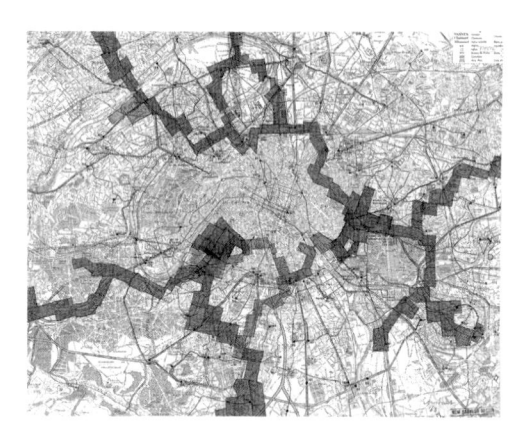

FIGURES 11 AND 12 *La Cittá Nuova, casa a gradinata.* Sant'Elia, 1914 (top); New Babylon Paris. Constant Nieuwenhuys, 1963 (below).

encased within the perimeters of windowless warehouses. In each case a ruthless cultural reduction masks itself by the rhetoric of *kitsch* or by the celebration of technique as an end in itself.[25]

THE IDENTITY OF CONSUMPTION AND THE WORLDLESSNESS OF PLAY

The earliest concentrations of labor-power, beginning first with the workhouse and then with the mill, brought about the uprooting of agrarian populations who then became as alienated from their traditional culture as they were from the objects of industrial production. This loss of "vernacular" was to return to haunt the descendants of these populations as soon as they became the "emancipated" consumers of their own output. While the specific form of "worldlessness" that resulted from this induced consumption varied with successive generations and from class to class, the initial loss of identity enforced by the conditions of industrial production was eventually sublimated, irrespective of class, by an identity to be instantly acquired through consumption. The phenomena of *kitsch*—from *Verkitschen*, "to fake"—appears with the advent of the department store, around the middle of the nineteenth century, when bourgeois civilization achieves for the first time an excessive productive capacity and is brought to create a widespread culture of its own—a culture that was to remain strangely suspended between the useful and the useless, between the sheer utility of its own puritan work ethic and a compulsive desire to mimic the licentiousness of aristocratic taste.[26]

While Marx, writing just before mass consumption began in earnest, projected the eventual liberation of all mankind from the necessity of remorseless labor, he failed to account for the latent potential of machine production to promote a voracious consumer society wherein, to quote Arendt, "nearly all human labor-power will be spent in consuming, with concomitant serious consequences for leisure."[27] In such a society the basic problem is no longer production but rather

---

[25] Innumerable examples exist of the specific displacement of the public realm in contemporary building. Among the more recent instances, one might cite the following: The Ford Foundation Building, New York, for its provision of a false "public" foyer which is programmed in such a way as to assure that no public realm may be allowed to come into existence. The Centre Pompidou, Paris, for its reduction of its "users" to the same status as the "services"—the users being piped-in, so to speak, on one side, and the services fed into the structure on the other. In short, the reduction of a museum to the status and the model expressiveness of an oil refinery! The Richards Laboratories at the University of Pennsylvania where service towers are rendered as monumental elements and where the whole structure is pervaded by a sense of "religiosity" inappropriate to the processal nature of a laboratory building. In this last example a misplaced monumentality fails to transcend the manifest absence of an appropriately "representative" or "commemorative" program, whereas in the first case the presence of a "representative" program is rendered null and void by the rhetoric of the machine. Consciously designed as a cultural supermarket, art in the name of populism is reduced to a commodity.

[26] See Hermann Broch, "Notes on the Problem of Kitsch," in Gillo Dorfles, ed., *Kitsch: The World of Bad Taste* (New York: Universe Books, 1969), p. 54.

[27] Arendt, *The Human Condition*, p. 131.

the creation of sufficient daily waste to sustain the inexhaustible capacity for consumption. Arendt's subsequent observation that this supposedly painless consumption only augments the devouring capacity of life, finds its corroboration in a world where shorter working hours, suburbanization, and the mass ownership of the automobile have together secured for the realm of consumption the ever-accelerating rate of daily commutation within the megalopolis, a situation in which the hours saved from production are precisely "compensated" by the hours wasted in the consumptive journey to work.

The victory of the *animal laborans* with which Arendt concludes her study of the dilemmas facing modern man turns not only on the reduction of art to the problematic "worldlessness" of free play, but also on the substitution of social gratification for the fabricating standards of function and use.[28] [...] Art, on the other hand, as the essence of inutility—and this of course includes the non-functional aspect of architecture—is rendered worldless in such a society, insofar as it is reduced to introspective abstraction or vulgarized in the idiosyncratic vagaries of *kitsch*. In the first instance it cannot be easily shared and in the second it is reduced to an illusory commodity. If, as Arendt insists, the world must be constructed with thought rather than cognition[29] then insomuch as it is not essential to the life processes of a laboring society, art loses its original worldliness and comes to be subsumed under play. This, of course, raises the problematic question as to the conditions under which play may be considered to be worldly. Be this as it may, freedom in laboring society is perceived solely as release from labor, namely, as play, and it is Arendt's recognition of this fact that makes her text such a perceptive, if partial, critique of Marx.[30]

[...]

THE HUMAN CONDITION AND CRITICAL THEORY: A POSTSCRIPT

Given Hannah Arendt's skepticism as to the redemption promised by the Marxist prognosis it will no doubt appear extraneous to compare her discourse to the critical theory of the Frankfurt School.[31] The reserve which Arendt publicly exercised in respect to this school of Marxist criticism should be sufficient caution against making such a comparison. Yet despite the disdain she seems to have felt for those whom she regarded as renegade Marxists, a common concern and even method may be found to relate the arguments developed in

---

[28] *Ibid.*, p. 101. See also footnote pp. 307, 308.

[29] *Ibid.*, p. 171. Arendt's distinction between "thought" and "cognition" is worth repeating here: "Thought and cognition are not the same. Thought, the source of art works, is manifest without transformation or transfiguration in all great philosophy, whereas the chief manifestation of the cognitive processes, by which we acquire and store up knowledge is the sciences."

[30] *Ibid.*, pp. 117, 118.

[31] For a historical account of the Frankfurt School and Institute of Social Research see Martin Jay, *The Dialectical Imagination* (Boston: Little, Brown, 1973).

The Human Condition to the socio-cultural analyses of the Frankfurt School. It is clear that both Arendt and the Frankfurt School were equally obsessed with the interaction of structure and superstructure in advanced industrial society, even if such terms were entirely foreign to her thought.

These qualifications accepted, one may argue that the succession of the Frankfurt School, specifically the theoretical progression that links the later thought of Herbert Marcuse to the writings of Jürgen Habermas—takes up a number of themes that were either suppressed or suspended at the conclusion of the *The Human Condition*. Amongst these issues one may arguably posit two. First, the problematic cultural status of play and pleasure in a future laboring society after its hypothetical liberation from the compulsion of consumption (Marcuse) and, second, the problematic possibility for mediating the autonomous rationality of science and technique through the reconstitution of the space of public appearance as an effective political realm (Habermas).

If one derives from *The Human Condition* the implication that a highly secular, laboring, and industrialized order must inevitably prevail in either state-capitalist, capitalist, or socialist societies, and if one posits some future state in which the "fatality" of an ever-accelerating consumption is, in some measure, redeemed, then the question arises as to what are the minimum environmental priorities that such a transformed state could realistically envisage?

While the *vita activa* in the ancient sense would no doubt initially remain in abeyance, some upgrading or the private habitat, essential to the quality or domestic life, would surely assert itself as a priority once this life was no longer subject to either rapacious consumption or optimized production. For while it is true, as Arendt asserts, that from the point of view of nature, it is *work* rather than *labor* that is destructive, this observation overlooks that qualitative dimension of consumption beyond which "man's metabolism with nature" becomes even more destructive of nature than *work*, beyond that frontier that we have already crossed, where non-renewable resources such as water and oxygen begin to become permanently contaminated or destroyed.[32] At this juncture, labor, as optimized consumption, stands opposed to its own Benthamite cult of life as the highest good, just as privacy *per se*, as the quintessence of labor and life, is undermined by the productive reduction of all built objects to the status of "consumer goods;" a threshold that has again been reached in the mobile-home industry of the United States.

Human adaptability notwithstanding, the basic criterion of privacy asserted by Barragán, posits itself not only as the necessary "figure" to the public ground, but also as the only standard by which a *balanced and rhythmic* life for the species could eventually be maintained. The urban consequences of applying such criteria as economic densities would be to spontaneously create the

---

[32] Earl F. Murphy, *Governing Nature* (Chicago: Quadrangle Books, 1967), p. 31. See also p. 118 for an interesting comment on the nature of industrial consumption: "Men have assumed that there was a direct line from production to consumption to disappearance. Now it is evident that man, whether as producer or consumer, is part of a cycle. The residue streaming from his production and consumption do *not* disappear . . . "

boundaries of a "negative" urban form—namely, some kind of public realm, even if this would not immediately constitute a "world" in the Arendtian sense. That the public space of the medieval city was the physical counterform of the private fabric Arendt herself has recognized in her assertion that it is the exterior perimeter of the private realm that effectively shapes the space of the city.

[. . .]

Whether architecture, as opposed to building, will ever be able to return to the representation of collective value is a moot point. At all events its representative role would have to be contingent on the establishment of a public realm in the political sense. Otherwise limited by definition to the act of commemoration it would remain exactly where Adolf Loos left it in 1910. That this commemorative impulse would remain alive even in a laboring society became manifest after the First World War in the numerous memorials to the "unknown soldier;" those testaments to an unidentifiable somebody whom four years of mass slaughter should have revealed.[33]

[. . .]

We are confronted [. . .] with an existential political perspective that for Arendt and Habermas alike is the only possible vehicle for the rational determination of human ends. Such a decentralized "cantonal" conception, tends, I would submit, to return us to the dependency of political power on its social and physical constitution, that is to say, on its derivation from the living proximity of men and from the physical manifestation of their public being in built form. For architecture at least, the relevance of *The Human Condition* resides in this—in its formulation of that political reciprocity that must of necessity obtain, for good or ill, between the status of men and the status of their objects.

---

[33] Arendt, *The Human Condition*, p. 181.

3 Industrialization and the Crises in Architecture (1973)

[...]

THE CRISIS OF 1851

Between 1830 and 1860, the sequential development of the ferrovitreous arcade, the market shed, the exhibition hall and the department store engendered a building typology dedicated to serve the processes of consumption. At this juncture engineering tended towards the spontaneous creation of a totally unprecedented syntax of building, wherein the essential modular technique of glass house construction would come to be combined at mid-century with the prefabricated process of the railway. The achievement of Paxton's gargantuan greenhouse, to serve as a gigantic international department store, could not have been realized in the necessary space of four months had it not been for the railway engineer Charles Fox, who was to be responsible for all its ingenious connections and for the invention and supervision of its prefabricated modular assembly.

With the Crystal Palace, the question of "how" began, at a public level, to take precedence over the issue of "what," the latter being simplistically characterized in the critical words of John Ruskin, "... as nothing but a large greenhouse." It is of significance that its size, particularly in respect to its length, was in no way limited by its form, for it could in theory have been extended well beyond its symbolic length of 1,851 feet. In short, the essence of the Crystal Palace resided in its fabric as a process, its combination of pane, sash bar, louvre, gutter, beam,

Source: Kenneth Frampton, "Industrialization and the Crises in Architecture," *Oppositions* no. 1 (September 1973), 57–82. "This paper was first read on November 25, 1972, at York University, Toronto, Canada before a conference dedicated to the work of Hannah Arendt given under the auspices of the Toronto Society for the Study of Social and Political Thought. The author was asked to prepare this paper on the basis of his previous study of Hannah Arendt's work, which had first appeared in 1969 under the title, 'Labour, Work & Architecture'." [This reference appears in the original text].

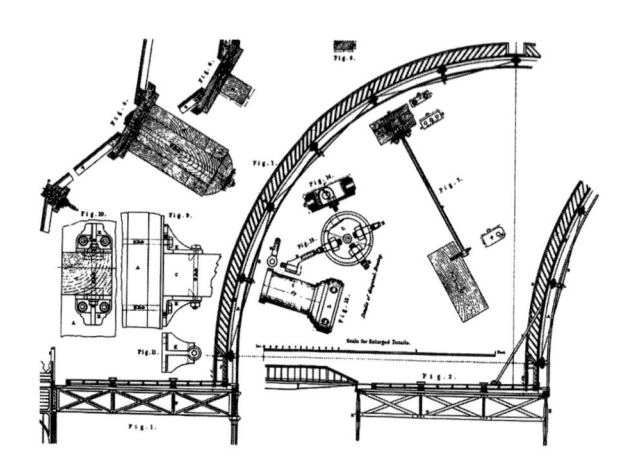

FIGURES 13 AND 14 Crystal Palace, London, United Kingdom. Joseph Paxton (with Fox and Henderson), 1851. Construction details (top) and the "Glazing Waggon" (below).

truss and column, to be endlessly repeated and rearranged just like the components of the railway system to which it was directly related. Paxton's Palace was infinitely extendable and capable of limitless permutation. Burton's proposal to reassemble its components into a tower 1000 feet high to be served by steam elevators (the vertical equivalent of the locomotive) testifies to the intrinsic openendedness of its system. Clearly the Palace would not in any classical sense of the word be said to have been composed and indeed, had it not been for a last minute outcry over tree preservation, it would have been erected without its central transept—the one feature which served to impart a certain fortuitous symmetry to its otherwise undifferentiated facade. The particular reversal that the Great Exhibition represents of the traditional hierarchic order of ends and means, merits some examination since the consequence of such a reversal is different in respect to the Palace itself and the objects it contained. In both instances the "how" took precedence over the "what," but with such different results that the dramatic discrepancies to be found between the exhibition as building and the exhibition as an array of objects demands some explanation. This may be accounted for in the assigned status of the objects involved, for whereas the former was essentially the crystallization of the *primary system of production and distribution*, identical in its paleotechnicity to the cast iron lathes and the rolling stock that were displayed within its machine hall, the latter was *the essential end product*, the creation of an instant culture of consumption, the provision of intimate artifacts for the theatrical establishment of a totally new class.

It is hardly an accident that the phenomena of wholesale kitsch appears exactly at this point of crisis, at this moment of the department store, in 1860, when bourgeois civilization, entering upon its first flood of affluence, finds itself equipped with a surplus of means over needs and is forced to create an instant culture of its own—that outside sheer utility is destined to lie suspended between the asceticism of production (the Puritan ethos) and the comfort of consumption (the heritage of license).

[...]

The bourgeois world, deprived by its sudden triumph of a traditional arena or time honored mode in which to ritualize its power, display its wealth and realize its image was forced by virtue of its inherent self-alienation to create an instant culture of aristocratic pretensions or alternatively to celebrate in liberal protest the lost tranquility of some pre-industrial world wherein production was founded in the communality of the medieval Guild. In the first instance it attempted to domesticate the aristocratic landscape of *libertinage*, to tame the Baroque excesses of the *ancien regime*. In this connection the charade of constitutional monarchy may be seen as the *mise en scene* for the ultimate bourgeois fantasy. By the same token, as Broch has put it, " . . . the middle classes deceived themselves by saying that they had won a complete victory;

throughout the nineteenth century they pretended that they had inaugurated great art and defeated *libertinage* for ever."[1]

All of the middle class that is save for its liberal thinkers, architects and designers who were not so easily deceived and who struggled in their critical confusion (even to the extent of falling into *kitsch*) against the ever overwhelming sea of *kitsch* into which they were pathetically projected. The connection between utilitarianism and *kitsch* can hardly be overlooked. Jeremy Bentham's precept, "... the greatest happiness of the greatest number" is surely sufficient justification for its perpetuation. At all events the Crystal Palace was one vast emporium of kitsch, notwithstanding the utilitarianism of its structure and the machine functionalism of some of its objects. No one was more aware of the crisis of 1851 than the German architect and liberal revolutionary Gottfried Semper [...who] was to find no cure for the despair that he felt at the prospect of the Great Exhibition.[2] The crisis that he so succinctly outlined was to remain unresolved both for him and for all the subsequent followers of Pugin, Ruskin and Morris—the many disciples of the English Arts and Crafts reaction to the tide of industrial production. All the craft guild revivals and the design reform movements were not to prosper in their vain attempts to countervail the flood of industrialism. Only the Deutsche Werkbund, founded in 1911 by Herman Muthesius, as a consortium of industrialists and designers, had the remotest chance of success and this intended in the last analysis (however deluded it might have been) not the cultural, social and political reformism of the Arts and Crafts movement, nor Muthesius' egalitarian world of *Gute Form*, but rather a further expansion in Prussia's share of world trade. In the interim William Morris, the socialist, had to resign himself to producing wall papers and Pre-Raphaelite pseudo mediaeval furnishings for the upper bourgeoisie—the industrial *nouveau riche*. Morris' dream of a utopia where wind and water would once again be the only source of power, where the agrarian commune would constitute the space of public appearance, and where the guild would be the only source of work, food and furnishing was not to be realized. As he was to put it at the end of his life, with regard to the prospect of creating a culturally valid architecture for the 19th century, an architecture free from alienation, "The hope of our ignorance has passed away. But it has not given place to the hope born of knowledge."[3]

---

[1] Herman Broch, "Notes on the Problem of Kitsch" in *Kitsch: The World of Bad Taste*, ed. Gillo Dorfles (New York: Universe Books, 1969), p. 65.

[2] Gottfried Semper, *Wissenschaft, Industrie and Kunst* (Braunschweig, 1852). Excerpts in English from H.M. Wingler, *The Bauhaus* (Cambridge, Mass.: The MIT Press, 1969), p. 18 [Footnote moved from its original place by the editor].

[3] William Morris, "The Revival of Architecture" (1888), *Some Architectural Writers of the Nineteenth Century*, ed. Nicholas Pevsner (Oxford: Clarendon Press, 1972), p. 323. Given the argument of this present essay, Morris' conclusions about architecture made at the end of his life are worth quoting in full. "History taught us the evolution of Architecture, it is now teaching us the evolution of society; and it is clear to us, and even to many who refuse to acknowledge it, that the society which is developing out of ours will not need or endure mechanical drudgery as the lot of the general population; that the new society will not be hagridden as we are by the necessity for producing ever more and more market wares for a profit, whether anyone needs them or not; that it will produce

In the last analysis the overall crisis suffered by architecture after its mid-18th century divorce from engineering turned as much on the initiation of comfort and domesticity and on the flowering of social intercourse, as it did on those transformations progressively effected after 1750 in the basic means of production. As Hannah Arendt has written, "The astonishing flowering of poetry and music from the middle of the 18th century until the last third of the 19th century, accompanied by the rise of the novel, the only entirely social art form, coinciding with a no less striking decline of all the more public arts, especially architecture, is sufficient testimony to a close relationship between the social and the intimate."[4]

Even if largely determined by a mid-century escalation in machine production and distribution, the proliferation of *kitsch* after 1860 is nothing if it is not a social manifestation, which sought spontaneously to provide through its pluralism of style that range of necessary fantasy for those emerging classes, who would have otherwise been bereft of style and who, in any event, irrespective of their status, lacked a fulfilling socio-cultural arena within which to reify and exercise their status and imminent power.

Meanwhile, what was already making mass society difficult to bear was not, to quote Hannah Arendt, "... the number of people involved or at least not primarily, but the fact that the world between them [had] lost its power to gather them together, to relate and to separate them."[5] It is surely this disintegration of the public realm that accounts for the overriding concern of 19th century thinkers, architects and reformers for the recreation of a culturally viable community in which the "space of public appearance" would be brought into being after the manner of the ancient Greek polis. Thus some form of pre-industrial social armature, often conceived as an agrarian craft building, became the hypothetical key to the recreation of a coherent and authentic culture.

[...]

THE CRISIS OF 1918

The hypostasized triumph of 19th century production and technique, formally expressed in the pompier manner of the Paris exhibition of 1900, prevailed without interruption until the outbreak of the First World War. With the eruption of Von

---

to live, and not live to produce, as we do. Under such conditions architecture as a part of the life of people in general, will again become possible, and I believe that when it is possible, it will have a real new birth, and add so much to the pleasure of life that we shall wonder how as people we ever were able to live without it. Meantime we are waiting for that new development of society, some of us in cowardly inaction, some of us amidst hopeful work towards the change; but at least we are all waiting for what must be the work, not of leisure and taste of a few scholars, authors and artists, but of the necessities and aspirations of the workmen throughout the civilized world."

[4] Hannah Arendt, *The Human Condition* (Chicago: University of Chicago Press, 1958; New York: Doubleday Anchor Book, 1959), p. 36.

[5] Arendt, *The Human Condition*, p. 36.

Moltke's so-called "time-table war" (wherein both the railway and machine tool technology were to play salient roles), industrial production and consumption acquired a new and horrific meaning, namely the mass production of death and the mass consumption of men. This holocaust, the first instance of "total war" directly involving the civilian population, had the effect of bursting the bubble of late 19th century romanticism—the largely private yet nonetheless xenophobic realms of the *Art Nouveau*, the *Jugendstijl* and the *Stile Floreale*. With Lenin's seizure of the Winter Palace in St. Petersburg in October 1917, the proud but fragile tower of the 19th century bourgeois culture collapsed and with it, not only the confident *fin de siecle* celebration of the State—the masquerade of constitutional monarchy—but also the claustrophobic individualism of the exotic *Gesamtkunstwerk*.

It is the German and Russian experience this time to arrive at "an architecture degree zero,"[6] and the difference of their respective attitudes to this experience is of significance in itself. Industrial production, now disrupted and in many instances totally destroyed by the war, creates an austere objectless world, a cultural hiatus wherein men hitherto overwhelmed by the nightmare of industrialization may briefly speculate on an alternative condition. For a moment following the armistice of 1918 they are unencumbered by the remorseless cycle

---

[6] I have borrowed the elusive term "degree zero" from Roland Barthes' study *Le Degre Zero de L'Ecriture*, Paris, 1953; translated from the French by Annette Lavers and Colin Smith and published by Jonathan Cope, London in 1967 as *Writing Degree Zero*. I have used this term to suggest a cultural break in which the traditional cultural system is totally vitiated, resulting in a "black hole" so to speak within which an unforeseen socio-cultural complex begins to accrete. Of the evolution of literature in the 19th and 20th centuries Barthes has written: "From an initial nonexistence in which thought, by happy miracle, seemed to stand out against a backcloth of words, writing thus passed through all the stages of a progressive solidification; it was first the object of a gaze, (Châteaubriand) then of creative action, finally of murder, (Mallarmé), and has reached in our time a last metamorphosis, absence: in those neutral modes of writing, called here 'the zero degree' of writing; we can easily discern a negative momentum, and an inability to maintain it within time's flow, as if literature, having tended for a hundred years now to transmute its surface into a form with no antecedents, could no longer find purity anywhere but in the absence of all signs, finally proposing the realization of this Orphean dream; a writer without Literature." At the end of his study Barthes concludes, "There is therefore in every present mode of writing a double postulation: there is the impetus of a break and the impetus of a coming to power, there is the very shape of every revolutionary situation, the fundamental ambiguity of which is that Revolution must of necessity borrow, from what it wants to destroy, the very image of what it wants to possess. Like modern art in its entirety, literary writing carries at the same time the alienation of History and the dream of History; as a Necessity, it testifies to the division of languages, which is inseparable from the division of classes; as Freedom, it is the consciousness of this division and the very effort which seeks to surmount it. Feeling permanently guilty of its own solitude, it is nonetheless an imagination eagerly desiring a felicity of words, it hastens towards a dreamed-of language whose freshness, by a kind of ideal anticipation, might portray the perfection of some new Adamic world where language would no longer be alienated. The proliferation of modes of writing brings a new Literature into being in so far as the latter invents its language only in order to be a project: Literature becomes the Utopia of language" [footnote moved from its original place by the editor].

FIGURES 15 AND 16 Lyonel Feininger, "Cathedral of the Future," woodcut, cover for the Bauhaus program, April 1919 (top); the 3rd Battle of Ypres Salient, 1917 (below).

of production and consumption; for an instant they are activated by the extreme socio-economic crises in which they are immersed, in Germany by the Sparticist Revolt of 1919, in Russia by the trauma of Civil War lasting from 1917 to 1921. Bourgeois professionalism, so painstakingly institutionalized throughout the 19th century, momentarily loosens its cultural hold. For a brief moment the mid-18th century division between architecture and engineering loses its significance. Art now rises into the ascendant as the potential embodiment of unalienated value and the artist briefly re-emerges as the highest form of the *homo faber*.

[. . .]

The situation in Russia immediately after the Revolution of 1917 was entirely different. The bourgeois world was suddenly terminated. The means of production, such as they were, were definitively in the hands of the State. The imminent era of State Capitalism, even with its incipient beginnings in the compromise of NEP of 1922, was hardly to be foreseen. Within the urbanized populace the intrinsic relations obtaining between man and man and men and objects now stood mutually and consciously transformed by a definitive break in history.

For the Russian workers' Soviets, the space of public appearance was no longer a fantastic *Narodnik* dream, as in Gropius' *Zukunftskathedrale* or in Taut's *Haus des Himmels*, but rather a living everyday reality.

[. . .]

Theoretically all objects, whether utilitarian or not, now stood oriented towards the same teleology, namely the fundamental disalienation of all men. The function of production was no longer solely the inverted process of consumption, and objects which had hitherto stood against the producers as the product of labor to be appropriated by capital, now embodied the very content of life and its necessary objectification. Both 19th century *Narodnik* reformism and bourgeois utilitarianism now became mutually absorbed within the object, and to this end the largely illiterate Soviet society provided the opportunity for the object to play a unique role in the space of public appearance, since everything required to be re-semanticized, as it were, in a situation where objects and their contextual disposition, rather than the written word, were to become the currency and the testament of the people. As in mediaeval times, the disposition of an object or a man in space now took on an informative role. By the same token, as in the traditional Russian *lubok* or icon, the slogan and the image of an object became almost mutually interchangeable, the word fusing into a sign while the object by virtue of its simplification began to function as inscription. At this juncture the most rudimentary open timber scaffolding became capable of evoking the total constructive intention of the Soviets, while soon after the Revolution of 1917, the block capital inscription of Lenin's name became the immediate icon of the new socialist state.

None succeeded more forcefully in inventing a theoretical superstructure for this process of *resemanticization* than the Social Democrat Alexander Malinovsky, otherwise known as Bogdanov (the God gifted), who was to abandon the Social Democrats for the Bolsheviks in the revolutionary crisis of 1903 and to found, three years later, the organization for Proletarian culture, otherwise known as the *Proletkult* movement. This movement was to dedicate itself to the regeneration of culture through a new unity of science, industry and art. *The Proletkult* was to afford the collectivity a means for transcending both traditional culture and its own production into a new order of unity.

The traditional fields of art, architecture and engineering now found themselves inundated and overrun by the world of objects in action. Buildings were no longer hermetic finished compositions but rather aggregations of elements in the process of being enacted. Their component parts were not only signs of actual productive relationships, as in Paxton's Crystal Palace, but also the context for more explicit iconography and information. Equipped with flags, clocks, searchlights, cinematic projectors, radio aerials, loudspeakers, slogans and billboards, they deliberately carried the dialectic of socialism into the street. They constituted both its manifest incarnation and its literal meaning. By the same token *Proletkult* furniture no longer optimized cushioned comfort as in the upholstered interiors of late 19th century bourgeois affluence but gave priority instead to the use of unworked standard timber sections and therein to the universal primitive nature of its production and to its inherent potential for disassembly, mobility, conversion and reuse. Furniture was thus returned to its etymological origins, as indicated by the French word *meubles*. In essence it became indistinguishable from the demountable set pieces or play machines of the *agit prop* stage, just as the acrobatic slapstick routines of the circus became fused into "agitatory" presentations of Western classical theatre. Art, life, theatre, circus, cinema, and architecture now began to be consciously merged into one continuum in which there was no longer any self-evident point of interruption. This "art of the street," as it were, manifested itself most intensely in the theatricalization of everyday life, in the agit prop propaganda trains and boats designed by the *Proletkult* and in the "monumental plan" launched by the authorities immediately after the Revolution, with the express purpose of covering every available surface with slogans and abstract icons representing the new order. All was process, yet all was public. At the same time all the categories of the old world momentarily ceased to have any significance. In the midst of hunger, crisis, civil war and political conflict the whole of life had become a total work of art through an emphasis on totality rather than on art. Overnight, fine artists vehemently abandoned their traditional calling and diverted their entire creative energies to the field of applied art. These men became preoccupied with the design of light, collapsible furniture, with the furnishing of durable worker's clothing, and with the design of more efficient pieces of equipment. Something of their essential position may be gleaned from the rhetorical polemic of the *Program of the Productivist Group* which concluded with the words, "Down with Art! Long live the Technic! Religion is a lie! Art is a lie! Down with guarding the traditions of art! Long live the constructivist technician!"[7]

The post-war cultural impact of 1918, which was first a triumph and then a debacle, remains with us today, and the way in which we still experience its effect merits some examination. There is no question but that the whole object of modern design received its basic paradigm via the Bauhaus of 1923 from the Proletarian Culture of the Russian Revolution. For although much of the origin of modern functionalism lies embedded in the utilitarianism of the 19th century, its elevation into a value and a sign—as the *Ding an sich* of human culture—is the prime contribution of the *Proletkult* of the early Russian Soviets. In a sense it is this essence that the Bauhaus assimilated and "translated" into the product design ethos of the mid-20th century.[8]

This origin more than anything else may go far towards explaining the perennial incompatibility that obtains between rigorous modern design and the world in which we live. For whereas the one presupposes, despite its subtle reabsorption into the production cycle, some predetermined state of scarcity or of homeostasis (where objects are not produced for the purpose of their instant consumption), the latter remains in or alternatively has regressed into, a state where the possibilities of an unalienated culture have been vitiated either by bureaucratic loss of nerve in the East or by "admass somnambulism" in the West. Where the former presupposes some sterile orthodoxy divorced from life, the latter predicates the apparent and deceptive pluralism of *kitsch*. In both instances the common crisis indicates a crisis of identity and power: the failure of the center to know who it is or by what ultimate right it rules; the failure of the periphery to know not only its own historical identity but also to understand why it is ruled and to what end. As Hannah Arendt reminds us, the triumph of 1789 caused the bourgeoisie to

---

[7] For the full text of the program see *Gabo* (Cambridge: Harvard University Press, 1957), p. 153. This program was signed by Vladimir Tatlin and Alexei Gan. A parallel text, entitled "Constructivism" was written by Alexei Gan in Moscow in 1920. It was first published by Tver in 1922. In this essay, Gan quotes Bogdanov to the following effect: "During the primitive age, art was not the basis of a formal expression of ideologies. It served purely practical purposes and had only a utilitarian significance: it was the organising element in work, creating that 'unity of mood' among those taking part and a coordination of this mood with the work in hand." See Camilla Gray, *The Great Experiment: Russian Art 1863–1922* (London: Thames & Hudson, 1962), pp. 284–87.

[8] The orientation of the Bauhaus workshops changed after the spring of 1923 when Johannes Itten resigned, yielding this key position on the Bauhaus faculty to László Moholy-Nagy. Before joining the Bauhaus, Moholy-Nagy had made contact with Alexander Rodchenko and El Lissitzky, both of whom had taught in the Soviet *Vchutemas*, after their foundation in the early '20s. The translation referred to is one in which the so-called production art of the *Vchutemas*, the object design that derived its authority from an economic culture of materials, came to be aestheticized in the Bauhaus workshops. The aluminum tube and canvas chair designed under Rodchenko's direction in 1926 contrasts with Marcel Breuer's Vassily chair designed in the Bauhaus metal workshop in 1925. The respective dates, according to Quilici and Wingler, give precedence to the latter but one is left with an uncomfortable feeling that the position is the reverse.

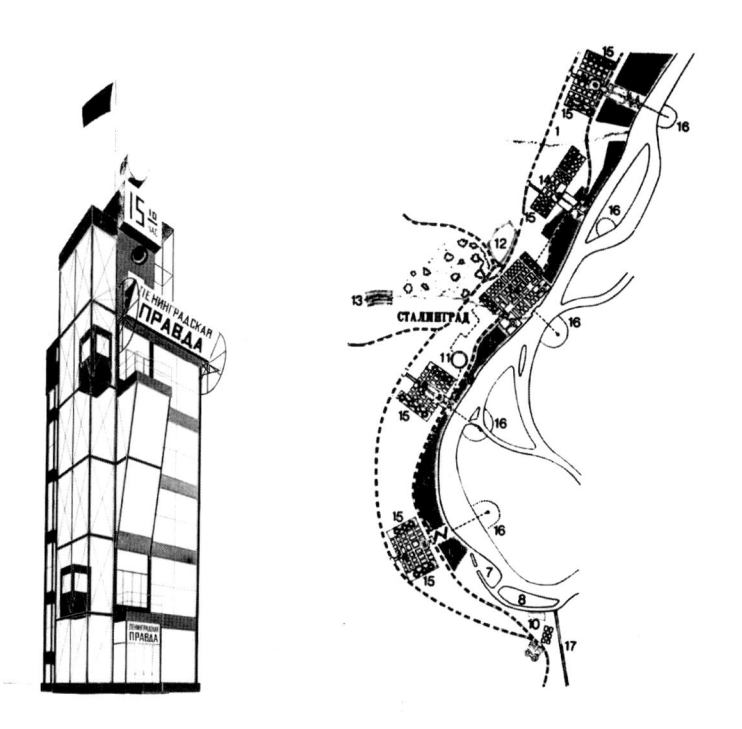

FIGURES 17 AND 18 Design for the Pravda newspaper building, Leningrad (St. Petersburg), Russia. Leonid, Viktor, and Alexander Vesnin, 1924 (left). V. Semenov's plan for Stalingrad, 1930 (right).

acquire the trappings of the deposed aristocracy and to imitate their noble style of life. By something of the same token the revolutionaries of 1917 fell into the simulation of the bourgeois state and culture they had previously overthrown; as a direct means of asserting and maintaining the legitimacy of their absolute power.

The constructivist technician may well have failed the Revolution through his failure to acknowledge the reality of such psychological dependency or, more seriously, through his technical incapacity or through his inability to realize that a rhetoric of technique must perforce give way to the struggle to transform an underdeveloped economy into a modern industrial state. Conversely, one may argue that the party bureaucrat failed the Revolution in as much as he could not permit the participatory culture of the *Proletkult* to continue, particularly as it was predicated on its own spontaneous space of public appearance. In the name of power and security he needed instead to assert art as the codification of disciplinary values oriented not towards the evolution of a more human way of life but rather towards the statistical determination of productive behaviour, the paradigm of the *Stakhanovite*.

Within this historical paradox the basic crisis of a teleology re-emerges not only for architecture but for the orientation of human culture as a whole. Bogdanov was more than fully aware of this problem when, as James Billington has written: "In the manner of Saint Simon, rather than Marx, Bogdanov argued that the destructive conflicts of the past would never be resolved without a positive new religion; that the unifying role once played in society by a central temple of worship and religious faith must now be played by the living temple of the proletariat and by a pragmatic socially oriented philosophy 'empirion-ism.'"[9]

As we rush headlong into the reverberating crisis of the future, it becomes increasingly clear that what transpired in Russia in 1918 determined both the predicament and cultural threshold of all that we have subsequently experienced as men set within the raceway of the 20th century. With Bogdanov architecture arrived at a "degree zero" from which it has not been possible to return despite the *kitsch* consumerism of much of the building in which we are largely destined to live out our lives. It stood then at the threshold of a promise that remains unresolved. With its commitment to advancing the proletariat on three parallel fronts, the political, the economic and the cultural, it posited culture as a space of public appearance in itself. To Lenin's outrage it postulated the cultural as a formative element equal to the jurisdiction of the party. It advocated the social determination of the environment as the very substance and meaning of human culture. It implied a continuum of objects reduced to their non-fantasized significance; to their intrinsic meaning in relation to society as a whole. At one level functionalism for the *Proletkult* meant that things were not produced in order to be consumed, at another it committed itself to production as some ultimate end. In this it participated in the dilemma that still bedevils both East and West, namely how one may escape the endless cyclical chain

---

[9] J. Billington, *The Icon and the Axe* (New York: Knopf, 1968), p. 489.

of means and ends without admitting to any telos or end in itself—or to put it another way, how one may determine any final form without having a model of some ultimate state. One may appreciate all too clearly why Bogdanov was preoccupied with the idea of a new religion; with the challenge of interjecting some ultimate ideal into the spectrum of materialism.

The crisis of 1918 was the crisis of architecture in as much as men acknowledged for the first time that there was no escape from the processes of history, that the unity of antiquity was lost forever and the production without end, without any limiting theory of material and spiritual need presupposed a limitless consumption—the never ending fantasmagoria of *kitsch*. Today, we are caught up within an ideology of waste, whereof as Hannah Arendt has written: "In our need for more and more rapid replacement of the worldly things around us, we can no longer afford to use them, to respect and preserve their inherent durability, we must consume, devour, as it were, our houses and furniture and cars as though they were the good things of life which would spoil uselessly if they are not drawn swiftly into the never ending cycle of man's metabolism with nature. It is as though we had forced open the distinguishing boundaries which protected the world, the human artifice from nature, from the biological processes which surround it, delivering and abandoning to them the always threatened stability of a human world."[10]

In this passage architecture as opposed to cyclical production is revealed by Arendt as being fully contingent on the preservation of a truly political realm at an effective scale, since rationality itself, i.e., rational truth or as Habermas has characterized it, *purposeful rational action,* in no way guarantees the appearance of the human world upon which architecture reflexively depends.[11] For lacking an ultimate end, lacking the metaphysical unity of antiquity or of Christendom, lacking above all even the possibility of a scientific determination of needs, architecture can only be predicated ultimately on the political arena. In this respect it becomes increasingly apparent that the only way in which our self consuming ideology of waste will be overcome and architecture redeemed is through the participatory democratic determination of the nature of our environment. The alternative is to remain subject to that which Arendt has described as the most tyrannical government of all, namely, the government of nobody—the totalitarianism of technique.

---

[10] Arendt, *The Human Condition*, p. 109.

[11] Jürgen Habermas, "Technology and Science as 'Ideology,'" *Toward a Rational Society*, trans. Jeremy J. Shapiro (Boston: Beacon Press, 1971), pp. 81–122.

4 Apropos Ulm: Curriculum and Critical Theory (1974)

INTRODUCTION

There is little doubt that the Hochschule für Gestaltung, Ulm, has been the most significant school of design to come into existence since the end of World War II, not so much for what it achieved in terms of actual production, nor for the large number of designers it effectively educated, but for the extraordinary high level of critical consciousness that it managed to sustain in its daily work. In many respects the Hochschule was a pioneer, not only in terms of its evolution of design methods and the quality of the designs it achieved with these methods, but also because of the crisis of identity it suffered as a consequence of its dialectical rationality. The questions that the Hochschule began to ask a decade ago are now being asked, consciously or unconsciously, by every design and architecture school throughout the country, and the crisis of identity that befell the Hochschule has now become a universal *malaise*. For, over the past ten years it has become increasingly clear that certain lines of rational inquiry lead very promptly to an abyss where the relation between the design product and the society becomes extremely problematic; or, put in other terms, to a situation where the impossibility of an overall rational projection, under present circumstances, becomes clearly manifest.

Once design has reached this level of consciousness, it is inevitably confronted with a dilemma in which, in the broadest terms, it is usually faced with two choices. Either, as in the case of the famous Bertrand Russell paradox, it may choose to exclude a certain area of enquiry—a gesture which, although it sufficed to sustain mathematics, is difficult to maintain without rupture in the social world—or it may choose to continue to confront the immanent contradictions

Source: Kenneth Frampton, "Apropos Ulm: Curriculum and Critical Theory," *Oppositions*. no. 3 (May 1974): 17–36.

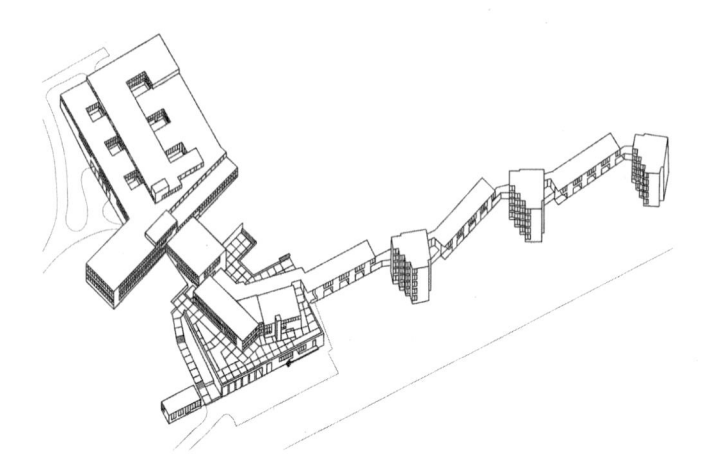

FIGURES 19 AND 20 Hochschule für Gestaltung Ulm, Germany. Max Bill, 1952–1955. Axonometric (top), and a view of the building in 1955 with the Ulm Münster Cathedral behind (below).

of the projection of rational human goals in relation to the dominant processes of the society. Should it choose the latter course, there is little doubt but that, as in the experience of the Hochschule, the liberal consensus of pluralism would be placed in jeopardy and relations with the establishment would become increasingly strained. This much is evident from the accounts of the development of the Hochschule given in the journal *Ulm*, numbers 1 to 21, which have been the main source for the study that follows here. It is clear even from a most cursory reading of this publication that, contrary to popular myth, there was never any monolithic position obtained at the Hochschule, for the discourse that was carried on in its journal came into being solely through interchange of individual opinion. In this respect, by virtue of quoting extensively, I have largely let the protagonists speak for themselves, although, as always, the choice of text for excerption must inevitably support one interpretation rather than another.

In my treatment of the curriculum and the pedagogical method employed, I have only been able to outline the circumstances of a very complex development, partly because the material published in the journal is insufficient for an exhaustive analysis, and partly because this has not been my main intention. My aim has been to trace the evolution of the general ideology of the curriculum rather than to reveal the multiple vicissitudes of the teaching method, and in this, I should add, I have used throughout the term "ideology" in the non-pejorative sense, to mean, as in the Oxford English Dictionary, "a system of ideas concerning phenomena especially those of a social life." I have also deliberately adopted the term "critical theory" to suggest that there was something more than just a casual connection between the critical consciousness of the Hochschule and the critical theory developed by the Frankfurt School of Social Research.

[...]

THE IDEOLOGY OF A CURRICULUM

In an indirect way, the Hochschule für Gestaltung was a product of the German resistance to the Nazi regime, for the Hochschule was created, in principle, in 1950 by the Geschwister-Scholl Foundation, in memory of two young members of the Scholl family, Hans and Sophie Scholl, who had been executed by the Nazis some seven years before. It was the purpose of the foundation to establish a school which would, in the words of the constitution, combine "as one entity, professional ability, cultural design and political responsibility."

According to Konrad Wachsmann, the Hochschule had its origins in a move on the part of the American High Commissioner for Germany, John J. McCloy, to sponsor, with considerable American aid, the foundation of a school of social research and political science as part of the American programme for the postwar reconstruction of Germany.[1] It would seem, if Wachsmann is

---

[1] Donald Drew Egbert, *Social Radicalism and the Arts*, New York: Alfred A Knopf, 1970, p. 700. Egbert makes it clear that John McCloy was involved in the founding of the school. It is evident that in the late 1950s the HfG still received American financial support: "In

correct, that this initiative was officially channeled through the Geschwister-Scholl Foundation and that it was Max Bill who, on being commissioned to design the building, persuaded Inge Aicher Scholl, and presumably the American High Commission, to found not a school of politics but rather a school of design. Nonetheless, a vestige of this initial political intent remained in the curriculum of the school, and this element contributed significantly to the shaping of its destiny.

Apart from this political legacy, the Hochschule was a conscious continuation of the German Applied Art School reform movement,[2] begun in the last decade of the nineteenth century, out of which the Bauhaus emerged in all its various incarnations. Even the name Hochschule für Gestaltung derives directly from the Bauhaus, since this was already a sub-title for the Dessau Bauhaus before Walter Gropius's resignation in 1928.[3] In any event, the connection was made explicit in Max Bill's first public statement as the director of the Hochschule in 1953.[4]

[. . .]

---

the last few years, the industry of West Germany gave an average of DM100,000 per year for further expansion of the school, for the scholarship fund and to balance the budget. The Rockefeller Foundation donated DM40,000 for the completion of school buildings and workshops. The Ford Foundation gave DM65,000 for the establishment at an Institute for Visual Perception" (Appendix to *Ulm*, No. 2. October 1958). If Wachsmann is correct in asserting that the original intent had been to found a school of politics then an interesting parallel would emerge with the Frankfurt School of Social Research, since this was re-established in Frankfurt under the auspices of McCloy in July 1949. See Martin Jay, *The Dialectical Imagination*, Boston, MA: Little. Brown & Co., 1973, p. 282.

[2] The founding of the Grand Ducal School of Arts and Crafts at Weimar in 1906, under the directorship of Henry Van de Velde, was a direct outcome of the German Kunstgewerbeschule reform movement, as was Peter Behrens's appointment to the head of the School of Applied Art, Dusseldorf, in 1903.

[3] Hans Maria Wingler, *The Bauhaus*, Cambridge, MA: MIT Press, 1969, p. 125. The Bauhaus newspaper also bore the name *Zeitschrift für Gestaltung*.

[4] "The founders of the Ulm School believe art to be the highest expression of human life and their aim is therefore to help in turning life into a work of art. In the words of that memorable challenge thrown down by Henry Van der Velde over 50 years ago, we mean 'to wage war on ugliness,' and ugliness can only be combated with what is intrinsically good . . . 'good' because at once seemly and practical. As the direct heir to Van de Velde's School at Weimar, the Dessau Bauhaus had set itself precisely the same objects. If we intend to go further at Ulm than they did at Dessau, this is because postwar requirements clearly postulate the necessity for certain additions to the curriculum. For instance, we mean to give still greater prominence to the design of ordinary things in everyday use; to foster the widest possible development of town and regional planning; and to bring visual design up to the standard which the latest technical advances have made possible. There will also be an entirely new department for the collection and dissemination of useful information." Max Bill, "The Bauhaus Idea from Weimar to Ulm," in Trevor Dannatt, ed., *Architects' Yearbook*, No. 5, trans. P. Morton Shand, London: Elek, 1953, pp. 29–32 [Quote converted to footnote by the editor].

The resignation of Bill in 1956, and his replacement by a triumvirate, found its reflection in these discreetly formulated goals from which any reference to city and regional planning had been eliminated. It also found reflection in the four-year curriculum outline that followed, above all in the foundation course which was mandatory for all first-year students. This course, which was established as a *Grundlehre* by the Argentinian painter/designer Tomás Maldonado,[5] ostensibly comprised the following subjects: visual method, workshop practice, presentation methods, design methodology, sociology, perception theory, twentieth-century cultural history and a remedial course in mathematics, physics and chemistry. Judging from the highly schematic exposition given in *Ulm 1*, this course attempted to place a distinct and unusual emphasis on mathematics; first, on the creative and manipulative use of mathematical constructs in pragmatic design training, and second, on mathematical logic as the conceptual basis of design method. At the same time, the sociological and cultural aspects of the course emphasized Western super-structural transformations since the Industrial Revolution. One should note in passing that the workshop practice was markedly different from that of the Bauhaus, its emphasis being entirely away from any kind of craft production and towards the photo-reproduction of material and the making of prototypes. In fact, training was only given in wood, metal, plaster and photography.[6]

[5] Tomás Maldonado was born in Buenos Aires in 1922. Trained at the Fine Arts Academy of Buenos Aires from 1938 to 1942, he thereafter worked as a painter and a writer. From 1951 he was editor of the magazine *Nueva Vision*, an Argentine publication dedicated to art, typography, architecture and industrial design. He joined the foundation faculty of the Hochschule für Gestaltung at Ulm in 1954 and became chairman of the triumvirate board in 1956. The initial contact would seem to have been established during the preparation of Maldonado's monograph on the work of Bill, *Max Bill* (Buenos Aires: Editorial Nueva Vision, 1955). Maldonado, who was present at some of the earliest planning meetings with Inge Scholl, has confirmed the Wachsmann thesis that the idea for a "New Bauhaus" had come from Bill. Maldonado's own position in the mid-1950s is evident from his text on the school published in *Nueva Vision* in 1955: "In the years following the First World War the necessity for a generic modern culture was strongly felt. This programme now seems too vague and deficient: we could not use it as a basis for a current programme, or at least, not without certain reservations . . . The HfG we are building in Ulm intends to redefine the terms of the new culture. Unlike Moholy-Nagy in Chicago, it does not merely want to form men who would be able to create and express themselves. The school at Ulm . . . wants to indicate what the social goal of this creativity should be; in other words, which forms deserve to be created and which do not. That is, generic modernity and creativity hold no place in its programme . . . An example can better clarify the nature of the phenomena to which we are referring. It is a widespread belief, at least in certain circles, that the industrial designer, the planner who works for mass production, has only one function: that of catering to the sales programme of large scale industry, while simulating the mechanism of competition. In contrast to this view, the HfG proposes that the designer, even while working for industry, must continue to absolve himself of his responsibilities with regard to society." It is obvious that Maldonado sensed from the outset the contradiction of industrial design in a neo-capitalist society; although at this date, it is clear that the prime hope was to evolve a workable strategy for the mediating role of design [Footnote moved from original place by the editor].

[6] For a detailed breakdown of the 1957 curriculum see *Ulm*, No. 2. October 1958.

That there had been a major shift in orientation between Bill's brief tenure and the triumvirate rule of 1958 is also reflected in the curricula of the four departmental courses of industrial design, building, visual communication and information. If the heritage of the Bauhaus, initially acclaimed by Bill, still manifested itself in the recreation of a common foundation course and in the importance attached to some form of workshop practice, the departure from the Bauhaus tradition found clear expression in three sets of academic courses that were common to all four departments. First, in the return to socio-cultural history, a subject which had never been regarded as having any kind of validity within the millennial perspective of the Bauhaus; second, in a course known as operational research, comprising group theory, set theory, statistics and linear programming; and finally, in courses dealing with the theory and epistemology of science, branching out into behavior theory and the theory of machines. Irrespective of the level initially attained in this ambitious programme, there is no reason to doubt but that this curriculum served not only to structure the pedagogic programme but also to publicly proclaim the ideology of the school; and, lest there should be any doubt as to the changed nature of the school, this schematic statement of intent was followed in the same month by the second issue of the journal, *Ulm 2*, which was largely devoted to a transcript of Tomás Maldonado's address to Brussels World Fair, given in September 1958, under the title "New Developments in Industry and the Training of the Designer." This, as far as I know, was Maldonado's first public declaration; the range and complexity of the argument warrants a brief analysis of its salient points, particularly as this discourse clearly exerted a major influence on the formation of school policy. In retrospect, one cannot see that either of the other members of the triumvirate—neither the graphic designer Otl Aicher, who in any event betrayed little taste for intellectual discourse at this time, nor the sociologist Hanno Kesting, whose critical sociological position could not have been very far removed from that of Maldonado, and whose studies into the nature of industrial society had been published in the previous year[7]—would have much cause for disagreement with Maldonado's position.

Given the inescapable, almost fatal orientation of the Hochschule towards an updating of the Bauhaus, the initial point of interest in Maldonado's 1958 address lies in his measured critique of that legendary institution, and in particular for the distance he took in placing this legend in its proper historical context. [...]

Aside from these complex issues turning on the nature of industrial production and consumption, Maldonado praised the progressive aspects of the Bauhaus for its commitment to the "learning through doing" approach of Hildebrandt, Kerschensteiner, Montessori and Dewey, and for its pragmatic opposition to the verbal emphasis of the humanist tradition. Nevertheless, it was clear that this

---

[7] Hanno Kesting, *Technik und Industriearbeit and das Gesellschaftsbild des Arbeiters*, Tübingen: Mohr Siebeck, 1957.

particular pedagogical approach had now outlived its usefulness and that a new philosophy of praxis was needed. To this end, Maldonado proposed scientific operationalism, which he remarked, "it is no longer a question... of knowledge, but of operational, manipulable knowledge."[8]

By "operationalism" Maldonado seems to have been referring to that philosophical system developed in the early Fifties by Anatol Rapoport and published by him, in 1953, under the title *Operational Philosophy*. Given the persistence of the Bauhaus heritage, it is hardly surprising to find that Rapoport's philosophy was really a methodological updating of John Dewey's pragmatic-instrumentalism. The appeal of Rapoport's method lay in his attempt to provide a precise system for the evaluation of alternative courses of action. It is a measure of his discretion that, despite his dependence on mathematical logic, Rapoport was at pains to distinguish both his and Dewey's system from that of the logical positivists, with their belief that philosophy should become a purely analytic discipline, akin to mathematics. Instead, Rapoport thought of his operationalism as being a synthetic action-oriented discipline. In 1953, he wrote that operationalism "is the philosophy of action-directed goals. It starts with logical analysis but transcends it by relating this analysis to society."[9] At the time this seems to have been relatively close to Maldonado's own notion of scientific operationalism, of which he has since written, "By scientific operationalism I intended then a model of action oriented towards overcoming the dichotomy between theory and practice. Later on, following Kotarbinski, I preferred to call it 'praxiology'—and even more recently, 'the philosophy of praxis,' as seen in Gramsci."[10]

Rejecting its Arts and Crafts origins and ever conscious of the perspectives of Marxist analysis, the Hochschule, bound to the service of neo-capitalism, had little choice in the Fifties but to look beyond the limits of these traditions for a mediatory ideology from which to develop not only a satisfactory heuristic method, but also a theory of design. A theoretical basis seems to have been proffered by Rapoport's operationalism, save for its incapacity to deal in an adequate manner with the intrinsic significance of form itself. For this the Hochschule seems to have turned first to Max Bense, whose communications approach to the determination of aesthetic need was first outlined in his book *Aesthetica*, published in 1954;[11] and then to the writings of Charles Morris,

---

[8] Tomás Maldonado, in *Ulm*, No. 2, October 1958, p. 40.

[9] Anatol Rapoport, *Operational Philosophy*, New York: Harper & Row, 1953.

[10] Tomás Maldonado, "Colloquium con Maldonado é Ohl," *Design-Italia*, September 1972, p. 32.

[11] Max Bense, *Aesthetica*, Stuttgart: Verlag-Anstalt, Baden-Baden, 1954; Idem, *Aesthetische Information*, Krefeld/ Baden-Baden, 1956. In a recent letter to the author [Kenneth Frampton] Maldonado has attempted to clarify something of Bense's relation to the HfG: "As for Max Bense, I am convinced that he played an extremely important role in the first years of Ulm, with his tremendous interest in the application of scientific disciplines to the various areas which we dealt with. Probably for generational reasons he sided with Bill in our conflict, even if his own attitude—given his interest in the scientific approach etc.—should have placed him among the younger faculty members, of whom I was one."

whose first semiotic works had appeared in the *Unified Science* publications of the late Thirties.[12] Operation and communication: these are the two "poles" that are to play major roles in the evolution of Hochschule theory.

[. . .]

THE DEVELOPMENT OF A CRITICAL THEORY

Despite the reorientation of the school under Aicher's stewardship [1962–1968], the socio-cultural criticism emanating from the Hochschule continued to grow over the next five years, most particularly through the contribution of Maldonado, Claude Schnaidt and Gui Bonsiepe. These three happened to announce their common critical attitude in the review section of *Ulm 7*, published in 1963, wherein their notes were respectively addressed; first, to a criticism of the intrusion of neo-Dada into the field of industrial design;[13] second, to an appraisal of Leonardo Benevolo's *History of Modern Architecture*; and finally, to a review of Georg Klaus's critique of Norbert Wiener's information theory, which had then just appeared in Klaus's book *Cybernetics in the Light of Philosophy*. The aim of the Klaus study was to refute the Weiner reduction of information to a mere quantifiable assessment of its relative density and predictability. Rejecting the implicit Wiener split of sign from import and his classification of information as a mere quantum, akin to energy, Klaus argued that, "All information must rather have a definite meaning, must be a carrier of some significance."[14]

This apparently banal but nonetheless anti-positivist statement had of course, been the basic assumption behind the Maldonado seminars in semiotics, given as a regular course in the Hochschule from 1957 to 1960, the first fruits of which were the Maldonado essay "Communication and Semiotics" that appeared in *Ulm 5* in 1959, and the Bonsiepe text "*Über Formale und Informale Sprachanalyse: Carnap und Ryle*" that was written in 1960.[15] Strangely enough, the only adequate publication of the work of these seminars did not appear in the journal *Ulm*, but in a little known publication entitled *Uppercase*, edited by Theo Crosby. Thus, *Uppercase 5* of 1963, dedicated in the main to work of the Hochschule, featured texts by Maldonado and Bonsiepe, a design case study by Walter Muller and a semiotic glossary.[16]

---

[12]See Charles William Morris, "Scientific Empiricism," *International Encyclopedia of Unified Science*, Vol. I, No. 1, 1938; *Idem*, "Foundations of the Theory of Signs," *International Encyclopedia of Unified Science*, Vol. I, No. 2, 1938.

[13]Tomás Maldonado, "Design-Objects and Art-Objects," *Ulm*, No.7, January 1963, pp. 18–22. Review of an exhibition of consumer product designed as though they were art objects.

[14]Gui Bonsiepe, "Information/Machines/Consciousness," *Ulm*, No. 7, January 1963, p. 24. Bonsiepe quotes from Georg Klaus's book *Kybernetik in Philosophischer Sicht*, Berlin, 1961.

[15]*Uppercase*, No. 5, London: Whitefriars Press, 1963, p. 60.

[16]*Ibid.*, pp. 47–60. In addition to the Maldonado text and the semiotic glossary, this special issue of *Uppercase* also featured an article by Gui Bonsiepe on verbal and visual rhetoric.

In retrospect, the most significant aspect of this approach was the distance it implicitly took from a positivistic design approach and the corresponding stress it placed on form as a necessary communicative element. In his "Notes on Communication," Maldonado refused the positivistic split of operation from communication in a text that is remarkable for its perception of function as being an integral part of culture, and *vice versa* [...] Maldonado extended this argument to embrace the field of ergonomics and in particular the province of machine design, where the operative and communicative aspects become dramatically intermeshed and where the critical "man-machine" relationship of advanced industrialization acquires an undeniably concrete dimension. In this respect, the advanced ergonomic theories of Chapanis, Fitts and Taylor[17] were welcomed by Maldonado for the stress they placed on the redesign of the machine and for their mutual intent to resolve the "man-machine" couple in such a way as to liberate a man as much as possible from the tyranny of the machine.

This measured critique was extended in the Maldonado–Bonsiepe essay "Science and Design," which appeared in 1964 in *Ulm 10/11*. Broadly speaking, this paper was an attack on the simplistic borrowing of design methods from the field of "human engineering," beginning with a critique of the established methods of experimental psychology for their untenable linearity of approach and going on to upbraid that aspect of ergonomics which grounded itself in a servo-mechanical model of the human being—a schema whereby the complexity of man becomes reduced (usually under conditions of extremis) to the so-called H-factor. The authors concluded their survey of heuristic methods, derived from the margins of applied science, with a highly skeptical appraisal of the procedures of market and motivational research and for the propensity of such research to convert "undifferentiated needs into definite demands"[18] [...] Maldonado and Bonsiepe clearly felt they had no choice but to promote disquiet. Not for its own sake, since there is little enough anarchy in their thought, but as a direct consequence of their analysis. While simultaneously practising and teaching industrial design, they could not fail to become aware of the overall predicament of the designer in a neo-capitalist economy. Unlike the Pre-Raphaelites or the artists of the Weimar Bauhaus, they were neither romantic iconoclasts nor Spenglerian critics of science. On the contrary, they sought, in accordance with the initial orientation of the Hochschule, to come to terms with the realities of industrial production and distribution. But it was precisely this determination to comprehend reality that led them into the uncomfortable lucidity of their analyses. In collaboration with their colleague, Claude Schnaidt, in the HfG building department, they saw all too clearly the present highly problematic situation of the architect and the industrial designer.

[17] Paul M. Fitts, "Engineering Psychology and Engineering Design," in Stanley S. Stevens, *Handbook of Experimental Psychology*, New York: Wiley, 1951; Alphonse Chapanis, "Engineering Psychology," *Annual Review of Psychology*, Vol. 14, Palo Alto, CA: Annual Reviews, Inc., 1963. See also the pioneering work of Frederick Winslow Taylor, *The Principles of Scientific Management*, New York and London: Harper, 1911.

[18] Tomás Maldonado and Gui Bonsiepe, "Science and Design," *Ulm*, No. 10/11, May 1964, p. 29 [footnote moved from original place by the editor].

[...]

For Maldonado, design in general, after a dialectical overcoming of both the "degeneracies" of admass populism and the paradoxical "alienations" of bureaucratic socialism, has to be returned to a strict distinction in practice between puristic formalism on the one hand and formal order in its broadest sense on the other. In the last analysis, for Maldonado, this distinction can only be made in the context of preserving human values, an issue with which the second half of the twentieth century has yet to come to terms. Given the economic and highly abstract imperatives of our present society, this is understandable, since the reintegration of such values ultimately presupposes a dialectical definition of "needs" which would have to transcend, without excluding them, the primary demands of production and use. Such a definition would have to assimilate these basic criteria into a perspective that takes cognizance of the fundamental limitations of human life, *eros* and *thanatos*, hedonism and mortality.

The position taken by Schnaidt and Maldonado[19] with regard to the particular predicament of architecture, as it was then being practised and taught in the Sixties, remains remarkably timely. Their views, now almost ten years old and strongly influenced by the conditions of the time, retain nonetheless a certain general validity that makes them as applicable today as when they were first written. In fact, in a decade, little has changed except that the opportunities for the architect to make significant contribution to the society are possibly even more limited now than they were in the early Sixties. In his essay "Prefabricated Hope," which appeared in *Ulm 10/11*, Schnaidt attempted a comprehensive analysis of the failure of industrialized building. He then argued against the by now familiar sterility of treating this prospect from a purely technical standpoint[20]

---

[19] Tomás Maldonado, "Design Education," in György Kepes, ed., *Education of Vision*, Vision and Value Series, New York: George Braziller, 1965 [footnote moved from original place by the editor].

[20] "It is difficult to apply profitably industrial production methods in the building of housing estates containing less than 500 dwellings. Given the current density of population, 500 dwellings require at least 2.5 hectares of land . . . To create such sites one must acquire many small lots, paying the owners a surplus value estimated according to the expected value of the lot after mains supplies and sewerage pipes have been laid. This is where speculation is let loose. The sale and resale of building sites to the profit of the few is a curse which is becoming increasingly ruinous to the community. On the outskirts of numerous major European cities, the price of real estate has increased ten-fold in the last ten years; in 1950, the ground rates represented about ten percent of the selling price of a house; by 1960, it had risen to 45 percent. The reduction in the cost of housing which can be achieved by industrializing building seems ridiculously small in comparison with the increase caused by land-speculation . . . The future of the industrialization of building will depend on the solution found to all these problems. This is why it is erroneous, if not dishonest, to speak solely of technical matters when evoking decisions that affect this future. The choice is not, as they would have us believe, between so-called traditional building and prefabrication. It is between a disordered, slow and precarious development of technical progress in building as a whole and a coherent, rapid and planned industrialization for the benefit of the community." Claude Schnaidt, "Prefabricated Hope," *Ulm*, No. 10/11, May 1964, pp. 2–9 [quote converted to footnote by the editor].

[...] One need hardly add that this critique was, in many respects, an implicit attack on the work of the Hochschule building department in which Schnaidt himself functioned as a teacher. In a parallel criticism of architectural education given as the Lethaby Lecture at the Royal College of Art, in 1965, under the title "The Emergent World: A Challenge to Architectural and Industrial Design Training," Maldonado was to argue that the upgrading of architectural school curricula had largely resulted in a shifting of the academic scenery, in which the fundamental pedagogical orientation had remained unchanged. A primary aspect of this apparent transformation had clearly been the universal adoption of basic design courses, along the lines of the Bauhaus, while the most common secondary change, largely unrelated to the first, had been the wholesale acceptance of modern architecture. Of this Maldonado remarked, "On the altar where Palladio was worshipped, Wright, Le Corbusier, Gropius, Mies van der Rohe, Fuller, Louis Kahn or Kenzo Tange are now being honoured. The idols have changed but not the doctrines."[21] Yet for Maldonado not even those schools which had attempted to restructure their curricula along scientific lines were entirely free from criticism, for he could see all too clearly, after his own experiences at the Hochschule, how a naive worship of scientific method could lead to designs even more abstracted from any legitimate form of sociocultural reality than before.

It would seem that by 1966 the "critical theory" of the Hochschule had already reached the threshold of disputing by implication the viability of design schools *per se*, and there is little reason to doubt but that Otl Aicher's essay "Planning All Awry?" which appeared in *Ulm 17/18* of that year, was nothing but an oblique attempt to counter the auto-criticism of his "left wing" faculty; Aicher urging all designers, not only planners, to accommodate themselves to the power constraints of neo-capitalism.[22] It is interesting to note that the anti-monumentalism of his position would have been shared by Schnaidt, but not the ultimately apolitical, mystifying scientism of his conclusions [...] Aicher did not go unanswered, first inadvertently by Maldonado, in the same issue of the journal, *Ulm 17/18*, in a text with the provocative title, "How to Fight Complacency in Design Education," and then in the penultimate issue of the journal, *Ulm 19/20*, in 1967, in a seminar report by Abraham Moles addressed to "Functionalism in Crisis," and in an essay by Claude Schnaidt titled "Architecture and Political Commitment."

Where Maldonado, while pleading the case for C.S. Peirce's "university of methods,"[23] stressed conflict and disorder and the reciprocal link that existed

---

[21] Tomás Maldonado, "The Emergent World: A Challenge to Architectural and Industrial Design Training," *Ulm*, No. 12/13, March 1965, p. 6.

[22] Otl Aicher, "Planning All Awry?" *Ulm*, No. 17/18, June 1966 [footnote moved from original place by the editor].

[23] Tomás Maldonado, "How to Fight Complacency in Design Education," *Ulm*, No. 17/18, June 1966, p. 20.

in the Third World between violence and necessity, Moles went straight to the *raison d'être* of the Hochschule and argued in effect that its basis had been overtaken by the success of the "economic miracle," since the pure functionalism it professed was no longer required by the economic system it was pledged to serve[24] [. . .] It was left to Schnaidt to articulate in unequivocal terms the consequences of this crisis in its wider ramifications, and in many respects his text was to be the last major contribution to the critical theory of the Hochschule before its self-dissolution in February 1968. His indirect response to the Aicher model of planning reality requires little comment, save that his arguments led him to advocate regional decentralization:

> While architects take refuge in aestheticism, fantasy and technocracy, man's environment and everyday life are steadily deteriorating. The megalopolises which are taking shape are stricken at the least failure of their over-burdened infrastructures. They call for prodigious amounts of money to function at all . . . The annual subsidy received by the Paris Passenger Transport Board is four times larger than all the allocations made to help the industrialization in Brittany during the past ten years . . . The concentration of industries and their head offices in and around the metropolis, and the continuous increase in rents which compels those working there to put up their homes far afield, have made certain reductions in working hours a purely illusory gain. After all, a cut of six to eight hours a week means very little when two to three hours a day are lost travelling to and from work. And all this lost time comes off the leisure which people are forever talking about . . . Apart from the loss of time, money and lives, the problem of home-to-job distance causes another kind of trouble, this time of a social nature with repercussions on both the individual citizen and the urban region. The latter has gone onto 'half-time' and its inhabitants have followed suit. Thus a man sets off at dawn from his village, his suburb, his satellite town which provides the labour needed for the big city. He is away the whole day and he comes home in the evening depleted of energy and longing for nothing else but peace and quiet. And for this reason, it is rare for him to contribute anything to the community in which he lives; he has no ideas, no criticism, no impetus to give it. As far as his environment is concerned, he might just as well be dead . . . What is the basic cause of concentration? When a manufacturer sets up in a developed area, he can use the existing infrastructure and equipment. And these—water, gas, electricity, telephones, sewage, communications, public transport services, public buildings—are paid for by the community. Thus, the manufacturer is enabled to avoid the expenditure involved in setting up, renewing and adapting this infrastructure . . . He is thus able to increase his profit margin. Put differently, the community has to bear what has been called the 'social cost of private enterprise.' Political commitment requires

---

[24] Abraham Moles, "Functionalism in Crisis," *Ulm*, No. 19/20, August 1967, p. 24 [footnote moved from original place by the editor].

one to demand that the brunt of the social cost of private enterprise should no longer be borne by the community.[25]

The unequivocal and sometimes simplistic remedies that Schnaidt prescribes in "Planning All Awry?" categorically reveal the radical nature of his own political affiliations, but this in no way detracts from the general accuracy of his analysis nor from the pertinence of his revolutionary perspective.

The critical theory of Bonsiepe, Maldonado and Schnaidt was fated to return the Hochschule to its point of departure. Having started its existence as a school of design, *in lieu* of a school of politics, it was paradoxically returned to its political destiny by men whose lives were dedicated to design. The vicissitudes that their respective theories passed through, over a decade, tend to confirm that this development arose naturally out of adopting a certain attitude towards design. For design as the self-determination of man on earth, through the exercise of his collective consciousness, still remains with us as a positive legacy of the Enlightenment. Despite the admass absorption of the Modern Movement, the fundamental frustration of its genuine realization in every domain of life still testifies to the present containment of its liberating force. This much was stated by Schnaidt when he wrote of the historical co-option of the movement that, "Modern architecture which wanted to play its part in the liberation of mankind by creating a new environment to live in, was transformed into a giant enterprise for the degradation of the human habitat,"[26] and by Bonsiepe when he wrote [his resignation] in the last issue of the journal, *Ulm 21*.[27]

---

[25] Claude Schnaidt, "Architecture and Political Commitment," *ibid.*, pp. 30–32.

[26] *Ibid.*, p. 26.

[27] "Admittedly, there is little evidence of realization in training institutions that the communications industry is a consciousness industry, whether it is concerned with the engendering of truth or untruth in consciousness, with enlightenment or ideology. The more visual designers concentrated on the aesthetic perfection of the designs, the more the communications industry was able to keep its power out of sight. The insistence on the aesthetic as one aspect of design is undoubtedly warranted and was capable of retaining its validity over the years. But the aesthetic cannot be maintained in unsullied and apolitical detachment from the social. Formerly, the aesthetic figured as the anticipation of a state of affairs which implied liberation from the constraints of necessity. But the aesthetic met with a fate which could not have been foreseen. It was found that it could very readily be pressed into the service of repression. The forms of power have been sublimated. In the course of this sublimation, the aesthetic—which was and still is a promise of the state of liberation of mankind—has been harnessed by the agencies of power and thus used to acquire and maintain power. No consequences have as yet been drawn from this change in the role of the aesthetic insofar as it affects either the theory or practice of training in visual communication." Gui Bonsiepe, "Communication and Power," *Ulm*, No. 21, April 1968, p. 16 [quote converted to footnote by the editor].

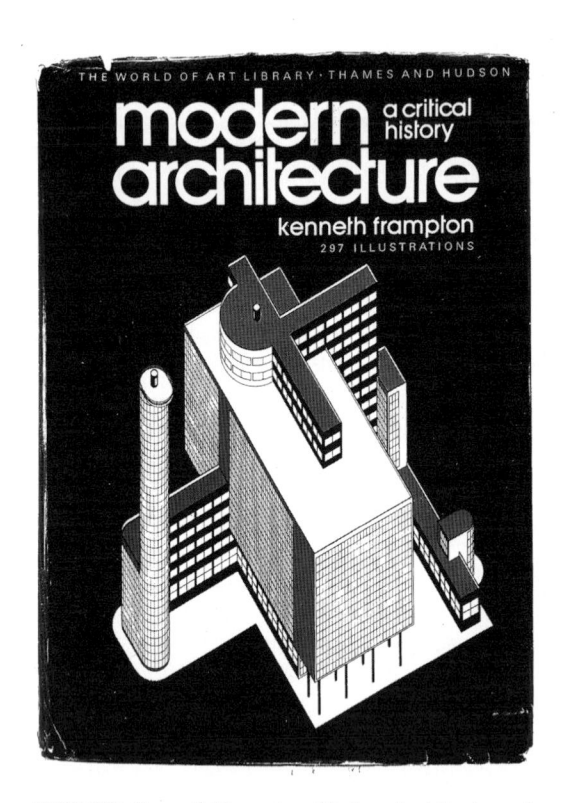

FIGURE 21 Kenneth Frampton, *Modern Architecture: A Critical History*, cover of the first Thames & Hudson edition, 1980. Cover of Kenneth Frampton's personal copy.

5 *Modern Architecture: A Critical History*, Introduction to the 1st Edition (1980)

INTRODUCTION

A Klee painting named 'Angelus Nevus' shows an angel looking as though he is about to move away from something he is fixedly contemplating. His eyes are staring, his mouth is open, his wings are spread. This is how one pictures the angel of history. His face is turned towards the past. Where we perceive a chain of events, he sees one single catastrophe which keeps piling wreckage upon wreckage and hurls it in front of his feet. The angel would like to stay, awaken the dead, and make whole what has been smashed. But a storm is blowing from Paradise: it has got caught in his wings with such violence that the angel can no longer close them. This storm irresistibly propels him into the future to which his back is turned, while the pile of debris before him grows skyward. This storm is what we call progress.
 Walter Benjamin, *Theses on the Philosophy of History*, 1940

One of the first tasks to be faced in attempting to write a history of modern architecture is to establish the beginning of the period. The more rigorously one searches for the origin of modernity, however, the further back it seems to lie. One tends to project it back, if not to the Renaissance, then to that moment in the mid-18th century when a new view of history brought architects to question the Classical canons of Vitruvius and to document the remains of the antique world in order to establish a more objective basis on which to work. This, together with the extraordinary technical changes that followed throughout the century, suggests that the necessary conditions for modern architecture

Source: Kenneth Frampton, "Introduction," in *Modern Architecture: A Critical History* (Thames & Hudson, 1980, first edition), 8–10.

appeared some time between the physician-architect Claude Perrault's late 17th-century challenge to the universal validity of Vitruvian proportions and the definitive split between engineering and architecture which is sometimes dated to the foundation in Paris of the École Nationale des Ponts et Chaussées, the first engineering school, in 1747.

Here it has been possible to give only the barest outline of this prehistory of the Modern Movement. The first three chapters, therefore, are to be read in a different light from the rest of the book. They treat of the cultural, territorial and technical transformations from which modern architecture emerged, offering short accounts of architecture, urban development and engineering as these fields evolved between 1750 and 1939.

The critical issues to be broached in writing a comprehensive but concise history are first, to decide what material should be included, and second, to maintain some kind of consistency in the interpretation of the facts. I have to admit that on both counts I have not been as consistent as I would have wished; partly because information often had to take priority over interpretation, partly because not all the material has been studied to the same degree of depth, and partly because my interpretative stance has varied according to the subject under consideration. In some instances I have tried to show how a particular approach derives from socio-economic or ideological circumstances, while in others I have restricted myself to formal analysis. This variation is reflected in the structure of the book itself, which is divided into a mosaic of fairly short chapters that deal either with the work of particularly significant architects or with major collective developments. As far as possible I have tried to allow for the possibility of reading the text in more than one way. Thus it may be followed as a continuous account or dipped into at random. While the sequence has been organized with the lay reader or undergraduate in mind, I hope that a casual reading may serve to stimulate graduate work and prove useful to the specialist who wishes to develop a particular point.

Apart from this, the structure of the text is related to the general tone of the book, inasmuch as I have tried whenever possible to let the protagonists speak for themselves. Each chapter is introduced by a quotation, chosen either for its insight into a particular cultural situation or for its capacity to reveal the content of the work. I have endeavoured to use these "voices" to illustrate the way in which modern architecture has evolved as a continuous cultural effort and to demonstrate how certain issues might lose their relevance at one moment in history only to return at a later date with increased vigour. Many unbuilt works feature in this account, since for me the history of modern architecture is as much about consciousness and polemical intent as it is about buildings themselves.

Like many others of my generation I have been influenced by a Marxist interpretation of history, although even the most cursory reading of this text will reveal that none of the established methods of Marxist analysis has been applied. On the other hand, my affinity for the critical theory of the Frankfurt School has no doubt coloured my view of the whole period and made me acutely aware of the dark side of the Enlightenment which, in the name of an unreasonable reason, has brought man to a situation where he begins to be as alienated from his own production as from the natural world.

The development of modern architecture after the Enlightenment seems to have been divided between the utopianism of the avant garde, first formulated at the beginning of the 19th century in the ideal physiocratic city of Ledoux, and that anti-Classical, anti-rational and anti-utilitarian attitude of Christian reform first declared in Pugin's *Contrasts* of 1836. Ever since, in its effort to transcend the division of labour and the harsh realities of industrial production and urbanization, bourgeois culture has oscillated between the extremes of totally planned and industrialized utopias on the one hand, and, on the other, a denial of the actual historical reality of machine production.

While all the arts are in some degree limited by the means of their production and reproduction, this is doubly so in the case of architecture, which is conditioned not only by its own technical methods but also by productive forces lying outside itself. Nowhere has this been more evident than in the case of the city, where the split between architecture and urban development has led to a situation in which the possibility of the former contributing to the latter and vice versa, over a long period of time, has suddenly become extremely limited. Increasingly subject to the imperatives of a continuously expanding consumer economy, the city has largely lost its capacity to maintain its significance as a whole. That it has been dissipated by forces lying beyond its control is demonstrated by the rapid erosion of the American provincial city after the end of the Second World War, as a consequence of the combined effect of the freeway, the suburb and the supermarket.

The success and failure of modern architecture to date, and its possible role in the future, must finally be assessed against this rather complex background. In its most abstract form, architecture has, of course, played a certain role in the impoverishment of the environment—particularly where it has been instrumental in the rationalisation of both building types and methods, and where both the material finish and the plan form have been reduced to their lowest common denominator, in order to make production cheaper and to optimize use. In its well-intentioned but sometimes misguided concern to assimilate the technical and processal realities of the 20th century, architecture has adopted a language in which expression resides almost entirely in processal, secondary components, such as ramps, walkways, lifts, staircases, escalators, chimneys, ducts and garbage chutes. Nothing could be further from the language of Classical architecture, where such features were invariably concealed behind the facade and where the main body of the building was free to express itself—a suppression of empirical fact that enabled architecture to symbolize the power of reason through the rationality of its own discourse. Functionalism has been based on the opposed principle, namely the reduction of all expression to utility or to the processes of fabrication.

Given the inroads of this modern reductionist tradition, we are now being urged once again to return to traditional forms and to render our new buildings—almost without regard for their status—in the iconography of a kitsch vernacular. We are told that popular will demands the reassuring image of homely, hand-crafted comfort and that 'Classical' references, however abstract, are as incomprehensible as they are patronizing. Only rarely does this critical opinion extend the scope of its advice beyond the surface issue of style to demand that architectural practice should readdress itself to the issue of place creation, to a critical yet creative redefinition of the concrete qualities of the built domain.

The vulgarization of architecture and its progressive isolation from society have of late driven the discipline in upon itself, so that we are now confronted with the paradoxical situation in which many of the more intelligent, younger members of the profession have already abandoned all ideas of realization. At its most intellectual this tendency reduces architectonic elements to pure syntactical signs that signify nothing outside their own 'structural' operation; at its most nostalgic it celebrates the loss of the city through metaphorical and ironic proposals that are either projected into 'astral wastes' or set in the metaphysical space of 19th-century urban splendour.

Of the courses of action which are still open to contemporary architecture—courses which in one way or another have already been entered upon—only two seem to offer the possibility of a significant outcome. While the first of these is totally coherent with the prevailing modes of production and consumption, the second establishes itself as a measured opposition to both. The former, following Mies van der Rohe's ideal of *beinahe nichts* or 'almost nothing,' seeks to reduce the building task to the status of industrial design on an enormous scale. Since its concern is with optimizing production, it has little or no interest in the city. It projects a well-serviced, well packaged, non-rhetorical functionalism whose glazed 'invisibility' reduces form to silence. The latter, on the other hand, is patently 'visible' and often takes the form of a masonry enclosure that establishes within its limited 'monastic' domain a reasonably open but nonetheless concrete set of relationships linking man to man and man to nature. The fact that this 'enclave' is often introverted and relatively indifferent to the physical and temporal continuum in which it is situated characterizes the general thrust of this approach as an attempt to escape, however partially, from the conditioning perspectives of the Enlightenment. The sole hope for a significant discourse in the immediate future lies, in my view, in a creative contact between these two extreme points of view.

6 Towards an Ontological Architecture: A Philosophical Excursus (2015)

> A work of architecture extends beyond itself in two ways. It is as much determined by the aim which it is to serve as by the place it is to take up in a total spatial context. Every architect has to consider both these things. His plan is influenced by the fact that the building has to serve a particular living purpose and must be adapted to particular architectural circumstances. Hence we call a successful building a 'happy solution', and mean by this both that it perfectly fulfills its purpose and that its construction has added something new to the spatial dimensions of a town or a landscape. Through this dual ordering the building presents a true increase of being: it is a work of art . . . A building is never primarily a work of art. Its purpose, through which it belongs in the context of life, cannot be separated from itself without its losing some of its reality. If it has become merely an object of the aesthetic consciousness, then it has merely a shadowy reality and lives a distorted life only in the degenerate form of an object of interest to tourists, or a subject for photography. The work of art in itself proves to be a pure abstraction.[1]
>
> Hans Georg Gadamer, *Truth and Method*, 1960

Although this exercise in the comparative analysis of built form is exclusively predicated on photographic, orthographic, and descriptive material, the buildings are nonetheless envisaged as being directly experienced in tactile terms as the subject passes through space. In my view, architecture is consummated by the "body-being" at both a sensuous and a referential level, rather than as an aesthetic manifestation that is exclusively visual and abstract. This move

---

Source: Kenneth Frampton, *A Genealogy of Modern Architecture: Comparative Critical Analysis of Built Form*, ed. Ashley Simone (Zürich: Lars Müller Publishers), 8–27.

[1] Hans-Georg Gadamer, *Truth and Method*. New York: Seabury Press, 1975, pp. 138–9.

away from formal aestheticization in favor of an all-encompassing ontological experience of the environment has something of its origin in Edmund Husserl's phenomenology as this was fully elaborated towards the end of his life in his magnum opus, *The Crisis of European Sciences and Transcendental Philosophy* of 1937. He writes herein on the ontic presence of things:

> Perception is related only to the present. But this present is always meant as having an endless past behind it and an open future before it. We soon see that we need the intentional analysis of recollection as the original manner of being conscious of the past, but we also see that such an analysis presupposes in principle that of perception, since memory, curiously enough, implies having perceived. If we consider perception abstractly, by itself, we find its intentional accomplishment to be presentation, making something present: the object gives itself as 'there,' originally there, present.[2]

Husserl's insistence on the primacy of the "life-world," along with his slogan "back to the things themselves" is the origin of a line of thought that engages a wide range of philosophers who, while of diverse affiliations, nonetheless belong to a continuous line of development extending from Husserl and his protégé Martin Heidegger to include, in addition to Gadamer, such figures as Hannah Arendt, Herbert Marcuse, Karl Jaspers, and, at one remove, Jean-Paul Sartre and Maurice Merleau-Ponty, who assimilated this line of thought into France. This line has culminated most recently in the thought of Gadamer's pupil Gianni Vattimo. This tradition has the potential of complementing the dialectical legacy of socialism by emphasizing the ontological sensitivity of the subject with respect to the environment. With the above citation from Husserl in mind, it is important to acknowledge that, besides its tectonic and abstract character, architecture, unlike the other arts, is as much a presentation as it is a representation, and vice versa, whereby the "body-being" encounters both aspects simultaneously.

There is perhaps no single text that is more evocative of the ontological scope of architecture than Heidegger's characterization of the anchoring of a Greek temple into its site, as this appears in his essay "The Origin of the Work of Art" of 1936:

> The temple work, in its standing there, first gives to the things their look and to men their outlook on themselves . . . When a work is created, brought forth out of material—stone, wood, metal, color, language, tone—we say also that it is made, set forth out of it . . . Thinking of it within this perspective, what is the nature of that in the work which is usually called the work material? . . . In fabricating equipment—e.g., an ax—stone is used, and used up. It disappears into usefulness. The material is all the better and more

---

[2] Edmund Husserl, *The Crisis of European Science and Transcendental Philosophy: An Introduction to Phenomenological Philosophy*. Evanston: Northwestern University Press, 1970, p. 160.

suitable the less it resists perishing in the equipmental being of the equipment. By contrast the temple-work, in setting up a world, does not cause the material to disappear, but rather causes it to come forth for the very first time and to come into the Open of the work's world. The rock comes to bear and rest and so first becomes rock; metals come to glitter and shimmer, colors to grow, tones to sing, the word to speak. All this comes forth as the work sets itself back into the massiveness and heaviness of stone, into the firmness and pliancy of wood, into the hardness and luster of metal, into the lighting and darkening of color, into the clang of tone, and into the naming power of the word.[3]

Although Hannah Arendt's seminal work, *The Human Condition* of 1958, does not refer either to Husserl or Heidegger, her disquisition on the way in which the "lifeworld" comes into being justifies, in my view, our reading of her *magnum opus* as an ontological discourse. We may note in this regard that instead of focusing on the "things themselves," to cite Husserl's famous slogan, Arendt emphasizes the existential conditions under which things come into being. In this regard she differentiates between different experiential categories of production as these determine the different destinies of the things produced.[4]

Arendt amplifies her distinction between work and labor by contrasting the relative durability of the work of the *homo faber* (i.e. man as fabricator) to the fungibility of the product of the *animal laborans* (i.e. man as laboring animal) whereby what is produced is intended for consumption. She will argue that where work aspires to the realization of things that are static, public, and permanent, labor is inherently processal, private, and impermanent. For Arendt, the human condition as such depends on the durability of the world, that is to say, on the capacity of built objects to resist the erosive forces of time, nature, and use.[5]

[...]

While Arendt's *The Human Condition* makes no reference whatsoever to phenomenology, her thesis is nonetheless concerned with the constitution of things and with our inter-subjective experience of them in relation to our being. To the same end, the comparative analyses which follow stress the hierarchical organization of space with the intention of avoiding a reductive rendering of architecture as nothing more than a combination of function with aesthetics, as opposed to being an ontological presence that transcends both. In other

---

[3] Martin Heidegger, "The Origin of the Work of Art," in *Poetry, Language, Thought*. New York: Harper Row, 1971, p. 46.

[4] Hannah Arendt, *The Human Condition*. Chicago/London: University of Chicago Press, 1958. p. 7. [editor's note: For Frampton's discussion of differences between "labor" and "work," see "The Status of Man and the Status of his Objects: A Reading of *The Human Condition*" in this section].

[5] *Ibid.*, p. 173. [editor's note: for the discussion of the concept of "artificial worldliness" see "The Status of Man and the Status of his Objects: A Reading of *The Human Condition*" in this section.]

words, the analytical emphasis falls on the implied status of both space and materiality, and on our corporeal relationship with each aspect. At the same time, this method of comparative critique takes into consideration the relationship between the intrinsic structure of the built fabric and its extrinsic appearance as representational form. It includes the connotational aspects of both material finishes and details, bearing in mind the ramifications which any single material or detail might have in relation to both the spatial hierarchy and the sensuous experience of a particular form. In this way, comparative critique is developed so as to reveal the ways in which values are evoked through the detailed inflection of space, structure and material.

Merleau-Ponty's *Phenomenology of Perception*, first published in French in 1945, augments the ontological implications of *The Human Condition* by introducing the concept of the body-being as the prime agency through which we experience the world. This recognition is intimately linked to our motility as the pre-condition through which we experience space.

> In the action of the hand which is raised toward an object is contained a reference to the object, not as an object represented, but as that highly specific thing towards which we project ourselves, near which we are, in anticipation, and which we haunt. Consciousness is being-towards-the-thing through the intermediary of the body . . . These elucidations enable us clearly to understand motility as basic intentionality . . . Sight and movement are specific ways of entering into relationships with objects and if, through all these experiences some unique function finds its expression, it is the momentum of existence which does not cancel out the radical diversity of contents, because it links them to each other, not by placing them under the control of an 'I think' but by guiding them towards the intermediary unity of 'a world.'[6]

Merleau-Ponty's world view implies the possibility of a condition in which the body-being is not only sustained by the physical and institutional environment within which it is housed, but is also endowed with the potential to interpret and experience the environment so as to transcend our literal placement within history. The multi-sensory apprehension of the environment in terms of our corporeal experience of space, light, sound and form, is an aspect of political subjectivity.

The primary assumption underlying the interpretive critique of architecture contained in this volume [*A Genealogy of Modern Architecture*] is that the values embodied in a work of architecture are to be apprehended not only through the sensuous tactility of the space but also through cultural associations incorporated into the articulation of its form. This reciprocal interplay between conception and perception, and vice versa, necessitates acknowledging the role played by

---

[6] Maurice Merleau-Ponty, *Phenomenology of Perception*. London & New York: Routledge, 1962.

tradition in the constitution of the form, including the tradition of the new. Of this continual interaction, the Polish philosopher Zygmunt Bauman has written:

> The ambiguity which truly matters, the sense-giving ambivalence, the genuine foundation on which the cognitive usefulness of conceiving human habitat as the 'world of culture' rests, is the ambivalence between 'creativity' and 'normative regulation'. The two ideas could not be further apart, yet both are—and must remain—present in the composite idea of culture. Culture is as much about inventing as it is about preserving; about discontinuity as it is about continuation, about novelty as about tradition; about norm-following as much as about the transcendence of norm; about the unique as much as about the regular; about change as about the monotony of reproduction; about the unexpected as much as about the predictable.[7]

In all of the above I have attempted to trace a mode of beholding that Jonathan Hale has recently characterized as critical phenomenology.[8] What these discourses have in common is the inseparability of the body from the mind, which according to Hale was first formulated by the Austrian psychoanalyst Paul Schilder, in his book *Das Körperschema*. This thesis, first published in Berlin in 1923, was eventually translated into English in 1935 as *The Image and Appearance of the Human Body*. The subjectively experienced "body image" is inseparable from the "body being," which in its turn is embedded in the body politic, in the social, as Merleau-Ponty was to put it in *The Phenomenology of Perception*:

> We must return to the social with which we are in contact through the mere fact of existing and which we carry about inseparably with us before any objectification. Objective and scientific consciousness would be impossible had I not, through the intermediary of my society and my cultural world and their horizons, at least a possible communication with . . . the Athenian Republic or the Roman Empire were they not somewhere marked on the borders of my own history . . .[9]

This concept of cultural continuity is echoed in Gadamer's concept of the 'fusion of horizons' as set forth in his book *Truth and Method*:

> Every encounter with tradition that takes place within historical consciousness involves the experience of the tension between the text and the present. The hermeneutic task consists in not covering up this tension by attempting

---

[7] Zygmunt Bauman, *Culture as Praxis*. London: Sage Publications, 1999, p. xiv.

[8] See Jonathan Hale, "Critical Phenomenology: Architecture and Embodiment," in *A Carefully Folded Ham Sandwich: Towards a Critical Phenomenology*, The Inaugural Frascari Symposium. Edited by Roger Connah. FAD Design House, Montreal, Canada, 2014, pp. 31–49.

[9] Op. cit., Merleau-Ponty, p. 362.

a naïve assimilation but consciously bringing it out. This is why it is part of the hermeneutic approach to project an historical horizon that is different from the horizon of the present. Historical consciousness is aware of its own otherness and hence distinguishes the horizon of tradition from its own. On the other hand, it is itself, as we are trying to show, only something laid over a continuing tradition, and hence it immediately recombines what it has distinguished in order, in the unity of the historical horizon that it thus acquires, to become again one with itself.[10]

Architecture is a singular material culture in that by its very nature it has the potential to resist the current pervasive drive to commodify the entire world. The emerging impulse towards sustainable development, in response to the warming of the earth's climate, returns us to the necessity of achieving a balance between the gratification of desire through consumption and the attainment of a certain level of homeostatic equilibrium essential to the survival of the species. It is already clear that our rampant consumption of non-renewable resources and the concomitant toxification of the environment will have a negative outcome. The multiplicity of language games, which is the legacy of the postmodern condition, is double-edged. On the one hand, it constitutes the basis for a decentralized resistance to global domination. On the other, particularly in regards to architecture, it tends towards the iteration of meaningless aesthetic differentiations. It is just at this juncture that criticism and creativity converge to provide an opening for the ontological architecture to which the title of this essay refers. What is intended by this term is an architecture in which the corporeal potential of the subject is envisaged as being realized both individually and collectively through the referential experience and articulation of the built-form.

---

[10]Gadamer, *Truth and Method*, p. 273.

SECTION 2
Urban Landscape and the Eclipse of the Public Realm

7 Introduction to Section 2

One of the central lines of inquiry in Frampton's work since the mid-1960s has been epitomized by the following question: "By what means, both as a society and as a profession, may we hope to be able to maintain 'spaces of human appearance' within an exceptionally privatized and highly commodified process of unending urbanization?"[1] This section provides a closer look into the consistency with which Frampton has engaged in the ferocious critique of capitalism-driven global urbanization and the proliferation of megalopolitan conditions predicated on the primacy of private property and the never-ending proliferation of free-standing built forms. The resulting landscape degradation and environmental destruction, as well as the erosion of the public realm and the dissolution of the common world, have been insistently addressed by Frampton in a series of publications that span the past fifty years.

"America 1960–1970: Notes on Urban Images & Theory," published in *Casabella* in 1971,[2] is the very first essay in which Frampton fervently confronts the inability of American architects, urban designers, and planners to stand up to the wholesale commodification of culture and landscape, wherein he asks whether the celebration of consumer folk culture and the triumph of kitsch are essentially testament "that our urban society is organized towards self-defeating ends, on a sociopolitical basis that is totally invalid." That issue of *Casabella* was titled "The City as an Artifact" and dedicated to the work of the Institute for Architecture and Urban Studies (IAUS), directed by Peter Eisenman. Frampton would join the IAUS in 1972, co-edit its journal *Oppositions*,

---

[1] Kenneth Frampton, "Megaform as Urban Landscape," Senior Loeb Scholar Lecture, Harvard Graduate School of Design, 25 October 2017, YouTube video, https://www.youtube.com/watch?v=USRaFhH7jIw.

[2] Kenneth Frampton, "America 1960–1970: Notes on Urban Images and Theory," *Casabella*, no. 359–360 (1971): 25–40.

and remain a fellow until 1982. The issue was edited by a team that included Eisenman, Frampton, Franco Alberti, and Piero Sartogo. Frampton assembled a group of authors whose essays exemplified current debates regarding American urbanization, including Denise Scott Brown, Stanford Anderson, Joseph Rykwert, Tom Schumacher, and others.

In his essay, Frampton directs his criticism mainly toward Denise Scott Brown and Robert Venturi for their enthusiastic embrace of populism in general and Las Vegas kitsch in particular, but also toward planners such as Kevin Lynch and Donald Appleyard for their "picturesque pluralism," which brought together a Sittesque method of urban design with the Gestalt theory; Richard L. Meier for his *A Communications Theory of Urban Growth*;[3] and finally Melvin Webber for his concepts of "community without propinquity" and of "nonplace urban realm."[4] In his critique, Frampton departs from two of his central references: Clement Greenberg (in relation to kitsch)[5] and Hannah Arendt (in relation to the "space of appearance"). "It is ironic that Denise Scott Brown should attempt to bestow upon such reservoirs of process and pseudo points of arrival, as parking lots, those very attributes which previous cultures reserved for 'space of human appearance,'"[6] writes Frampton. For him, the appallingly politically conservative, cynical, and above all complicit ("marginally tolerant," in his words) attitude of the above-mentioned practitioners implied a "deactivation" of design disciplines and a tendency to occupy themselves largely with theorizing, "with describing, eulogizing and extrapolating upon the triumph of mid-cult which already exists." The issue at stake for Frampton is foremost political, but also cultural ("the implicit divorce between form and content is culturally invalid") and economic, inasmuch as it presents a methodological dilemma to the design professions. The pinnacle of Frampton's critique of the relationship between human artifice and the public realm is addressed through his keen reading of Venturi's *Complexity and Contradiction in Architecture*, in which Venturi states that the public square is "un-American" because "Americans feel uncomfortable sitting in a square: they should be working at

---

[3] Richard L. Meier, *A Communications Theory of Urban Growth* (Cambridge, MA: MIT Press, 1962). The book was published for the Joint Center for Urban Studies of the Massachusetts Institute of Technology and Harvard University.

[4] Melvin Webber et al., eds., *Explorations into Urban Structure* (Philadelphia: University of Pennsylvania Press, 1964).

[5] Clement Greenberg, "Avant-Garde and Kitsch," in *Kitsch: The World of Bad Taste*, ed. Gillo Dorfles (New York: Universe Books, 1969).

[6] Frampton's criticism was specifically directed at Scott Brown's essay "Learning from Pop" in the same issue of *Casabella* and was followed by her reflection on Frampton's editorial, titled "Pop Off: Reply to Kenneth Frampton," also published in R. Venturi and D. Scott Brown, *A View from the Campidoglio: Selected Essays 1953–1984* (New York: Harper and Row, 1984), 34–37.

the office or home with the family looking at television."[7] Frampton elegantly argues that Venturi's cynical, conservative rhetorical formalism can hardly form an ethical response to the social, political, and environmental challenges American society was facing in the 1960s. This *tour de force* critical essay is Frampton's first attempt to evaluate the American architecture and urbanism of the period. Furthermore, it is an eloquent attempt to draw clear boundaries between the work of the IAUS in New York and at Princeton University, and the work of Venturi and Scott Brown at Yale, Lynch at MIT, Meier and Webber at Berkeley, and the like.

In parallel with this critique, Frampton advanced arguments for the remedial possibilities embedded in existing civic and public typologies. In 1978, as part of a larger project conceived at the IAUS, Frampton contributed to *On Streets*, a volume edited by Stanford Anderson, with his essay "The Generic Street as a Continuous Built Form."[8] This was the first time Frampton published his method of critical comparative analysis of built form—in this case, in relation to the ability of environmental form to articulate Arendt's "space of human appearance." Frampton had begun to teach the method in the mid-1960s at Princeton and had continued to employ it at Columbia University and elsewhere ever since. It was not until 2015 and the publication of *A Genealogy of Modern Architecture: Comparative Critical Analysis of Built Form*,[9] however, that his approach was carefully edited by Ashley Simone and published in its most elaborated form to date. In "The Generic Street," Frampton proceeds from Alison and Peter Simpson's theoretical formulation of the eponymous term "generic street" from 1955, in order to advance his own proto-theory of both "place-form" and "megaform" via the comparative method. Namely, Frampton questions how to address the parallel problematic: First, to what extent does megastructural form (not yet "megaform," such as mass social housing and the like) serve as spatial and symbolic anchors (i.e., landmarks) in the context of megalopolitan developments? And second, how can such forms simultaneously "situate" residents in the urban landscape and reproduce the sociocultural vitality of the traditional street? Frampton's argument here is that large, megastructural built forms must be designed so as to produce public spaces, "breaks in the abstract motopian system, which are identifiable

---

[7] Robert Venturi, *Complexity and Contradiction in Architecture* (New York: Museum of Modern Art, 1966), 133.

[8] Kenneth Frampton, "The Generic Street as a Continuous Built Form," in *On Streets*, ed. Stanford Anderson (Cambridge, MA: MIT Press, 1978), 309–37.

[9] Kenneth Frampton, *A Genealogy of Modern Architecture: Comparative Critical Analysis of Built Form*, ed. Ashley Simone (Zürich: Lars Müller Publishers, 2015). See Section 1 of this volume.

and sustainable as public enclaves of varying density and capacity." While the "living together of people" is, for Arendt, a prerequisite for the emergence of the spaces of appearance, the role of megastructural form is to articulate the public realm at the micro scale.

Frampton explores these ideas further in the brief essay "The Atrium as Surrogate Public Form," delivered as an introduction to the "Public Building, Form and Influence" session at the 1996 Jerusalem Seminar in Architecture. The seminar, organized by Frampton under the label "Technology, Place and Architecture,"[10] gathered some of the most prominent architects and urbanists of the day. Frampton's outstanding introduction declares that the fundamental task of the gathering was to explore building technology—specifically, the reintegration of land-form into built fabric in order to mediate the results of global megalopolitan developments and to produce culturally significant work. Frampton goes on to propose that the ethical role for architects, in the face of wholesale "technocratic commodification" and the "depoliticized aestheticization and technification of the architectural *modus operandi*," is to insist that the future of democracy itself depends on the ability to design and erect what he calls the "provocative public micro-realm."

Returning to the arguments made in "The Generic Street," Frampton suggests in "Civic Form"[11] that a civic institution experienced as a space of public appearance can simultaneously, through its typographic character, be experienced as a landmark. He expands on the cultural and political potential of the civic form and on the representation of the civic institution as a space of assembly. As in the section's previous essay, Frampton here provides examples of realized civic forms mostly in the work of European architects, arguing that the articulation and manifestation of social values through civic form can provide the necessary resistance to wholesale commodification and universal consumerism. His key reference in this respect has been the work of Alvar Aalto, and in the essay that follows here—"The Legacy of Alvar Aalto: Evolution and Influence"[12]—Frampton discusses Aalto's civic architecture, his robust regional planning work, and describes Aalto's public work as particularly important in

---

[10] The event was documented in the Rizzoli published volume with the same title in 1998. For reference, see Kenneth Frampton, Arthur Spector, and Lynne Reed Rosman, eds., *Technology, Place & Architecture: The Jerusalem Seminar in Architecture* (New York: Rizzoli, 1998).

[11] "Civic Form" appears within "Afterword: Architecture in the Age of Globalization" in the fifth edition of *Modern Architecture: A Critical History* (pp. 636–42). Arguments made in this essay build most directly on Frampton's "Megaform as Urban Landscape" lecture of 1999. See Kenneth Frampton, *Megaform as Urban Landscape: 1999 Raoul Wallenberg Lecture* (Ann Arbor, MI: The University of Michigan A. Alfred Taubman College of Architecture and Urban Planning, 1999).

[12] Kenneth Frampton, "The Legacy of Alvar Aalto: Evolution and Influence," in *Alvar Aalto: Between Humanism and Materialism*, ed. Peter Reed (New York: Museum of Modern Art, 1998), 118–39.

relation to the space of public appearance: for example, the way Aalto builds the entry sequence from the street to the core of the building, which is often conceptualized as the atrium.[13]

The split between architecture and planning professions, so alarmingly evident in the 1990s under the assault of neoliberal policies, had in Frampton's view resulted in the rendering of environmental planning as a technocratic, value-free practice of management and applied science. In 1995's "Toward an Urban Landscape,"[14] Frampton argues that this separation has enabled the wholesale destruction of the North American landscape. As in much of this volume, Frampton refers to Serge Chermayeff and Christopher Alexander's *Community and Privacy: Toward a New Architecture of Humanism*[15] of 1963, which from his perspective provided "a rational model for suburban development." Although highly imperfect, and characterized by Frampton as "a neocapitalist, automotive land-settlement pattern,"[16] their proposal offered a new standard for suburban land settlement based on low-rise, high-density courtyard houses—a sensitive approach to land-form that also is "capable of sustaining a modicum of public space" (Figures 52 and 53). Frampton saw value in their effort to create a place for building and sustaining communal and public forms of social life while simultaneously taking part in megalopolitan, automotive developments. Such public micro-realms would indeed offer at least the possibility of democratic participation within a bounded environment conducive to face-to-face political deliberations. In reflecting on and responding to *What U Can Do*,[17] Shadrach Woods' call to action of 1970, Frampton herein develops a twelve-point assessment as to where the field stands a quarter century later. Landscape and landform emerge as his central concerns; as Frampton asserts, "priority should now be accorded to landscape, rather than to freestanding built form." If architecture assumes "an ecological stance in the broadest possible sense,"

---

[13] "Interview with Kenneth Frampton on Alvar Aalto," Vitra Design Museum, 5 October 2015, YouTube video, https://www.youtube.com/watch?v=SmBi_T-3ZAA. For a more elaborate study of Aalto, see also Kenneth Frampton, "The Legacy of Alvar Aalto: Evolution and Influence," in *Alvar Aalto: Between Humanism and Materialism*, ed. Peter Reed (New York: Museum of Modern Art, 1998), 118–39.

[14] Kenneth Frampton, "Toward an Urban Landscape," *D: Columbia Documents of Architecture and Theory*, no.4 (1995): 83–93.

[15] Serge Chermayeff and Christopher Alexander, *Community and Privacy: Toward a New Architecture of Humanism* (Garden City, NY: Doubleday, 1965).

[16] Kenneth Frampton, "Land Settlement, Architecture, and the Eclipse of the Public Realm" in *The Pragmatist Imagination: Thinking About "Things in the Making,"* ed. Joan Ockman (New York: Princeton Architectural Press, 2000), 104–11. The essay is included later in this section of the book.

[17] Shadrach Woods, *What U Can Do: Architecture at Rice 27* (Houston: Rice University School of Architecture, 1970), 33–35.

Frampton argues, it may be capable of credibly proposing remedial landscapes as "critical counter forms" to the ongoing destructive commodification of the man-made world.[18]

As a direct extension of the arguments made above, Frampton authored another seminal work: "Megaform as Urban Landscape," first given in 1999 as a public lecture at the University of Michigan in Ann Arbor.[19] In this essay, Frampton for the first time defines the term "megaform" in reference to the form-giving potential of horizontally extending urban fabric with a strong topographical character capable of effecting topographic transformation and densification. Moreover, he renders megaform a unifying environmental trope in twentieth-century architecture, urbanism, and civic design—an urban project whose anthropogeographic dimensions are characterized by the attempt to integrate the human experience of a place with the rationality and abstraction of architectural and urban design (via Vittorio Gregotti's notion of "critical rationalism"[20]) at the regional if not territorial scale. In a situation where, as Frampton writes, "late capitalism seems reluctant to commit itself to any form of land settlement that would be consistent with the production of coherent civic form," megaforms act as "civic microcosms": distinguishable spaces of public appearance within the ever more commodified global megalopolis.

Many of the issues addressed in this section were reworked into Frampton's formidable and evocative contribution to Joan Ockman's 2000 edited volume *The Pragmatist Imagination: Thinking About "Things in the Making"*: the essay that closes this section, titled "Land Settlement, Architecture, and the Eclipse of the Public Realm."[21] Frampton here reminds us of the dangers of technocratic commodification so rampant at the close of the twentieth century—a process that tends to depoliticize architectural practice and reduce it to a spectacle of technical productivity. Building on his earlier arguments, Frampton maintains

---

[18] The term "remedial landscape" refers to Peter Rowe's thesis advanced in his book *Making a Middle Landscape* (Cambridge, MA: MIT Press, 1991), which Frampton cites in the "Megaform as Urban Landscape" essay in this section.

[19] Delivered as the 1999 Raoul Wallenberg Memorial Lecture, the essay was subsequently published by the A. Alfred Taubman College of Architecture and Urban Planning under the same title.

[20] See Vittorio Gregotti, *Il Territorio dell'Architettura* (Milan, Italy: Feltrinelli, 1966). See also V. Gregotti, *Inside Architecture*, trans. Peter Wong and Francesca Zaccheo (Cambridge, MA: MIT Press, 1996). The latter volume includes a foreword by Frampton and was originally published in Italian as *Dentro l'architettura* (Turin, Italy: Bollati Boringhieri, 1991).

[21] Frampton, "Land Settlement, Architecture, and the Eclipse of the Public Realm," 104–11.

that under conditions where the public realm is withdrawn, we must insist on establishing direct causalities between democracy and spaces of public appearance. It is the architect's task, he asserts, to act as an agent capable of articulating instances of the public realm in order to gather people specifically at the thresholds between public institutions and society. Acting in this capacity is, strictly speaking, a political challenge—and Frampton insists it ought to be addressed by the contribution architecture should make to "the realization of a more liberative society."

Normally, we don't make a distinction between architecture and building, but I think it's important to recognize that there are these two words in almost every language. Architecture with the capital 'A' has always been about public building . . . Architecture guarantees the public realm; it has that kind of political, cultural, and social importance. The philosopher Hannah Arendt coined the term 'the space of appearance.' Architecture ultimately is about the space of public appearance.

Kenneth Frampton, "What Is Architecture?" *Arch Daily* Interviews, 14 July 2014, YouTube video, https://www.youtube.com/watch?v=OsqH6D64LkI.

8 America 1960–1970: Notes on Urban Images and Theory (1971)

The recent writings of Denise Scott Brown and Robert Venturi extend the syncretic capacity of the English picturesque tradition beyond its traceable limits. Their joint text, "A Significance of A&P Parking Lots or Learning from Las Vegas" of 1968, extols the virtues of that city as a paramount example of an urbanity, worthy of serious study by future architects and planners.[1] Amongst other things, they seem to imply, to quote Ferrari [. . .] that modern architecture, now irrelevant and isolated, should seek, "for its social-economic integration in the field of the production and consumption of single objects, that is objects considered independently of the entire field of relationships between them and their consumer."[2]

[. . .]

Scott Brown and Venturi are prompt to reassure us, lest we should become squeamish, that their Las Vegas "analysis" is merely a phenomenal study in architectural communication and that this being so, its values are not questioned. They continue: "There is no reason, however, why the methods of commercial persuasion and the skyline of signs should not serve the purpose of civic and cultural enhancement", and indeed there is not, as Oscar Nitschke, Johannes Duiker and the Vesnin Brothers, amongst many others, have long ago demonstrated.[3] "But this is not entirely up to the architect", they advisedly conclude, and in architecturally unencumbered Las Vegas it is obviously not, for it is presumably up to the holding "interests" to decide whether or not they will pay for the erection of a giant sky sign.

Source: Kenneth Frampton, "America 1960–1970: Notes on Urban Images and Theory," *Casabella*, no. 359–360 (1971): 25–40.

[1] Venturi, R. and Scott Brown, D., "A Significance for A & P Parking Lots, or Learning from Las Vegas", *Architectural Forum*, March 1968.

[2] Ferrari, A., "La Lettura dell'Ambiente Fisico Nella Cultura Inglese", *Zodiac* 18, Milano 1969.

[3] Prior to Nitschke's building there was of course Johannes Duiker's Cineac Building, built in Amsterdam in 1934 and the Vesnin Brothers famous Pravda project of 1926.

This essentially picturesque prospect of Las Vegas relates however elliptically to the English "townscape" position, first initiated in *The Architectural Review* in the late 40's as an integral part of that post-war Anglo-Saxon concern to "humanize" the modern movement. This "humanization" was a popular success and by the mid-50's Townscape had been academicized into a Sittesque "method" of urban design, that was commonly accepted and practiced in the States. Townscape was introduced into "respectable" American planning circles via the development of an M.I.T. methodology that was first publicly presented in 1960, in Kevin Lynch's *The Image of the City*.[4] This work, appearing in retrospect as a pioneering piece of populist urbanism (almost in anticipation of advocacy planning), largely had the intended effect of rationalizing the post-war erosion of the American city by the automobile. Of the ruthless superposition of federally subsidized highways and of the sporadic speculative urban renewal, contingent upon the displacement of the urban poor, that followed predictably in their wake, it passed no comment. Once again, no doubt, such value judgments were regarded as being extraneous to the study. Thus, other than urging that an uncommon sensibility be statistically complied from common consensus to serve as the basis of future urban design—a collective sensibility to express itself in terms of "edge", "district", "landmark" and other similar nuances, as are of course invariably respected by real estate interests—it had no comment to make, in respect of the then imminent dissolution of the existing structure of Boston. To distract from this instant institutionalized vandalism, it posited the creation of urban "image" maps, employing a graphic notation, compounded out of a sophisticated infusion of Sitte with latter day Gestalt theory. This ingenious instrument of a picturesque pluralism was succeeded a few years later by an automotive kinetic version along similar lines which was co-authored with Donald Appleyard and John R. Myer and significantly entitled *A View from the Road*.[5] With an admirable concentration on essentials, which GM would have appreciated, this report concluded that elevated highways were preferable in respect of such a view. Aware that in their conclusion there lay an irresolvable conflict of interest, the authors wisely chose to exclude from their report any consideration of those who, out of the unfortunate necessity of remaining in the city, would look at such highways from the ground.

In "Learning from Pop", Denise Scott Brown advocates a very similar cinematic use of sophisticated technology. She writes: "New analytical techniques must use film and video tape to convey the dynamism of sign architecture and the sequential experience of vast landscapes; and computers are needed to aggregate mass repeated data into comprehensible patterns".[6] Is this because they are incomprehensible otherwise, or is it that like Trajan's Column, the Stardust

---

[4] Lynch, K., The Image of the City, MIT Press, 1960.

[5] Lynch, K., *The View From the Road*, co-authors Donald Appleyard and John Meyer, MIT Press, 1964.

[6] Scott Brown, Denise, "Learning from Pop", *Casabella* 359–60, December 1971. [From the editor: Frampton's and Scott Brown's essays appear in the same issue of *Casabella*.]

Sign is imperially destined to be codified and then disseminated throughout the world?

There is no doubt that such research, properly programmed, would yield useful operational and aesthetic data, in respect of kino-graphic communication vis-à-vis visibility, reaction time, etc.—yet once informational/computational processes are emphasized, as they are now, above places of arrival and departure, the very notion of place itself tends to become threatened, to the potential detriment of "human" experience. As Hannah Arendt has put it, "The 'in order to' (becomes) the content of the 'for sake of' (and) utility established as meaning generates meaninglessness".[7] It is ironic that Denise Scott Brown should attempt to bestow upon such reservoirs of process and pseudo points of arrival, as parking lots, those very attributes which previous cultures reserved for "space of human appearance"[8]—such as those churches, so clearly revealed as "res publica" in Nolli's maps of Rome. Of the latter she writes: "Nolli's late 18th Century mapping technique which he applied to Rome, when it is adapted to parking lots, throws considerable light on Las Vegas". Rather less light, one would have thought, than that already thrown by Eduard Ruscha who has exhaustively demonstrated, to arcane ends, that parking lots, unlike swimming pools and gasoline stations, are at their best when seen from the air; that is when alienated from the normal field of human vision.[9] Pop clearly has little feel for a "camp" historicism such as would see A & P parking lots as corresponding to the *tapis verts* of Versailles.

What then are we to learn from two phenomena so superficially similar yet so different in ultimate intent as Motopia (i.e., Las Vegas, Los Angeles, Levittown, etc.) and Pop Art, for surely Pop Art is not quite synonymous with consumer folk culture, as now industrially mass-produced and marketed? Do designers really need elaborate sociological ratification *à la* Gans, to tell them that what the people want is what they already have?[10] No doubt Levittown could be brought to yield an equally affirmative consensus in regard to current American repressive policies, domestic and foreign. Should designers like politicians wait upon dictates of a silent majority, and if so, how are they to interpret them?

[7] Arendt, H., *The Human Condition*, Doubleday Anchor Books Edition, 1959, page 135. See also Venturi, R., "Complexity and Contradiction in Architecture", MoMA Papers, No. 1, Museum of Modern Art, New York, 1966, page 133—wherein the space of human appearance is to be seen as having "unpatriotic" connotations. Venturi writes: "The piazza, in fact, is 'un-American'. Americans feel uncomfortable sitting in a square: they should be working at the office or home with the family looking at television". There are only two possibilities presumably. This argument is twisted with nice sophistry in the last sentences of Venturi's book which reads: "We are in the habit of thinking that open space is precious in the city. It is not. Except in Manhattan perhaps, our cities have too much open space, in the ubiquitous parking lots, in the not-so-temporary deserts created by Urban Renewal and in the amorphous suburbs around".

[8] Arendt, H., *The Human Condition*, op. cit., p. 45.

[9] Ruscha, E., *Thirty Four Parking Lots*, Los Angeles, 1967. See also other books by Ruscha: *Twenty Six Gasoline Stations*, 1963; *Every Building on Sunset Strip*, 1968.

[10] Gans, H.J., *The Levittowners: Ways of Life and Politics in a New Suburban Community*, New York, 1967.

Design oriented expertise in Western European and American universities stands largely transfixed before the technical prowess and success of Western Neo-Capitalism—inhibited by a mass consensus, its socio-political critical faculty has been seriously undermined—entranced by the so-called democratization of consumption and by the inevitability of that, which I have elsewhere characterized as the "instant utopia" of Los Angeles, it largely occupies itself with describing, eulogizing and extrapolating upon the triumph of mid-cult which already exists. These anti-utopian New Utopians are to be gainfully engaged in the *"post facto"* rationalization of our already "polluted" environments. The architectural, planning, and sociological disciplines, now semi-derelict through inept or trivial use, are particularly prone to these occupationally "therapeutic" activities, primarily because these disciplines are largely restrained by powerful interests, from any significant realization of their most socially progressive prescriptions.

The dilemma is as much socio-cultural and economic as it is methodological. Architects and planners are embedded in a society which having become exclusively preoccupied with industrial growth, is structurally inimical to their inherently synthetic approach. This is not to discredit the current realistic wave of anti-utopianism, nor to disclaim the past failure of formalist "dogmatic" design, but rather it is to place any critique of the design profession in a more comprehensive context. Jerzy Soltan characterized the predicament with great exactitude when he wrote in 1967: "It is an unhealthy paradox that in a domain so pragmatic, in a science and art so very much 'applied' as urban design, theorizing is what remains to the majority of practitioners. What would become of applied physics if it should be limited to theories of medicine without practice? How many major urban design projects are born every day? Published in architectural magazines? How many of them reach realization? What is the relation between philosophy, the spirit of the overwhelming majority of the projects and the occasionally realized urban units? Aren't they often representing complete extremes? Can one obtain useful feedback for an intransigently forward-looking project, from a conservative or even backward-looking realization? How long can one discuss without acting?"[11]

This deactivation of the design profession—in particular architecture and planning—no doubt accounts for our current preoccupation with the redefinition of our professional scope, aim and methodology. This commonly leads to the not entirely reasonable but nonetheless publicly plausible conclusion that it is not the society but only these professions which are in need of such restructuring and from this it is but a step to that which Tomás Maldonado has characterized as the "status quo" school of environmental design.[12] Despite ever escalating evidence as to the scale of the world's ecological imbalance,

---

[11] See *Team 10 Primer*, edited by Alison Smithson, M.I.T. Press, 1968, page 14.

[12] Maldonado, T., "La Speranza Progettuale", *Ambiente e Società*, Nuovo Politecnico 35, Einaudi, Torino, 1970, pages 101–13.

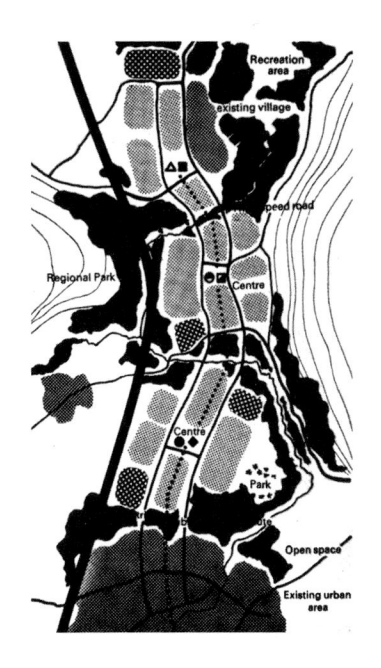

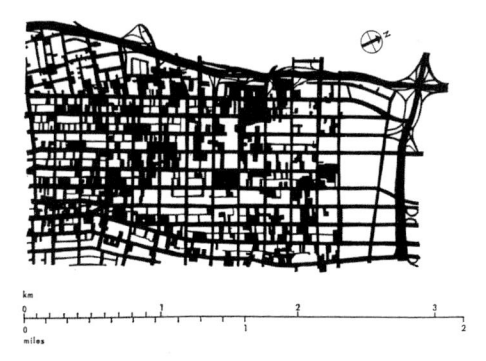

FIGURES 22 AND 23 A "three-strand" Linear City Proposal for linked townships in Central Lancashire, UK. J.R. James for the British Ministry of Housing and Local Government, 1967 (top); Analysis of the ground surfaces in downtown Los Angeles, California. Konstantinos Doxiades, 1968 (below).

the implicit attitude of this "school" remains one in which the design professions are to be reactivated only through greater conformity to the sacrosanct "populist" goals of our affluent society. First variously formulated in America in the early 60's by planners, so widely polarized as Kevin Lynch and Melvin Webber, and since heavily mythologized and aestheticized by men such as Tom Wolfe[13] and Eduard Ruscha, this attitude now evidently numbers among its adherents Denise Scott Brown and Robert Venturi.

In his book "Complexity and Contradiction in Architecture" of 1966,[14] Venturi declared his ultimately mannerist attitude in a text and title that nicely reflected his predilections for an illusory monumentality and for the transformation of abstract geometry into alienating form. In contrast to a Scharoun or to an Aalto, Venturi's symbolism is neither anthropomorphic nor, in Jungian terms, archetypal. It restricts itself to detached empirical comment upon the inherent frailty of man and his institutional structures. It sustains itself through the construction of elaborate aesthetic metaphors and through the projection of paradoxes which, far from being subversive, verge on the cynical. The cavalier attitude to material, the monumental gesture that dissolves into historicism, the justification of an elite mannerism on the ground of feasibility and social concern, the overt use of outsized Pop imagery that may be read by the initiated as some comic cut-out reference to a piece of outdated American folklore, all testify to a "popular" wit that is ultimately conservative. Unlike Kahn's heroic monumentality, to which it is related, Venturi's work does not gravitate towards the values of the archaic. Instead, it adopts a marginally tolerant attitude towards those values which are already desecrating large tracts of our physical environment. It flirts with an industrially brutalized folk culture in order to engender that which has since been proclaimed by Ada Louise Huxtable as the cult of the "dumb and the ordinary".[15] The ordinary, of course, constitutes the basis of any true vernacular and from this suburbia cannot be excepted. However, the "creative" recapitula-

---

[13] Wolfe, T., *The Kandy-Kolored Tangerine-Flake Streamline Baby*, Farrar, Straus and Giroux, New York, 1965.

[14] Venturi, R., "Complexity and Contradiction in Architecture", MoMA Papers No. I, Museum of Modem Art, New York, 1966.

[15] See the *New York Times*, January 18, 1970, "Heroics Are Out Ordinary Is In", by Ada Louise Huxtable. Despite its irreducible achievements, such as the Seagram Building in New York, one cannot but welcome this much proclaimed move away from Venturi's Guild House, Philadelphia, from the Corporate Neo-Classicism that has dominated American post-war architecture. "Ordinariness" as both Ada Louise Huxtable and Robert Venturi maintain does indeed afford a refreshing alternative to this Neo-Classicism, now in its decadence. However, this alternative is clearly to be more easily achieved in some instances than in others. Thus, the Scott, Venturi, Rauch 1968 project for Transportation Square in Washington maintains only a tenuous hold on the "ordinary" in a context that is overridingly monumental. Elsewhere the "ordinary" is seen to vary, here it borders on the deliberately "gauche", to that studied and syntactically anomalous mixture of intricate elegance and banality which characterizes the Moore, Lyndon, Turnbull design for Pembroke College at Brown University, Rhode Island. Ordinariness in any event is

tion of the ordinary on economic grounds and its fashionable elevation into a "camp" cult concern for banal or quaint effects, may be just as inappropriate to a given design as any piece of rhetorical formalism. Moreover, architectural practice, however provisionally removed from the canons of high art does not absolve itself from an implicit environmental responsibility that devolves upon designers to declare their opposition to public building programs which are either socio-culturally false or fiscally inadequate. The issue is political, yet suprapartisan. Thus, to canonize, from a quasi-town-scape standpoint, the mid-cult kitsch of Las Vegas as a general model of urbanity is hardly a progressive level of response. Despite the declared value-free demonstration of method involved, the implicit divorce between form and content is culturally invalid.

[. . .]

Webber's perspective of 1963[16] was eminently the non-critical social science perspective, first synthesized into "A Communications Theory of Urban Growth", in Richard Meier's book of this title published in 1962. The Meier thesis paradoxically prepared the way for the political awareness of Webber's later writing. Growth was then regarded by Meier as an attribute to be avidly sought for by urban civilizations irrespective of their natural tendency to grow through demographic increase. The implication was that an urbanized open system must conserve negative entropy in terms of information if it was to survive. The underlying assumption was economic, in as much as the urban production of wealth and power and hence the GNP, was seen as being a direct or indirect result of information growth. The value questions as to information for what ends and survival under what conditions—those questions later to be posited by E.J. Mishan, in his book *The Costs of Economic Growth* of 1967—were not asked.[17] However, Meier did anticipate a scenario of violence and conflict for he wrote, "In a very real sense 'information' brings with it a capacity to form an ensemble of alternatives, whoever has this information is in a position to

---

not new in 20th century architecture. There are plenty of precedents from Hannes Meyer to Hugo Häring and from De Klerk to Alvar Aalto. What distinguishes the Philadelphia/West Coast School from such work is clearly its camp flirtation with Pop Art on the one hand and its somewhat inconsistent ties to the classic and the archaic, through its formal sources in the work of Louis Kahn, on the other. Whether or not this school will be able to transcend its self-imposed "gaucheness", to achieve, as it promises to do, environments which are truly responsive to current human needs, both operationally and culturally, remains to be seen. As it is, only Joseph Esberick's Cannery Building in San Francisco seems to have passed beyond the cult of the "ordinary" to arrive at a mode of building which is at once appropriate, articulate and liberating [Footnote moved from its original place by the editor].

[16] Webber, M., "The Urban Place and the Non-Place Urban Realm," in Webber, M.M., Dyckman, J.W., Foley, D.L. et al. (Eds) *Explorations in Urban Structure*, Philadelphia: University of Pennsylvania Press, 1964, pages 13–44 [footnote inserted by the editor].

[17] Mishan, E.J., *The Costs of Economic Growth*, New York, 1967.

discover that some alternatives yield more of the commodities that are temporarily scarce than others".[18]

This is surely close to being the information thesis of the performance principle itself, characterized by Marcuse as defining the standard of living solely in terms of automobiles, television sets and air-planes.[19] Mishan's postulation that information proliferation and industrialized production, in respect of their redundancy or pollution factor, constitute a megalopolitan system, profligate in its maximized energy consumption and hence by definition rapidly running down in a non-informational sense (to human detriment) appears as totally foreign to Meier's thought.

There is a marked difference between the early and later writings of Melvin Webber—in particular between his conference text of 1963 entitled "Comprehensive Planning and Social Responsibility"[20] and his essay of 1965 entitled "The Role of Intelligence Systems in Urban Design".[21] Whereas in his early polemical essays and in his AIP conference text he betrayed an apolitical easy confidence in the late maturity of the planning profession (through its assimilation of advanced social science), proclaiming its broad social mandate and its, as then unproven, new instrumental ability to act effectively, by 1965 he was concerned to reveal the inherently political predicament of any urban planning perspective. He was then to write: "Whether we like it or not, social science,

---

[18] Meier, R.L., *Communications Theory of Urban Growth*, MIT Press, 1962.

[19] Marcuse, H., *Eros and Civilization*, Vintage Books, New York, 1962, page 139.

[20] Webber, Melvin M., "Comprehensive Planning and Social Responsibility (Towards an A.I.P. Consensus on the Profession's Roles and Purposes)", *AIP Journal*, November 1963, pages 232–41. Although this was a far more socially conscious essay than his polemical "Order in Diversity: Community Without Propinquity" of approximately the same date, its somewhat complacent conclusions were directly challenged by Francis Piven in the *AIP Journal*, November 1964, pages 229–30 when she wrote as follows: "Webber raises some of the major value dilemmas which our society faces, and the professional and political problems which follow from these dilemmas. He puts them aside however with a somewhat awesome *braggadocio*. Thus, the abstract idea that planning is a process by which the community seeks to increase the individual's opportunities to choose for himself contains extremely perplexing philosophical problems. And the empirical assertion that our society demonstrates a growing appreciation of cultural diversity is open to serious question. Webber recommends centralization–decentralization combinations as administrative solutions without specification, giving no attention to the organizational complexities which are involved. Some of those difficulties and dilemmas have recently been highlighted in the very model Webber points to—the public education system. Few of its recent critics have acknowledged its success as an institution which expands individual choices. Rather, it has been attacked for expanding the choice of some at the expense of others and for wielding tremendous social control in terms of the interests and values of dominant groups".

[21] Webber, Melvin M., "The Role of Intelligence Systems in Urban Systems Planning", *AIP Journal*, November 1965, pages 289–296. This paper may be taken as responding to some of the aspects of the Francis Piven critique. For example, one finds Webber writing, despite his faith in pluralism, that: "A master plan that showed some desired future state for the presently poor without also showing the methods for attaining it could scarcely command much attention".

and especially policy-oriented social science, cannot be value-free science . . . Seemingly straightforward facts about societal things and events are seldom, if ever, neutral. They inevitably intervene into the workings of the systems they describe. The information supplier, whatever his motives and methods, is therefore inevitably immersed in politics. The kinds of facts he selects to report, the way he presents them, the groups they are distributed to, and the inferences he invites, each work to shape subsequent outcomes, subsequent facts."[22]

[. . .]

There is little doubt that it is the measure of a highly developed mannerist taste (not at all popular) that against one's instinctive reaction, one should like such Ruscha material as Denise Scott Brown claims she does in her article "On Pop Art, Permissiveness and Planning" wherein she writes: "This is not to abandon planned action for judgement. Judgment is merely deferred a while in order to make it more sensitive. Liking what you hate is exhilarating and liberating, but finally confirming for judgement."[23] Taken at face value, "liking what one hates" seems a Newspeak with which to make value judgements or through which to arrive at desired future state—the latter presumably being the "*sine qua non*" of all planning activity. Such a sophisticated rationalization leaves one with two outstanding questions of a highly critical nature. Is it the inevitability of kitsch only to be transcended through such a perverse exultation of our industrial capacity to induce and satisfy mass taste in the endless promotion and repetition of kitsch? Or, is it that present triumph of kitsch is testament in itself, without the illuminations of Pop Art, that our urban society is organized towards self-defeating ends, on a sociopolitical basis that is totally invalid?

---

[22] Webber, Melvin M., "The Role of Intelligence Systems in Urban Systems Planning".

[23] Scott Brown, Denise, "On Pop Art, Permissiveness and Planning", *AIP Journal*, May 1968. In her review of the work of Eduard Ruscha, Scott Brown states that evidence of a parallel new sensibility to the spontaneous man-made landscape is to be found in the avant-garde cinema; she cites by way of example Michelangelo Antonioni's, *La Notte*, *Deserto Rosso*, and *Blow-Up*. Certainly, Eduard Ruscha is as obsessed as Antonioni with the "presence of absence", i.e., the scenes of the crime. However, she does not comment on the complexity of this director's attitude to his chosen material. Surely *Deserto Rosso* makes unequivocally clear the self-alienation of man from nature, through detached causality of thought and industrialization—an alienation that is as much metaphysical as it is environmental. There is again the position rendered in *Zabriskie Point* where the "production power house" of the Los Angeles strip, is cut against the opening sequences of militant students discussing their intended revolt, in Marxist terminology. As the hero remarks: "I am sick of kids talking about violence and the cops handing it out". The final frames of the film may be taken as a violent exposure of the consumer society in which the house of consumable objects explodes. This sequence is preceded by a sequence in which the businessmen-heroes, the land speculators etc., of the real estate world plot their "para-military" campaign for the future exploitation of the Californian desert.

9 The Generic Street as a Continuous Built Form (1978)

[...]

INTRODUCTION: THE STREET AND THE AVANT GARDE

While the "nonplace urban realms"[1] as characterized by [Kenneth] Boulding[2] may be resistant to any kind of large-scale modification, the fact remains that an existential need for something that may be identified as a street seems to persist. In this respect, it is instructive to note that little more than twenty years separates the antistreet thesis of Le Corbusier from the prostreet preoccupations

---

Source: Kenneth Frampton, "The Generic Street as a Continuous Built Form," in *On Streets*, ed. Stanford Anderson (Cambridge, MA: MIT Press, 1978), 309–37.

[1] See Melvin M. Webber, *Explorations into Urban Structure* (Philadelphia: University of Pennsylvania Press, 1964). Webber's coinage of the term "nonplace urban realm" has surely helped to further the ideology of the motopian open city, as has his rationalizing phrase "community without propinquity."

[2] "A high level post-civilized stable technology would almost have to be based on the oceans for sources, for its basic raw materials, as the mines and the fossil fuels will very soon be gone. There will, therefore, be some manufacturing concentrations around the shores of the world. We may even see a revival of the form of the classical city for pure pleasure where people can enjoy the luxury of walking and of face-to-face communication. Inequality of income in such a society is likely to be reflected in the fact that the poor will drive vehicles and the rich will walk. We are already, I think, beginning to see this movement in the movement of the rich into the city centers and the development of the mall. These cities, however, will be stage sets—they will arise out of the very freedom and luxury of the society rather than out of its necessities," Kenneth E. Boulding, "The Death of the City: A Frightening Look at Post-Civilization," in Oscar Handlin and John Burchard. eds., *The Historian and the City* (Cambridge, Mass.: The MIT Press, 1966) [Quote converted to footnote by the editor].

of Alison and Peter Smithson, a concern that first became evident in their Golden Lane Housing of 1952. Where Le Corbusier, true to his Enlightenment heritage, castigated the traditional street for being, "no more than a trench, a deep cleft, a narrow passage"[3] that in his opinion did nothing but oppress the spirit, the Smithsons by the early fifties had become acutely aware of the sociocultural vitality of the street—particularly as they had then experienced it in the still-existing London bye-law housing dating from the turn of the century.

Their appreciation of this street formulated for the first time in modern theory the idea of the generic street: that is, of a street that may not be recognizable as such but would have, nonetheless, many of the psychosocial attributes of the traditional street. Thus they wrote under a heading entitled *Patterns of Association* the following appreciation of the bye-law street:

> In a tight knit society inhabiting a tight knit development such as the byelaw streets there is an inherent feeling of safety and social bond which has much to do with the obviousness and simple order form of the street: about 40 houses facing a common open space. The street is not only a means of access but also an arena for social expression. In these "slum" streets is found a simple relationship between house and street.[4]

What failed to follow from this appraisal of the street was a convincing idea as to how a generic form of this order could be generated within the prevailing megalopolitan milieu, and from this time onward the work of the Smithsons, together with that of the Team 10 formation, may be regarded as a loosely coordinated effort at inventing such a form.

What this form could validly be, in the increasingly abstract context of motopia, was no clearer to the Smithsons than to any other member of Team 10, a fact that is brought home from the relative failure of Golden Lane's [1952] single-loaded access gallery to function as a genuine substitute for the traditional street (cf. Parkhill Housing, Sheffield of 1962). That the Smithsons were not capable at this time of sensing the existential and phenomenological limits of the street per se, namely its essential doublesidedness[5] and its lateral continuity with the ground, not only points to the extent to which they, in their turn, were conditioned by the abstract rationality of the modern movement but also touches on another dilemma which has confronted architectural thought over the past

---

[3] See "La Rue" by Le Corbusier which appears in Le Corbusier et Pierre Jeanneret, *Oeuvre Complète de 1910–1929* (Zürich: Girsberger, 3rd edition, 1943) pp. 112–15. This by now famous anti street polemic of Le Corbusier first appeared in the Journal *L'intransigeant* in May 1929.

[4] A. and P. Smithson, *Urban Structuring* (London: Studio-Vista, 1967). The text first appeared in *Uppercase 3*. ed. Theo Crosby (Tunbridge, Kent: Whitefriars Press, 1955).

[5] *The Shorter Oxford English Dictionary*, 3rd edition, 1966 points to the essential double-sided nature of a street as a cultural phenomenon, as we may judge from the second definition. "2. A road in a town or village . . . running between two lines of houses of shops. Also the road together with the adjacent houses. Used for the inhabitants of the street; also, the people of the street, late M.E."

decade. This parallel problematic essentially poses two questions: first, in what way may megastructural forms, such as the freeway, be used to impart landmark identity to the large-scale megalopolitan reality; and second, the related issue as to what may be an appropriate formulation for large urban elements such as mass housing so that these will not only relate to the megalopolitan scale but at the same time "situate" man and provide for those fundamental needs of association and identity. That this dichotomous issue has led on occasion to the generation of poetic but operationally inconsistent models is evident from a good deal of architectural speculation over the last twenty years, as we may well judge from many of the designs projected by Team 10 during this period. Two projects stand out as being particularly exemplary of this dilemma—Louis Kahn's midtown Philadelphia proposal of 1953 and the Smithsons' Hauptstadt Berlin competition entry of 1958.

Where in the one instance the periphery of a pedestrianized center is shown as being lined by cylindrical parking silos, in the other a multileveled pedestrian esplanade, linking randomly placed office towers, is shown as being indifferent to the continuity of the "grain"[6] in the existing city despite its frequent connection to the sidewalk infrastructure through an elaborate system of escalator access. What is problematic about both these proposals is not only their mutual indifference to the historical limits of their respective urban contexts (which even in the case of Berlin still persists) but also their incapacity to formulate a convincing model for the generic interface between the automotive infrastructure and the pedestrian street. In these two projects, as in a great deal of our everyday urban reality, the separate realms of freeway and pedestrian street tend to cancel each other out, with the former invariably emerging as the dominant force.

But the most telling point about these examples is not their specific shortcomings—the vague differentiation made between automotive and pedestrian movement (which is particularly chronic in the case of Philadelphia) or the climatic and commercial inviability of the pedestrian decks in the case of Berlin—but rather these disjunctive propositions as the manifestation of a general theoretical block, wherein the true limitations and needs of the present appear to be inimical to any kind of adequate formulation. At this juncture the endemic utopianism of the architectural profession seems to limit its creative and critical capacity, for the reality of the "nonplace urban realm" is hardly to be mediated by such imaginative, but ultimately inviable, essays in the grandmaster manner. Ultimately, Kahn's Philadelphia looks more to Piranesi's Rome than it does to the existential realities of the American downtown, while the Smithsons' Berlin is more concerned with the iconography of San Gimignano

---

[6] For the concept of grain, see R.C. Stones, "Grain Theory in Practice: Redevelopment in Manchester at Longsight," *Town Planning Review*, 41 (October 1970), pp. 354–56. Although ultimately of picturesque origin, grain theory derives primarily from concern not only for the continuity of the street pattern but also for maintaining the general mass volume at a given sector of the city (See also R.C. Stones, "Housing and Redevelopment," *Town Planning Review* 37 (January 1967), pp. 237–54.

than it is with the programming of public life in a convincing way. Their particular failure with regard to this last seems to be borne out by the absence of any viable public or commercial function on the podium of their Economist Building completed in London in 1965.[7]

It is clear that the responsibilities of the architect must increasingly lie with the realities of the past-in-the-present as they must with postulations for the immediate future, since he is the sole professional who is situated by definition in a mediatory historical role. This being so, the architect must endeavour to divest himself of a millennial view of history in which, at one and the same time, we overrate the future and underrate the past. For in the last analysis, the irreversibility of history has its own implacable but ambiguous meaning, namely, that while we cannot exchange one moment in time for some future or past golden age, we have nonetheless, by virtue of this, little choice but to integrate the past into the realizations of the present. Thus while we cannot hope to revoke the loss of the traditional street at a global level, we may hope still to maintain within limits, those physical continuities that are capable of sustaining something of its living social history.

Furthermore, there seems to be a necessity to reintroduce into the abstract anonymity of the megalopolis type forms which are capable of generating something of that sense of public space or rather place that has always characterized the denser parts of the traditional city; to engender, as it were, breaks in the abstract motopian system, which are identifiable and sustainable as public enclaves of varying density and capacity.

As was noted at the outset, such an approach is hardly original, since many members of the so-called avant garde have long since attempted to come to terms with this issue, not only Team 10 (the Smithsons in their London Roads Study of 1960 or Stefen Werwerka in his Berlin U-Bahn megastructures of 1956) but also the Japanese metabolists men such as Maki and Ohtaka, in their "group form" proposals, their design for the Shinjuku district, and their prototypical shopping enclaves projected for Tokyo in 1962.[8]

Two factors, however, have since become extremely self-evident from our experience of the recent past. The first concerns the whole technical and experiential problematic surrounding the viability and desirability of the megastructure per se; the second addresses itself to the limits and usefulness of the whole design strategy known by the name "open aesthetic." In the first instance the megastructure itself guarantees very little, either from the point of view of its own realization in a reasonable time span or from the point of view of the appropriateness of its scale. Enough megastructures have already been built which, at one and the same time, not only establish a violent rift between their own form and the existing urban context but also engender an internal landscape of such a size and programmatic vacuity that the pedestrian is largely

---

[7] See my essay "The Economist and the Hauptstadt," *Architectural Design* (February 1965), pp. 61–62.

[8] See Fumihiko Maki and Masato Ohtaka, "Some Thoughts on Collective Form," in *Structure in Art and in Science*, ed. György Kepes (New York: George Braziller, 1965), pp. 116–27.

bereft of any "living" relation to his immediate context. In this perspective, there remains the possibility of the limited intervention of the generic street or enclave and it is to an examination of this possibility that the remainder of this chapter is devoted.

A COMPARATIVE SURVEY OF THREE GENERIC STREET ALTERNATIVES: THE PERIMETER BLOCK, THE LINEAR ARCADE AND THE MULTILEVEL MEGASTRUCTURE

Criteria for Categories and Examples

While these three alternatives may appear to have been rather arbitrarily selected according to the abstraction of point, line, and plane, and while the first two may be developed by a simple process of extension into the third, they nonetheless seem to conform to the generic types available for immediate and limited intervention in the field of urban form. From the many projected and realized examples that could have been chosen, these three generic types are here primarily represented by the following examples:

The Perimeter Block: Spangen Housing, Rotterdam, by M.A. Brinkman, completed in 1919, and Cooper Square Housing, New York, by Roger A. Cumming, Architect, with Waldtraud Schleicher Woods, designed in 1974.

The Linear Arcade: Royal Mint Square Housing, London, by Nigel Greenhill and John Jenner, designed in 1974, and Students' Union Housing for the University of Alberta. Edmonton, Canada, by A.J. Diamond and Barton Myers, completed in 1973.

The Multilevel Megastructure: Frankfurt-Römerberg Center, Frankfurt-am-Main, designed in 1963 by Shadrach Woods and Manfried Schiedhelm of Candilis, Josic and Woods, and the Brunswick Center, London, by Patrick Hodgkinson, of 1973.

[Two] criteria were generally applied to the selection of these models: (a) that they should demonstrate an evident capacity for maintaining social and physical continuity in relation to existing urban fabrics; (b) that they should be capable of differentiating identifiable and usable public space within their own aggregate built form.

[. . .]

THE PERIMETER BLOCK: APPLICABILITY AND VARIATION

The applicability of Spangen [housing] in its own time was inseparable from the gridded European city extensions of the twenties when the perimeter block form became a generic housing prototype, as applicable to the new sections of Rotterdam as it then was to Amsterdam or to Berlin. The greatest range of variation in this type occurred in the socialist housing built around the periphery of Vienna in the twenties.[9]

The subsequent mass ownership of the automobile has necessarily posed problems for the further application of this type, and variations have since been developed that have tried to come to terms with the integration of the automobile within the perimeter form. The reinvention of the perimeter block by Shadrach Woods, from his Hamburg-Steilshoop proposal of 1966[10] to his Karlsruhe project of 1971—the latter having been designed with Ilhan Zeybekoglu—are two attempts at just such an integration. The on-grade parking, which is only partially integrated into the Hamburg-Steilshoop proposal, becomes more fully incorporated in the subterranean parking of Karlsruhe. This is also true for an extension of the Karlsruhe concept, designed by Zeybekoglu, for application to downtown Santiago as an entry to the Santiago international competition of 1973.

Hamburg-Steilshoop, Karlsruhe, and Santiago represent three different variants of the same type, where the interface conditions between pedestrian movement, parking, and automobile access vary in each case. Hamburg-Steilshoop and Karlsruhe are two versions based on the same principle of intermixing restricted slow-moving service access with pedestrian street movement. These schemes differ not so much in respect of their approach to parking but rather in their attitude to the street space as volume: the continuous perimeter blocks of Karlsruhe assure continuity in the urban space. Santiago, on the other hand, relegates both parking and service to a volume immediately below grade and maintains the internal courts of the blocks as vehicular-free enclaves. In this respect the Cooper Square model is closely related to the Karlsruhe prototype but makes no provision whatsoever for either off-street parking or servicing.

A unique variation on the Spangen model, where the integration of the automobile was to result in an all but total disintegration of the perimeter form, was projected by J. Whitney Huber of Princeton University, in a low-rise, high-density housing scheme for Trenton, New Jersey [1972]. This scheme, which, unlike either Hamburg-Steilshoop or Karlsruhe, integrated the cars by distributing them over the site, sacrificed in the process of doing so the desirable proximity of built form and street. Thus while a vestigial perimeter still remained in the continuity of this aggregate form, it in itself was all but totally disassociated from the street: first, by a perimeter wall surrounding the site, and second, by a service road, which, apart from serving the cluster parking, would have acted like a moat, in dividing the built form from the continuity of the sidewalk [. . .] this arrangement would have tended to drain all pedestrian movement into the center of the site, despite the fact that regular cuts through the containing wall would have been maintained to the sidewalk. In many respects this version of the perimeter block has more in common with the walled mobile-home sites of

---

[9] See Helmut Kunze, "Housing in Vienna in the 1920s," *Bauwelt* (1969, No. 12–13), pp. 44–49.

[10] The Hamburg-Steilshoop scheme, as requested by the city commission, indicated access, building lines, perimeters, and height limits. Hamburg-Steilshoop has now been largely realized by various architects working within the guidelines established by Woods.

FIGURES 24 AND 25 Bochum University competition entry. Candilis, Josic and Woods, 1962 (top); Student Housing Union Building (HUB), University of Alberta, Edmonton, Canada. A. J. Diamond and Barton Myers, 1973 (below).

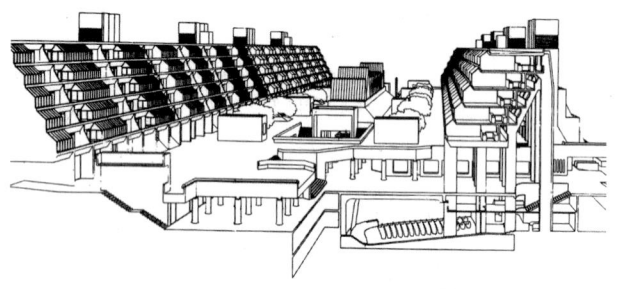

FIGURES 26 AND 27 Frankfurt-Römerberg Center competition entry, Frankfurt-am-Main, Germany. Shadrach Woods and Manfried Schiedhelm of Candilis, Josic and Woods, 1963 (top); Brunswick Center, London, United Kingdom. Patrick Hodgkinson, 1973 (below).

the West Coast than it does with the traditional perimeter model and a certain indifference to the living continuity of the urban fabric separates this scheme from the whole of the perimeter block sequence developed by Shadrach Woods.
[...]

THE LINEAR ARCADE: APPLICABILITY AND VARIATION

In morphological or topological terms the linear arcade appears as the inversion of the perimeter block, which, if it is extended, will tend to become transformed, as in the case of Moscow's Gum Store of 1893, into a network of introverted streets totally enclosed and lit from above. Where the perimeter block guarantees two contrasting spaces or places, as exemplified in the *outer active* and *inner tranquil* spaces of Woods' Karlsruhe scheme, the linear arcade only assures one; namely, the *inner active* realm. This city in miniature—the "unreal" counterform of the "real" city—has always gained its substance from being inlaid into the fabric of the city proper. The arcade or, more strictly, the galleria has invariably arisen like a parasitical labyrinth, dependent for its form on the public mass within which it is concealed. Where this context does not exist the arcade seems to have little capacity for contributing to the continuity of the exterior urban space. By virtue of its closure as a system it necessarily involves a break in the continuity of the open city, irrespective of the ease of its connection to the general level of circulation. This break is, of course, less marked where the normal sidewalk datum is maintained throughout, as in the case of most nineteenth-century arcades.

Thus we see that for all of its brilliance the student housing at Edmonton seems to possess little scope for general urban application, other than serving as a spine for a free-standing structure whose exterior facade would have the effect of reconstituting the continuum of the street space (cf. Spangen). And this, as we have seen, would be a paradoxical outcome since, on completing the elevated system of public circulation, the urban space at grade would no longer carry any significant movement. On the other hand there is little doubt that the arcade is capable of establishing a convincing sense of place through simulating the street experience of the traditional city, although this is perhaps less true of the model posited in the Royal Mint Square Housing where the private status of the flanking elements effectively determines the semiprivate nature of the enclosed space.

Both the Edmonton student housing and the Candilis, Josic, and Woods design for the University of Bochum of 1962 make one aware of the space-creating limits of the arcade as a linear organizing spine. In Bochum, as in the Edmonton scheme, the only significant space, both volumetrically and operationally, is that which is internal to the arcade and its branchlike extensions. Once again the space external to the arcade—in the case of Bochum the open field of the unbuilt campus—is left bereft of both meaning and use—a sort of rustic no-man's-land surrounding the internal coherence of the arcaded artifact.
[...]

THE MULTILEVEL MEGASTRUCTURE: APPLICABILITY AND VARIATION

As stated at the beginning of this chapter, the megastructure is a paradigm for urban intervention that, apart from the difficulties attending its formulation, has rarely, if ever, been satisfactorily achieved. At the same time one has to admit that a precise definition of the term tends to prove elusive. Josep Lluís Sert's Holyoke Center [1963] in Cambridge, Massachusetts, for example would hardly qualify as a megastructure, but nonetheless it seems to achieve a satisfactory intervention at a megastructural scale.

In general, the megastructure with its intrinsic virtues of affording density and internal continuity is characterized by exactly those attributes that generally make for discontinuity in relation to an existing urban context. For all of its many virtues, Brunswick Center is exemplary of this, an enclave solution that appears, in its ingenious sectional organization, to be too closed and disassociative to be able to sustain any kind of adequate continuity at grade. Frankfurt-Römerberg, on the other hand, postulates a model of disarming simplicity that not only affords urban enclosure and continuity, but also posits a city-in-miniature whose internal order is appropriately differentiated according to status, scale and use. The range of urban situations to which the Woods/Schiedhelm Frankfurt model could be successfully applied seems to be both wide and varied, for while it affords a convincing sense of place in situations where the larger context is relatively discontinuous, it is equally capable of being integrated into a preexisting continuous whole. Where the specifics of the Frankfurt-Römerberg scheme are exemplary of the second condition, Woods's application of the same idea to his project for the Free University of Berlin of 1963 is clearly a demonstration of the first.

It may be argued that Frankfurt-Römerberg is a rationalization of a model for urban intervention that had first been posited in the 1932–1939 development of Rockefeller Center, New York, to the designs of Reinhard and Hofmeister, Corbet, Harrison, Hood and Fouilloux. Despite major differences in scale, profile, structure, and, above all, in motivation, certain similarities obtain between the two models which are worthy of comment. In the first instance they are both irrigated by continuous systems of pedestrian access which serve to unite a disparate series of identifiably different volumes and users. In the second they are equally articulated structures whose modular increments relate to the urban context and scale in which they are situated. The modulation of the Rockefeller Center profile along the Fifth Avenue frontage has become a classic in this respect. By a similar token, its extensive mezzanine-concourse network has been copied in a number of recent urban developments, including Place Ville Marie and the Place Bonaventure complex, both built in Montreal in the mid-1960s.

CONCLUSION: THE RATIONALE AND POTENTIAL OF THE GENERIC STREET

From the foregoing it is possible to develop the following argument for the use of the generic street as a device for urban intervention.

1 The traditional city can no longer be sustained or perpetuated. The prevailing mode of automotive distribution mitigates against the dense concentration of the traditional city.
2 *Tabula rasa* planning has already proven its ineffectiveness and inhumanity. The utopian *a priori* approach has invariably resulted either in the irrelevance of large scale schemes which are destined never to be realized or in the alienation of an abstract motopia. The corollary to *tabula rasa* planning, namely, the wholesale erosion of existing urban fabrics through the abrasive intrusion of the automobile, suggests the urgent need for alternative piecemeal strategies.
3 This false choice between two crude models of urban planning—namely, between abstract idealism and opportunist pragmatism—suggests that organic urban strategy must of necessity be incremental and hierarchically structured.
4 The success of any incremental transformation will be dependent on the creation of a significant hierarchical order. Such an order may be established through the application of a viable type that possesses certain concrete qualities.
5 In this respect there remains the possibility of creating and/or sustaining generic street forms of limited extent.
6 The generic street is here defined as a building that automatically engenders active street space, either adjacent to its perimeter or within its own corporeal form. The oriental bazaar is the archetypical paradigm of such a street.
7 From the comparative analysis given earlier, it would seem that such generic forms should meet at least most, if not all, of the following criteria if they are to prove effective from both a social and a plastic point of view:

> a. *Continuity:* Such forms should maintain as far as possible the existing urban continuity in terms of (i) pedestrian movement and activity, (ii) the sustenance of urban space as place, and (iii) the perpetuation of an urban grain that is compatible with the existing context;
> b. *Hierarchy and Enclosure:* Such forms should engender a sense of enclosure and establish clearly a differentiation between public and private domains;
> c. *Interface:* The interface conditions established by such forms are critical, in concrete terms, to the overall sense of hierarchy, enclosure, and continuity.

10 Technology, Place & Architecture (1998)

INTRODUCTION

Since the emergence of the profession, a salient, often undeclared aspect of architectural practice has been the reconciliation of conflicting values through the creation of inflected form, irrespective of whether the work be a private dwelling, a public institution, or a piece of urban development. This critical dimension has become more difficult to sustain due to the constantly escalating rate of technological change and the greatly increased scale of urbanization. The deleterious environments of the nineteenth-century industrial city notwithstanding, architecture and planning in the first half of this century still aspired to achieve a balance between industrialization and more traditional forms of agrarian land settlement and use. The turn of the century was attended by a proliferation of attempts to mediate between the two economies, largely through the creation of satellite communities designed by such garden city pioneers as Ebenezer Howard and Georges Benôit Lévy, or through the semi-spontaneous emergence of the dormitory suburb that followed in the wake of extending rail transit out into the countryside.

With the advent of universal car ownership after 1945, accompanied by the exponential expansion of tertiary industry and the maximization of agricultural production, this promise of achieving a new environmental equilibrium was constantly frustrated. Over the last fifty years, large areas of the so-called developed world have become placeless domains where each shopping mall looks like the next and a disjointed conglomeration of exurban fragments spreads across the landscape. This has been accompanied by intense but random levels of commercial high-rise speculation in one downtown after another.

One needs to set these transformations within a wider context, one which, while recognizing the broader consequences of regional urbanization, also

Source: Kenneth Frampton, "Introduction" and "Public Building, Form and Influence: The Atrium as Surrogate Public Form," in Kenneth Frampton, Arthur Spector, and Lynne Reed Rosman, eds., *Technology, Place & Architecture: The Jerusalem Seminar in Architecture* (New York: Rizzoli, 1998), 12–15, 272–73.

acknowledges the way in which building technology has radically changed over the last half century. These innovations have brought about a dematerialization of building together with a literal mechanization/electrification of its fabric. The development of tungsten lighting, electrical elevators, two-pipe plumbing, central heating, and air-conditioning between 1880 and 1904 coincided with the simultaneous perfection of steel-frame and reinforced concrete construction. These innovations had the effect of separating the non-load-bearing skin from the structural frame of the building. As R. Gregory Turner has shown in his 1986 study, *Construction Economics and Building Design*, these changes shifted the focus away from undifferential masonry mass toward the articulation of built form into *podium, services, framework*, and *envelope*. Turner shows that, during the past thirty-five years, these sectors have grown increasingly independent, each with its own criteria and consultants. He also demonstrates that while the cost of the podium has remained relatively stable at twelve and one-half percent of the budget, the cost of electro-mechanical services has risen since the turn of the century to some thirty-five percent of the total. The chances are that this figure will only increase with the emergence of telematic communication. Conversely, the amount devoted to the basic structure has dropped from approximately eighty percent in the previous century to some twenty percent today. That we tend to spend more today on electro-mechanical equipment than on any other single item is surely indicative of the importance we now attach to comfort and communicative efficiency rather than to durability and the representational value of built form.

Despite the undeniable progress of techno-science and the beneficial effect it has had on the quality of human life, one has sufficient reason to be apprehensive about the tendency of technology to become a new nature covering the surface of the earth while simultaneously destabilizing both the natural and the man-made worlds.

Admittedly we have an overall tendency rather than an absolute condition applying to all building everywhere at any given historical moment. Moreover, as Cecil D. Elliot has written in his book, *Technics and Architecture* (1992):

> It would be convenient, but only somewhat accurate, to attribute twentieth-century changes in architecture to the influence of technology as it was applied to building. Architecture is a complex art having many a master. A building is at the same time an object, an investment and a cultural and personal expression of beliefs. Any change in the way buildings are built or the way they look must be tested by a variety of standards, their relative importance being somewhat different for every project. This truism explains why certain technological aspects of architecture have been readily adopted and others have been long delayed . . .

What Elliot does not say is that building, like agriculture, tends to be a somewhat anachronistic procedure, one that by standards of techno-science cannot be truly regarded as being "high-tech." We need look no further than to the typical foundation in order to have proof of this. I am alluding to the tangled mass of mud, rock, and preexisting pipes, etc., that even today is still the prelude to almost every building operation. It is precisely this schism between wet and dry construction, together with the split between craft-practice and industrial technique, that compels one to acknowledge the hybrid character of building. Within this mixed activity, it is possible to apply various levels of production to different parts of a given work, not only for reasons of economy and efficiency but also for the realization of certain expressive values. Technological maximization as an end in itself is categorically opposed to the expressive potential of the consciously hybrid approach, since this last yields a range of forms that are more open to inflection. The very opposite of this mediatory attitude is made evident by the maximization of technique. I am thinking, say, of the optimization of air-conditioning in hot-dry climates where protection from the sun has been traditionally provided by thick walls, over-hangs, and cross-ventilation, or in this century by the provision of *brise soleil* and by the possibility of opening and closing windows and shutters at will. The capacity to open a structure to natural ventilation is equally crucial in temperate climates. Who has not experienced the situation where in fine weather it is impossible to open a window because the fenestration has been fixed in order to maximize the efficiency of the air-conditioning system? Similar observations may be applied to the traditional roof and its capacity to shield a building from inclement weather. Moreover, all such responsive elements can be said to be automatically expressive of the climate and hence of the place in which the structure happens to be situated.

From this it follows that technological maximization as such is often antithetical to the creation and maintenance of the place-form. We may note how the maximization of one technique will sometimes necessitate the equally excessive use of another. Thus, the prevalence of air-conditioning is in part a compensatory response to automotive noise and petro-chemical pollution. This double bind of using one technique to correct a dysfunction caused by another may be compared to similar syndromes in other fields. I have in mind the over-prescription of antibiotics together with the optimized use of invasive high-tech surgical methods in the practice of allopathic medicine, or, let us say, the excessive use of artificial fertilizers in agriculture with the corresponding undermining of the immune system and equally deleterious effects on the water table and long-term fertility of the land. As against such maximizing techniques, often applied for economic or ideological reasons, we may posit the judicious application of technology to the real issues confronting society. The challenge is to maintain cultural *quality* in an epoch largely devoted to the instrumentalization of *quantity*.

Thus, one is brought to recognize the perennial demand for rationalized production and constructional innovation, including such recent developments as the use of structural glass over wide spans or the employment of high-strength glues and sealants in almost every aspect of building construction. Such new materials and jointing methods have shifted the focus away from load-bearing masonry towards "dematerialized" modes of assembly. This transformation has been accompanied by the proliferation of other "dry" techniques from gypsum plasterboard to glass-reinforced fiber, from heat-resistant glass to thin, machine-cut stone capable of simulating heavy-weight masonry. Whether or not one elects to exploit such applications to unsatisfactory ends is one of the ethical and cultural dilemmas confronting architectural design today. The ubiquitous curtain wall is a case in point, for it has often been applied in unsuitable cultural and climatic situations—ostensibly for economic expediency. In India, for example, the intense radiant heat gain and the accompanying glare make it a questionable technique.

Technological maximization, irrespective of whether it is bureaucratically enforced or ideologically adopted, also has the tendency to reduce the creation of built-form to the production of freestanding objects, whether the object in question is merely a technological instrument or the occasion for a spectacular aesthetic display. Against this, we may posit the critical strategy of the place-form, the ecological obligation that each new structure be inscribed into its site in such a way as to permit the creation of an articulated earthwork. Thus Mario Botta's slogan "building the site" means to engender a condition in which it is all but impossible to discern where the ground ends and the building begins. Hence the critical import of the *tectonic* and the *topographical* values in the development of built form, or, to put it more directly, the protective value of the *roofwork* and sustaining value of the *earthwork*.

This evocation of the earthwork returns us to the issue of global urbanization and to the fact that the reintegration of land-form into built-fabric is crucial today if we are to be able to mediate in any way the consequences of megalopolitan development. Aside from the application of minimum standards, as these are essential to the regulation of highway construction and suburban zoning, regional urbanization over the past fifty years has shown little regard for the cultural and ecological impact that scattered suburban settlement has had on the overall character of the landscape. This impact has been felt on land that, within living memory, was almost exclusively devoted to agriculture or forestry, and on areas previously classified as desert, which have been transformed into verdant automotive suburbs largely through the profligate use of irrigation. While much of this rapacious development will be difficult to reintegrate in cultural and ecological terms (one thinks of the infinitely extended American strip, most of which will become ruined long before it is either demolished or rebuilt), it is nonetheless desirable that every architectural commission be conceived as a potential place-form, or that, where necessary, the work should create its own micro-environmental context. In this sense, the art of landscape is absolutely critical. At the same time one must remain open to the use of advanced techniques, particularly where judiciously applied and inflected so as to create a culturally significant work.

[. . .]

PUBLIC BUILDING, FORM AND INFLUENCE: THE ATRIUM AS SURROGATE PUBLIC FORM

I want to broach the theme of the public building through the prototype of the atrium considered as a paradigmatic city-in-miniature. The role of the atrium over the last two hundred years has been to compensate, either consciously or unconsciously, for the gradual erosion of the public realm in the traditional city and even, later, for the disappearance of the traditional city itself. It is significant that Frank Lloyd Wright invariably regarded his public buildings as introspective domains where the representational space and its corresponding public facade were on the interior rather than the exterior. Wright seems to have sensed from the very outset of his career that there was "no more there, there," to coin Gertrude Stein's overfamiliar phrase. He sensed from the beginning that the public realm in the American city was not reliable. This would explain why all of his quasi-public buildings had blank exteriors, from the Larkin Building in Buffalo, New York, of 1904, to the S.C. Johnson Administration Building in Racine, Wisconsin, of 1939; from the Morris Gift Shop in San Francisco, of 1948, to the Guggenheim Museum in New York, of 1959. In each instance, the representative public face of the building was on the interior, as in the traditional mosque.

This phenomenon of progressively internalizing the public realm did not begin with Wright, of course. It first appeared perhaps in the mid-seventeenth century, with Cardinal Richelieu's development of the Palais Royale as a space set apart from the continuous fabric of the city of Paris. The Palais Royale was not just another royal square; it was a microcosmos consisting of a large elongated garden court surrounded on four sides by a continuous open-sided arcade with apartments above. This paradigm was augmented over time by another layer of residential development built during the reign of Louis-Philippe at the end of the eighteenth century, when, as Michel Verne points out, life within the Palais Royale became synonymous with everything one might associate with the French term *commerce*, from trade in luxury goods to prostitution, and from theatrical performances to the organization of political clubs. The Palais Royale was a kind of urban "free port" within which certain license was granted that was not available elsewhere. Hence, it is no accident that Camille Desmoulins would incite a mob to revolution in the garden of the Palais Royale in 1798. The ultimate quintessential glazed gallery or arcade, the so-called Galerie d'Orléans, was built there in 1825 to the designs of Percier and Fontaine.

Over time the Palais Royale became inseparable from the labyrinth of the Parisian arcades extending from it into the interstices of the surrounding urban fabric; the galleries Colbert and Vivienne were typical in this regard. These top-lit *passages*, celebrated by Walter Benjamin in his essay "Paris, Capital of the Nineteenth Century," were superseded after the middle of the nineteenth century by the emergence of the department store, the first of which was the Bon Marche store dating from 1852. Like Wright's Larkin Building, the department store was not only a microcosmos but also a semipublic realm where one went to see and be seen. And, like Charles Garnier's opera house in Paris, it was in fact a surrogate space of public appearance. Other examples of top-lit, ferro-vitreous, surrogate public places dating from the last half of the nineteenth century include, of course, the great railway terminals of the major European

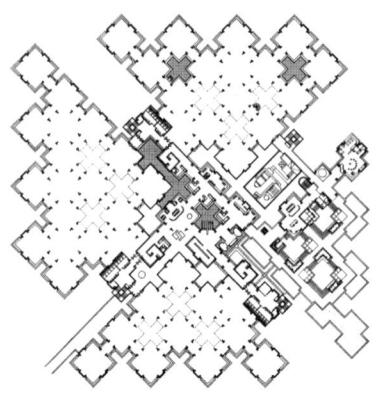

FIGURES 28 AND 29 The Centraal Beheergebouw insurance company office building, Apeldoorn, The Netherlands. Herman Hertzberger, 1965–1972. Section and diagrammatic plan (top), and interior space (below).

capitals, along with mega-gallerias such as Giuseppe Mengoni's Galleria Vittorio Emmanuele in Milan; this last project is inseparable symbolically and politically from the rise of the Italian State.

Once these typological continuities are pointed out, one can easily understand how the atrium came to reassert itself as a type in contemporary practice, even as a way of creating a clearly defined pseudo-public space in what was otherwise a processional urban domain. One thinks not only of Wright's Larkin Building and Raymond Hood's Rockefeller Center in Manhattan (1936) but also of more recent "surrogate" public buildings such as Herman Hertzberger's Centraal Beheer in Apeldoorn, The Netherlands (1965), or Norman Foster's Willis, Faber, Dunmar Building in Ipswich, England (1975). Both of these were essentially introspective *burolandschaft* office buildings built for insurance companies in the mid-1970s. The link between the internal spaces of Centraal Beheer and the Larkin Building is obvious although the two buildings have quite different plan forms, just as the Foster building and the nineteenth-century department store share spatial and formal correspondences. I have in mind the center void of the "doughnut" plan, with escalators rising inside the void to serve the office floors on all sides. This is a kind of atrium building, and it is clear that a marked sense of commonality is provided by the central volume. Here, this surrogate public space is reinforced by the presence of a restaurant on the roof and a swimming pool on the ground floor, both allocated for use by the employees, as in the Larkin Building. And while the Larkin Building did not provide a swimming pool, it did have a conservatory and restaurant on the roof as well as an organ in the central space.

Other modern atria that come readily to mind are John Portman's Hyatt Regency Hotel at the Atlanta Peachtree Center (1967)—his invention of the "atrium hotel"—or Barton Myers and Jack Diamond's student dormitory block in the form of a top lit galleria at the University of Alberta (1969). Richard Rogers's Lloyds Building in London (1978–1986) is yet another variation on the same theme, as is Richard Meier's City Hall and Central Library in The Hague, The Netherlands (1986–1995). Here it is clear that the vast atrium of Meier's city hall functions as a totally new space of public appearance within the pre-existing, low-rise brick fabric that until the end of the 1970s made up the basic residential fabric of The Hague. Despite the fact that no one actually lives in the city hall, it is the quintessential "city-in-miniature." It makes up for the fact that the traditional city fabric has been totally disrupted by the rather random superimposition of new office slabs throughout the downtown over approximately the same time. The new atrium of the city hall is able to mediate between the scale of these slabs and the more discreet, tessellated grain of the surrounding city fabric.

11 Civic Form (2020)

In a world increasingly depoliticized by the media, "the space of public appearance" (to use Hannah Arendt's memorable phrase) still remains as a democratic ideal for both architecture and society, particularly at a time when a homeostatically balanced way of life is increasingly undermined by the commodification of both the natural and the man-made worlds. What Arendt intends by this term is made explicit in her study *The Human Condition* of 1958:

> The only indispensable material factor in the generation of power is the living together of people. Only when men live so close together that the potentialities of action are always present can power remain with them, and the foundation of cities, which as city-states have remained paradigmatic for all Western political organization, is therefore indeed the most important material prerequisite for power.[1]

With these words Arendt characterized not only the latent political and cultural potential of civic form, but also the space of assembly wherever this may still be found within public institutions in general. Over the past few decades civic building of quality has been particularly noticeable in France, above all in the work of Henri Ciriani and Jean Nouvel, with the former subtly continuing the programmatic approach of Le Corbusier, and the latter favouring a technocratic aesthetic that is, at times, equally concerned with the representation of the cultural institution as a space of public appearance.

In the case of Ciriani, the emphasis has fallen not only on the museum as a microcosmos, but also on its potential to serve as a surrogate for the socially unifying religious building. This aspect manifests itself particularly forcefully in

---

Source: Kenneth Frampton, "Afterword: Architecture in the Age of Globalization," in *Modern Architecture: A Critical History* (Thames & Hudson, 2020, fifth edition), 636–42 (excerpt).

[1] H. Arendt, "Specifically Republican Enthusiasm", in *The Human Condition* (1958), p. 201.

two museums realized by Ciriani towards the end of his career: the Archaeological Museum at Arles, completed in 1991, and the Museum for the First World War at Peronne, which was integrated into the remains of a 17th-century fortress in 1994. Notwithstanding the undeniably arresting image of a building faced completely in cobalt-blue glass, the museum in Arles is not easily accessible, largely because, detached from the urban core, it can only be approached via a ring road encircling the city. The articulation of its internal space, with freestanding cylindrical columns, conveys the impression of a Neo-Purist enclave, as removed from everyday life as the collection it houses. Such hermeticism does not arise in the case of the Peronne museum, on account of the immediate proximity of the urban fabric and the presence of an adjacent riverside park. Moreover, the elevation of its concrete mass on *pilotis* enables a carefully orchestrated promenade through the sombre relics of the 1914–18 war to be relieved by views over the park that flanks the building on its south-western face.

The eventual size of museums is limited if they are to retain their institutional viability and civic significance. As Le Corbusier's 1934 proposal for a "Musée à Croissance Illimitée" demonstrated, a museum of unlimited expansion is self-contradictory both conceptually and urbanistically. This limit, difficult to specify in advance, may partially explain why the new Museum of Modern Art in New York (2004) has now attained a size at which it has begun to lose its capacity to be read within the city as a discrete civic institution. This has come about despite the brilliant orchestration of its penultimate extension by the Japanese architect Yoshio Taniguchi, who attempted to compensate for its extraordinary size and scale by introducing a public galleria, as a virtual right of way through the building, within the street grid of its Manhattan mid-block site.

Richard Meier's Getty Center, completed as a city-in-miniature on a prominent hilltop site in the Brentwood area of Los Angeles in 1997, has an indisputable civic character, as does his Hague City Hall complex, realized in 1995. Apart from being a megaform accommodating offices, shops, a municipal library and a council chamber, what is decisive about this institution is the fact that its thirteen-storey mass encloses a top-lit galleria 183 metres (600 feet) long, modulated by footbridges, fed by freestanding elevators, which link the corridors of the flanking offices. This is a civic volume rivalling in its extent and height the largest galleria of the 19th century, the Galleria Umberto I erected in Naples in 1891. In a city that in recent years has seen its intimate, low-rise, brick-lined street fabric overwhelmed by random high-rise development, Meier's City Hall presents itself as a civic oasis, capable of consolidating a new scale around itself while compensating for the loss of urbanity in the city as a whole. The civic appeal of the galleria itself stems in no small measure from the fact that it is a large, top-lit public space permanently shielded from the inclemencies of the Dutch climate.

A sense of *civitas* on a heroic scale is to be found in the work of the Berlin architects Axel Schultes and Charlotte Frank, most notably in their winning Spreebogen competition entry of 1993. The scheme assumed the form of a temenos—a strip of federal buildings to be known as the "Band des Bundes"—initially projected as the administrative centre of a reunified

FIGURE 30 The British Library, London, United Kingdom. Colin St John Wilson and Mary Jay Long, 1963–1997. Panoramic view of the library.

Germany four years after the fall of the Berlin Wall in 1989. The Wall had hitherto divided not only East and West Berlin, but also, on a global scale, the democratic West from the Communist East. The Schultes–Frank entry for this international competition was the only scheme to capture the urbanistic and symbolic importance of the site, in terms both of the history of the previous half-century and of the way in which this void in the heart of the city had served repeatedly as the context for tragically contrasting conceptions of Germany's destiny.

Out of this proposal came the architects' German Chancellery, completed in 2001 as a partial realization of their original scheme, the full extent of which will not now be realized—a regrettable circumstance given the representational status of the building, remarkable not only for its vivacity but also for the lightness of its Neo-Baroque manner, executed in concrete and painted white. Defying convention, the architects chose to represent the German state through an allusion to the scale and deportment of the Ali Qapu palace in Isfahan. Bounded by five-storey ministerial offices to the north and south, this central pavilion faces eastwards onto a *cour d'honneur* and westwards onto the Spree River. Patently influenced by Louis Kahn's sense of monumentality but totally removed from his syntax, the sky lobby of the Chancellery affords a panoramic view over the new Reichstag realized to the designs of Paul Wallot in 1894 and reconstructed by Foster Associates in 1999.

The manifestation of civil society in built form is difficult to achieve in our commodified world of universal consumerism, wherein—as Arendt wrote in 1958—"we consume . . . our houses and furniture and cars as though they were the 'good things' of nature which would spoil uselessly if they are not drawn swiftly into the neverending cycle of man's metabolism with nature".

Nothing could be further from this than Colin St John Wilson's British Library, realized in London at virtually the same time as the French Bibliothèque Nationale after a delay of more than two decades. Strongly influenced by the work of Alvar Aalto, this building assumes a more overtly contextual character on account of its organic composition and its facing in red brick, which links it empathetically, in terms of both material and scale, to the Gothic Revival head building of the adjacent St Pancras Station, completed in 1874. While it lacks the axial monumentality of its Parisian counterpart, the British Library is obviously predicated on a more expressively organic and contextual articulation of the institution. Within and without, the vast scale and complexity of the programme are broken down into a number of discretely articulated collections, each subtly connected to the others.

Like most of the works featured in this postscript, the British Library may be seen as a megaform, that is to say as a civic institution that may be experienced by the society as a representation and as a 'space of public appearance', while having, at the same time, the typographic character and the scale of a landmark. It is evident that certain programmes lend themselves to this form of embodiment and interpretation more readily than others. I have in mind such institutions as town halls, theatres, museums, hospitals, universities and

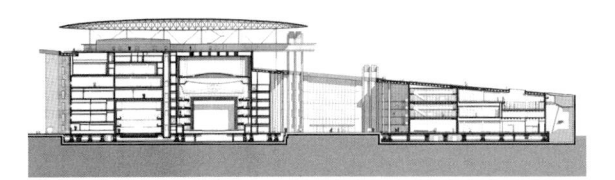

FIGURES 31 AND 32 The Stavros Niarchos Foundation Cultural Center, Athens, Greece. Renzo Piano Building Workshop with Betaplan, 2008–2016. Section (top) and view towards the Falírou Bay (Órmos Falírou) (below).

airports, of which Richard Rogers's ultimate masterwork, his Barajas Airport, Madrid (2006) is an outstanding example.

It is fitting given their mutual authorship of the Centre Pompidou at the very beginning of their separate careers that an equally arresting megaform should have been realized recently to the designs of Renzo Piano, namely the half-kilometre-long Stavros Niarchos Foundation Cultural Center, built just outside Athens as a gargantuan earthwork in 2016. Within this lushly landscaped artificial outcrop are housed two subterranean auditoria, which may be accessed on foot at grade via a so-called agora let into the side of the earthwork. These large and small auditoria have seating capacities of 2,000 and 400 respectively. The other civic institution situated within the body of the megaform is the Greek National Library, in addition to the provision of parking. It is perhaps even more pertinent, given the context, that this 'acropolis' should culminate at its highest point in a belvedere, sheltered by a typical 'high-tech', lightweight canopy set before the turbulence of a wine-dark sea.

The urban architecture of Aalto is really impressive. Of course, The National Pensions Institute is a case in point, but also Rautatalo, for example, where it's just a curtain wall office building, and he's able to transform a curtain wall—an infill curtain wall office building—into a public realm so that when you enter the building you have this courtyard that is beautifully lit from above and with its own vegetation and water elements. The normative office building is transformed, and that's also true of the Engineers Union building, which is a little infill block. That was extraordinary: the work has a kind of normative character, but at the same time it is always inflected; and that's true of his urban work and also of his so-called rural work, but it's particularly striking in the urban situation . . . The two spaces [in Aalto's buildings] that really are always so carefully dealt with: one is the entrance and the foyer, the point at which people are gathered together before they fulfil the main promenade of the building; and then is the space of arrival. I think that these two spaces are always so carefully elaborated and balanced in relation to each other . . . This question of scale is also very interesting, and also a certain idea about threshold and the direct tactile experience of the human subject as this subject enters the space.

Kenneth Frampton, "Interview with Kenneth Frampton on Alvar Aalto,"
Vitra Design Museum, 5 October 2015, YouTube video,
https://www.youtube.com/watch?v=SmBi_T-3ZAA.

12 The Legacy of Alvar Aalto: Evolution and Influence (1998)

> The structures which were means to create a new architecture have been wrested from us and turned into commercialized decorative ends in themselves with no inner value. There was a time when a misconstrued, lifeless traditionalism was the chief enemy of good architecture. Today its worst enemy is the superficial decorative misuse of the means acquired during the breakthrough... The contrast between deep social responsibility and decorative "surface effects" is perhaps the oldest and certainly the most topical issue in the debate on architecture. Please do not think that I wish to disparage beauty in rejecting decorativeness. Architecture must have charm; it is a factor of beauty in society. But real beauty is not a conception of form which can be taught, it is the result of harmony between several intrinsic factors, not least the social.[1]
>
> Alvar Aalto

[...]

In an age in which we are overwhelmed by ephemeral images of every kind, we may justly see Aalto as an architect whose oeuvre was totally antithetical to the reduction of building to modular spatial arrangements largely determined by proximal or productive considerations, or to provisional assemblies predominantly conceived to provide a spectacular image—the cult of the "decorated shed" against which he reacted throughout his life. While this did not render him immune to the picturesque in European culture, Aalto's predisposition for asymmetrical compositions was always qualified by a deep concern for an appropriately organic aggregation of the parts and for the integration of the resultant assembly into the site.

> Source: Kenneth Frampton, "The Legacy of Alvar Aalto: Evolution and Influence," in *Alvar Aalto: Between Humanism and Materialism*, ed. Peter Reed (New York: Museum of Modern Art, 1998), 118–39.

[1] Alvar Aalto, interview in *Pagens Nyheter* (Stockholm), October 28, 1936; repr. in Göran Schildt, *Alvar Aalto: The Decisive Years*, trans. Timothy Binham (Rizzoli: New York, 1986), pp. 202–3.

Aalto belonged to that "existential" generation of northern European intellectuals in which, to put it in terms of Martin Heidegger, "building, being, dwelling and cultivating"[2] were seen as part and parcel of the same socio-organic response to the conditions of existence. And while he was too democratic and realistic to have anything to do with the chauvinistic politics that were fatally associated with this view, Aalto's ecological propensity brought him nonetheless close to Hugo Häring's *Neues Bauen* movement, that is to say, to that alternative line in modern architecture identified by St. John Wilson as "the other tradition."[3] This tradition, loosely associated with northern European expressionism, would be more precisely defined through the work of Häring and Hans Scharoun and, above all, perhaps through Häring's famous Gut Garkau farm complex of 1924, which came closest to anticipating Aalto's heterotopic syntax.

The work of Aalto is of critical import at the end of the twentieth century because, while he was by no means antithetical to the manifest advantages of modern technoscience and industrial production, he was, simultaneously, far from sanguine about the tendency to regard technological advance as an end in itself rather than as a means to a liberative end. He thought that the habitat in general, should be able to respond easily and freely to cyclical life changes and to fluctuations in the daily pattern of existence, particularly as these affected psychic mood as well as physical well being. Like the Franco-Irish architect Eileen Gray, he thought that "a window without a shutter was like an eye without an eyelid"[4] and that the interior of the living volume should, within limits, be freely modifiable by the occupant.

[...]

For Aalto, building culture was to be given the widest possible interpretation rather than be narrowly understood in a classical or modern avant-gardist sense. Hence, despite his lifelong attachment to Italy, he displayed no interest whatsoever in humanistic proportional systems or, for that matter, in any radically hermetic intellectual proposition. And, while he was not averse to employing organizing grids and modules, and indeed would frequently do so, he was totally opposed to the use of modular systems as ends in themselves. His intuitive, biomorphically inspired approach to environmental design caused him to place an enormous emphasis on the capacity of built form to modify equally both the landscape and the urban fabric. In this regard he would have been sympathetic to the architect Mario Botta's slogan, "building the site."[5] All of Aalto's sites were built in this topographical sense, and his achievements as

---

[2] Martin Heidegger, "Building, Dwelling, Thinking" (1934), in English in Albert Hofstadter, *Poetry, Language, and Thought* (New York: Harper Colophon, 1975), pp. 145–61.

[3] Colin St. John Wilson, *The Other Tradition of Modern Architecture: The Uncompleted Project* (London: Academy Editions, 1995), p. 16.

[4] See Jean Badovici and Eileen Gray, "From Eclecticism to Doubt," *L'Architecture vivante* (Autumn 1929). See also St. John Wilson, *The Other Tradition of Modern Architecture*, p. 117.

[5] See Francesco Dal Co, Mario Botta: *Architetture 1960–1985* (Milan: Electa, 1985), p. 17.

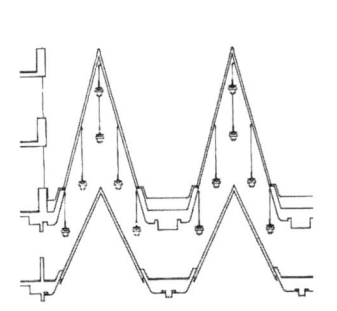

FIGURES 33–35 National Pensions Institute, Helsinki, Finland. Alvar Aalto, 1952–1956. Aerial view of the Institute (top); construction detail drawing of the skylights (below left) and interior of the customer service facilities (below right).

an architect cannot be separated at any stage of his career from his capacity as a designer of landscapes.

FROM CONSTRUCTIVISM TO ORGANICISM

Aalto's mature career seems to break down into two interconnected but distinct episodes: on the one hand, the early *constructivist* work that he designed and realized in Turku in close collaboration with Erik Bryggman, such as the Turku 700th Anniversary Exhibition and Trade Fair of 1929, and, on the other, the shift toward *organicism*, as this was first unequivocally expressed in his own house and studio, completed in the Helsinki suburb of Munkkiniemi in 1935–36.[6] In retrospect, it is clear that the laconic character of Finnish constructivism derived from its origin in the severity of Nordic classical form.[7] In Aalto's case, this is at once evident in the Southwestern Finland Agricultural Cooperative Building in Turku of 1927–30 and in the different phases of his competition entry for the Viipuri City Library of 1927–35, wherein one may witness the gradual evolution of classical norms into constructivist tropes. However, unlike the extravagant engineering forms adopted by the Russian Constructivists, Aalto eschewed the technological rhetoric of the Soviet avant-garde in the name of an objective propriety. This much is at once clear when one compares the main elevation of Aalto's Turun Sanomat Building of 1928–30 to the Vesnin brothers' project for the Pravda newspaper building in Moscow of 1923, with which Aalto was surely familiar. We find the same singular display device in both, namely the projection of the front page of their respective newspapers onto a large glass wall facing the street. While the Russians augmented this ultramodern gesture with all sorts of technological paraphernalia, from transparent elevator cabins to digital clocks, the large display window of Aalto's building was simply juxtaposed with sober, steel-framed ribbon windows, typical of a functionalist facade of the late 1920s.

Aalto's gradual recasting of neoclassical tropes into the sobriety of the *Neue Sachlichkeit*[8] may be readily perceived if we not only follow the stages of the

---

[6] The break to a kind of organic collage has been seen, in part, as a return to Finnish national romanticism of the 1890s. This affinity was not missed by Aalto's long-standing friend, the architect and architectural critic, Gustaf Strengell, who, just prior to his tragic suicide, characterized the architect's house as the new Niemelä farm. This referred to a collection of eighteenth- and nineteenth-century timber structures clustered around a central yard and exhibited in close proximity to their original forest setting. See Schildt, *Alvar Aalto: The Decisive Years*, p. 130.

[7] See Simo Paavilainen, ed., *Nordic Classicism, 1910–1930* (Helsinki: Museum of Finnish Architecture, 1982).

[8] The term *Sachlichkeit* had been current in German cultural circles long before 1924, when the art critic G.F. Hartlaub hit upon the phrase *die neue Sachlichkeit* [the new objectivity] to identify a postwar school of anti-Expressionist painting. *Sachlichkeit* seems to have been first used in an architectural context in a series of articles written by Hermann Muthesius for the journal, *Dekorative Kunst*, between 1897 and 1903. These

Viipuri City Library but also if we observe the development of the Southwestern Finland Agricultural Cooperative Building at the level of its interior detailing, particularly the treatment devised for its 500-seat theater. While the first version of this auditorium was a Nordic classic essay after the manner of Erik Gunnar Asplund's Skandia Cinema in Stockholm of 1922–23, the second was an objective, prismatic volume of similar proportions, wherein discrete technical components assumed the space-modulating role that had been previously afforded by the classically romantic mural depicted in the initial perspective. Where the mural had previously articulated the wall surface and the volume into upper and lower zones, this division now depended upon the virtual plane established by Poul Henningsen's light fittings, hung in a U-formation around the sides of the auditorium. A similar functional articulation, in ornamental terms, is evident in the retractable footlights that pop out of the stage and in the severe reveals of the vomitoria leading into the hall.

The subtle shift that occurred in Aalto's work at this time, as he passed from the neoclassical formality of Nordic classicism to the "product-form" of the *Neue Sachlichkeit*, was never more evident than in the Tapani Standard Apartment Block in Turku of 1927–29. Commissioned by Juho Tapani of the Tapani Construction Company, this block was constructed out of standard precast, light-weight concrete units, namely 50-cm-wide beams and 30-cm-thick wall units, both components being hollow in order to lighten their weight and accommodate mechanical services within the void. [. . .]

Immediately after completing this building, the Aalto office began to produce a series of standard drawings, featuring normative solutions for windows, doors, and a wide range of other components, with the ostensible aim of reusing these solutions in future work. Thus, while Aalto's typological approach had its roots in Nordic classicism, it became technologically focused through the work of the German and Dutch left-wing functionalists with whom he became familiar between 1929 and 1932. As Elina Standertskjöld has shown, the effects of this influence are particularly evident in Aalto's emerging sense of the creative potential of the typical object in the evolution of modern environmental culture.[9] Aalto's interest in perfecting quasi-industrial prototypes was stimulated further by his decision to attend the second Congrès Internationaux d'Architecture Moderne (CIAM), held in Frankfurt in 1929. Aside from the ingenious solutions he devised for light fittings, handrails, and doors, together with the standard signs that he developed for both the Turun Sanomat Building of 1928–30 and

---

articles attributed the quality of *Sachlichkeit* to the English Arts and Crafts movement, particularly as manifested in the handicraft guilds (such as that founded by C.R. Ashbee) and the application of the craft ethic to early garden-city suburbs. For Muthesius, *Sachlichkeit* seems to have meant an objective, functionalist, eminently yeoman approach to the design of objects, implying the ultimate reform of industrial society itself. In the second half of the 1920s, the term was closely associated with the left-wing functionalist architects of Germany's Weimar Republic, Switzerland, and the Netherlands.

[9] See Elina Standertskjöld, "Alvar Aalto and Standardization" and "Alvar Aalto's Standard Drawings 1929–32," *Acanthus 1992* (Helsinki: Museum of Finnish Architecture, 1992), pp. 84–111.

the Paimio Tuberculosis Sanatorium of 1929–33, Aalto also evolved standard solutions for prototypical casement and sliding double-glazed windows, in both timber and steel, which were subsequently exhibited at the Frankfurt congress.

This preoccupation with norms reached its apotheosis with the Stockholm Exhibition of 1930, held under the auspices of the newly constituted Swedish welfare state. Aalto wrote of this exhibition with great enthusiasm and perspicacity on two separate occasions.[10] [. . .] In a second article, he adopted a more critical attitude, discriminating between the evolutionary character of a refined material culture, as opposed to the pursuit of superficial radicalism as an end in itself. This was already an articulation of the ethical position that he would assume throughout the remainder of his career.

The international socialist challenge to provide decent minimum residential accommodation for all was patently the inspiration behind Aino and Alvar Aalto's 60-square-meter, one-bedroom apartment designed for the *Rationalization of the Minimum Dwelling* exhibition staged in Helsinki in 1930. In addition to modern furnishings, this exhibition featured a range of prototypical products pioneered by Finnish manufacturers, including rubber and linoleum floor finishes and the Enso-Gutzeit company's standard plywood doors, which served as the prototype for the plywood doors that Aalto installed in Paimio. Aalto's first plywood and tubular-metal chair, the so-called Hybrid Chair, also dates from this time, making its debut in the furnishing of Paimio. His general preoccupation with standardized serial production at this time led finally to the development of the Paimio Chair of 1931–32, made entirely out of bent, laminated plywood. This chair, with its cantilevering organic form, was poised on the dividing line between Aalto's early constructivism and the organicism of his later career.

---

[10] In May 1930, [Aalto] wrote: "I see it as a very positive manifestation that the artist is in a sense denying himself by going outside of his traditional sphere of work, that he is democratizing his production and bringing it out of a narrow circle to a wider public. The artist thus steps in among the people to help create a harmonious existence with the help of his intrusive sensibility, instead of obstinately upholding the conflict between art and nonart which leads to acute tragedies and a hopeless life. The biased social manifestation which the Stockholm Exhibition wants to be has been clad in an architectural language of pure and unconstrained joy. There is a festive refinement but also a childish lack of restraint to the whole. Asplund's architecture explodes all the boundaries. The purpose is a celebration with no preconceived notions as to whether it should be achieved with architectural or other means. It is not a composition in stone, glass, and steel, as the functionalist-hating exhibition visitor might imagine, but rather is a composition in houses, flags, searchlights, flowers . . . and clean tablecloths." Alvar Aalto, "The Stockholm Exhibition I," summary of interview in *Åbo Underrättelser* (May 22, 1930); repr. in Göran Schildt, ed., *Sketches: Alvar Aalto*, trans. Stuart Wrede (Cambridge, Mass., and London: MIT Press, 1978), p. 16. Inspired by the vision of Gregor Paulsson, the leading figures of the so-called *acceptera* faction were the architects Erik Gunnar Asplund, Uno Åhren, Wolter Gran, Sven Markelius, and Eskil Sundahl. They were also the leading designers of the 1930 Stockholm Exhibition. They were closely connected to the socialist *Clarté* movement, which helped develop the program for the exhibition. Gunnar and Alva Myrdal were part of this intellectual circle, while Viola Markelius was the editor of the group's radical journal to which Aalto contributed. See Schildt, *Decisive Years*, p. 49 [Main text converted to the footnote by the editor].

Aalto's next attempt at an organic inflection of structural form came with his "bent-knee" leg of 1933, which was the key to the production of his famous three-legged, stackable stool, first shown in London that year.[11] This leg was produced by inserting slivers of wood into a series of saw cuts and then bending and gluing it into position. With this diminutive "column," as the architectural critic Gustaf Strengell termed it, Aalto was able to transform not only his furniture but also his entire architectural syntax, even though he continued to design the occasional piece in tubular steel, such as the convertible sofabed, specially designed for Sigfried Giedion's *Wohnbedarf* furniture store in Zurich in 1932. From this date onward however, Aalto's furniture tended to be exclusively of wood, with an ever-expanding repertoire of birch pieces, ranging from the triangular, laminated bookshelf brackets to the so-called sledge tea trolley of 1937.

[. . .]

There is no single work in Aalto's long career that is more synthetically symptomatic of his critical response to [rationalization and standardization] than his Apartment Building for the Interbau Exhibition in the Hansaviertel, Berlin, of 1954–57, for it is here, perhaps more than anywhere else, that he brought together two ostensibly opposed impulses. On the one hand, there was his lifelong recognition that the most urgent problem confronting the species was some satisfactory solution to the perennial social problem that Friedrich Engels had identified as the "housing question"; on the other hand, there was his growing conviction that the vernacular in general and the Finnish vernacular, in particular, embodied within its form a key to the solution of this crisis. As far as Aalto was concerned, this potential stemmed from the fact that the Karelian agrarian tradition was quintessentially additive in character and, therefore, perennially open to the process of agglutinative growth. He returned to this theme in the midst of the Continuation War of 1941–44, when eastern Karelia was occupied by Finnish troops, in an essay simply titled "Architecture in Karelia":

> The first essential feature of interest is Karelian architecture's uniformity. There are few comparable examples in Europe. It is a pure forest-settlement architecture in which wood dominates . . . in most cases naked, without the dematerializing effect that a layer of paint gives. In addition, wood is often used in as natural proportions as possible, on the scale typical of the material . . . Another significant special feature is the manner in which the Karelian house . . . is in a way a building that begins with a single modest cell or with an imperfect embryo building, shelter for man and animals and which then figuratively speaking grows year by year. "The expanded Karelian house" can in a way be compared with a biological cell formation. The possibility of a larger and more complete building is always open.[12]

---

[11] This exhibition was organized by P. Morton Shand in the London department store, Fortnum & Mason. The success of this show led to the establishment of Finmar, a company that was especially dedicated to the sale of Aalto furniture. See Schildt, *Decisive Years*, pp. 103–28.

[12] Alvar Aalto, "Karjalan rakennustaide" [Architecture in Karelia]; repr. in Schildt, ed., *Sketches: Alvar Aalto*, p. 82.

From this, he went on to argue that the inevitably tight economic constraints governing the period of postwar reconstruction would, by definition, necessitate a similar additive approach. As he put it:

> The task presupposes an architectural system according to which houses can grow and be enlarged over the years. We cannot accomplish our work with the conventional cultural loans or the "technocratic" rationalism and buildings that have been dominant in Europe in recent times. The system must be created here and must take our own circumstances into consideration; but certain features in the Karelian building system that I have just mentioned can give us some excellent help in finding the right system, at least to the extent that larger population groupings, thanks to this architecture, become accessory to the necessary self-confidence and feeling that we are not taking the wrong path.[13]

With these words, Aalto categorically rejected the technocratic rationalism of the early modern movement as unacceptably reductive, while recognizing that without the popular support of society one cannot achieve anything of lasting consequence as far as the habitat is concerned. This Karelian thesis evidently implied some form of topographically inflected, low-rise, high-density housing, such as Aalto had already demonstrated in the Sunila Pulp Mill and Housing of 1936–38 and the Standard Terrace Housing in Kauttua of 1937–38. Thus, while he was not totally opposed to high-rise construction, it is clear that for him, as for Frank Lloyd Wright, the preferred line was horizontal, since, as he put it in 1946: "Highrise apartments must be regarded, both socially and architecturally, as a considerably more dangerous form of building than single-family houses or lowrise apartments."[14] Last, but not least, there was the clear implication that the key to ecologically responsible housing production in the future lay in the "ready-made" model of the Finnish vernacular, just as this had once served as the point of departure for the Finnish national romantic architects of the 1890s. It was just this Finnish tradition that led Aalto back to the Land U-shaped plans of the English Arts and Crafts house, and to type plans that, in their turn, had been derived from vernacular forms. As we have noted, his own house in Munkkiniemi signaled this return as early as 1935, and this would find further elaboration in the adjacent timber ambulatory and courtyard that was designed to receive Aino Aalto's grave after her premature death in 1949.

It is virtually the same Finnish vernacular paradigm that resurfaced with full force in his highrise Hansaviertel apartment building of 1954–57. In this instance, each apartment is, in effect, a small single-story patio house, and we may say

---

[13] *Ibid.*, pp. 82–83.

[14] Alvar Aalto, "Rakennuskorkeus sosiaalisesa kysymyksenä" [Building Heights as a Social Problem], *Arkkitehti* (1946); repr. in *ibid.*, p. 93.

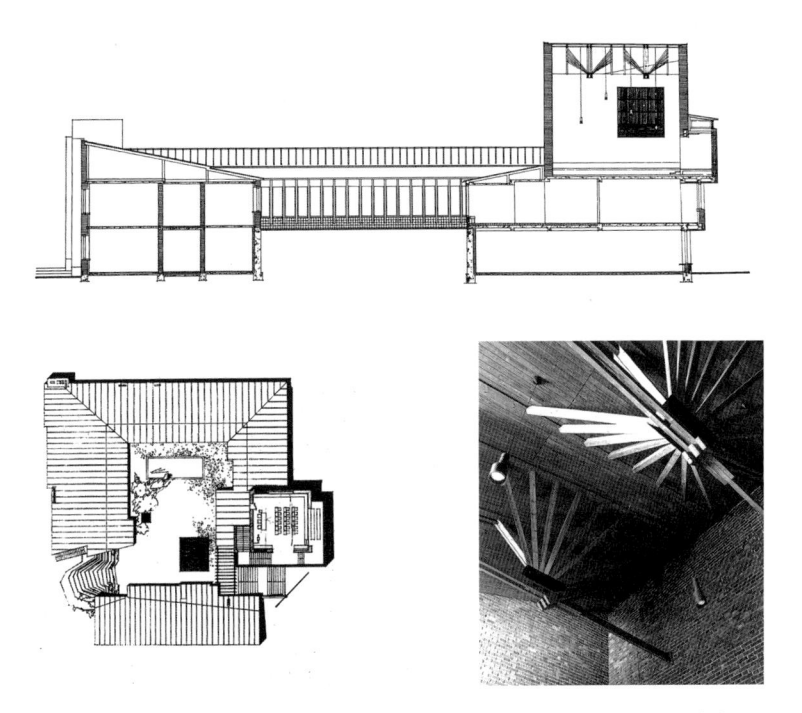

FIGURES 36–38 The Säynätsalo Town Hall, Säynätsalo, Finland. Alvar Aalto, 1949–1951. Section through the courtyard (top), plan (below left), and the radiating trusses of the Council Chamber hall ceiling (below right).

FIGURE 39 Kenneth Frampton in front of the Säynätsalo Town Hall, 1980s.

that their syncopated aggregation creates the semblance of a diminutive village on each floor. The basic apartment is an assembly of three bedrooms, plus a bathroom and a kitchen, grouped around three sides of a central living room that opens directly to the exterior through a generously proportioned terrace partially inset into the corpus of the building. Each terrace is shielded from the next, and from the ground, by virtue of the way it is incorporated into the staggered plan of the block. A galley-kitchen gives direct access to this terrace for the purposes of eating outdoors, while the kitchen is directly accessed from a generously proportioned internal foyer. Acoustical and visual privacy is facilitated throughout by a pattern of circulation that serves the flanking bedrooms while being partially screened from the central living volume.

This carefully modulated arrangement is matched by the generosity of the glazed elevator hall, which is wide, naturally lit, and well-ventilated. It is a room, rather than an access corridor in the usual sense. In ergonomic terms, this apartment layout plan is one of the most brilliant, middle-class apartment plans invented in the entire span of the twentieth century, and the mystery is that neither Aalto nor anyone else would have the occasion or the desire to replicate its form or develop a further variation of its patio organization.[15]

[...]

The virtues of Aalto's Hansaviertel prototype do not end with the units themselves, for the modular rhythm of the block, established through its precast concrete, modular wall system, sets up a significant interplay with the inset terraces that are automatically incorporated into its form. These terraces are rhythmic at another scale in that the raised soffits above the living rooms impart a "noble" identity to each apartment. Furthermore, the gray concrete panels, cast from steel formwork, are rhythmically jointed, so as to create a coursed effect reminiscent of stone facing on a gigantic scale—the merest hint, one might say, of a latent Nordic classical sensibility. At the same time, the partially protruding terraces, opening toward the south and thereby imparting a direction to the massing, serve to distance the overall form from any sense of classical propriety, except for the entry portico, which, framed by a peristyle of concrete columns, imparts a classic touch to the entrance. Aalto's intention in developing this apartment type and block formation is confirmed by the description that appears in the first volume of his complete works, published in 1963:

> The conventional apartment house is a sort of collective dwelling; it can never possess the same qualities as, say, a private house, which has a direct relation to the landscape. Nevertheless, the private house, which is often placed as a box in a small garden without a protected interior court, has its

---

[15] Aalto did, in fact, deploy the Hansaviertel block type and apartment plan in his unrealized housing projects for Kampementsbacken, Stockholm (1958) and for Björnholm on the southern Finnish coast (1959).

negative sides, while, on the other hand, the apartment block can present some positive advantages. Therefore an attempt should be made to combine, in an ideal manner, the specific advantages of an apartment block with the merits of the individual house . . .

The conventional small corridor-like balconies were here transformed into patios around which the rooms of the apartments were grouped. This grouping around the open-air room created an intimate, private atmosphere.[16]

This cluster organization entailed the provision of balconies, which, by virtue of the manner of their enclosure, ensured both privacy and a sense of being in the open air. At the same time, their chevron formation implied a biomorphic organization similar to that analyzed in D'Arcy Thompson's *On Growth and Form* of 1917.[17] Unlike the modular cubic character of Le Corbusier's Pavillon L'Esprit Nouveau, at the Exposition Internationale des Arts Décoratifs et Industriel Moderne in Paris of 1925 (which was also designed as a prototypical highrise dwelling), Aalto's Hansaviertel apartments could have been readily adapted to form clusters of single-story houses at grade, aggregating into picturesque assemblies with each house stepping down to follow the contours of the site, much like the format that Jørn Utzon adopted in his Kingo Housing, completed near Helsingør in Denmark in 1956.

[. . .]

MEGALOPOLITAN ECOLOGY

Like Ludwig Mies van der Rohe and Ludwig Hilberseimer, both of whom were subject to the influential proto-ecological writings of Raoul francé,[18] Aalto envisaged a more-or-less continual urbanization of the earth's surface, one in which his all but mythical "forest town" would come to be universally adopted in northern Europe and, to some extent, elsewhere as a kind of regional Gaia

---

[16] Karl Fleig, ed., *Alvar Aalto* (London: Tiranti, 1963), p. 168.

[17] See D'Arcy Wentworth Thompson, *On Growth and Form*, ed. J.T. Bonner (Cambridge: Cambridge University Press, 1971). First published in 1917, the book was expanded and revised in 1942.

[18] See Fritz Neumeyer, *The Artless Word: Mies van der Rohe on Building Art* (Cambridge, Mass.: MIT Press, 1991), pp. 102–106. Mies was profoundly influenced by Raoul francé's protoecological writings. In the mid-1920s, one finds Mies in total accord with francé's dictum: "The best one can do is to find a compromise between the I and this law (of ecology) and to adjust to it according to the variables of the surroundings." Here we encounter a surprising affinity between Mies and Aalto, particularly concerning their respective attitudes toward regional planning.

System,[19] equally devoted to agrarian and industrial development, the one continuously fusing into the other. Aalto first posited his concept of the forest town in his 1936 master plan for the industrial community of Sunila, near Kotka, of which he remarked in a lecture of 1956: "The housing is placed wholly on the southern slopes leaving the northern slopes to the forest . . . Both the housing developments and the factory itself are designed to grow without disrupting their harmony."[20] Here, the heroic monumental Sunila Pulp Mill built for a consortium of major paper producers as a gridded, brick-faced matrix on an island promontory facing the sea was complemented by low-rise workers' housing laid out in a fan formation on an adjacent mainland site. [. . .]

Aalto's green-city ideology seems to have been informed by a number of countervailing open-city planning models developed during the first four decades of the century, from N.A. Ladovsky's formalistic planning precepts, which seem to have influenced a prototypical new town, "An American Town in Finland", designed by MIT students under Aalto's direction in 1940, to the Anglo-Saxon garden-city model refined by Clarence Stein and Henry Wright in Radburn, New Jersey, and in their green-belt New Towns. Aalto would have become familiar with the latter through his friend Lewis Mumford, whose influential *The Culture of Cities* had been published in 1938. The other primary influence on Aalto's approach to planning at this time was unquestionably the Tennessee Valley Authority (TVA) Regional Plan promulgated under the auspices of Franklin Delano Roosevelt's New Deal after 1933. This was surely the inspiration behind Aalto's Kokemäenjoki River Valley Regional Plan of 1940-42, when Harry Gullichsen persuaded several river-based municipalities, from Pori to Kokemaki, to unite in commissioning Finland's first regional plan from Alvar Aalto. [. . .]

Aalto's master plan was, in his words, a "formation of trees, planted areas, meadows, and fields, providing a distinctive feature characteristic of Imatra and separating the built-up areas"[21] thereby obviating the need for formal parks of any kind. This diffusion of tended woodland justified the title, "forest town." As Jussi Rautsi has written of the Imatra plan: "There is thus no need to plan artificial parks in the midst of settlement, especially as the forest often penetrates all the way to the central areas. The Finnish character of the parks must be preserved, even further accentuated. The

---

[19] The name of this hypothesis derives from the Greek goddess of the earth, Gaia. The term was coined by James Lovelock in the 1970s and refers to his hypothesis that the homeostatic balance of the earth's biomass is regulated by a complex network of interwoven feedback systems. See James Lovelock, *Gaia: A New Look at Earth* (London: Oxford University Press, 1979) and *The Ages of Gaia: A Biography of Our Living Earth* (New York: Norton, 1995). See also Max Oelschlaeger, *Postmodern Environmental Ethics* (New York: SUNY, 1995).

[20] Alvar Aalto, "Problemi di architettura" (1956); repr. in Göran Schildt, *Alvar Aalto: The Complete Catalogue of Architecture, Design and Art*, trans. Timothy Binham (New York: Rizzoli, 1994), p. 14.

[21] Alvar Aalto, *Arkkitehti*, nos. 1–2 (1957); cited in *ibid.*, p. 22.

FIGURE 40 Alvar Aalto's Structural Map of the General Town Plan of Imatra, Finland. Dated 1 August 1951.

unique beauty of Finnish nature is not based on luxuriant growth or colours or enormous scale. Our nature is marked by a realistic beauty, and should be kept that way."[22]

Aalto justified his forest-town approach in terms that were reminiscent of Bruno Taut's deurbanizing thesis, as set forth in his 1920 publication, *Die Auflösung der Städte oder die Erde eine gute Wohnung* [The Dissolution of Cities]. Thus, we find Aalto writing of the Kokemäenjoki River Valley Regional Plan: "Exactly as the medieval cities once upon a time lost their fortification walls and the modern city grew out beyond them, the concept of the city today is in the process of shedding its constraints. But this time it is happening, not to lead once again to the creation of a larger unit, but rather so that the city will become part of the countryside. The underlying meaning of such regional plans is that they synchronize country and city."[23]

Despite their organic flexible character, Aalto's regional plans remained largely unrealized due to speculation and other economic constraints.[24] Such interests did not prevent the realization of Aalto's smaller civic complexes however, where the geological metaphor assisted him in establishing the identity of the place through the way in which the profile of the built form extends into the site. This is at once evident in the case of Säynätsalo Town Hall of 1948–52, where the municipal structure is the cumulative element of a chevron formation of lowrise structures running through the center of the town. Here, Bruno Taut's concept of the "city crown"[25] returns in the mono-pitched roof of the council chamber, which rises up as an indicator, so to speak, of the way in which the town ought to grow. A similar roof crowned most of Aalto's later civic centers with the same basic intention, namely, to serve as a symbolic core around which the rest of the municipality would develop.

Resisting closure around either a classical paradigm or a technological norm, Aalto strove for an organic flexibility, wherein function and production would play their appointed roles without being over-determined and where, within the megalopolis, agriculture and industry would interact with nature in such a way as to create an environmental ecology satisfying to fundamental human needs.

[. . .]

---

[22] See Jussi Rautsi "Alvar Aalto's Urban Plans 1940–1970," *DATUTOP 13* (Tampere) (1988), p. 52.

[23] Alvar Aalto, "Valtakunnansuunnittelu ja kulttuurimme tavoittet" [National Planning and Cultural Goals], *Suomalainen Suomi* (1949); repr. in Schildt, *Sketches*, p. 100.

[24] Rautsi, "Alvar Aalto's Urban Plans 1940-1970," p. 55.

[25] Bruno Taut, *Die Stadtkrone* (Jena: Diederichs, 1919).

AALTO AT THE MILLENIUM

In June 1977, in the commemorative issue of *L' Architecture d'aujourd'hui* following Aalto's death, the Italian architect, Leonardo Mosso, analyzed the underlying substance and method of Aalto's work in the following profound and moving terms:

> Each project has a double system of requirements: those that are material and those that are social. Material requirements must absolutely be resolved or else the very reasons for a project's existence are compromised ... As for the social requirements, Aalto attempts to solve the material problems of the individual within the framework of social organization, by inserting qualities of sociability into the system of objective requirements. He seeks to overcome man's egoism (in the sense of a primacy of self over others) by combining functions that tend to be more collective than individualistic, while at the same time, he fights against alienating aspects by including insulating and protective qualities. Aalto incorporates physically into his spaces the basic attributes of this dialectic ... The aphorism "to achieve Paradise on earth through the sole means of the art of the building" means (as the whole of Aalto's practice demonstrates) the recreating of a unity between urban tissue and natural surroundings. In other words, permitting the entire population to recover urban spaces colonized by capitalist commercialism and profit seeking, by all that destroys the identity of man and of social man.[26]

Now, twenty years later, on the occasion of the centenary of his birth, we have cause to reassess, in comparable terms, the relevance of Aalto's work to the architecture of the emerging future, above all, because of the fragmented character of contemporary development and the ever-widening domain of the megalopolis in the late modern world. As far as this last is concerned, it is clear that Aalto embraced a critically realistic view in which ecologically tempered tracts of regional urbanization would become the universal norm, however much they may be layered and inflected, as his vision of the forest town implies.

[...]

While Aalto exploited the sensuous potential of the heterotopic method for what he called its unpremeditated style creating power, the significance of this strategy at the end of the century, resides in its categorical antipathy to building as a proliferation of freestanding objects. Like the comparable architecture of Hugo Häring and Hans Scharoun, with whom, as Colin St. John Wilson reminded us,[27] there was always an affinity, Aalto's buildings were either landscapes in themselves, as in the case of the Wolfsburg Cultural Center of 1958–62 or, alternatively, they extended into the surroundings in such a way as to transform the

---

[26] Leonardo Mosso, "Aalto: Architect of Social and Cultural Reintegration," *L'Architecture d'aujourd'hui*, no. 191 (June 1977), p. 122.

[27] St. John Wilson, *The Other Tradition of Modern Architecture*, pp. 27–35.

preexisting ground, as in the case of the Maison Carré of 1956–59 or Seinäjoki Civic Center of 1958–87. Of parallel ontological consequence was the way in which his buildings were constituted as topographic structures rather than as gratuitous sculptural gestures, which, by definition, can never transcend their freestanding isolation. This is the paradox of Aalto's heterotopic legacy, for while it is an idiosyncratic response to the specificity of both site and program, it remains open, almost by design, to the subsequent collective transformation of the work across time. It anticipates, in terms of the larger future, that which is already inherent in the design process itself. It is the precondition, one might say, for Álvaro Siza's insistence that the main task of architecture resides in transformation rather than invention.[28]

Thus, the ultimate significance of Aalto's work for the coming century resides in his conviction that the built work always has to be rendered, in large measure, as a landscape, thereby fusing and *con*fusing both figure and ground, in a ceaseless interplay between natural constraint and cultural ingenuity. This surely is the critical essence of what Aalto leaves to us, as we contemplate a totalizing limitless environment in which we can no longer say where city ends and country begins. And, while the ruthless rapacity of late-modern development takes us further and further from the ecological ethic of Aalto's forest town, the hope remains that all the ill-considered, ill-related, half-abandoned objects of our time may, one day, be redeemed through an ad hoc creation of layered, topographic assemblies, irrespective of whether these be roofworks or earthworks or, as is more often the case, an inseparable mixture of both.

---

[28] See Álvaro Siza, "Interview," *Plan Construction* (May 1980). "Architects invent nothing. They work continuously with models which they transform in response to problems they encounter."

13 Toward an Urban Landscape (1995)

The split between the architecture and planning professions, already an established fact by the late fifties, has been sustained without any reconsideration over the last forty years. This separation of powers naturally entailed reducing the art of environmental planning to the value-free, applied science of land-use and transportation management. In this form, the dominant planning strategy became logistical and managerial. Symptomatic of this development is the fact that in 1974 the municipality of Rotterdam finally substituted a so-called "structure plan" for the "physical plan" that had hitherto guided the development of the city. Since 1945 the plan of the city had been maintained and regularly upgraded. Its replacement by the strategy of Melvin Webber's *non-place urban* realm[1] was presumably to maximize the economic development of the region, as previously unbuilt areas of reclaimed land were freed for speculation through the expansion of the national road system. In America as elsewhere, this infrastructure would be subsidized by the federal government, under the direct influence of the automobile and oil industry lobbies. In the United States the postwar GI Bill and the pro-suburban Federal Housing Administration mortgage regulations were directly integrated into this broad instrumental maneuver. This policy was furthered by consciously adopting a strategy of benign neglect toward the railroad infrastructure and by the general elimination of all existing forms of public transport. This policy was advanced to the point of encouraging the clandestine purchase of public transit lines for the express purpose of shutting them down. General Motors was directly involved in such an operation in Los Angeles, which up to the mid-fifties had an extensive and highly convenient

---

Source: Kenneth Frampton, "Toward an Urban Landscape," *D: Columbia Documents of Architecture and Theory*, no.4 (1995): 83–93. This text is a transcript of the lecture originally delivered as part of a faculty symposium entitled "Cities at the Limit" at Columbia University on 4 October 1993.

[1] Melvin Webber et al., *Explorations into Urban Structure* (Philadelphia: University of Pennsylvania Press, 1964).

system of suburban rail transit. This network was closed down and the rights-of-way previously employed by the rail lines appropriated for the freeway system.

The joint result of such policies was the seemingly unwitting destruction of the American provincial town and the concomitant proliferation of the car-accessed suburban supermarket, which led inevitably to the economic destruction of the traditional American main street. After forty years of attrition, this process continues unabated, as we may judge from the current expansion of Mega-supermarket chains. None of these developments have come into being entirely by accident. In one way or another, this was and still is a global operation, contrived to further the interests of deregulated land speculation and to sustain larger units of corporate industrial production—above, of course, the symbiotic functioning of the oil and automobile industries. In all of this, we need to remember that 85 percent of this built production in the United States is realized without the intervention of the architectural profession, while planning, where effectively applied, usually does little more than facilitate the overall operation. This contrasts markedly with the Spanish situation, in which until recently the law required that every building be designed by an architect.

As markets become increasingly global and capital increasingly fluid, the multinational market system disseminates itself over the face of the earth and with it, of course, the ubiquitous megalopolis. While all of this has been well known for some time, the architectural and planning professions are still faced with the unenviable task of attempting to reintegrate themselves into a global building process that is only too capable of proceeding without them. Current deregulation operations now being considered at the highest level of government policy making in Europe and elsewhere point in the same direction, and we are fooling ourselves if we think that this is not further evidence of the interests of maximizing multinational finance together with the building industry's drive to rationalize and monopolize its output through the so-called package-deal approach. We may thus establish a link between the undermining of the American architectural profession in the late seventies by the American antitrust laws and the current attempt of the European building industry to revoke the protected status of the title of architect. The aim of these moves is obvious, namely to dispose of any vestige of critical resistance coming from the profession to the maximizing thrust of free-market development. Architects may still intervene today in 15 to 25 percent of significant public work, a percentage apparently more than most builder-developers are willing to tolerate. The tendency today to fund public works with private money patently favors the interests of the builder-developer over the critical acumen of the architect.

It is necessary to acknowledge these tendencies openly because we too easily deceive ourselves into thinking that the cultural and ecological predicament of the megalopolis is not a direct result of conscious political and ideological decisions made at the highest level of the power system. To this we must add the paradoxical and tragic fact that the popular, not to say populist, consumerist taste and world view is oriented away from any kind of more rational land settlement, largely on psycho-symbolic grounds. This seemingly spontaneous hostility is also largely engineered, in part by a lumpen home-building industry that does its best to make sure that what people want is what it already provides, and in large and full measure by the banks, which are strongly inclined to disallow mortgages for any form of planned unit-development, especially where the dwelling units are contiguous. Proof resides in the fate of the mediatory land settlement model proposed by Serge Chermayeff and Christopher Alexander in the early sixties. I am referring, of course, to their largely forgotten joint study *Community and Privacy*[2] of 1963. The general prognosis of this study is that the city core as a civic center is becoming decentralized in terms of both administrative convenience and shopping. The authors remark that the main street as a shopping street had already given way to more conveniently located suburban shopping centers linked to rapid-transit systems lying outside the city proper. As a consequence, Chermayeff and Alexander argued:

> The suburb fails to be countryside ... because it is not dense enough or organized enough. Countless scattered houses dropped like stones on neat rows of development lots do not create an order, or generate community. Neighbor remains a stranger and the real friends are most often far away ... The husband suffers the necessity of long-distance commuting ... the [wife] finds herself either behind the wheel of a car, an unpaid chauffeur, or in front of the television set, a captive spectator.[3]

All of this is of course so familiar by now as to be unremarkable but was less familiar thirty years ago, as the Chermayeff and Alexander critical response to this condition remains unfamiliar today. *Community and Privacy* proposed a new standard for suburban land settlement based on low-rise, high-density courtyard houses. The attributes of this largely untried form of modern land settlement (which was compatible with automobile access and suburban development) are as follows: (1) the assurance of complete privacy inside and outside the unit; (2) the provision of efficient car and service access to every dwelling together with the provision of corresponding communal space; (3) the automatically economic organization of service infrastructure; and (4) an economically and ecologically sound pattern of development in terms of land use, thereby minimizing ground coverage, infrastructural investment and so on.

While this remains, in my view, a rational model for suburban development, it has in fact had little influence over the past thirty years. Thus while we are aware of viable alternative models for "motopian" development, these are largely ignored for economic, political and speculative reasons. We live in a time when the species seems to be incapable of devising an ecologically rational mode of land settlement. *Community and Privacy* can hardly be dismissed as an otherworldly, revolutionary proposition. It was and still is a well-articulated response to changed technological and socioeconomic conditions. While I would be the first to concede that we cannot reduce the predicament of the urbanized

---

[2] Serge Chermayeff and Christopher Alexander, *Community and Privacy: Toward a New Architecture of Humanism* (Garden City, N.Y.: Doubleday, 1965).

[3] *Ibid.*, 63.

region to a matter of simply finding and applying new forms of appropriate land settlement, it is important to recognize that the dysfunctional and wasteful dimensions of the ever-expanding megalopolis cannot be adequately answered through inventing new aesthetic criteria or through the hypothetical application of revitalized avant-gardist stratagems in new guises and at new scales, such as we find say in Rem Koolhaas's recent proposal for the megalopolis of Lille.

What beyond this can one reasonably imagine or propose in terms of significant interventions in the supposedly spontaneous "motopian" city? Before responding to this complex, somewhat rhetorical question, I would like to posit the following provisional polemic and critique. Architects have been attempting to come to terms with the historic reality of the megalopolis for at least sixty years, so we can hardly claim that the crisis is new or that appropriate forms of response have hitherto remained unimagined. One thinks of Robert Moses's expansion of the parkway system into the urban region or the Le Corbusian seven-route strategy, particularly as this was proposed as a means of reordering the Marseilles hinterland and the area around his Marseilles *Unité d'habitation* of 1952: the rhizome *avant la lettre*.[4] One thinks of Alison and Peter Smithson's London Roads Study[5] of 1953 and of their "land-castle" and "mat-building" concepts;[6] of Peter Land's organization of the Previ experimental quarter outside Lima, Peru;[7] of the Aktion Schweiz movement on the occasion of the Swiss National Exhibition of 1963;[8] of J.R. James's linear city proposal for the British Home Counties around London;[9] of John Turner's strategy for the so-called housing deficit of the Third World.[10] One thinks of Doxiades's "Dynapolis" model of directional linear urban development[11] and of Shadrach Woods's pamphlet *What U Can Do*. Woods opens his short tract with a citation from a text written ten years earlier: "Urbanism and architecture are parts of a continuous process. Planning [urbanism] is the correlating of human activities; architecture is the housing of these activities . . . [Urbanism] remains abstract until it generates architecture." He ends in 1970 with an unequivocal appeal to the future promulgation of a rational welfare state:

---

[4] Le Corbusier, *Oeuvre Complète*, Vol. 5: 1946–1952, Vol. 6: 1952–1957, Vol. 7: 1957–65 (Zurich: Les Editions d'Architecture, 1967).

[5] Alison Smithson, *Urban Structuring: Studies of Alison and Peter Smithson* (London: Studio Vista; New York: Reinhold, 1967).

[6] Alison Smithson, "How to Recognize and Read Mat-Building," *Architectural Design*, Vol. 44, No. 9 (1974): 573–90.

[7] *Atelier 5: 26 Selected Works* (Zurich: Ammann Verlag, 1986), 174.

[8] Achtung, die Schweiz: Ein Gespräch über Unsere Lage und ein Vorschlag zur Tat (Basel: F. Handschin, 1955).

[9] J.R. James, "Planning for the 1970s," *RIBA Journal*, Vol. 74 (October 1967): 419–28.

[10] John Turner, *Housing by People: Towards Autonomy in Building Environments* (New York: Pantheon Books, 1977).

[11] Konstantinos Doxiades, *Ekistics: An Introduction to the Science of Human Settlements* (New York: Oxford University Press, 1968).

For urbanists and architects a saner future means that we can at last rid ourselves of all those nutty ideas about throw-away buildings, built-in obsolescence, high energy consuming schemes and walk-around cities on the one hand—but it also means that we must reconsider extreme low-density development, with its enormous waste potential and over-extended supply lines, on the other. We come at last to the useful end of the "waste produces wealth" period, having discovered that the wealth produced by waste is ill-gotten, a two-edged sword, a poisoned gift. Architects and urbanists will make their plans and develop them in light of economic, rather than merely financial considerations, for instance. Decisions will be made on the basis of reason, perhaps, and not merely in the light of political opportunism. Reason will dictate continuous renewal of the environment at every scale, not massive blight followed by massive reconstruction.[12]

As with *Community and Privacy*, a quarter of a century has passed since these challenging words were set to paper, and we are no further along. By way of an equally tendentious anachronistic echo, let me respond to Woods's appeal with the following twelve-point assessment as to where we seem to stand as opposed to what we might do.

1. The dystopia of the megalopolis is already an irreversible historical fact: it has long since installed a new way of life, not to say a new nature.
2. The scale of this urbanizing explosion or implosion, depending on how one looks at it, is without precedent in human history. It has nothing whatsoever to do with the traditional city.
3. Attempts to reconstruct the classical city as advanced by the Italian *tendenza* movement in the sixties, exemplified in Aldo Rossi's *The Architecture of the City*[13] or Leon Krier's *Rationalist Architecture*,[14] were and remain destined for rather limited application: witness the recent fate of Krier's Poundbury new town proposal as sponsored by the Prince of Wales, where the traffic turning circles required by modern automobile access inhibited Krier's wish to return to the enclosure and scale of an eighteenth-century street grid.
4. The classical center city, where it still exists as a living entity, is increasingly threatened by a subtle tendency to transform it into a kind of theme park. The pedestrianization of traditional city centers, a policy dating back to the early sixties, is the first symptom of this tendency.

---

[12] Shadrach Woods, *What U Can Do: Architecture at Rice 27* (Houston: Rice University School of Architecture, 1970), 33–5.

[13] Aldo Rossi, *The Architecture of the City* (Cambridge, Mass.: MIT Press, 1982).

[14] Leon Krier, *Rationalist Architecture* (Milan: Franco Angell, 1973).

5 From the aerial viewpoint the megalopolis appears to assume a quasi-orderly, biological character, yet this is invariably imperceptible from the ground.
6 Ordered or not, such a perspective heightens our awareness of the megalopolis as a new nature. This has led some critics to evoke a new kind of pastoralism as a mediatory force capable of transcending the impasse outlined above. At the same time they would like to recognize the architectonic potential of an emerging set of unprecedented megalopolitan forms. This seems to be the argument advanced by Peter Rowe in his book *Making a Middle Landscape*.[15] Rowe regards such ex-urban corporate establishments as Kevin Roche's General Foods or his Union Carbide Headquarters as an occasion for the creation of local parterres, although what benefits such landscapes necessarily bestow upon society is left rather unclear.
7 Two salient factors may be derived from Rowe's thesis however: first, that priority should now be accorded to landscape, rather than to freestanding built form; and second, that there is a pressing need to transform certain megalopolitan types such as shopping malls, parking lots and office parks into landscaped built forms.
8 These new types may well become the foci of future design interventions in the urbanized region, along with the pressing need to find new uses for abandoned postindustrial "scar tissue" left behind by obsolete, abandoned nineteenth- and early twentieth-century factories. However, all such development or modification will obviously remain subject to stringent economic constraint.
9 The accepted process of amortization is likely to remain a constraint in almost all future urban development. This economic paradigm is closely linked to a global tendency toward total commodification. The Venturian model of the decorated shed remains the commodifying instrument *par excellence*, regardless of whether the decor veers toward historical pastiche or toward the deconstructive speculations of the neo-avant-garde. We should also note that whereas a corporation may be prepared to invest large sums in the creation of a representational landscape, it is unlikely that the lower end of the speculative market will act in an equally responsible way.
10 Cities have always been constructed, in one way or another, out of fragments, and one cannot expect the megalopolis to be any different. Building invariably proceeds by fits and starts. A certain amount of capital is amassed, and when this has been expended, the one-off building process summarily ceases. As architects, we need to conceive of future urban interventions in such a way as they have a wide-ranging catalytic effect for a given amount of investment.

---

[15] Peter Rowe, *Making a Middle Landscape* (Cambridge, Mass.: MIT Press, 1991).

Their "open" character in this regard should also be capable of being "closed" when necessary.
11 With what power is left to us, it is our ethical responsibility to use our ingenuity to engender an urban fabric aggregated out of topographic fragments within the metabolic interstices of the megalopolis.
12 We should not allow ourselves to be deceived by the free-market deregulatory impulses of late capitalist development. We should not underestimate the reductive aim of such provisions, which surely seeks to mask its maximizing thrust under the superficial gloss of culture. At the same time we have no choice but to respond to opportunities that arise in order to create a critical counter form within the existing situation.

In a recent address on the theme of *atopy* or dystopia, given at a conference in Barcelona in 1992, the Italian architect Vittorio Gregotti reminded us that internationalism today is based on intangible financial transactions, the exchange of scientific and technical information and forms of mass communication having their own rules. In this situation, where everything is possible, subjectivity is weakened as a source of differentiation. This would seem to have negative consequences for architecture. Gregotti writes:

> Even the relative diversity of the increasing number of interesting things produced in the field of art seems to be an obstacle to the establishment of an authentic differentiation, guided as they are by the very homogenization of the unified market of mass communications which demands the continuous invention of undifferentiated articles.[16]

After arguing that the increasing number of "interesting" things makes it increasingly difficult to establish an authentic differentiation, Gregotti makes the following point about the nature of *atopicity:*

> There is no doubt that atopicity could be interpreted as the sign of an inevitable mechanism of international interdependence which has a cultural, political and economic structure, a sign that has not yet found a meaningful spatial organization in the territory of architecture.

> This is an interdependence which still seems to involve control and domination, thus opposing the attempt of the existing community to ensure in the process of unification the maximum expression of their traditional values. This atopicity is still widely at the service of the brutal exploitation of the economic differences between social classes.

---

[16] Vittorio Gregotti, "On Atopy," *Urbanismo Revista: Periphery as a Project*, No. 9–10 (1992): 79.

Could it move instead in the direction of solidarity, towards that "communicative public action" of which some philosophers speak? This is probably a naively optimistic interpretation, but one which is also dictated by an intimate necessity and, at least as a hypothesis, one which is perhaps able to transfer into the territory of architecture the destructive impetus of atopicity, transforming it into a dialogue of solidarity, even with regard to the context.[17]

This discreet call to action ought to be sufficient to make us rethink our rather unreflecting submission to arcane theories that have no discernible *practical* or *ethical* application in the field of architecture and urban design. There is no reason to assume that an obtuse theoretical discourse drawn more or less directly from either literature or philosophy is necessarily applicable in any cogent way to the design of the urban fabric. I would submit that instead we need to conceive of a remedial landscape that is capable of playing a critical and compensatory role in relation to the ongoing, destructive commodification of the man-made world. Architecture must assume an *ecological* stance in the broadest possible sense. Thus we should encourage the Taoist strategy of "acting by not acting," that is to say we should look toward the cultivation of a quiet but pertinent minimalism. This is surely of more consequence than "acting by overacting" in the name of art, media pressure or intraprofessional competition. By the same token we may assert that *landscaped form* as the fundamental material of a fragmentary urbanism is of greater consequence than the free-standing aestheticized object.

---

[17] *Ibid.*, 80.

My theme this evening, 'Megaform as Urban Landscape' has something of its origin half a century ago when my initial experience of the urbanized region of the scale of the Boston–Washington corridor was impressed upon my mind, for the first time, by actually taking a helicopter ride from Newark Airport at 5PM on a summer evening, and back to Kennedy Airport to fly back to London. I had never seen so much electrical power—this is the mid-'60s—or gasoline burning before my eyes as one of those sublime panoramas that you are never likely to forget.

There are two things that coincided at this time. One was this experience of the urbanized region, and the other was Hannah Arendt's book *The Human Condition* which first appeared in 1958 and from which I will never really recover in terms of the way she influenced my total attitude to architecture and to life in general. Where the first, the urbanized region, made me aware of the process of continuous, never-ending urbanization, the continual assembly of totally unrelated free-standing objects, the other introduced me to the provocative phrase 'the space of human appearance,' with all the political and cultural connotations that this implies. And thus, I first became preoccupied with something that has haunted me ever since. Namely, by what means, both as a society and as a profession, may we hope to be able to maintain 'spaces of human appearance' within an exceptionally privatized and highly commodified process of unending urbanization?

Kenneth Frampton, Senior Loeb Scholar Lecture, Harvard University, Graduate School of Design, 25 October 2017.

14 Megaform as Urban Landscape (1999)

[...]

Since 1961 when the French geographer Jean Gottmann first employed the term megalopolis to allude to the northeastern seaboard of the United States, the world population has become increasingly dense with the result that most of us now live in some form of continuous urbanized region. One of the paradoxical consequences of this population shift is that today we are largely unable to project urban form with any degree of confidence, neither as a *tabula rasa* operation nor as a piecemeal aggregation to be achieved through such devices as zoning codes maintained over a long period of time. The constant expansion of the autoroute infrastructure throughout the world continues to open up increasing tracts of former agricultural land to suburban subdivision. Despite this endless suburbanized development throughout the world and most particularly in North America, there remains the occasional capital city where some kind of urban planning process is still being significantly maintained such as Helsinki or the recent refurbishing of Barcelona which is yet another example of an exception to the megalopolitan norm.

In the main, however, the urban future tends to be projected largely in terms of remedial operations as these may be applied to existing urban cores or, with less certainty, to selected parts of the megalopolis. Meanwhile, the urbanized region continues to consolidate its hold over vast areas of land as in the Randstad in the Netherlands or the Tokyo-Hokkaido corridor in Japan. These urbanized regions are subject to sporadic waves of urban expansion that either escalate out of control or enter into periods of stagnation. It is a predicament that confronts the urbanist with an all but impossible task, one in which civic intervention has to be capable not only of sustaining a sense of place but also of serving as an effective catalyst for the further development of the region.

Source: Kenneth Frampton, *Megaform as Urban Landscape: 1999 Raoul Wallenberg Lecture* (Ann Arbor, MI: The University of Michigan A. Alfred Taubman College of Architecture and Urban Planning, 1999).

Owing to the dissolution of the city as a bounded domain, dating from the mid-nineteenth century, architects have long since been aware that any contribution they might make to the urban form would of necessity be extremely limited. This resignation is already implicit in Camillo Sitte's remedial urban strategy of 1889. In his book, *City Planning According to Artistic Principles*, he attempted to respond to the "space-endlessness" of the Viennese Ringstrasse by recommending the redefinition of the Ring in terms of bounded form. Sitte was evidently disturbed by the fact that the main monuments of the Ring had been built as free-standing objects and he recommended enclosing them with built fabric in order to establish relationships similar to those that had once existed in the medieval city, such as that between the *parvis* and the *cathedral*.

Inspired by Sitte's revisionism, I have coined the term megaform in order to refer to the form-giving potential of certain kinds of horizontal urban fabric capable of effecting topographic transformation in the megalopolitan landscape. It has to be admitted at the outset that this term may read as being synonymous with the term megastructure, as this was first coined in the 1960s. In my view, the two terms may be differentiated from one another in terms of the relative continuity of their form. Thus, while a megaform may incorporate a megastructure, a megastructure is not necessarily a megaform.

One may illustrate this distinction by comparing the Centre Pompidou in Paris, which is surely a megastructure, to Arthur Erickson's Robson Square development in Vancouver which is ultimately a megaform. This is largely due to the way in which its continuously stepped layered form serves to modulate and unify the existing urban fabric of downtown Vancouver. This particular example also happens to have been enriched by an exceptionally fertile collaboration between its architect, Arthur Erickson, and the landscape architect, Cornelia Oberlander.

It seems that our capacity to imagine megaforms may well have originated with our first experiences of the world as seen from the air. This, on his own admission, was the catalyst behind Le Corbusier's Plan Obus for Algiers of 1931 that was directly inspired by the volcanic topography of Rio de Janeiro which he first surveyed from the air in 1929. This sweeping panorama led him to imagine a continuous urban form in which one could no longer discriminate between the building and the landscape. A corollary to this topographic approach was to treat the built fabric as a form of artificial ground, upon which and within which the occupant would be free to build in whatever way he saw fit. Hence, while postulating the continuity of the megaform, Le Corbusier left its interstitial fabric open and accessible to popular taste. In its failure to conform to any received urban model, the Plan Obus was hardly a feasible proposal from either a productive or a cultural standpoint. It was totally removed, let us say, from Joseph Stübben's codification of regularized urban space as this had been set forth in his book *Die Städtebau* of 1890. Nor did it owe anything to the perimeter block type, as this would be applied to urban extensions from around 1890 to 1924 and of which Berlage's Amsterdam South plan of 1915 is a prime example. At the same time neither did it conform to the Zeilenbau row

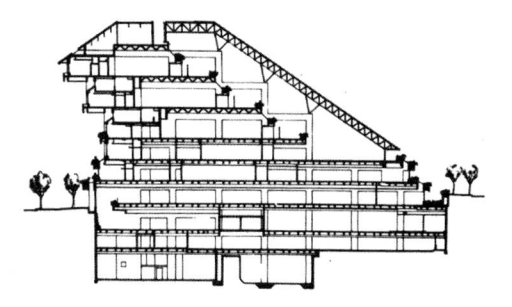

FIGURES 41 AND 42 Robson Square, Vancouver, Canada. Arthur Erickson and Cornelia Hahn Oberlander, 1979–1983. Section (top) and a panoramic view of Robson Square and the Law Courts complex (1986) (below).

house model which was adopted in the Weimar Republic and elsewhere from around 1924 onwards.

For our purposes, the megaform may be defined as the displaying the following characteristics: 1) a large form extending horizontally rather than vertically; 2) a complex form which, unlike the megastructure, is not necessarily articulated into a series of structural and mechanical subsets as we find for example in the Centre Pompidou; 3) a form capable of inflecting the existing urban landscape as found because of its strong topographical character; 4) a form that is not freestanding but rather insinuates itself as a continuation of the surrounding topography; and last but not least, 5) a form that is oriented towards a densification of the urban fabric.

Beyond the dense historical core, a megaform may be identified as an urban nexus set within the "space-endlessness" of the megalopolis. Henri Ciriani's concept of *une piece urbaine* as first formulated in his so-called Barre à Marne or Noissy I complex, realized in Marne la Vallée in 1980, certainly seems to have been conceived along these lines and something similar may be claimed for Rafael Moneo and Manuel de Sola Morales' L'Illa Block as realized in Barcelona in 1997.

The idea of megaform is also implicit as a strategy in Vittorio Gregotti's concept of the anthrogeographic landscape as this is set forth in his book, *Il territorio di architettura* of 1966. Drawing on the work of the German geographer Friedrich Ratzel, who first coined the term anthrogeographic, Gregotti was able to evolve a territorial approach to urban design that, among his Neo-Rationalist colleagues, put him in a class apart. While not opposing the Neo-Rationalist project of reconstructing the neoclassical European city along traditional, typological lines as hypothesized by Aldo Rossi, Leon Krier et al., Gregotti was more intent on responding to the challenge of the megalopolis at a regional scale – at a scale that was closer to that of Le Corbusier's Plan Obus which he recognized as a precedent. Hence his Zen housing scheme for Palermo of 1965 may be seen as combining the Zeilenbau pattern of Weimar with the perimeter block approach of Amsterdam. His scheme for the University of Florence designed two years later was much more territorial with its long blocks running out into the agrarian landscape. This approach took on an even more expansive geographic dimension in his proposal for the University of Calabria of 1973, where the "spine" of the university cuts across five hills between a take-off from the regional autoroute and a railroad station. Partially realized, this infrastructure remains a canonical piece in as much as it is both ordered and yet open to random development. Blocks were designed to be freely attached to the spine without compromising its ability to impinge on the landscape at a panoramic scale.

If one looks for the origin of the megaform in the history of the Modem Movement one tends to find it in Northern Europe rather than the Mediterranean. One first encounters it in Bruno Taut's concept of the "city crown" as this appears in his book *Die Stadtkrone* of 1919. This becomes manifest in the ensuing decade in the German cult of the big building form as it appears in the work of a number of Expressionist architects of the 1920s, including such figures as Hans Scharoun, Hugo Häring, Fritz Höger and Hans Poelzig. One finds in these architects a predisposition for creating large, dynamic urban entities in opposition to the dematerialized spatial dynamics of the twentieth century avant-garde. One thinks of such canonical works as Hans Poelzig's House of Friendship projected for Istanbul in 1916, Hugo Häring's Gut Garkau of 1924, Fritz Roger's Chilehaus in Hamburg of 1925 and Hans Scharoun's Breslau Werkbund exhibition building of 1929. In the case of Poelzig's Istanbul project, one is struck by the way in which the distant silhouette of the building rises diagonally out of the horizontal profile of the city, so that it assumes the form of an artificial escarpment, replete with hanging gardens.

There were of course other German architects in this period who were to embrace a similar topographic strategy—above all Erich Mendelsohn, whose project for Alexanderplatz, Berlin of 1927 rises out of the existing street fabric like a dynamic force. The megaform seems to be an embryonic presence in almost all of Mendelsohn's work from his diminutive Einstein Tower in Potsdam of 1920 to his commercial center for Haifa of 1924 and his heroic Hadassah Hospital projected for Mount Scorpus in 1935. The megaform was also evident in the work of Austrian architect Lois Welzenbacher, above all in his competition entry for Berlin Hazelhorst housing of 1928.

Among Scandinavian architects, the one who lies closest to this German tradition is Alvar Aalto, as is most evident perhaps from his Baker Dormitory, completed on the edge of the Charles River in Cambridge, Massachusetts in 1944. However, a perennial topographic syndrome is manifest in Aalto's work throughout his mature career, from the "tented-mountain" he projected for the Vogelweidplatz Sports Center in Vienna in 1953 to the Pensions Institute realized in Helsinki in 1956. A similar stress upon megaform is also evident in his proposal of the mid-sixties for a new cultural district in the Tooloo area of Helsinki wherein a terraced autoroute system transforms the morphology of the center, serving as a topographic link and a dynamic binder between a series of cultural buildings lining the lake and the major rail head entering the city.

Something approaching a megaform strategy may also be found in the work of Team X, above all perhaps in Jacob Bakema's Bochum University proposal of 1962, his plan for Tel Aviv of 1963 and his Pampas Plan for Rotterdam of 1965. Both Bakema and the British architects Alison and Peter Smithson seem to have regarded the autoroute infrastructure as the sole element which could be depended upon when projecting the future of urban form. This accounts for the Smithsons' Berlin Hauptstadt Competition entry of 1958. The megaform theme also plays a role in the work of Ralph Erskine, above all in his Svappavaara proposal for Lapland of 1963 and in his later Byker Wall housing complex completed in 1981 at Newcastle in England.

To my knowledge the term megaform as opposed to megastructure is first used rather coincidentally by Fumihiko Maki and Masato Ohtaka in their essay "Some Thoughts on Collective Form" of 1965. They introduce the term when

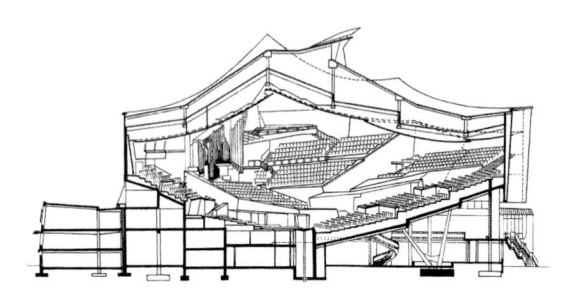

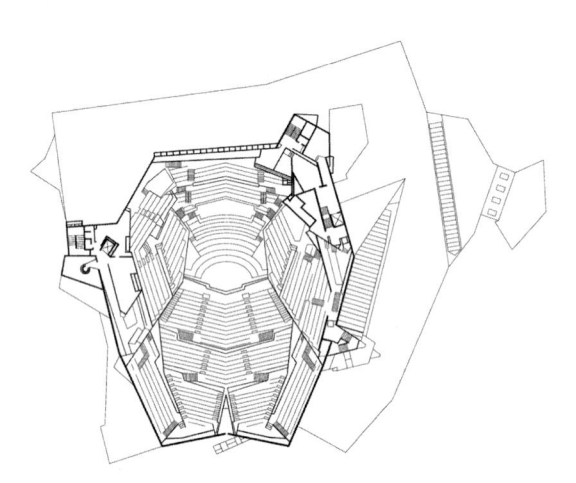

FIGURES 43 AND 44 The Berlin Philharmonic, Berlin, Germany. Hans Scharoun, 1960–1963. Section of the building (top) and plan (below).

writing an appreciation of Kenzo Tange's Tokyo Bay Project of 1960 to the effect that:

> One of the most interesting developments of the megaform has been suggested by Kenzo Tange in connection with the Tokyo Bay Project. He presents a proposal for a mass-human scale form which includes a megaform and discrete, rapidly changing, functional units which fit within the larger framework. He reasons that short-lived items are becoming more and more short-lived and the cycle of change is shrinking at a corresponding rate. On the other hand, the accumulation of capital has made it possible to build in large scale operations . . .

For Maki and Ohtaka, the megaform concept depended upon the idea that change would occur less rapidly in some realms than others. On this basis, they introduced the idea of group form, with the notion that a podium may be inserted into an urban fabric in order to provide for a long term stability while the structures on its surface would be subject to a faster cycle of change and replacement. This concept was exemplified at the time in their joint proposal for the Shinjuku area of Tokyo in which they proposed building a podium above the Shinjuku transit terminal, while at the same time introducing new shopping facilities at grade with parking beneath and rather random, medium rise offices and residential structures above.

Maki's subsequent work has contributed to the theme of the megaform. Like the "city-crown" projects of Jørn Utzon, it is a form that generally manifests itself at two levels, so that while it emphasizes the importance of the podium/earthwork, almost as a precondition, it also depends on the roofwork as an element that is essential to the hill-like character of the final form, as we find this in Bruno Taut's vision of the "city-crown." This double paradigm of earthwork/roofwork first fully emerges in Maki's Fujisawa Gymnasium of 1980 and reappears in his Tokyo Metropolitan Gymnasium of 1985 and in his Makahari Convention Center, Chiba of 1989.

[. . .]

In his archery building for the 1992 Barcelona Olympics, Catalan architects Enric Miralles [with Carme Pinós] designed a building which is extremely sensitive to the landscape and which becomes the landscape. In his scheme for the Igualada Cemetery, realized in a disused quarry and dating from the same year, it is difficult to say whether this is a building, a series of buildings, the city of the dead or the landscape. It is so much a landscape form that it is difficult to say where landscape ends and building begins. Miralles has always striven to give his architecture a topographic character, one that either animates a flat site or fuses it with pre-existing heavily contoured form. Clearly landform as a radical reshaping of the ground may be used to impart shape to a terrain that would otherwise be totally formless.

One may object that the megaform approach gives sufficient attention to the transport infrastructure or, conversely, that the physical form of the city is of little consequence in a telematic age. Alternatively, one may claim that urban

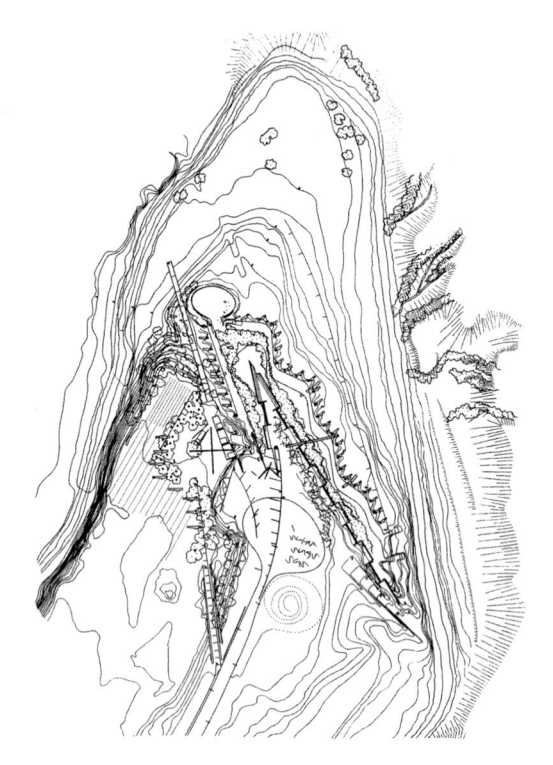

FIGURE 45 Igualada Cemetery, Barcelona, Spain. Enric Miralles and Carme Pinós, 1984–1994. Site plan.

culture in a classical sense can only be reconstituted typologically, or, conversely, that the traditional context of the historical city is no longer pertinent. Each of these polarized positions seem to be somewhat evasive to the extent that they fail to confront the responsibility of giving an identifiable shape or inflection to the late modem megalopolis.

Given the ruthless forms of motopian development that are currently transforming vast tracts of the Asian continent, we are again reminded that cities can no longer be realized as coherent entities according to the dictates of some master plan, nor can they always be developed in culturally significant ways on an incremental basis. While this last may have always been the case, what has changed dramatically in the last fifty years is the rate of technological change and the rapacity of development, occurring at a speed and scale which totally outstrips anything that urbanized society had experienced in the past. In addition to this, we may note that in many parts of the world the land is no longer significantly productive, that is to say, it is no longer used as a site for either agricultural or industrial production. Instead, there is a noticeable tendency to reduce the ground itself to a commodity through the interrelated processes of tourism, land speculation and the global expansion of the service industry. Under these conditions, late capitalism seems reluctant to commit itself to any form of land settlement that would be consistent with the production of coherent civic form.

Thus we may conclude that architects can only intervene urbanistically in an increasingly remedial manner and that one effective instrument for this is the large building program that may be rendered as a megaform—as an element which due to its size, content and direction has the capacity to inflect the surrounding landscape and give it a particular orientation and identity. I believe that such forms are capable of returning us to a time when the prime object of architecture was not the proliferation of freestanding objects but rather the marking of ground.

[...]

I have attempted to trace the recurrence of the megaform as a unifying environmental trope in twentieth century architecture and civic design in an effort to suggest that it may be one of the only formal legacies that remain available for the realistic mediation of the random megalopolis as an iterated form. Clearly not all the examples I have cited are pitched at the same scale or at an equal level of abstraction nor do they possess the same potential feasibility. Despite these variations, they all tend to blur in different ways the conventional differentiation between architecture and landscape. Like canals, railway cuttings, autoroutes, dykes and other artificial earthworks, they all have the potential of gathering up the contingent landscape around them by virtue of their anthrogeographic status, so much so that they may, at some juncture, appear to merge with the ground or alternatively to become, through their topographic presence, the status of being a landmark.

A certain "kinetic horizontality" is almost a precondition for the emergence of such forms, and in this regard it is important to observe that free-standing high-rise structures, for all their rival potential as landmarks, do not attain the same anthrogeographic status, unless they happen to be of the same height and rhythmically linked in a compelling way at grade. While this may seem to be a prescription verging on formalism, it should be evident that the arbitrary horizontal packaging of the program, irrespective of content, is not desirable. It is essential that our horizontal megaforms serve as civic microcosms and that they function as identifiable spaces of public appearance within the universal, ever-expanding context of Melvin Webber's "non-place urban realm." Hence it is not so difficult to adumbrate the programmatic types that seem to have the potential of engendering such forms. Aside from the unlikely prospect of being able to achieve extended areas of low-rise, high-density housing, one thinks, in no particular order, of shopping malls, air terminals, transport interchanges, hospitals, hotels, sports facilities, and universities—a series of type-forms in fact that still have a certain currency, not to say urgency, within the ever-expanding domain of the megalopolis [. . .].

15 Land Settlement, Architecture, and the Eclipse of the Public Realm (2000)

It is perhaps somewhat extraneous to approach the issue of pragmatics with an observation about the status of the *homo faber* at different moments in time. All the same, it is instructive to note that in the medieval period the master builder largely served the spiritual and temporal powers, the priest and the prince. Beginning in the French Enlightenment the responsibility of the architect turned toward designing institutions of the state. With the emergence of architecture as a bourgeois profession in the 19th century the client base became more secular and middle class, while in the 20th century radical socialism came to conceive of the architect as serving society as a whole. As the Dutch architect Aldo van Eyck once put it, "Previously the architect served the priest and the prince, now the priest and the prince are disestablished. Thus if not an architecture for all then no architecture at all." This aphoristic statement ought to remind us how removed we are from the various public housing programs promulgated in Europe and America between the two world wars as well as from the welfare state assumptions of the post-Second World War era.

Prior to the mass ownership of the automobile, a certain reciprocity existed between the distribution of civic amenities and the density of the residential fabric. Despite the advent of the street-car suburb, the railroad seems to have had only a limited impact on traditional patterns of land settlement. People still lived relatively close together because they could hardly do otherwise. What Hannah Arendt calls the "space of public appearance" was assured by the street and the civic institutions to which it gave access: the village green, the town hall, the school, the public library. However, after the Second World

Source: Kenneth Frampton, "Land Settlement, Architecture, and the Eclipse of the Public Realm" in *The Pragmatist Imagination: Thinking About "Things in the Making,"* ed. Joan Ockman (New York: Princeton Architectural Press, 2000), 104–11.

War "main street," which had hitherto served as the public spine of the provincial city or village, came to be undermined by the symbiotic effects of the interstate freeway system and the proliferation of shopping malls. The subsequent destruction of the traditional street by the suburban strip was an all-pervasive condition by the time Serge Chermayeff and Christopher Alexander published their seminal thesis in 1963, *Community and Privacy*. In retrospect, we may regard their low-rise, high-density housing paradigm as a neocapitalist, automotive land-settlement pattern capable of sustaining a modicum of public space while simultaneously resisting the tendency to commodify the landscape with regard to not only residential stock but also natural topography. *Community and Privacy* postulated an alternative pattern for decentralized land settlement that was neither the sedate garden city of the turn of the century nor the speculative subdivision that had come to dominate megalopolitan development in the second half of the 20th century. The very title of the book suggests a pattern of settlement capable of mediating between the privacy of the family and the communality of the public realm.

While metropolises were already being surrounded by suburbs by the middle of the 19th century, suburbanization did not really emerge as a global process until the mid-20th century. Soon after, the French geographer Jean Gottmann coined the term *megalopolis* to describe an urbanized region like the Bos–Wash corridor—the built-up, urbanized continuum extending from Boston to Washington, D.C.

Once the continental autoroute infrastructure was laid in place, suburbanization proved to have no natural limit, as attested by the fact that the number of people in North America living in suburbia has doubled since 1960. Today only a third of the population still lives in cities. The post-1945 suburbanization of the United States was facilitated through massive state subvention of the interstate freeway system. Combined with the not-so-benign neglect of rail transit and the kind of assisted suburban housing encouraged under the GI Bill and FHA mortgage regulations, this new network converged with the vested interests of the oil and automobile lobbies. The extent to which zoning codes and building regulations have been far from neutral in this regard is evident to any architect who has ever attempted to provide an alternative form of land settlement in a suburban context.

[. . .]

So much for the relevance of the architectural profession to the megalopolitan situation in which we find ourselves. If suburban privatization has led to negative political, cultural, social, and ecological consequences, from a more positive perspective we must insist on the dependence of democracy on spaces of public appearance. It is Arendt, again, who has put this most clearly in her book *The Human Condition*: "The only indispensable material factor in the generation of power is the living together of people. Only where men live so close together that the potentialities for action are always present can power remain with them, and the foundation of cities, which as city-states have remained paradigmatic for all Western political organization, is therefore indeed the most important material prerequisite for power."[1]

While such a classical formulation may fairly be challenged in our internet age with all its rhetoric of popular democracy, we have sufficient reason to be skeptical about the political benefits of this form of free-floating telematic interchange. It is here, perhaps, with the potential of physical space for sustaining face-to-face, confrontational discussion and debate, that the architect resurfaces as an agent who still has some marginal critical relevance in the late-modern world. How else, other than by providing a provocative public micro-realm, can the architectural profession significantly intervene in the universal megalopolis?

This question has hardly been addressed by the recent proliferation of prestigious museums, which are the late-modern equivalent of those 19th-century representational buildings that were once largely dedicated to the ministration of the spirit or the governance of the state.

Whether public micro-realms such as I have in mind come to be fully consummated by society in political terms cannot, of course, be predetermined; and in any case such a direct, naive hypothesis would be a regression into behaviorism. On the other hand, the consequences of the absence of real spaces of discourse—that is, the inadequate environmental articulation of such spaces—become manifest, in my view, in situations where face-to-face discourse has been inhibited or prohibited. It is significant that at the time of the late shah of Iran's so-called White Revolution the brief for the design of a university campus outside Isphahan carried the stipulation that the campus be designed in such a way that there would be no areas conducive to spontaneous public assembly.

It is symptomatic of the privatized suburbanization of our "motopian" society that such basic civic amenities as schools, sports arenas, shopping centers, and health facilities are invariably disaggregated from one another, either by unwalkable distances or by equally forbidding tracts of black-top parking unrelieved by any kind of planting or shelter. Thus, instead of augmenting and strengthening the space of public appearance that each institutional threshold potentially contributes to the public domain, the various civic and service institutions are split apart in such a way as to assure that only a single, specific function will be served, more or less in isolation, as efficiently as possible. While the recent emergence of the mega-mall as a quasi "city-in-miniature" can possibly be explained in part as a way of compensating for the extreme alienation experienced by society, this space too is exclusively dedicated to consumerism. Needless to say, it guarantees little in social or political terms. It is worth noting that such centralized marketing institutions are forbidden by law in Norway, where the citizenry has opted to preserve traditional shopping streets rather than ruin them economically through suburban mega-marketing methods.

---

[1] Hannah Arendt, *The Human Condition* (Chicago: University of Chicago Press, 1998 [1958]), p. 201.

It is a sign of the current confusion in architectural education and practice that we have largely lost our capacity to address ourselves critically to such socially degenerative manifestations. Surely, though, architecture has the capacity to concern itself with the specifics of such a program. The fact that it does not do so today speaks all too clearly to the issue at hand.

What we have witnessed over the past two decades largely amounts to a depoliticized aestheticization and technification of the architectural *modus operandi*—the relegation of the architectural program, that is, to a factor that is satisfied in the most immediate and rudimentary way imaginable, either through spectacular imagery or technical efficiency.

In contrast to this, we may evoke the kind of delicately nuanced programmatic design that used to make itself regularly manifest in the heyday of the modern movement, let us say between 1925 and 1975, especially in the design of such public amenities as high schools and hospitals. In these instances, particular attention was paid not only to aesthetic and representational values but also to the threshold or interface between the institution and society. Within these micro-spaces there was an adequate hierarchical articulation of the relationship of the public domain to the private, culture to nature, and so forth. We may perhaps exonerate the degeneration of this system of values in contemporary architectural practice by arguing that our current *modus* is nothing more than a direct reflection of the depoliticization of society as a whole. Indeed, the fact that one can hardly think of an exemplary school or hospital built in the United States in the last thirty years (let alone affordable housing) speaks to the fundamental malaise that lies at the base of all this: that is to say, our society's current incapacity to guarantee the fundamental civilized rights of education and health to all.

There are, however, two other basic issues with which the pragmatics of building culture must surely come to terms. The first is the time-honored issue of durability, that is, the degree to which any structure is capable of withstanding the ravages of time as well as its own inevitable transformation over time. The second is the emerging issue of sustainability, in the broad sense of the overall ecological fit between the building and its environment. Both of these factors have fundamental implications for the pragmatics of built culture, and both leave much to be desired with regard to the way in which architecture is generally taught and practiced in the United States today. In the first instance, there is the current fashion of deprecating detailed design in favor of an overall sculptural dynamism and three-dimensional gestalt, ignoring the intrinsic quality of the joints and seams that must necessarily be present in the constitution of any tectonic form. In the second instance—and it goes without saying—architectural culture stands to be enriched rather than impoverished by being modulated appropriately in ecological terms.

This implies a distancing from the globalizing technology that aspires to reduce built culture to a universal technique equally applicable all over the world irrespective of manifest variations in climate and topography, not to mention in local materials, techniques, and regional values. It is difficult to interrelate all these factors in a single synergetic entity and to demonstrate the dynamic relationships that obtain among land settlement patterns, welfare provisions (or lack thereof), building practices, and governmental ecological policies, in both a macro and a micro sense. If we could do so, however, we would more clearly grasp the web of symbiotic causalities necessary to assure specific desirable environmental qualities. These include not only a poetics of architecture but a potential contribution to the realization of a more liberative society.

Nevertheless, it is at least possible to indicate through a prognosis such as this one where the problem areas lie. As I have suggested, the latter are not only cultural but also political. To be sure, saying so changes nothing. Nonetheless, it appears a crucial if quixotic undertaking to articulate the condition, if for no other reason than that it is a way of contravening our prevalent tendency to fall into a kind of post-socialist euphoria—or should we say somnambulism—in which technocratic commodification is seen as inevitably determining every field of human endeavor without any redress.

SECTION 3
Cross-Cultural Trajectories, Place Creation, and the Politics of Counter Form

16 Introduction to Section 3

In the context of the quadripartite configuration of architecture–place–culture–the public realm, which has provided a critical framework for Frampton's work, the built form acts as the locus of their entanglements and also as the agent for creating dispositions towards both politics and action. In Frampton's view, such politically charged critical counter form is capable of resisting the pressures inherent in global modernization and universal technological civilization, and of simultaneously articulating the public realm in specific bounded domains. The section opens with "On Reading Heidegger,"[1] which appeared in the fourth issue of *Oppositions* in 1974 and offers Frampton's astute reading of the German philosopher's influential text "Building Dwelling Thinking,"[2] inflected with Frampton's commitment to Arendt. K. Michael Hays has suggested that in that "inaugural moment," the essay "defined what we call contemporary architecture theory."[3] After establishing important dialectical opposition between place (qualitative and static) and production (quantitative, dynamic, and abstract)—both via Arendt's distinction between the "what" and the "how"—Frampton returns to the idea that design goals may be legitimized only by the activation of the political realm as the embodiment of the collective. This essay also provides us with the phenomenological–hermeneutical basis for Frampton's critical theory of building as situated between the infrastructural and superstructural domains of human activity.

---

[1] Kenneth Frampton, "On Reading Heidegger," *Oppositions*, no. 4 (October 1974): Editorial Statement.

[2] It was originally published in German in 1954 as "*Bauen Wohnen Denken*" from a lecture Heidegger presented in 1951 in Germany, and then translated to English in 1971. See Martin Heidegger, *Poetry, Language, Thought*, trans. Albert Hofstadter (New York: Harper Colophon Books, 1971).

[3] K. Michael Hays, introductory notes to Kenneth Frampton's, "Megaform as Urban Landscape," Senior Loeb Scholar Lecture, Harvard Graduate School of Design, 25 October 2017, YouTube video, https://www.youtube.com/watch?v=USRaFhH7jIw.

Frampton's seminal 1983 essay "Towards a Critical Regionalism: Six Points for an Architecture of Resistance"[4] is commonly perceived as Frampton's single most influential piece of writing: Mary McLeod asserted that it "has probably had more impact on architects than any single essay published in the last fifty years,"[5] while Hays called it a "masterwork."[6] As is clear from the interview and the other essays included in this book, "Towards a Critical Regionalism" is a six-point manifesto that emerged at a critical moment for Frampton and for modern architecture alike. Three years earlier—in 1980, the same year *Modern Architecture: A Critical History* was published—Frampton had been invited to join the jury for the first Architectural Biennale in Venice, curated by Paolo Portoghesi. The exhibition was staged as a postmodern spectacle organized along *Strada Novissima*, complete with a series of scenographic fronts built by Cinecittà technicians. After realizing what was planned for the Biennale, Frampton resigned from the jury.[7] Other problematic influences occurring in parallel, as Frampton often notes, included the growing negative impact of Robert Stern on the culture of the Graduate School of Architecture, Planning and Preservation at Columbia University (where Frampton taught) and the overwhelming orientation of architecture schools toward the postmodern ideology. These issues prompted Frampton to put forth the cultural strategy of Critical Regionalism, first in an essay titled "Prospects for a Critical Regionalism," which appeared in 1983 in the journal *Perspecta*,[8] and then in Foster's *The Anti-Aesthetic* later the same year.[9]

---

[4] Kenneth Frampton, "Towards a Critical Regionalism: Six Points for an Architecture of Resistance," in *The Anti-Aesthetic: Essays in Postmodern Culture*, ed. Hal Foster (Port Townsend, Washington: Bay Press, 1983), 16–30. This essay appeared only three years after Frampton's *Modern Architecture: A Critical History* (London: Thames & Hudson, 1980) and a year after Frampton edited *Modern Architecture and the Critical Present* (London: Architectural Design, 1982).

[5] Mary McLeod, "Kenneth Frampton's Idea of the 'Critical,'" in Karla Cavarra Britton and Robert McCarter, eds., *Modern Architecture and the Lifeworld: Essays in Honor of Kenneth Frampton* (London: Thames & Hudson, 2020), 20.

[6] K. Michael Hays, introductory notes to Kenneth Frampton's "Megaform as Urban Landscape," Senior Loeb Scholar Lecture.

[7] The first Architectural Biennale had also prompted Jürgen Habermas to write his seminal essay "Modernity—An Incomplete Project," which was likewise included in *The Anti-Aesthetic* and later became critical to Frampton's scholarship. See Jürgen Habermas, "Modernity—An Incomplete Project," in *The Anti-Aesthetic: Essays in Postmodern Culture*, ed. Hal Foster (Port Townsend, Washington: Bay Press, 1983), 3–15. This essay was originally delivered as a talk in September 1980 when Habermas was awarded the Theodor W. Adorno prize. It was subsequently delivered as a James Lecture at the New York Institute for the Humanities at New York University in March 1981, and published as "Modernity versus Postmodernity" in *New German Critique* (Winter 1981).

[8] Kenneth Frampton, "Prospects for a Critical Regionalism," *Perspecta*, no. 20 (1983): 147–61.

[9] Both texts have their origin in Chapter 4 of *Modern Architecture: A Critical History*, titled "Place, Production and Architecture." For a recent critical take on the significance of Frampton's critical regionalism, see T. Avermaete, V. Patteeuw, H. Teerds, and L. C. Szacka, *Critical Regionalism Revisited*, *OASE* no. 103 (2019) Rotterdam: NAi 010 Publishers.

Noting that architectural production has shifted toward either pure technique or pure scenography—or both—Frampton argues that architecture can be conceived of as a critical practice only if it assumes an *arrière-garde* position that simultaneously "distances itself equally from the Enlightenment myth of progress and from a reactionary, unrealistic impulse to return to the architectonic forms of the preindustrial past." As Fredric Jameson suggested, Frampton's theory of Critical Regionalism—as both "descriptive and prescriptive" in intent—can thus be seen as simultaneously anti-modern and anti-postmodern, a double negative ("negation of the negation"), which intends neither to coax us to the ur-time of modernism nor to propose a belated form of it.[10] As a resistant counter practice, Hal Foster writes, Critical Regionalism stands in opposition "not only to the official culture of modernism but also to the 'false normativity' of a reactionary postmodernism."[11] In point number 4 of the manifesto—"The Resistance of the Place-Form"—Frampton evokes Heidegger's concept of "bounded domain" and argues that establishing a sovereign domain is the absolute precondition for the creation of an architecture of resistance. The resulting bounded place-form, as an institutional-physical form "in public mode," thus creates preconditions for the emergence of the Arendtian public realm in order to withstand "the endless processal flux of the Megalopolis." Frampton writes, "The tactile and the tectonic jointly have the capacity to transcend the mere appearance of the technical in much the same way as the place-form has the potential to withstand the relentless onslaught of global modernization."[12] This line serves as the pretext for Frampton 1984 essay "Tadao Ando's Critical Modernism"[13] published in a volume edited by Frampton—*Tadao Ando: Buildings, Projects, Writings* which also includes essays by Ando, Koji Taki, and Toshio Okumura—in which Frampton for the first time discusses Ando's "critical modernism" in the context of the just published Critical Regionalism framework.

Frampton advances the concept of place-form further through a less known but significant essay titled "Place-Form and Cultural Identity" (1988),[14] in which he confirms his intellectual trajectory as belonging to a certain generation of post-World War II architects. By the mid-1960s, he claims, "without the radical cultural and political programmes of the revolutionary modern movement," these architects had found themselves without a plausible and operative theoretical basis for their work, particularly in the context of the emerging influence of "reactionary" figures such as Leon Krier, Robert Venturi, and Charles Jencks. Returning to Paul Ricoeur's paradox—how to become modern and yet return

---

[10] Fredric Jameson, *The Seeds of Time* (New York: Columbia University Press, 1994), 189–90.

[11] Foster, *The Anti-Aesthetic*, xii.

[12] Frampton, "Towards a Critical Regionalism," 29.

[13] Kenneth Frampton, "Tadao Ando's Critical Modernism," in *Tadao Ando: Buildings, Projects, Writings*, ed. Kenneth Frampton (New York: Rizzoli, 1984), 6–9.

[14] Kenneth Frampton, "Place-Form and Cultural Identity," in *Design After Modernism: Beyond the Object*, ed. John Thackara (London: Thames & Hudson, 1988), 51–66.

to sources[15] (which had also opened "Towards a Critical Regionalism"), Frampton posits that a self-conscious "culture of place" and thereby more relevant architectural cultures ought to be found "on the periphery"—an idea he further explores in a series of published works, some of which are featured in this book. Even though this particular essay's "Five Points for Architecture of Resistance" are analogous to the titular "Six Points" of 1983, most important here is how Frampton explicitly acknowledges for the first time the aim of his work on Critical Regionalism since 1980: to develop a *critical theory of an architecture of resistance*.[16] Such a theory, Frampton writes, "demands a more fundamental reappraisal of the limits of the field, from both an ontological and a normative standpoint. It is nothing less than this last which I have attempted in elaborating this theory of 'place-form and cultural identity.'" Significant as well is this essay's conclusion, "Critical culture and the post-modern condition," in which Frampton discusses the contemporaneous debate between Jürgen Habermas and Jean-François Lyotard, and concludes with his ongoing commitment to Habermas' concept of "undistorted communication" and to the notion of "condition-situation" as the fundamental ground upon which a critical practice of architecture will have to locate its *métier*.

As a juror for the 2001 Aga Khan Award for Architecture,[17] Frampton co-edited the resulting publication, *Modernity and Community: Architecture in the Islamic World*.[18] Frampton's essay "Modernization and Local Culture," included in the present section, addresses the advancement of "sensibly reformed" modernist architectural practices that are capable of resisting the impact of technology-driven modernization in what he calls "degree zero"[19] local building

---

[15] Paul Ricoeur, "Universal Civilization and National Cultures" (1961), in *History and Truth*, trans. Charles A. Kelbley (Evanston, IL: Northwestern University Press, 1965), 276–77.

[16] Stylianos Giamarelos' research in the Kenneth Frampton archives at the Canadian Center for Architecture reveals an unpublished 1978 manuscript: "The Resistance of Architecture," a thirty-four-page typescript (CCA IAUS, C1-36 @ C1-83, IAUS files, 57–006, B 50 5 03, C1-42). An essay with the same title appears as "An Anthological Postscript" in Frampton's 1982 edited volume *Modern Architecture and the Critical Present* (pp. 85–119). At the time of writing "Place-Form and Cultural Identity" in 1988, Frampton was preparing a manuscript on Critical Regionalism to be published by Rizzoli, and this essay does seem to encapsulate key aspects of that proposal, completed the following year in 1989. As Giamarelos reports, by 1990, Frampton had given up on this book project and become skeptical about further prospects for the Critical Regionalism thesis. For reference, see Stylianos Giamarelos, *Resisting Postmodern Architecture: Critical Regionalism Before Globalisation* (London: UCL Press, 2022), 153–54.

[17] Aga Khan Award for Architecture (AKAA) is an architectural prize that recognizes architectural excellence in the Muslim world. For reference, see https://www.akdn.org/architecture.

[18] Kenneth Frampton, Charles Correa, and David Robson, eds., *Modernity and Community: Architecture in the Islamic World* (London: Thames & Hudson and The Aga Khan Award for Architecture, 2002).

[19] Frampton borrows the term "degree zero" from Roland Barthes to indicate a cultural break in which the traditional cultural system is weakened to the point where unforeseen socio-cultural phenomena begin to emerge. For further explication, see "Industrialization and the Crises in Architecture" in Section 1 of this book. The degree-zero building

cultures. The evidence of this Frampton finds in the Barefoot College campus in Tilonia, Rajasthan, India (1986–1999), designed by architect Neehar Raina after months of living with the local villagers and learning about local idioms, materials, and techniques.[20] Raina then handed his plans over to a collective of Barefoot Architects—local people with no formal education—who interpreted Raina's design and built the campus using locally available materials and techniques. Frampton focuses on what he calls "the cultural and collective core of the college," a central theatrical space at the center of the scheme that simultaneously employs the regional building syntax (the work of local builders) and implicitly evokes a "neo-Kahnian layout" with its main diagonal axis (the work of an academically educated young architect). An analogously topographic place-form was devised in 2000 by Heikkinen-Komonen Architects for the Kahere Eila Poultry Farming School in Koliagbe, Guinea, where its central courtyard serves as the collective core of the community. In these and other projects awarded in 2001, Frampton sees successful, ecologically minded local responses to the impacts of globalized forms of modernization that often are implemented through direct foreign investments in infrastructure and the built environment alike. In their refusal to abandon the emancipatory and progressive dimensions of the modern architectural legacy, the architects for these projects aspire to improve the living conditions of ordinary people in ordinary places, through designs that are sensitive to the regional culture yet also critical of its shortcomings—and in the process, they create what Frampton sees as paradigms of a "future hybrid civilization."

Such hybridity stands at the core of Frampton's concept of "world architecture," which appears in his public talks after 2010, and as Part IV in the fifth edition (2020) of his *Modern Architecture*. Inspired by Milan Kundera's concept of the emerging "world literature,"[21] Frampton focuses on anthropogeographic

---

culture is to be differentiated from vernacular architecture as defined by, for example, Bernard Rudofsky. "The term regional is not intended to denote the vernacular," Frampton writes, "as this was once spontaneously produced by the combined interaction of climate, culture and craft, but rather to identify those regional 'schools' whose aim has been to represent and serve particular constituencies. Such regionalism depends, by definition, on an explicit or implicit rapport between body politic and the architectural profession." For reference, see Kenneth Frampton, "The Isms of Contemporary Architecture," in *Modern Architecture and the Critical Present* (London: Architectural Design, 1982), 77. This essay has its origin in Kenneth Frampton, "*Du Néo-Productivisme au Post-Modernisme*," in *Architecture d'Aujourd'hui*, no. 213 (1981): 2–7. See also Bernard Rudofsky, *Architecture Without Architect: A Short Introduction to Non-Pedigreed Architecture* (New York: Museum of Modern Art, 1969).

[20] For the controversy surrounding the 2001 Aga Khan Award for Architecture, see Sonu Jain, "Tilonia's Barefoot Campus: Now the Bare Facts," *The Indian Express*, 30 June 2002.

[21] Kundera borrows the term from Johann Wolfgang Goethe. For reference, see Milan Kundera, "*Die Weltliteratur*: How We Read One Another," *The New Yorker* (8 January 2007).

building cultures that possess a creative yet fragile poetic character, explaining, "This is the key of momentary culture that I seek to identify and recognize."[22] Mobilization of the key values, principles, and tropes of modern architecture across cultural and national boundaries, including translations (with both intended and unintended slippages), has been the vehicle for the development of a world architecture that simultaneously challenges the modernist master narratives with discourses of "others." This line of inquiry is exemplified here by two essays: In the first, "The Predicament of the Place-Form: Notes from New York" (1997),[23] Frampton explores low-rise, high-density aggregate housing proposals by Indian architects and planners who have developed economical models of residential settlements in response to accelerating degrees of urbanization that parallels or exceeds that of the Western world. Tracing the mobility of ideas and models between European and American architects and their Indian colleagues, Frampton discusses the work of prominent Indian architects Charles Correa, Balkrishna Doshi, Kamran Diba, and others, arguing that the courtyard housing model developed in India (unlike the mainstream land settlement models in the United States) secures spaces of public appearance at various scales. In the second such essay, "Plan Form and Topography in the Work of Kashef Chowdhury" (2016),[24] Frampton primarily discusses Chowdhury's Friendship Centre (2010–2012) in Gaibandha, Bangladesh, and the architect's heightened sensibility to the intricacies of this geo-cultural region. This "mat building" creates an elevated datum so as to register the public realm—to which all private and semi-public spaces are connected through its labyrinthine Piranesian volume—yet it also emerges "out of the collective Bengal memory of ancient Buddhist monasteries as out of the increased threat of inundation due to escalating climate change."

Typical of Kenneth Frampton, on the occasion of being made a Fellow of the Society of Architectural Historians (SAH) in 2018, he declared himself a teacher of architecture and not an architectural historian.[25] In his plenary talk for that conference, which concludes this section, Frampton revisits his most cited and influential scholarly accomplishments, aligning them through a career-long attempt to determine the basis upon which a responsible culture of architecture can be pursued. One line of inquiry emphasized in this talk, through Frampton's own writing and through Fredric Jameson's critique,[26] is

---

[22] Kenneth Frampton, *Modern Architecture: A Critical History*, 5th ed. (London: Thames & Hudson, 2020), 368.

[23] Kenneth Frampton, "The Predicament of the Place-Form: Notes from New York," in *Contemporary Architecture and City Form: The South Asian Paradigm*, ed. Farooq Ameen (Mumbai: Marg Publications, 1997), 101–9.

[24] Kenneth Frampton, "Plan Form and Topography in the Work of Kashef Chowdhury," in Kenneth Frampton and Robert Wilson, *Kashef Chowdhury: The Friendship Centre, Gaibandha, Bangladesh* (Zürich: Park Books, 2016), 8–12.

[25] Kenneth Frampton, Plenary Talk at the 71st Annual International Conference of the Society of Architectural Historians, 20 April 2018, Saint Paul, MN.

[26] Jameson, *The Seeds of Time*, 189–90.

the "rapport" between some European architects and the "city-states" in which they live and work—distinctive regional cultures with a "cantonal sense of political sovereignty," which Frampton recognizes as the necessary precondition for the establishment of a region-specific, responsible culture of architecture. Frampton refers here to his reading of Arendt's discussion of *polis*, but also returns to the Heideggerian notion of "bounded domain," within which such a rooted culture of architecture presents a model of the *rear-garde* practice. As Jameson points out, the strength of the entire Critical Regionalist argument is predicated on the capacity of the building to "transfigure the burden of the modern" by the critical operations of "enclosing" and "reopening."[27] However, one of the crucial points that remain open, as Frampton never addressed it directly, is the connotations of "resistance" in the Critical Regionalist discourse vis-à-vis more contemporary notions of multi- and interculturalism (as Jameson suggests) but also in relation to the operation of "pluralizing modernity," which, as Arturo Escobar rightly proposes, unintentionally risks reinforcing "the universality of dominant modern ways of seeing."[28]

As if in direct response to such assertions, Frampton writes the following in a 2013 opinion essay in *Domus*:

> Even if we have no choice but to forego any naïve assumptions as to local sovereignty, regionally counter-hegemonic tectonic form surely still retains at the grass roots level the capacity to resist the variously reductive forms of stylistic postmodernism with which the hegemonic power of the centre prefers to surround itself . . . Thus, for me, a liberative promise for the future resides in an agonistic architecture of the periphery as opposed to the subtle nonjudgmental conformism of ruling taste emanating from the centre.[29]

While Jameson's critique of Critical Regionalism—which Frampton accepted as a staunch Marxist take and also called "outstanding"—resides in his skepticism about the political and cultural viability of the concept of the semi-autonomous regional city-state, Frampton insists that the constitution of city-states as political and cultural entities resides in their ability to develop (or preserve) a culture of real political strength and identity, and thereby their power to constitute the public realm.

---

[27] Jameson, *The Seeds of Time*, 201.

[28] Arturo Escobar, *Designs for the Pluriverse: Radical Interdependence, Autonomy, and the Making of Worlds* (Durham, NC: Duke University Press, 2018), 210.

[29] Kenneth Frampton, "Towards an Agonistic Architecture," *Domus* 972 (September 2013), https://www.domusweb.it/en/opinion/2013/10/03/_towards_an_agonistic_architecture.html. See also Section 4 in this volume.

As there are many ways of practicing architecture, there are many ways of writing history, and many different kinds of historians and architects. And the question whether I am, strictly speaking, a historian is a moot point. I'm someone who thinks that it's very difficult to enter into any theoretical discussion of architecture without historical references, without the processing of history in relation to the present. I'm also someone who thinks, along with E.H. Carr, that each age writes its own history, that there is no final, definitive, objective history because history is also a cultural activity. Having said that, the question of whether one works as a historian or not is another issue: when I put together a collection of essays [*Labour, Work and Architecture*] published by Phaidon, maybe much too self-consciously I went out of the way saying I don't know if I am strictly speaking a historian: the reason being that they decided to organize the book into sections called 'history,' 'theory,' and 'criticism.' I felt compelled because it wasn't my decision, it was the editor's decision to do that; maybe it was a good decision, by the way. It's one way of arranging an otherwise heterogeneous mass of writings . . . Nonetheless, I felt obliged to say, well, 'Am I strictly a historian?' I'm not sure I am. Am I strictly a theoretician? I don't think I am. Am I a critic? Also, again, it was negative. I sort of settled for the title of *writer*, for what it's worth. That's very evasive, but I do think it's important to try to be engaged *now*, you know. 'Those that can, do; those that can't, teach,' and there are people who both do and teach—but not me! They're the best, probably, as in the time of apprenticeship before universities. But if one is going to teach, or engage in teaching activities closely, I think it is quite important to try to—I'm going to use the word *calibrate*—present production, to try to find a way of *beholding it*, which is productive, enlightening. I don't know if I can say anything more than that.

Kenneth Frampton, "Architecture in the Age of Globalization"
(lecture, Harvard Graduate School of Design, 25 July 2013).

17 On Reading Heidegger
(1975)

> The nature of building is letting dwell. Building accomplishes its nature in the raising of locations by the joining of their spaces. Only if we are capable of dwelling, only then can we build.
>
> Martin Heidegger, Building Dwelling Thinking

It becomes increasingly clear, as the utopian hallucinations of the Enlightenment fade, that we have long been in the habit of using too many synonyms; not only in our everyday speech but also in our more specialized languages. We still fail, for example, to make any satisfactory distinction between architecture and building, despite the fact that we are, at the same time, inconscionably aware that such a distinction should be made. We know, for instance, that Mies van der Rohe was at pains throughout his life to recognize this distinction and that in his own work he asserted the mediatory realm of *Baukunst* (the "art of building"), a Teutonic term for which there is no satisfactory English equivalent. All of this would be mere etymological speculation were we not constantly being reminded of the issue by those cultural and operational discrepancies that invariably arise between the generation of built form and its reception by society. This *lapsus* is sufficient to suggest that these everyday disjunctions must have at least some of their origins in our persistent failure to make such a distinction in building practice. There, in the physical realm of the built world, we seem to be presented with dramatic proof of the paradoxical Heideggerian thesis that language, far from being the servant of man, is all too often his master. We would, for instance, invariably prefer to posit the ideal of architecture—the monument in every circumstance be it public or private, the major opus—for situations that simply demand "building" and we are commonly led to realize the irreducibility of this fact, fatally after the event.

As with that which we would fain idealize in the projection, so with that which we would rationalize after the misconception and here we find that the

Source: Kenneth Frampton, "On Reading Heidegger," *Oppositions* no. 4 (1974): Editorial Statement.

ironic mystifications of Candide have much in common with the deception of our own more recent ideologies. Surely this was never more evident than in, say, Daniel Bell's presumptuous announcement of the end of ideology or in Melvin Webber's ingenious celebration of the "non-place urban realm"; that apotheosis of late liberal capitalism posited, not to say "deposited," as the existing paradise of Los Angeles. In this last context, we are supposed (according to the received program of the idealogues) not only to recognize but further even to welcome with enthusiasm the utopian advent of this "community without propinquity," to quote yet another appealing phrase of more than a decade ago.

The intervening lapse of time has done little to neutralize such rationalization. The actual phrases may have passed from our lips but the mental sets largely remain and it is these that unavoidably condition us as we go about our work. Should we choose, through some inner inadequacy or protracted sense of responsibility, to eschew autonomous art or the liberating promise of the poetic intellect, then all too often, we will find ourselves conflating in the name of populism the objects of elitist culture with elaborate rationalizations of the environment as found. In such a vein, we will seek to sublimate the frustrations of utopia with the sadness of suburbia or with the enervations of the strip; and while we will self-consciously appeal, by way of justification, to an illusory vernacular, the true nature of our Western predicament will continue to escape us. Between the Charybdis of elitism and the Scylla of populism, the full dimension of our historical dilemma will remain hidden.

Nowhere are the turns of this labyrinth more evident, as Heidegger tries to make clear, than in our language, than in our persistent use of, say, the Latin term "space" or *"spatium"* instead of "place" or the Germanic word *"Raum"*—the latter carrying with it, as it does, the explicit connotations of a clearing in which *to be*, a place in which to come into being. We have only to compare the respective Oxford English Dictionary definitions to appreciate the abstract connotations of "space" as opposed to the socially experienced nature of "place"; to confront construction *in extensio* with the act of significant containment.

This, again, would be empty speculation could we not point directly to our present all but total incapacity to create places; an incapacity that is as prevalent in our architectural schools and in the monuments of the elite, as it is in "motopia" at large. Place now appears as inimical to our received mental set, not only as architects but also as a society. In our ubiquitous "non-place" we congratulate ourselves regularly on our pathological capacity for abstraction; on our commitment to the norms of statistical coordination; on our bondage to the transactional processes of objectification that will admit to neither the luxury nor the necessity of place. We exonerate the strip, ever fearful to admit that we might have eliminated, once and for all, the possibility of ever being anywhere. We vaunt our much prized mobility, our "rush city," to coin Neutra's innocent phrase, our consumption of frenetic traction, only to realize that should we stop, there are few places within which any of us might significantly choose to be. Blithely, we exchange our already tenuous hold on the public sphere for the electronic distractions of the private future. Despite this, outside the "mass" engineered somnambulism of television, we still indulge in the proliferation of roadside kitsch—in the fabricated mirage of "somewhere" made out of billboard facades and token theatrical paraphernalia—the fantasmagoria of an escape clause from the landscape of alienation. In all this, the degeneration of the language speaks for itself. Terms such as "defoliation" and "pedestrianization" enter everyday speech as categories drawn from the same processes of technological rationalization. With "newspeak" overtones, they testify to a fundamental break in our rapport with nature (including our own), they speak of a laying waste that can only find its ultimate end in ourselves. Against this, it would seem that the apparent universal triumph of the "non-place urban realm" may only be modified through a profound consciousness of history and through a rigorous socio-political analysis of the present, seen as a continuing fulfillment of the past. We have no choice but to reformulate the dialectical constituents of the world, to determine more consciously the necessary links obtaining between *place* and *production*, between the "what" and the "how." This reciprocation of ends and mean binds us to an historical reality wherein the *tabula rasa* fantasies of the Enlightenment lose a deal of their authority. With the manifest exhaustion of non-renewable resources the technotopic myth of unlimited progress become somewhat discredited and, at this juncture, the *production of place* returns us by way of economic limit not to architecture but to *Baukunst* and to that which Aldo Van Eyck has already called the "timelessness of man."

Accepting the limits of our historical circumstance and the perennial conflict of end with means and of freedom with necessity, that which remains critical is the process by which decisive priorities are established; for in the last analysis, as Jürgen Habermas and Giancarlo De Carlo have reminded us, design goals, as the motives of our instrumentality, may only be legitimized through the activation of the public sphere—a political realm that, in its turn, is reciprocally dependent on the representational and physical embodiment of the collective. Place, at this juncture, irrespective of its scale, takes on its archetypal aspect, its ancient attribute which is as much political as it is ontological. Its sole legitimacy stems, as it must, from the social constituency it accommodates and represents.

The minimum physical pre-condition for place is the conscious placement of an object in nature, even if that artifice be nothing more than an object in the landscape or the rearrangement of nature herself. At the same time, the mere existence of an object in and of itself guarantees nothing. The cyclical processes of modern production and consumption seem to be more than adequately matched for the exhaustion of every resource and for the laying waste to all production irrespective of the rate at which it is generated. To rationalize this so-called optimization in the name of human adaptability and progress is to ideologize the self alienation of man. One has to recognize the dialectical opposition of place and production and not confuse the one with the other, that is, ends with means. For where *place* is essentially qualitative and in and of itself concrete and static, *production* tends to stress quantity and to be in and of itself dynamic and abstract.

Place, as an Aristotelean phenomenon, arises at a symbolic level with the conscious signification of social meaning and at a concrete level with the establishment of an articulate realm on which man or men may come into being. The receptivity and sensitive resonance of a place—to wit its sensate validity *qua* place—depends first on its stability in the everyday sense and second on the appropriateness and richness of the socio-cultural experiences it offers.

Production, on the other hand, clearly has its own laws, which are tied into a reality that none of us can escape. But the margin of choice that always remains, demands to be fully exploited, less we arrive by default at the government of nobody, at that so-called utilitarian tyranny of technique. Since the "what" is fatally tied to the "how," everything resides in how and to what end we choose to modify the relevant optimal sub-categories of production, not only those of the built form itself, but also those structurally productive force that implacably shape the built environment as elements in the general economy of our relations to nature.

A state of affairs, in which on the threshold of famine large amounts of prime agricultural land are continually lost to urbanization and mining without the exercise of adequate restraint, can hardly be regarded as economic in any fundamental sense, just as the proliferation of suburban sprawl can have little significance beyond stimulating land speculation and maximizing the amortization of investment in certain lines of consumer production. Certainly the creation of place, in both an ontological and political sense is generally ill-served by our persistent policies of laissez-faire dispersal, and what is true for the essence of the *res publica* applies with equal force to the "catchment" limits of public transportation. All discourse on the built environment that does not make at least a reference to these kinds of basic contradictions, between the so-called short and long term interests in the society, tends toward a mystification of the historical circumstances in which we work.

At the more specific level of built form, production considered solely as an economy of method has the unfortunate tendency of inhibiting rather than facilitating the creation of receptive places. A case in point is the universal tendency toward stereometric high-rise flat slab construction where economy in erection is granted absolute priority over any other morphological consideration. By a similar token, the industrialization or rationalization of building, as the unavoidable consequence of the inviability of high craft production in a mass society, should not be regarded as beneficial in itself, particularly where such methods lead, through an abstract optimization, to a manifest impoverishment of the environment. And here, in this hypothetical confrontation between the *macro-scaled environmental desirability* of urban containment and *micro-scaled environmental undesirability* of high-rise construction, we have perhaps a convenient if highly schematic example of what one might regard as *an environmental dialectic of production*, that is, a state of affairs wherein the quantitative and qualitative gains at one level should be evaluated against the quantitative and qualitative losses at another.

The necessary relations obtaining between *place, production, and nature* implacably suggest the biological concept of the "homeostatic plateau," wherein the energy feedback loops of an organic metabolism serve to sustain the steady state of its overall system—the "zero-growth" feedback syndrome in nature.

Comparable structural models in the field of the built environment have long since been posited at varying levels of detail from N.A. Miliutin's linear agro-industrial city to Ralph Knowles' metabolic profiling of the built environment, as though it were a climatic and topographic extension of the landscape itself. The rooted ecological nature of such otherwise abstract models finds its reflection in the direct recycling of body-waste for the purpose of horticultural production, or in the conservation of the overall energy required for the tasks of heating and cooling. It should come as no surprise that up to now, despite the current fad for solar energy studies, short-term interests have effectively inhibited anything but the most limited application of such models and one may take it as a reflection of these interests that architectural schools have largely ceased to concern themselves with such matters.

This aloof critique of current design praxis and its pedagogical substance bring us to the question once again of the full nature of the art of building. The present tendency to polarize the quintessence of built form as though it were of necessity one single thing appears to my mind to be nothing other than an ideological refusal to confront historical reality. The building task intrinsically resists such polarization. It remains fatally situated at that phenomenological interface between the infrastructural and superstructural realms of human production. There it ministers to the self-realization of man in nature and mediates as an essential catalyst between the three states of his existence: first, his status as an organism of primal need; second, his status as a sensate, hedonistic being; and finally, his status as a cognitive, self-affirmative consciousness. Autonomous artistic production certainly has many provinces but the task of place creation, in its broadest sense, is not necessarily one of them. The compensatory drive of autonomous art tends to remove it from the concrete realization of man in the world and to the extent that architecture seeks to preempt all culture it consciously divorces itself from both building and the realm of historical reality. This much Adolf Loos has already intimated by 1910, when he wrote with characteristic but understandable overstatement: "Only a very small part of architecture belongs to art: the tomb and the monument."

18 Towards a Critical Regionalism: Six Points for an Architecture of Resistance (1983)

The phenomenon of universalization, while being an advancement of mankind, at the same time constitutes a sort of subtle destruction, not only of traditional cultures, which might not be an irreparable wrong, but also of what I shall call for the time being the creative nucleus of great cultures, that nucleus on the basis of which we interpret life, what I shall call in advance the ethical and mythical nucleus of mankind. The conflict springs up from there. We have the feeling that this single world civilization at the same time exerts a sort of attrition or wearing away at the expense of the cultural resources which have made the great civilizations of the past. This threat is expressed, among other disturbing effects, by the spreading before our eyes of a mediocre civilization which is the absurd counterpart of what I was just calling elementary culture. Everywhere throughout the world, one finds the same bad movie, the same slot machines, the same plastic or aluminum atrocities, the same twisting of language by propaganda, etc. It seems as if mankind, by approaching *en masse* a basic consumer culture, were also stopped *en masse* at a subcultural level. Thus we come to the crucial problem confronting nations just rising from underdevelopment. In order to get on to the road toward modernization, is it necessary to jettison the old cultural past which has been the *raison d'être* of a nation? . . . Whence the paradox: on the one hand, it has to root itself in the soil of its past, forge a national spirit, and unfurl this spiritual and cultural revindication before the colonialist's personality. But in order to take part in modern civilization, it is necessary at the same time to take part in scientific, technical, and political rationality, something which very often requires the pure and simple abandon of a whole cultural past. It is a fact: every culture cannot sustain and absorb the shock of modern civilization. There is the paradox: how to become modern and to return to sources; how to revive an old, dormant civilization and take part in universal civilization.[1]

Paul Ricoeur, *History and Truth*

Source: Kenneth Frampton, "Towards a Critical Regionalism: Six Points for an Architecture of Resistance," in *The Anti-Aesthetic: Essays in Postmodern Culture*, ed. Hal Foster (Port Townsend, Washington: Bay Press, 1983), 16–30.

[1] Paul Ricoeur, "Universal Civilization and National Cultures" (1961), *History and Truth*, trans. Chas. A. Kelbley (Evanston: Northwestern University Press, 1965), pp. 276–7.

1. CULTURE AND CIVILIZATION

Modern building is now so universally conditioned by optimized technology that the possibility of creating significant urban form has become extremely limited. The restrictions jointly imposed by automotive distribution and the volatile play of land speculation serve to limit the scope of urban design to such a degree that any intervention tends to be reduced either to the manipulation of elements predetermined by the imperatives of production, or to a kind of superficial masking which modern development requires for the facilitation of marketing and the maintenance of social control. Today the practice of architecture seems to be increasingly polarized between, on the one hand, a so-called "high-tech" approach predicated exclusively upon production and, on the other, the provision of a "compensatory facade" to cover up the harsh realities of this universal system.[2]

Twenty years ago the dialectical interplay between civilization and culture still afforded the possibility of maintaining some general control over the shape and significance of the urban fabric. The last two decades, however, have radically transformed the metropolitan centers of the developed world. What were still essentially 19th-century city fabrics in the early 1960s have since become progressively overlaid by the two symbiotic instruments of Megalopolitan development—the freestanding high-rise and the serpentine freeway. The former has finally come into its own as the prime device for realizing the increased land value brought into being by the latter. The typical downtown which, up to twenty years ago, still presented a mixture of residential stock with tertiary and secondary industry has now become little more than a *burolandschaft* city-scape: the victory of universal civilization over locally inflected culture. The predicament posed by Ricoeur—namely, "how to become modern and to return to sources"[3]—now seems to be circumvented by the apocalyptic thrust of modernization, while the ground in which the mytho-ethical nucleus of a society might take root has become eroded by the rapacity of development.[4]

---

[2] That these are but two sides of the same coin has perhaps been most dramatically demonstrated in the Portland City Annex completed in Portland, Oregon in 1982 to the designs of Michael Graves. The constructional fabric of this building bears no relation whatsoever to the "representative" scenography that is applied to the building both inside and out.

[3] Ricoeur, p. 277.

[4] Fernand Braudel informs us that the term "culture" hardly existed before the beginning of the 19th century when, as far as Anglo-Saxon letters are concerned, it already finds itself opposed to "civilization" in the writings of Samuel Taylor Coleridge—above all, in Coleridge's *On the Constitution of Church and State* of 1830. The noun "civilization" has a somewhat longer history, first appearing in 1766, although its verb and participle forms date to the 16th and 17th centuries. The use that Ricoeur makes of the opposition between these two terms relates to the work of 20th-century German thinkers and writers such as Osvald Spengler, Ferdinand Tönnies, Alfred Weber and Thomas Mann.

Ever since the beginning of the Enlightenment, *civilization* has been primarily concerned with instrumental reason, while *culture* has addressed itself to the specifics of expression—to the realization of the being and the evolution of its *collective* psycho-social reality. Today civilization tends to be increasingly embroiled in a never-ending chain of "means and ends" wherein, according to Hannah Arendt, "The 'in order to' has become the content of the 'for the sake of' utility established as meaning generates meaninglessness."[5]

2. THE RISE AND FALL OF THE AVANT-GARDE

The emergence of the avant-garde is inseparable from the modernization of both society and architecture. Over the past century-and-a-half avant-garde culture has assumed different roles, at times facilitating the process of modernization and thereby acting, in part, as a progressive, liberative form, at times being virulently opposed to the positivism of bourgeois culture. [. . .]

The progressive avant-garde emerges in full force, however, soon after the turn of the century with the advent of Futurism. This unequivocal critique of the *ancien régime* gives rise to the primary positive cultural formations of the 1920s: to Purism, Neoplasticism and Constructivism. These movements are the last occasion on which radical avant-gardism is able to identify itself wholeheartedly with the process of modernization. In the immediate aftermath of World War I—"the war to end all wars"—the triumphs of science, medicine and industry seemed to confirm the liberative promise of the modern project. In the 1930s, however, the prevailing backwardness and chronic insecurity of the newly urbanized masses, the upheavals caused by war, revolution and economic depression, followed by a sudden and crucial need for psycho-social stability in the face of global political and economic crises, all induce a state of affairs in which the interests of both monopoly and state capitalism are, for the first time in modern history, divorced from the liberative drives of cultural modernization. Universal civilization and world culture cannot be drawn upon to sustain "the myth of the State," and one reaction-formation succeeds another as the historical avant-garde founders on the rocks of the Spanish Civil War.

Not least among these reactions is the reassertion of Neo-Kantian aesthetics as a substitute for the culturally liberative modern project. Confused by the political and cultural politics of Stalinism, former left-wing protagonists of socio-cultural modernization now recommend a strategic withdrawal from the project of totally transforming the existing reality. This renunciation is predicated on the belief that as long as the struggle between socialism and capitalism

---

[5] Hannah Arendt, *The Human Condition* (Chicago: University of Chicago Press, 1958), p. 154.

persists (with the manipulative mass-culture politics that this conflict necessarily entails), the modern world cannot continue to entertain the prospect of evolving a marginal, liberative, avant-gardist culture which would break (or speak of the break) with the history of bourgeois repression. Close to *l'art pour l'art*, this position was first advanced as a "holding pattern" in Clement Greenberg's "Avant-Garde and Kitsch" of 1939; this essay concludes somewhat ambiguously with the words: "Today we look to socialism *simply* for the preservation of whatever living culture we have right now."[6] Greenberg reformulated this position in specifically formalist terms in his essay "Modernist Painting" of 1965.[7]

[...]

Despite this defensive intellectual stance, the arts have nonetheless continued to gravitate, if not towards entertainment, then certainly towards commodity and—in the case of that which Charles Jencks has since classified as Post-Modern Architectures[8]—towards pure technique or pure scenography. In the latter case, the so-called postmodern architects are merely feeding the media-society with gratuitous, quietistic images rather than proffering, as they claim, a creative *rappel a l'ordre* after the supposedly proven bankruptcy of the liberative modern project. In this regard, as Andreas Huyssens has written, "The American postmodernist avant-garde, therefore, is not only the end game of avant-gardism. It also represents the fragmentation and decline of critical adversary culture."[9]

Nevertheless, it is true that modernization can no longer be simplistically identified as liberative *in se*, in part because of the domination of mass culture by the media-industry (above all television which, as Jerry Mander reminds us, expanded its persuasive power a thousandfold between 1945 and 1975)[10] and in part because the trajectory of modernization has brought us to the threshold

---

[6] Clement Greenberg, "Avant-Garde and Kitsch," in Gillo Dorfles, ed., *Kitsch* (New York: Universe Books, 1969), p. 126.

[7] "Having been denied by the Enlightenment of all tasks they could take seriously, they [the arts] looked as though they were going to be assimilated to entertainment pure and simple, and entertainment looked as though it was going to be assimilated, like religion, to therapy. The arts could save themselves from this leveling down only by demonstrating that the kind of experience they provided was valuable in its own right and not to be obtained from any other kind of activity." Greenberg, "Modernist Painting," in Gregory Battcock, ed., *The New Art* (New York: Dutton, 1966), pp. 101–2 [quote converted to footnote by the editor].

[8] See Charles Jencks, *The Language of Post-Modern Architecture* (New York: Rizzoli, 1977).

[9] Andreas Huyssens, "The Search for Tradition: Avant-Garde and Postmodernism in the 1970s," *New German Critique*, 22 (Winter 1981), p. 34.

[10] Jerry Mander, *Four Arguments for the Elimination of Television* (New York: Morrow Quill, 1978), p. 134.

of nuclear war and the annihilation of the entire species. So too, avant-gardism can no longer be sustained as a liberative moment, in part because its initial utopian promise has been overrun by the internal rationality of instrumental reason.[11]
[...]

3. CRITICAL REGIONALISM AND WORLD CULTURE

Architecture can only be sustained today as a critical practice if it assumes an *arrière-garde* position, that is to say, one which distances itself equally from the Enlightenment myth of progress and from a reactionary, unrealistic impulse to return to the architectonic forms of the preindustrial past. A critical arrière-garde has to remove itself from both the optimization of advanced technology and the ever-present tendency to regress into nostalgic historicism or the glibly decorative. It is my contention that only an arrière-garde has the capacity to cultivate a resistant, identity-giving culture while at the same time having discreet recourse to universal technique.

It is necessary to qualify the term arrière-garde so as to diminish its critical scope from such conservative policies as Populism or sentimental Regionalism with which it has often been associated. In order to ground arrière-garde in a rooted yet critical strategy, it is helpful to appropriate the term Critical Regionalism as coined by Alex Tzonis and Liliane Lefaivre in "The Grid and the Pathway" (1981); in this essay they caution against the ambiguity of regional reformism, as this has become occasionally manifest since the last quarter of the 19th century[12] [...]

---

[11] This "closure" was perhaps best formulated by Herbert Marcuse when he wrote: "The technological *apriori* is a political *apriori* inasmuch as the transformation of nature involves that of man, and inasmuch as the 'man-made creations' issue from and re-enter the societal ensemble. One may still insist that the machinery of the technological universe is 'as such' indifferent towards political ends—it can revolutionize or retard society ... However, when technics becomes the universal form of material production, it circumscribes an entire culture, it projects a historical totality—a 'world.'" Herbert Marcuse, *One-Dimensional Man* (Boston: Beacon Press, 1964), p. 156 [Quote converted to footnote by the editor].

[12] "Regionalism has dominated architecture in almost all countries at some time during the past two centuries and a half. By way of general definition we can say that it upholds the individual and local architectonic features against more universal and abstract ones. In addition, however, regionalism bears the hallmark of ambiguity. On the one hand, it has been associated with movements of reform and liberation; ... on the other, it has proved a powerful tool of repression and chauvinism ... Certainly, critical regionalism has its limitations. The upheaval of the populist movement—a more developed form of regionalism—has brought to light these weak points. No new architecture can emerge without a new kind of relations between designer and user, without new kinds of programs ... Despite these limitations critical regionalism is a bridge over which any humanistic architecture of the future must pass." Alexander Tzonis and Liliane Lefaivre, "The Grid and the Pathway: An Introduction to the Work of Dimitris and Susana Antonakakis," *Architecture in Greece*, 15 (Athens: 1981), p. 178 [Quote converted to footnote by the editor].

The fundamental strategy of Critical Regionalism is to mediate the impact of universal civilization with elements derived *indirectly* from the peculiarities of a particular place. It is clear from the above that Critical Regionalism depends upon maintaining a high level of critical self-consciousness. It may find its governing inspiration in such things as the range and quality of the local light, or in a *tectonic* derived from a peculiar structural mode, or in the topography of a given site.

But it is necessary, as I have already suggested, to distinguish between Critical Regionalism and simple-minded attempts to revive the hypothetical forms of a lost vernacular. In contradistinction to Critical Regionalism, the primary vehicle of Populism is the *communicative* or *instrumental* sign. Such a sign seeks to evoke not a critical perception of reality, but rather the sublimation of a desire for direct experience through the provision of information. Its tactical aim is to attain, as economically as possible, a preconceived level of gratification in behavioristic terms. In this respect, the strong affinity of Populism for the rhetorical techniques and imagery of advertising is hardly accidental. Unless one guards against such a convergence, one will confuse the resistant capacity of a critical practice with the demagogic tendencies of Populism.

The case can be made that Critical Regionalism as a cultural strategy is as much a bearer of *world culture* as it is a vehicle of *universal civilization*. And while it is obviously misleading to conceive of our inheriting world culture to the same degree as we are all heirs to universal civilization, it is nonetheless evident that since we are, in principle, subject to the impact of both, we have no choice but to take cognizance today of their interaction. In this regard the practice of Critical Regionalism is contingent upon a process of double mediation. In the first place, it has to "deconstruct" the overall spectrum of world culture which it inevitably inherits; in the second place, it has to achieve, through synthetic contradiction, a manifest critique of universal civilization. To deconstruct world culture is to remove oneself from that eclecticism of the *fin-de-siècle* which appropriated alien, exotic forms in order to revitalize the expressivity of an enervated society [. . .] On the other hand, the mediation of universal technique involves imposing limits on the optimization of industrial and postindustrial technology.[13] [. . .]

The scope for achieving a self-conscious synthesis between universal civilization and world culture may be specifically illustrated by Jørn Utzon's Bagsværd Church, built near Copenhagen in 1976, a work whose complex

---

[13] The future necessity for resynthesizing principles and elements drawn from diverse origins and quite different ideological sets seems to be alluded to by Ricoeur when he writes: "No one can say what will become of our civilization when it has really met different civilizations by means other than the shock of conquest and domination. But we have to admit that this encounter has not yet taken place at the level of an authentic dialogue. That is why we are in a kind of lull or interregnum in which we can no longer practice the dogmatism of a single truth and in which we are not yet capable of conquering the skepticism into which we have stepped." Ricoeur, p. 283 [Quote converted to footnote by the editor].

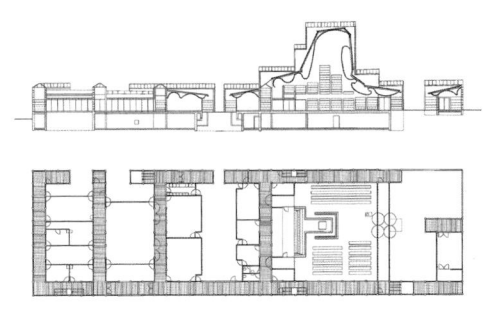

FIGURES 46 AND 47 Bagsværd Church, Bagsværd, Denmark. Jørn Utzon, 1968–1976. Section and plan (top); view of the main chamber (below).

meaning stems directly from a revealed conjunction between, on the one hand, the *rationality* of normative technique and, on the other, the *arationality* of idiosyncratic form.[14]

[...]

4. THE RESISTANCE OF THE PLACE-FORM

The Megalopolis recognized as such in 1961 by the geographer Jean Gottmann[15] continues to proliferate throughout the developed world to such an extent that, with the exception of cities which were laid in place before the turn of the century, we are no longer able to maintain defined urban forms. The last quarter of a century has seen the so-called field of urban design degenerate into a theoretical subject whose discourse bears little relation to the processal realities of modern development. Today even the super-managerial discipline of urban planning has entered into a state of crisis. The ultimate fate of the plan which was officially promulgated for the rebuilding of Rotterdam after World War II is symptomatic in this regard, since it testifies, in terms of its own recently changed status, to the current tendency to reduce all planning to little more than the allocation of land use and the logistics of distribution. Until relatively recently, the Rotterdam master plan was revised and upgraded every decade in the light of buildings which had been realized in the interim. In 1975, however, this progressive urban cultural procedure was unexpectedly abandoned in favor of publishing a nonphysical, infrastructure plan conceived at a regional scale. Such a plan concerns itself almost exclusively with the logistical projection of changes in land use and with the augmentation of existing distribution systems.

In his essay of 1954, "Building, Dwelling, Thinking," Martin Heidegger provides us with a critical vantage point from which to behold this phenomenon of universal placelessness. Against the Latin or, rather, the antique *abstract* concept of space as a more or less endless continuum of evenly subdivided spatial components or integers—what he terms *spatium* and *extensio*—Heidegger opposes the German word for space (or, rather, place), which is the term *Raum*. Heidegger argues that the phenomenological essence of such a space/place depends upon the *concrete*, clearly defined nature of its boundary, for, as he puts it, "A boundary is not that at which something stops, but, as the Greeks recognized, the boundary is that from which something begins its presencing."[16] Apart from confirming that Western abstract reason has its origins in the antique culture of the Mediterranean, Heidegger shows that

---

[14] Jørn Utzon, "Platforms and Plateaus: Ideas of a Danish Architect," *Zodiac* 10 (Milan: Edizioni Communità, 1963), pp. 112–14.

[15] Jean Gottmann, *Megalopolis: The Urbanized Northeastern Seaboard of the United States*. (Cambridge: MIT Press, 1961).

[16] Martin Heidegger, "Building, Dwelling, Thinking," in *Poetry, Language, Thought* (New York: Harper Colophon, 1971), p. 154. This essay first appeared in German in 1954.

etymologically the German gerund building is closely linked with the archaic forms of *being, cultivating* and *dwelling*, and goes on to state that the condition of "dwelling" and hence ultimately of "being" can only take place in a domain that is clearly bounded.

While we may well remain skeptical as to the merit of grounding critical practice in a concept so hermetically metaphysical as Being, we are, when confronted with the ubiquitous placelessness of our modern environment, nonetheless brought to posit, after Heidegger, the absolute precondition of a bounded domain in order to create an architecture of resistance. Only such a defined boundary will permit the built form to stand against—and hence literally to withstand in an institutional sense—the endless processal flux of the Megalopolis.

The bounded place-form, in its public mode, is also essential to what Hannah Arendt has termed "the space of human appearance," since the evolution of legitimate power has always been predicated upon the existence of the "polis" and upon comparable units of institutional and physical form.[17] While the political life of the Greek polis did not stem directly from the physical presence and representation of the city-state, it displayed in contrast to the Megalopolis the cantonal attributes of urban density.[18]

[...]

While the strategy of Critical Regionalism as outlined above addresses itself mainly to the maintenance of an *expressive density and resonance* in an architecture of resistance (a cultural density which under today's conditions could be said to be potentially liberative in and of itself since it opens the user to manifold *experiences*), the provision of a place-form is equally essential to critical practice, inasmuch as a resistant architecture, in an institutional sense, is necessarily dependent on a clearly defined domain. Perhaps the most generic example of such an urban form is the perimeter block, although other related,

---

[17] Thus Arendt writes in *The Human Condition*: "The only indispensable material factor in the generation of power is the living together of people. Only where men live so close together that the potentialities for action are always present will power remain with them and the foundation of cities, which as city states have remained paradigmatic for all Western political organization, is therefore the most important material prerequisite for power." Arendt, p. 201 [Quote converted to footnote by the editor].

[18] Nothing could be more removed from the political essence of the city-state than the rationalizations of positivistic urban planners such as Melvin Webber, whose ideological concepts of *community without propinquity* and the *non-place urban realm* are nothing if not slogans devised to rationalize the absence of any true public realm in the modern motopia [Melvin Webber, *Explorations in Urban Structure* (Philadelphia: University of Pennsylvania Press, 1964)]. The manipulative bias of such ideologies has never been more openly expressed than in Robert Venturi's *Complexity and Contradiction in Architecture* (1966) wherein the author asserts that Americans do not need piazzas, since they should be at home watching television [Robert Venturi, *Complexity and Contradiction in Architecture* (New York: Museum of Modern Art, 1966), p. 133]. Such reactionary attitudes emphasize the impotence of an urbanized populace which has paradoxically lost the object of its urbanization [Main text converted to footnote by the editor].

introspective types may be evoked, such as the galleria, the atrium, the forecourt and the labyrinth. And while these types have in many instances today simply become the vehicles for accommodating pseudo-public realms (one thinks of recent megastructures in housing, hotels, shopping centers, etc.), one cannot even in these instances entirely discount the latent political and resistant potential of the place-form.

5. CULTURE VERSUS NATURE: TOPOGRAPHY, CONTEXT, CLIMATE, LIGHT AND TECTONIC FORM

Critical Regionalism necessarily involves a more directly dialectical relation with nature than the more abstract, formal traditions of modern avant-garde architecture allow. It is self-evident that the *tabula rasa* tendency of modernization favors the optimum use of earth-moving equipment inasmuch as a totally flat datum is regarded as the most economic matrix upon which to predicate the rationalization of construction. Here again, one touches in concrete terms this fundamental opposition between universal civilization and autochthonous culture. The bulldozing of an irregular topography into a flat site is clearly a technocratic gesture which aspires to a condition of absolute *placelessness*, whereas the terracing of the same site to receive the stepped form of a building is an engagement in the act of "cultivating" the site.

Clearly such a mode of beholding and acting brings one close once again to Heidegger's etymology; at the same time, it evokes the method alluded to by the Swiss architect Mario Botta as "building the site." It is possible to argue that in this last instance the specific culture of the region—that is to say, its history in both a geological and agricultural sense—becomes inscribed into the form and realization of the work. This inscription, which arises out of "in-laying" the building into the site, has many levels of significance, for it has a capacity to embody, in built form, the prehistory of the place, its archeological past and its subsequent cultivation and transformation across time. Through this layering into the site the idiosyncrasies of place find their expression without falling into sentimentality.

What is evident in the case of topography applies to a similar degree in the case of an existing urban fabric, and the same can be claimed for the contingencies of climate and the temporally inflected qualities of local light. Once again, the sensitive modulation and incorporation of such factors must almost by definition be fundamentally opposed to the optimum use of universal technique. This is perhaps most clear in the case of light and climate control. The generic window is obviously the most delicate point at which these two natural forces impinge upon the outer membrane of the building, fenestration having an innate capacity to inscribe architecture with the character of a region and hence to express the place in which the work is situated.

[...]

Despite the critical importance of topography and light, the primary principle of architectural autonomy resides in the *tectonic* rather than the *scenographic*: that is to say, this autonomy is embodied in the revealed ligaments of the construction and in the way in which the syntactical form of the structure explicitly resists the action of gravity. It is obvious that this discourse of the load borne (the beam) and the load-bearing (the column) cannot be brought into being where the structure is masked or otherwise concealed. On the other hand, the tectonic is not to be confused with the purely technical, for it is more than the simple revelation of stereotomy or the expression of skeletal framework. Its essence was first defined by the German aesthetician Karl Bötticher in his book *Die Tektonik der Hellenen* (1852)[19] [. . .] The tectonic remains to us today as a potential means for distilling play between material, craftwork and gravity, so as to yield a component which is in fact a condensation of the entire structure. We may speak here of the presentation of a structural poetic rather than the re-presentation of a facade.

6. THE VISUAL VERSUS THE TACTILE

The tactile resilience of the place-form and the capacity of the body to read the environment in terms other than those of sight alone suggest a potential strategy for resisting the domination of universal technology. It is symptomatic of the priority given to sight that we find it necessary to remind ourselves that the tactile is an important dimension in the perception of built form. One has in mind a whole range of complementary sensory perceptions which are registered by the labile body: the intensity of light, darkness, heat and cold; the feeling of humidity; the aroma of material; the almost palpable presence of masonry as the body senses its own confinement; the momentum of an induced gait and the relative inertia of the body as it traverses the floor; the echoing resonance of our own footfall. Luchino Visconti was well aware of these factors when making the film *The Damned*, for he insisted that the main set of the Altona mansion should be paved in real wooden parquet. It was his belief that without a solid floor underfoot the actors would be incapable of assuming appropriate and convincing postures.

A similar tactile sensitivity is evident in the finishing of the public circulation in Alvar Aalto's Säynätsalo Town Hall of 1952. The main route leading to the second-floor council chamber is ultimately orchestrated in terms which are as much tactile as they are visual. Not only is the principal access stair lined in raked brickwork, but the treads and risers are also finished in brick. The kinetic

---

[19] It was perhaps best summarized by the architectural historian Stanford Anderson when he wrote: "'Tektonik' referred not just to the activity of making the materially requisite construction . . . but rather to the activity that raises this construction to an art form . . . The functionally adequate form must be adapted so as to give expression to its function. The sense of bearing provided by the entasis of Greek columns became the touchstone of this concept of *Tektonik*." Stanford Anderson, "Modern Architecture and Industry: Peter Behrens, the AEG, and Industrial Design," *Oppositions* 21 (Summer 1980), p. 83 [Quote converted to footnote by the editor].

impetus of the body in climbing the stair is thus checked by the friction of the steps, which are "read" soon after in contrast to the timber floor of the council chamber itself. This chamber asserts its honorific status through sound, smell and texture, not to mention the springy deflection of the floor underfoot (and a noticeable tendency to lose one's balance on its polished surface). From this example it is clear that the liberative importance of the tactile resides in the fact that it can only be decoded in terms of *experience* itself: it cannot be reduced to mere information, to representation or to the simple evocation of a simulacrum substituting for absent presences.

In this way, Critical Regionalism seeks to complement our normative visual experience by readdressing the tactile range of human perceptions. In so doing, it endeavors to balance the priority accorded to the image and to counter the Western tendency to interpret the environment in exclusively perspectival terms. According to its etymology, perspective means rationalized sight or clear seeing, and as such it presupposes a conscious suppression of the senses of smell, hearing and taste, and a consequent distancing from a more direct experience of the environment. This self-imposed limitation relates to that which Heidegger has called a "loss of nearness." In attempting to counter this loss, the tactile opposes itself to the scenographic and the drawing of veils over the surface of reality. Its capacity to arouse the impulse to touch returns the architect to the poetics of construction and to the erection of works in which the tectonic value of each component depends upon the density of its objecthood. The tactile and the tectonic jointly have the capacity to transcend the mere appearance of the technical in much the same way as the place-form has the potential to withstand the relentless onslaught of global modernization.

19 Tadao Ando's Critical Modernism (1984)

Tadao Ando belongs to that small circle of Japanese architects whose practice may be identified as critical on the grounds that it has assumed a culturally oppositional stance to the instrumentality of megalopolitan development. Like the Tokyo architects, Toyo Ito, Hiroshi Hara, and Kazuo Shinohara, Ando's architecture is critical in the sense that it resists being absorbed into the ever-escalating consumerism of the modern city. And while this resistance may seem redundant or even futile in view of the fact that radical architects are unlikely to receive large-scale commissions, it nonetheless retains its value as a rejection of consensus opinion, and as a sensitive contribution of import to the future development of architectural culture. In Ando's case, this resistance is predicated on emphasizing the boundary, thereby creating an introspective domain within which the homeowner may be granted sufficient private "ground" with which to withstand the alienating no-man's-land of the contemporary city.

At the same time, Ando remains aware that this pervasive modern predicament cannot be resolved by any kind of fictitious "homecoming"; that is to say, by the mere simulation of traditional Japanese timber construction or the use of evocative domestic components, such as the shoji screen or the tatami mat. And while such elements are still available, despite the industrialization of Japanese society, Ando has stoically refused the nostalgic ethos which such vernacular elements imply. He has, in fact, consistently rejected the current vogue for evoking another, more benign period of history, remote from the harsh facts of industrial and post-industrial society. Thus, the material conditions of modern society are always indirectly present in Ando's architecture, as implicit in its reinforced concrete walls as in the flood tide of development,

Source: Kenneth Frampton, "Tadao Ando's Critical Modernism," in *Tadao Ando: Buildings, Projects, Writings*, ed. Kenneth Frampton (New York: Rizzoli, 1984), 6–9.

which is only momentarily checked by these same massive boundaries. These walls reflect, through their surprising weight, not only the seismic conditions of the country, but also the "storm of progress" which rages throughout the Tokaido megalopolis.

Ando uses walls not only to establish "a human zone where the individual will can develop in the midst of the standardization of the surrounding society,"[1] but also as a means of countering the ubiquitous monotony of commercial architecture; "the use of the walls," as Ando puts it, is "to control walls."[2] And yet, while the wall on the exterior acts to delimit and reflect the surrounding urban chaos, on the interior it serves to encapsulate a "primitive" space which in Ando's own words "is able to symbolize relations between human beings and things,"[3] as these are mediated by the interaction of material with light, wind, and water.

Ando's dichotomous attitude towards the wall reflects the two primary themes which underlie the entire body of his work: on the one hand, there is a preoccupation with an *oppositional* perception of modern reality, on the other, there is a pronounced stress on the *ontological* experience of the sensate being rather than on the abstract processes demanded by the imperatives of industrialized society. This joint concern for what might be termed the "dialectic of being" has perhaps never been more comprehensively formulated by Ando than in his essay "From Self-Enclosed Modern Architecture Towards Universality"[4] of 1982, wherein modern architecture (now seen as a potential paradigm of place creation rather than space-endlessness) is posited as a counter thesis to the universal domination of history and technology. Indeed, throughout this essay Modernism appears as an ambiguous indication. It is perceived in its universal mode as leaving no room for autochthonous culture; but it is also recognized for its capacity to be inflected with regard to the attributes of a specific place. In a world overrun by media Ando values the "silence" of modern form for its resistance to consumption.

The critical distance which separates Ando from the universalism of the International Style is evident in the historical analysis with which this essay begins:

> Born and bred in Japan, I do my architectural work here. And I suppose it would be possible to say that the method I have selected is to apply the vocabulary and techniques developed by an open, universalist Modernism in an enclosed realm of individual life styles and regional differentiation. But it seems to me difficult to attempt to express the sensibilities, customs,

---

[1] Tadao Ando, "New Relations Between Space and the Person," *The Japan Architect*, October/November 1977, p.44.

[2] Tadao Ando, "The wall as Territorial Delineation," *The Japan Architect*, June 1978, p.13.

[3] Tadao Ando, "New Relations Between Space and the Person," p.44.

[4] Tadao Ando, "From Self-Enclosed Modern Architecture Towards Universality," *The Japan Architect*, May 1982, pp.8–12.

aesthetic awareness, distinctive culture and social traditions of a given race by means of the open internationalist vocabulary at Modernism.[5]

Following this passage, Ando asserts the role of modern architecture as a vehicle for enclosure rather than openness. Once again he situates his work within a precise historical context:

> After World War II, when Japan launched a course or rapid economic growth, the people's value criteria changed. The old, fundamentally feudal family system collapsed. Such social alterations as the concentration of information and places of work in the cities led to the overpopulation of urban centers and the underpopulation of agricultural and fishing villages and towns.... Overly dense urban and suburban populations made it impossible to preserve a feature that was formerly most characteristic of Japanese residential architecture: intimate connection with nature and openness to the natural world. What I refer to as enclosed Modern Architecture is a restoration of the unity between house and nature that Japanese houses have lost in the process of modernization.[6]

As the argument continues, one realizes that Ando's concept of nature is as removed from the apparent features of the Japanese landscape tradition as his architecture is distanced from the specific details of the traditional *Sukiya* style, by which at the same time it has been influenced.

It is possible to claim that Ando's work is critical on two interrelated counts. It criticizes universal modernity from within by establishing new goals and limits for modern architectural practice without at the same time denying its continuing validity as a vital cultural force. Yet it also evokes as a precedent for a more autochthonous critique, the enduring significance of the Sukiya teahouse style invented in the second half of the sixteenth century by Sen no Rikyū.

With regard to the first aspect, Ando has evidenced his breadth of critical understanding by remarking on the comparable devaluations suffered by the post and the colonnade as a consequence of the invention of the reinforced concrete frame. In his important essay on the use of the wall as a territorial delineator, Ando argues that the fundamental tropes of architecture in both the East and the West have been effectively nullified by the advent of the universal rigid frame. He cites the salient role played by the symbolic, non-structural post in traditional Japanese architecture, and he points out how the rhythm of the western colonnade—that is to say, the primary monumental format extending from the temple at Thebes to Perrault's east facade of the Louvre has been rendered technically obsolete and hence culturally inaccessible by the infinitely greater spanning capacity of the reinforced concrete frame:

---

[5] Tadao Ando, "From Self-Enclosed Modern Architecture Towards Universality," p.8.
[6] Tadao Ando, "From Self-Enclosed Modern Architecture Towards Universality," p.9.

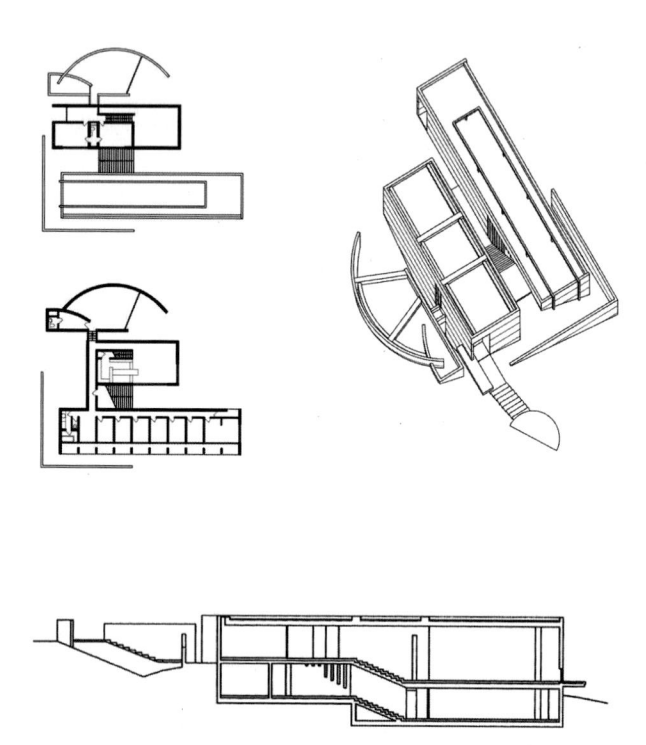

FIGURES 48 AND 49 Koshino House, Ashiya, Kobe, Japan. Tadao Ando, 1980–1984. Plans and axonometric (top), and section (below).

The rigid frame system is based on modernization and economic balance. It has robbed the post of its myths and the colonnade of its rhythm. Under such circumstances the wall emerges as a major theme. I am not attempting to make relative comparisons between the post and the wall or to claim that the wall is in any way superior to the post. Instead I have in mind an operation in which the wall and post just are rhetorically interrelated.[7]

As the above passage makes clear, Ando aspires to a form of cross-cultural criticism which attempts to compensate for the generic devaluations which architecture has suffered at the hands of technique. In this respect, his criticism is as valid for the West as for the East. But it is equally clear, as has been recently demonstrated, that Ando's work is at its most subversive in a Japanese context where the deeper significance of its Sukiya references can be readily appreciated. For evidently the original Sukiya style comprised certain fundamental characteristics which are consciously reinterpreted in Ando's work. Of the basic (non-stylistic) features which Ando's work and the Sukiya style have in common, Kiyoshi Takeyama cites calmness and purity, gentleness and clarity of mood.[8] Ando follows the Sukiya manner in his preference for dim lighting broken by shafts of light unexpectedly entering the darkness. Likewise, he attempts to create a feeling of spiritual expansiveness within a small domain. And while both expressions are patently artificial they succeed nonetheless in evoking a feeling for nature as an ineffable, all-pervasive presence. Thus, even in the midst of a highly congested urban fabric the tonal reference of the Sukiya style is ultimately rural. Takeyama enlightens us as to the subversive implications of this Zen Buddhist allusion to the aboriginal purity of rural culture when he writes:

Rikyū was striving to create spaces that though small could bring peace and calm, even for a short while, to members of the warrior class plagued by strife and conflict. In the rooms he designed, guests could become so absorbed in the affairs of the tea ceremony that they forgot the troubles of daily life. The methods he used to produce the kind of microcosm he wanted were enclosure and the adaptation of vernacular elements from folk dwellings. Through Rikyū's tea ceremony buildings (built in a style that came to be called *so-an* or grass thatched retreat) these elements became fashionable with the wealthy. Thus, the domestic architectural traditions of the common people exerted an influence on the design of the homes of the aristocracy and the military ruling class . . . the spirit of the tea ceremony and of everything associated with it as it was developed by and after Sen no Rikyū is often expressed by the Japanese word *wabi*, which means a deliberate striving for simplicity. But the word carries a connotation of dissatisfaction and is used to point out the falling of things or persons deemed worthy of criticism. For instance, the refined, quiet, calm *wabi* style is sometimes mentioned as

---

[7] Tadao Ando, "The wall as Territorial Delineation," p.12.
[8] Kiyoshi Takeyama, "Tadao Ando: Heir to a Tradition," *Perspecta* 20, 1983, pp.163–80.

an antonym for the gaudy, ostentatious taste associated with the great military leader, Tokyotomi Hideyoshi (who was a patron of Rikyū). The idea of *wabi* can stand for dissatisfaction with authority.[9]

The paradoxical nature of Ando's position—his capacity to develop critical themes in both accidental and oriental culture, his debt to Ludwig Wittgenstein and Adolf Loos for their anti-positivist objectivity—all of this is perhaps best summed up in Ando's ambivalent attitude towards functionalism as the one irreducible precept of the Modern Movement. However, when it comes to the evaluation of functional forms, Ando remains opposed to both bourgeois comfort and the ideals of ergonomic convenience, since for him such criteria are contaminated by consumerism. As he himself has written:

> I am interested in discovering what new life patterns can be extracted and developed from living under severe conditions. Furthermore I feel that order is necessary to give life dignity. Establishing order imposes restrictions, but I believe it cultivates extraordinary things in people. I believe in removing architecture from function after ensuring the observation of functional basics. In other words, I like to see how far architecture can pursue function and then, after the pursuit has been made, to see how far architecture can be removed from function. The significance of architecture is found in the distance between it and function.[10]

For Ando, architecture must always embody a double movement, it must accommodate daily life while remaining open to the symbolic. To this end his work has always been structured through absolutes: wall versus column, square versus circle, concrete versus glass, dark versus light, materiality versus immateriality. The essential character of his work resides finally in the *interaction* between these last four terms, in the way that light transforms both volume and mass; in the way in which it effects changes according to the hour, transforming dark into light and ponderous mass into scintillating surface. It is for this reason that Ando, unlike his peers, insists upon the paradoxical rendering of concrete as though it were a light material, like a paper screen, where all the energy is concentrated on the surface.

For Ando concrete "is the most suitable material for realizing surfaces created by rays of sunlight . . . [wherein] walls become abstract, are negated, and approach the ultimate limit of space. Their actuality is lost, and only the space they enclose gives a sense of really existing."[11]

---

[9] Kiyoshi Takeyama, "Tadao Ando: Heir to a Tradition," pp.164–165.

[10] Tadao Ando, "The Emotionally Made Architectural Spaces of Tadao Ando," *The Japan Architect*, April 1980, pp.45, 46.

[11] Tadao Ando, "From Self-Enclosed Modern Architecture Towards Universality," p.12.

From this last laconic passage we are able to perceive more clearly perhaps than elsewhere, the paradoxical nature of Ando's antipathy to abstraction or rather his rejection of abstraction as an end in itself. For Ando, as for the Shakers, whose culture he has long admired, the abstract, purified form is merely an agent for the realization of being. And yet this same abstraction also permits the apparent dematerialization of its form under the action of nature. As he was to write of the Koshino House, "I believe that the architectural materials do not end with wood and concrete that have tangible forms, but go beyond to include light and wind which appeal to the senses."[12]

---

[12] Tadao Ando, "Koshino Residence," *Space Design*, June 1961, p.15.

20 Place-Form and Cultural Identity (1988)

> We do not ask to be immortal beings, we only ask that things do not lose all their meaning.
>
> Antoine de Saint-Exupéry

THE VICISSITUDES OF IDEOLOGY: AN ANGLO-AMERICAN PERSPECTIVE

We live in a paradoxical moment when, while we are perhaps more obsessed with history than ever before, we have, simultaneously, the feeling that certain historical trajectory, or even, for some, history itself, is coming to an end. (See Gianni Vattimo, *La fine della modernità*, 1985).[1] This experience is so uncanny that we hardly know how to respond to it, for, faced with this apparent deliquescence of the modern world, we take comfort in the fact that the field of techno-science seems to be immune from this bewildering condition. Outwardly, scientists today appear to be just as modern now as Cavendish or Einstein did in their own time or, say, as Harvey and Volta did in the middle of the eighteenth century, a period which happens to coincide with the beginning of history in the modern sense. At the same time, and not only from a penchant for creature comforts, today's techno-scientists do not usually house themselves in modern environments. Like the man in the street, they gravitate towards a vaguely reassuring past, towards that suburban environment, the iconography of which is derived from a hypothetical agrarian culture which has disappeared forever. The humanists, on the other hand—that is to say, those whose vocation

---

Source: Kenneth Frampton, "Place-Form and Cultural Identity," in *Design After Modernism: Beyond the Object*, ed. John Thackara (London: Thames & Hudson, 1988), 51–66.

[1] See Vattimo, Gianni, 'Identità, differenza, confusione', *Casabella*, 519, December 1985, pp. 42, 43.

is to analyse and postulate the fundamental superstructure of the society—are the ones who find themselves enmeshed in the almost inexpressible aporias of the postmodern condition.

I am a member of that generation of so-called modern architects, who first came of age as active practitioners in the early sixties and whose concept of modernity (like that of the immediately previous generation) was already historically mediated; that is to say, unlike the pioneers of the inter-war period (1918–39) we did not conceive of ourselves as trying to engender an architecture whose form was totally unprecedented. Instead we already saw our task as a qualified restoration of the creative vigour of a movement which had become formally and programmatically compromised in the intervening years. It was, of course, quite impossible to recapture the energy and the optimistic belief systems of this previous epoch, but none the less we could still conceive of ourselves as returning to a modern line in architecture, irrespective of the different forms that this might assume.

It is hard to say exactly when this mediated but still modern *modus operandi* began to falter, but I suppose it must have coincided, at least in England, with the realization (and partial deformation) of the long-term programme of postwar reconstruction and with the mediocre results of the new towns policy which culminated in 1972 with the inauguration of Milton Keynes. We had been, in any event, the last generation of students to entertain the projection of utopian urban schemes in *both a programmatic and a formal sense*. Thereafter, the emerging Megalopolitan reality instantly transformed such projections into historical non sequiturs, with regard to which one could no longer suspend even a modicum of disbelief. It is significant in this regard that Leon Krier's theoretical urbanism of the late seventies should focus, not without a touch of caricature, on a form of *anti-utopia*: that is to say, on the end of history in a certain sense. I am alluding to his campaign for the wholesale "reconstruction" of the European city, in which the city would be reified in a kind of inaccessible past; frozen, as it were, at an ideal bourgeois moment, at some moment during the first half of the last century.

Throughout the sixties, Leslie Martin and his associates attempted to ground the practice of architecture in a normative typology. This approach was largely based on the architecture of two distinguished late modernists, Alvar Aalto and Louis Kahn, whose work seemed particularly appropriate to the British intellectual climate and its empirical traditions. The relevance of Martin's approach was to conceive of building as a background for life and thereby to limit its expressive scope.[2] It unconsciously recognized Walter Benjamin's aphorism that

---

[2] See *Buildings & Ideas 1933–1983. From the studio of Leslie Martin*, Cambridge, 1983. Among the more prominent members of Martin's office in the sixties were Colin St John Wilson and Patrick Hodgkinson. Although a typological point of departure was common to both Martin's practice and the research carried out under the auspices of the department of Land Form and Built Use Studies at Cambridge University, one needs to distinguish between the two. Where the former was pragmatic in its general orientation, the latter was logarithmic and abstract.

architecture, on the average, is appreciated in a state of distraction. In retrospect, it seems as if this normative attitude was replaced at the very end of the sixties by the British Productivist, or so-called High-Tech School. This shift is decisive at many levels, for it represents a political and symbolic move away from the institutional and residential fabric of the society, towards the productive imperatives of neo-capitalism. Pragmatically and ideologically, the High-Tech School responded to the new levels of productive and communicational efficiency then being demanded by the expansion of the tertiary economy.

Aside from the Martin school, there is little doubt that by the mid-sixties, we were increasingly bereft of a *realistic* theoretical basis on which to work. Without the radical cultural and political programmes of the revolutionary modern movement, we had no alternative theory to the reductive efforts, made from the late fifties onwards, to fill this void with ergonomic design methods; a positivistic approach which was not without its distant connections to both the Martin school and the later Productivist line of Richard Rogers and Norman Foster. Such methods, however, were soon to display their marked incapacity to synthesize building programmes of any complexity. The scientism of this attitude is evident from the ideological title changes suffered by prominent schools of architecture during this period, with one institution in particular passing through a brief period when it was known as a "school of environmental studies". The euphemistic use of the term "environment", with its "life-science" connotations is symptomatic of the time.

The redistribution of wealth brought about by the relative success of the post-war, neo-capitalist Welfare State, together with the capitalization of the unions and growth of the consumer society, were all factors which contributed to the universal campus crisis of the late sixties, euphemistically known, after the dramatic events which took place in Paris in 1968, as *les événements de mai*. And while it is true to say that few lasting political changes were introduced by this all too brief moment of student radicalism, it none the less left behind a critical legacy which eventually manifested itself in terms of both left- and right-wing ideologies; on the one hand, Marxist feminism and various radical factions deriving from radical psychoanalysis and the critical theory of the Frankfurt School, on the other, the ambiguities of French structuralism and *les nouveaux philosophes*.

This mixed legacy, together with the subsequent real move to the right in many Western countries and a new-found capacity to sustain, through welfare provisions, unprecedented levels of mass unemployment (while still maintaining some semblance of consumerism), are, together with the perennial nuclear threat, all determining factors of a context in which the postmodern phenomenon begins to emerge. As far as architecture is concerned, the postmodern, as an ideological category, if not as a style, announces itself in three somewhat interrelated events.

The first of these was the publication of Charles Jencks' *The Language of Post-Modern Architecture* in 1977, a work which argued for a free-floating pluralist populist architecture, primarily conceived in terms of accessible imagery. The second event was an exhibition entitled *Transformations*, staged in 1979 by Arthur Drexler at the Museum of Modern Art, New York. While this exhibition presented a more comprehensive survey than Jencks' book, ostensibly displaying the vicissitudes of modern architecture over the past twenty years, it adopted a very similar rhetoric; above all, it omitted any graphic information, presumably on the grounds that the general public are unable to read plans. Like Jencks' *magnum opus* it featured a large number of photographs (also at the rate of one shot per building) including large, back-lit, coloured transparencies of the typical curtain-wall, high-rise office structure of the period, invariably sealed in tinted, clear or mirrored glass and shot in the late evening sun. The third event was the architectural section of the Venice Biennale of 1980; an exhibition whose underlying supposedly liberative, populist bias was evident from the outset. This exhibition, mounted by Paolo Portoghesi and given the mildly demagogic, if ironic, title *The Presence of the Past: The End of Prohibition*, was precisely the occasion which prompted Jürgen Habermas to formulate his Theodor Adorno Prize address, given in Frankfurt in the same year under the title "Modernity—An Incomplete Project".[3]

By the early eighties it became clear that certain prominent figures in the American architectural establishment had been gradually moving towards reactionary position for some time; certainly since the publication in 1966 of Robert Venturi's *Complexity and Contradiction in Architecture*, which was first issued, one should note, by the Museum of Modern Art.[4] This ambiguously critical position paper gave rise to forms of populist architectural collage, theoretically realizing Venturi's vision of "the dumb and the ordinary" as an inexpensive and broadly understandable mode of building. This neo-Brechtian approach to architecture (made in this instance ironically complete by the use of outsize American flags to which Venturi, after Jasper Johns, was apparently so addicted) came to be popularized in the profession under the slogan "Main Street is almost all right"; a brand of cultural populism which shifted to the right with the publication of *Learning From Las Vegas* in 1972, with its characterization of the exploitative Las Vegas Strip as a paradigm of popularly gratified desire. Again, as in Jencks' *The Language of Post-Modern Architecture*, the instruments of semiotic and communicational analysis were scientifically adduced, as a means of bestowing an apparent legitimacy on what was little more than a manipulative form of admass advocacy.

Since the early eighties this conservative tendency in American architecture has become more dominant, with the vestigially modernist strategy of populist collage giving way to cannibalized forms of eclectic historicism, ranging from Robert Stern's *arriviste* neo-Edwardian suburban essays patterned after Luttyens, to Helmut Jahn's outsized neo-Art Deco parodies in curtain wall construction and to the more general use of the thin stone revetment to simulate, as inexpensively as possible, the past glories of Beaux Arts masonry.

---

[3] Habermas, Jürgen, 'Modernity—An Incomplete Project'. See *The Anti-Aesthetic: Essays on Postmodern Culture*, ed. Hal Foster, Port Townsend, Washington, 1983, pp. 3–15.

[4] Venturi, Robert, *Complexities and Contradiction in Architecture*, New York, 1966.

There is an understandable tendency for this historicism to be restricted to external finishes, since American builder-developers tend to favour an ad hoc "balloon-frame" approach to steel frame and sheet rock construction, thereby tending to eliminate both structure and volume as intrinsic forms of architectural expression. Under these conditions, the architect's task is reduced to the provision of a marketable image once an optimal rental return has been assured by the general arrangement of the plan. Needless to say, the increasingly rapid theoretical amortization of building stock is an important factor in promoting this relatively inexpensive form of development.[5]

In the face of these successive devaluations I have increasingly felt the need, as a critic and teacher, to develop some form of alternative theoretical position with which to continue, albeit interstitially, with the critical practice of architecture; one which while avoiding superannuated avantgardism, would somehow be able to build on the liberative and poetic legacy of the pre-war modern movement.

It appeared to me in 1980, that a more sensitive and relevant form of architecture could be found on the periphery of the so-called developed world rather than in the apparent centres of cultural and communicational power, such as New York, London and Paris. I perceived that these peripheral nodes were able to sustain a more multi-layered complexity of architectural culture. The reasons for this were manifold, ranging from conditions of local prosperity to an assumed or traditional cantonal identity. I sensed that these interstitial cultural manifestations arose when there was desire and willingness on the part of architects and their clients to develop a self-conscious and local contemporary expression; one which, while remaining committed to the modernization process, would none the less be able to qualify the received consumerist civilization through a consciously cultivated "culture of place". It had seemed to me in the early sixties that these peripheral, incidental works, irrespective of where they occurred—be it Zurich, Lugano, Udine, Athens, Venice, Porto, Helsinki, Stockholm, Copenhagen, Madrid, Barcelona, Amsterdam, New Delhi or Mexico City—always manifested themselves through sensuous, concrete and tactile elements of either a topographic or tectonic nature. And so by degrees I found myself gravitating towards the ideal of a self-consciously cultivated "regionalism" as a way of being able to continue with an architecture of resistance without falling into sentimentality, or into the false perpetuation of exhausted modern forms, or into the empty vagaries of historicism, placed at the service of optimized development.

---

[5] The current American administration has seen to fit to reduce the period over which a built-investment may be amortized for purposes of assessing taxation liability. This tends to reduce the investor's interest in assuring the durability of the structure in relation to the initial capital investment.

PLACE-FORM AND CULTURAL IDENTITY

I declared my allegiance to this hypothetical line in 1982, with an essay entitled 'Towards a Critical Regionalism', which first appeared in *Perspecta 20* and which was then presented in a more didactic form, under the same title, in Hal Foster's *The Anti-Aesthetic*.[6] The term 'critical regionalism' was not my invention; it was coined by Alex Tzonis and Liliane Lefaivre in their essay on the work of Dimitris and Susana Antonakakis in 1981.[7]

[. . .] By Critical Regionalism I did not mean any kind of style, nor did I have in mind some form of vernacular revival. Instead, I wished to employ the term to allude to a hypothetical and real condition in which a local culture of architecture is consciously evolved in express opposition to the domination of hegemonic power. In my view, this is a theory of building which, while accepting the potentially liberative role of modernization, resists being totally absorbed by forms of optimized production and consumption. In this regard, it has a latent affinity with political policies favouring some measure of autarchy.

Apart from indicating its presence in contemporary practice, the prime ground for my theoretical elaboration of Critical Regionalism derives from Paul Ricoeur and above all, from his essay of 1961 entitled 'Universal Civilization and National Cultures'. I am indebted to Ricoeur not only because this distinction between civilization and culture is fundamental to any clear understanding of our present situation, but also because it affords the oppositional structure from which the rest of my argument follows. In my view, the constituent elements of architecture are to be seen as being determined by the way in which such oppositions are mediated through form.

For Ricoeur, universal civilization means universal technology, and he sees this as being inseparable from the long-term liberative aims of modernization. As he points out, no developing country is able to forgo for long the benefits of universal civilization. On the other hand, he remains acutely aware of the fragility of local culture; of its tendency to crumble in the face of a totally alien technology and the implicitly antithetical, often positivistic values that this often brings in its wake. For Ricoeur, writing in the early sixties, this dilemma is particularly dramatic and difficult in the case of newly de-colonialized countries.[8] [. . .] This problem manifests itself throughout the contemporary world; and never more so, I would submit, then in the field of architecture.

Architecture, however, possesses the intrinsic advantage of being a particularly resistant *métier*. This is perhaps never more evident than in the fact that all attempts to industrialize building production over the past forty years have

---

[6] Frampton, Kenneth, 'Towards Critical Regionalism: Six Points for an Architecture of Resistance', in *The Anti-Aesthetic*, op.cit. (3), pp. 16–30.

[7] Tzonis, Alex, and Lefaivre, Liliane, 'The Grid and the Pathway: An Introduction to the Work of Dimitris and Susana Antonakakis', *Architecture in Greece*, 15, 1981, pp. 164–78.

[8] Paul Ricoeur, 'Universal Civilization and National Cultures' (1961), in *History and Truth*, trans. Charles A. Kelbley, Evanston, 1965, pp. 276–77.

met with only limited degrees of success, partly because the field is incapable of providing a sufficiently high level of repetition together with the requisite market to justify the large investment demanded by machine-tool production, and partly because the embedding of the product in the ground tends to retard the cycle of production and consumption favoured by modern industrial economy.[9] On all sides of the political spectrum every effort has been made to overcome this inherent resistance, above all in the many attempts made to construct high-rise residential fabric out of pre-cast concrete elements, usually to the ultimate detriment of both the fabric and its occupants. A comparable drive is evident in the current downtown, 'shrink-wrapped', mixed-use development now being realized on a mammoth scale in the United States. In both instances there is a discernible tendency to reduce architecture to a recalcitrant form of commodity, the quality of which is always severely limited by the need to justify the investment in *economic* terms, as though both 'left' and 'right' no longer possessed any other criteria by which to assess value.

As far as I am concerned, this recalcitrance of the *métier* vis-à-vis modernization is a blessing in disguise, since it provides the fundamental basis from which to cultivate a "critical" architecture. It affords, above all, a hybrid situation in which rationalized production (even partially industrialized production) may be combined with time-honoured craft practices, provided that the scale of the investment remains sufficiently modest to permit idiosyncratic forms of disjunction and that the local culture retains a capacity to evaluate the results in terms which are not exclusively economic.

This is why I have conceived of my theory of a Critical Regionalism as a field of resistance, and in the passages that follow I have attempted to elaborate this theory in terms of foci conceived as points of opposition. These points seem to parallel, to some degree, the confrontation between civilization and culture alluded to by Ricoeur. Before elaborating this further, however, two additional qualifications have to be made.

Firstly, I have come to realize that the suffix *ism* presupposes style. This ending is therefore etymologically antithetical to the cultural syndrome I would like to evoke. I do not want to deny style, but at the same time I do not wish to imply its necessary presence in advance. On these grounds I have opted for the present title 'place-form and cultural identity'. Secondly, it is necessary to add that the term *resistance* has a number of connotations; first, the resistance of the *métier* itself in all its intrinsic aspects; second, the resistance of built form to the erosive force of time (that aspect of *work* which Hannah Arendt once characterized as transcending individual mortality)[10] and last, but by no means least, the proposition that this cultural strategy implies a certain resistance to the forces of domination, wherever they may be found.

---

[9] Pike, Alexander, 'Failure of Industrialised Building/Housing Programme,' *Architectural Design*, Nov. 1967, p. 507.

[10] Arendt, Hannah, *The Human Condition*, Chicago, 1958.

CONCLUSION: CRITICAL CULTURE AND THE POST-MODERN CONDITION[11]

The protagonists of Postmodernity, that is to say, those who are convinced that the period of High Modernity has ended, seem to fall, at least initially, into two groups; the neo-Historicists and the neo-Situationists. The first of these, who happen to be the least intellectual and the more prominent in the eyes of the popular press, are those who feel that the entire ideology and stylistic apparatus of the modern avant garde has been discredited and that no choice remains but to abandon this ostensibly inhuman and radical discourse, together with its style, and to return to tradition in every conceivable sense; from figuration and expressionism in painting to tonality and classical form in music, from kitsch historicism in architecture, to outright neo-conservatism in culture-politics and even in politics itself. The neo-Situationists (and I have termed them thus in order to imply that there may be direct or indirect links here to the *Situationist* movement of the fifties) seem to welcome the continuing escalation of modernization as an inevitable and fundamentally radical process; one which, despite its predominantly utilitarian and positivistic character, embraces a constantly varying and unstable mosaic and hence the latent, liberative conjunctions of the future.

Of the two groups it may be claimed that the second is the more consistent, for where the former is culturally and politically retrogressive it remains committed to the benefits of universal civilization. It seeks to combine the optimization of techno-science with reactionary culture-politics, exploiting the latter to soften and mask the harsh realities induced by the former. Where the neo-Conservatives are schizophrenic and culturally *anti-modern*, the neo-Situationists are more strictly *post-modern* in that through repudiating the utopian legacy of the Enlightenment (which some of them see as inseparable from political terror) they proclaim the end of 'master narratives', in all fields, including that of science itself. Both groups seem, in fact, to envisage an end of Enlightenment history; the former by embracing historicism and thereby reducing the cultural present to a perpetual and meaningless regurgitation of a petrified past, the latter by renouncing history as the master narrative *par excellence*. Both groups, for different reasons, distance themselves from the redemptive end of bourgeois history prophesied by Marx, and yet in both the master-narrative of techno-science seems to return through the back door; in the first case, by virtue of unabashed reactionary politics, in the second, by assuming an apparently acritical attitude towards the seeming autonomy of techno-science.

This acriticality towards techno-science has been and is still being attacked by the contemporary heirs of the Frankfurt School, above all, of course, by Jürgen Habermas, whose essay 'Technology and Science as Ideology'[12] remains

---

[11] The preceding subchapter titled 'Five points for architecture of resistance' is omitted here due to its similarity with Frampton's 'Six points' which appear in the previous chapter [footnote inserted by the editor].

[12] Habermas, Jürgen, 'Technology and Science as Ideology' (1968), in *Towards a Rational Society*, Boston, 1970.

in my view a seminal work. Inasmuch as Habermas returns us to the necessity of some form of decentralized democratic control over the autonomous processes of techno-science (which tend where they merge into applied science to reproduce themselves, irrespective of the consequences for either the species or the cosmos), the later Frankfurt School remains, in my view, the only valid basis upon which to develop a form of (post) modern critical culture. There is herein a comparable departure from the cult of the master narrative, for a cultural politics of this order patently assumes a certain decentralization of power in the constitution of the modern state. This approximates to what Habermas intends by his concepts of consensus and undistorted communication and this *may* explain, by way of extension, why a peripheral or *interstitial* architecture may still be capable of generating a more appropriate, sensitive and responsive physical environment, than that generally found today in the centres of hegemonic power.

Despite the spontaneous devolution of power, such as we have recently witnessed in Spain, it would be naive, to say the least, to underestimate the staying power of the Jacobin state, along with its understandable interest in furthering the "autonomous" domain of techno-science, together with its 'value-free' application. In this sense, I would submit, we are finally justified in calling for a culture of resistance, or more specifically, in our case, for a critical practice of architecture, which, without falling into sentimental primitivism, would resist the universal commodification of the modern world and in doing so react against the further centralization of power and control. Here the confrontation between universal civilization and rooted culture takes on a decidedly political potential.

However, to acknowledge the interstitial existence of such a resistant architecture and to develop a general theory by which to further its aims are two different things. While we may achieve the former, through the exercise of descriptive procedure and critical analysis, the latter demands a more fundamental reappraisal of the limits of the field, from both an ontological and a normative standpoint. It is nothing less than this last which I have attempted in elaborating this theory of 'place-form and cultural identity'. It is evident that, in its present form, this theoretical schema owes much to the phenomenological existential traditions in Western thought, and to combine this mode of beholding with political stance drawn from the critical tradition of the Frankfurt School is contradictory, to say the least. However, there remains the outline of an ill-defined terrain in which these two fields of critical discourse may be said to intersect and even to complement one another. While there are intimations of this in their mutual commitment to the liberative traditions of the modern world, perhaps this complementarity may be best sensed in the correspondence which appears to obtain between Habermas's idea of modernity as the 'unfinished project' and Heidegger's insistence on 'being as becoming'.

In attempting to formulate a critical theory of postmodern architectural practice, it is difficult to escape the implications of the current debate between Jürgen Habermas and Jean-François Lyotard, particularly the different stances that they each assume towards the future of 'progress' and the continuity of modernity as an unfinished enterprise. Two issues of fundamental consequence seem to divide these thinkers. The first concerns the different way in which they each conceive of the 'postmodern' as being a continuation and/or metamorphosis of the 'modern'. For Habermas the issue finally turns on the question as to whether or not the liberative programme of the Enlightenment can still be seriously entertained as a realizable aim? For Lyotard it is this aim itself which has to be renounced; see his book *La Condition post-moderne*.[13] The second concerns the way in which each philosopher conceives of "value" as being determined by democratic discourse. Here the main difference arises from Habermas's insistence on the derivation of social and pragmatic value from what he regards as the 'finality' of consensus, with Lyotard categorically rejecting this concept for its latent totalitarianism. Paradoxically, both men subscribe to the principle that the self-realization of species and the just and intelligent resolution of conflict can only be achieved in relation to specific, local conditions. Where Habermas predicates this resolution on the existence and maintenance of undistorted communication—an idea which, in my view, implies the evolution and proliferation of semi-autarchic or cantonal democracies—Lyotard leaves the issue of power and manner of its mediation disturbingly vague. He seems to suggest that the plurality of techno-science and the multiplicity of circumscribed language-games will jointly serve to perpetuate a condition of liberative anarchy.

Given the violent (or potentially violent) trajectory of occidental applied science and the various dominant interests which are served by its optimization, it is difficult to be sanguine about the claims which Lyotard makes for the autonomous plurality of techno-science. On the other hand, it is equally difficult to comprehend the importance which Habermas attaches to the principle of *final* consensus. Both Lyotard and Habermas, however, seem to be equally concerned with the determination of an 'end'; with the former renouncing (denouncing?) all forms of unified history and the latter maintaining a certain commitment to the Enlightenment ideal. Both seem to reject as 'irrational' the ahistorical-ontological future as envisaged in the thought of Nietzsche and Heidegger—the eternal return and the end of progress. Hence both seem to dispute, to an equal degree, the seminal role of ontology in the future evolution of critical theory and practice, while at the same time they both seem to ignore the Eurocentric and occidental bias of their discourse. For me the controversy ought to be focused somewhere here, that is, in the way in which the species-being conceives of its relationship to nature, including its own nature. In this context one questions whether the future will perpetuate the occidental *end-games* of limitless wastage and pollution or whether new dimensions of ethical practice will arise out of a new-found respect for the symbiotic limits of both being and cosmos. While

---

[13]Lyotard, Jean-François, *The Post-Modern Condition: A Report on Knowledge*, Minneapolis, 1984. This 'neo-Situationist' work (my categorization) opens with a direct critique of Habermas's position. See also Stephen Watson, 'Jürgen Habermas and Jean-François Lyotard: Post-Modernism and the Crisis of Rationality', in *Philosophy & Social Criticism*, No. 2, Vol. 10, An International Disciplinary Quarterly Journal, Boston College, Cambridge, Mass., 1984.

nature is by definition dynamic rather than static, such a cultural symbiosis would imply an end of modernism *in se,* inasmuch as critical ecology would become the basis for limiting the aporia of occidental reason. Seen in this light, critical theory would have to define itself in terms of an organic practice wherein the myth of progress would encounter its natural limit. In such a prospect, conflict (including cultural-political conflict) would have to find its resolution in maintaining a 'homoeostatic' balance. Inasmuch as such a metabolic concept is dynamic, no consensus as to its detailed maintenance could ever be 'final' and yet within such a theoretical context Habermas's 'condition-situation' remains as the fundamental ground within which a critical practice of architecture will have to find its material.

21 Modernization and Local Culture (2002)

[...]

Ever since John Turner's pioneering work with squatter settlements in Latin America, documented in his "Dwelling Resources in South America" of 1963,[1] and since Hassan Fathy's *Architecture for the Poor*, first published in English in 1973,[2] we have been only too aware of the overwhelming scale of global poverty, and the limits of architecture as a bourgeois practice when confronted with the degree-zero of human habitation. Whether we like it or not, we are returned to these grass-roots circumstances by the Master Jury of the eighth cycle of the Aga Khan Award for Architecture. For four of the nine works premiated in this cycle focus once again, as in the past, on the all but unbridgeable gulf that separates the deprived millions of the late-modern world—those whom Frantz Fanon once called the 'wretched of the earth'[3]—from those of us who, by talent or by chance, find ourselves momentarily carried on the wave of global prosperity.

Source: Kenneth Frampton, "Modernization and Local Culture," in Kenneth Frampton, Charles Correa, and David Robson, eds., *Modernity and Community: Architecture in the Islamic World* (London: Thames & Hudson and The Aga Khan Award for Architecture, 2002), 9–16.

[1] John Turner, 'Dwelling Resources in South America' in *Architectural Design*, August 1963, pp 360–93. See also by the same author *Freedom to Build* (New York, Macmillian, 1972).

[2] Hassan Fathy, *Architecture for the Poor: an experiment in rural Egypt* (Chicago University Press, 1973).

[3] Frantz Fanon, *Les Damnés la terre* (Pans, F Maspero, 1961).

As Serageldin remarks elsewhere, much of the built environment in the Muslim world is in fact dependent on non-architects.[4] For this reason alone the Aga Khan Trust for Culture finds itself simultaneously patronizing the art of architecture with a capital A, while still acknowledging the harsh realities of a world that desperately needs its assistance at many levels, not least of which is the triennial disbursement of the Award. Fifteen of the seventy-eight projects selected by Award Master Juries between 1980 and 1998 were, in fact, largely devoted to housing schemes for those living at the low end of the economic spectrum in the Islamic World.

[...]

Among the numerous settlements nominated for this cycle, none perhaps is more directly representative of the interaction between modernization and local culture than the rehabilitation of the village of Aït Iktel in Morocco. The overall income of this remote community is complemented by migrant workers sending back a portion of their wages, and it was just this Berber diaspora that was galvanized into action by a local anthropologist, Dr Ali Arnahan, with the founding of the Association Aït Iktel de Développement. Two external factors stemming directly from the modernization process had a decisive impact on the formation of this organization: first, the closing of certain factories in France in the 1980s, where a number of Berber immigrant workers had been formerly employed: and second, the continuous drought induced in the High Atlas Mountains by changes in the global climate, which compelled village women to walk further and further to obtain water. Lest we conceive modernization solely as

---

[4] "Furthermore, outsiders cannot 'assume away' the local cultural milieu. It exists. Any outside assessment of a notable building will be 'read' by the milieu and the assessment itself will become a vector for change, in one way or another, that acts upon the milieu. This is particularly true of the attitudes of Western observers, who represent the dominant culture of the world today, vis-à-vis Muslim intellectual elites who seek to redefine their identity in non-Western terms in the face of a historical break in Muslim cultural continuity [...] The manifestations of the cultural situation also include another significant front: the advancing insertion of a modern, rapidly changing technology into everyday lives traditionally governed by other concerns. The suitability of the technology, its adaptation to the needs of the population and the societal context, is only one part of the issue. This is the part that has usually concerned architectural critics when looking at buildings. For both building as a process and building as a product, the technology issue has invariably been addressed in terms of suitability and adaptation. In more sophisticated analyses, the intrusion of technology into aesthetic precepts and norms has also been addressed. But the present discussion would add that technology, with its various facets and dimensions, involves a rationalist ordered universe, whose frame of reference is governed by a reductionist logic. That in turn confronts a manifest reality of semantic disorder due to the disintegration of semiotic frameworks referred to above. This confrontation is resolved when the rationalistic logic is used to provide new conditions that elicit a new set of cultural symbols, much as the Modern Movement in international (Western and Japanese) architecture came into being, thus liberating and broadening the horizons of an authentic yet contemporary cultural response within the Muslim world." Ismail Serageldin, 'The Search for Excellence in Muslim Societies', in *Space For Freedom* (Aga Khan Award for Architecture, 1986), p 62. [Quote moved to footnote by the editor]

a recent side effect of globalized First-World consumerism, we might note that the local climate had already been rendered more arid by the wholesale deforestation of the mountains throughout the nineteenth century. The insatiable demand of the poor for firewood and construction lumber led to the ravaging of the local forests, at a rate of depletion that, happily, has seen a significant reduction over the last decade.

Apart from affording access to basic education and providing itself with street lighting for the first time in its existence, Aït Iktel seems to have attained a significant improvement in its native culture, even if its basic housing stock remains essentially unaltered. Electrification and the provision of a reliable water supply has virtually eliminated the burden traditionally placed upon women, and Aït lktel has reduced its illiteracy rate to 75 percent as opposed to the national average of 81 percent. All of this is even more impressive when one realizes that the average village income per capita is US$90 per annum, as opposed to the national minimum wage of US$140 per month.

Clearly there is little here that may be subsumed under architecture in the professional sense, and indeed this degree-zero building culture seems to be as removed from the more sophisticated cultures documented in Bernard Rudofsky's *Architecture Without Architects* of 1969[5] as it is from the contemporary constructional norms of the developed world. This is perhaps what may be intended by the term local culture as opposed to the vernacular in a stylistic sense of the term. For here the vernacular, such as it is, can be seen as undergoing an all but invisible transformation as migrant building workers return home to build their own houses. Needless to say, they bring with them, however simple it may be, an alien building technology. However, even though the standard concrete frame is gradually being more generally adopted, along with the use of rendered block-work, traditional stone walls still hold their own against the seemingly infinite mountain range from which they have been quarried since time immemorial.

Equally removed from anything that we could possibly classify as traditional architectural practice is the work of the so-called Barefoot Architects, local people with no formal education who work at the Barefoot College in India. The college was established in 1972 by the sociologist Bunker Roy as a way of departing from the academic orientation of the Indian social-work tradition by engaging and training ordinary people so as to cultivate a kind of Deweyesque, self-reliant community. Once again, the process of modernization was the prime mover at more than one level: first, perhaps because the natural aridity of the climate has recently become exacerbated by global warming; and second, because the first five years of the institution would once again be largely spent in searching for a more reliable source of water and in electrifying some 110 villages in the district of Silora. This technological infrastructure was complemented over the next decade by improving the community's native

---

[5] Bernard Rudofsky, *Architecture Without Architect: A Short Introduction to Non-Pedigreed Architecture* (New York, Museum of Modern Art, 1969).

skills for agricultural and craft production, enabling, in turn, the construction of installations dedicated to the harvesting of rain and the harnessing of solar power. In addition, the Barefoot Architects built a campus for the college. Based on a design that seems to have been arrived at on a collective basis, the architectural result is at once both surprisingly formal and informal. The basic building syntax itself could hardly be more strict and severe, even though the technology employed is quite hybrid, so that it is not something one could possibly recognize as vernacular in the traditional sense.

In the last analysis, the Barefoot College displays all the traits of a Utopian community abstracted from another moment in history. One is irresistibly reminded to an equal degree of both Rabindranath Tagore's Santiniketan College and of Charles Fourier's paradigm of the *phalanstère*, even if there is no parade ground on which any kind of *phalanx* could possibly assemble. In its stead there is a central theatrical space and open-air stage flanked on its wings by the cultural and collective core of the college, made up of the main dining room, the puppet theatre and administrative offices. A great deal of attention is clearly given to the enrichment of the cultural life of the institution, as is suggested by the presence of smaller stage platforms in the courtyard of the residential blocks. It is difficult to ignore the implicit symbolism of this neo-Kahnian layout, with its main axis of diagonal symmetry bisecting both the rainwater-storage tank and the principal open-air stage. Buckminster Fuller's geodesic domes have been widely employed throughout, not only for the larger volumes but also for emergency shelter, invariably made out of scrap metal by the master craftsman Rafeek Mohammed. These temporary thatched shelters, often sided in mud-brick, recall the intermediate technology of the 1960s, along with the anarchic ethos of Drop City in Arizona and the ad hoc 'know-how' that was once commonly available in the pages of *The Whole Earth Catalog*.[6]

[...]

Irrespective of the official auspices under which they were realized, the works discussed so far have depended for their success on one or two visionary figures without whom they would never have been realized. The Kahere Eila Poultry Farming School in Koliagbe, Guinea is no exception to this rubric. It is the outcome of an unlikely collaboration between a local veterinarian, Bachir Diallo, and a wealthy Finnish woman, Eila Kivekäs, the school being created as a way of addressing the appalling lack of protein in the average Guinean diet. It was the first of many local initiatives supported by Kivekäs and her development association, Indigo, which eventually led her to settle in Mali town in 1993.

As a result, she commissioned a house for her own occupation, to be designed by the Finnish architects Markku Komonen and Mikko Heikkinen. This simple

---

[6] *The Whole Earth Catalog* (Menlo Park, California, Portola Institute Inc, 1969). Influenced by Buckminster Fuller's techno-anarchic views as to the need to develop proto-ecological, synergetic systems on a world scale, this catalogue contains self-help survival information in almost every conceivable field, from simple shelter construction to hydroponics and the exploitation of solar energy.

but somewhat mannered house, known as the Villa Eila [1995], was supposed to have been a demonstration of the latent cultural potential of arts and crafts in Guinea.

A number of its features, above all the roof and the bamboo sunscreening, do succeed in reflecting some aspects of local building technique, while suggesting the possibility of combining these tropes with modern spatial concepts and conveniences. The overall result, however, has apparently not withstood the ravages of the climate, together with a general lack of maintenance, particularly after Kivekäs' demise in 1999.

The modestly monumental Kahere Eila Poultry Farming School [2000], by the same architects, seems to have fared much better, and in this regard, we might note that its design was based on a more rational plan. The confrontation here between modernization and vernacular culture is oddly provoked by the use of Nordic timber techniques ingeniously employed by the Finnish architects in the construction of the mono-pitched roofs. In addition, cable-tied timber joists are used for the wider spans covering the central classroom and its monumentally symbolic portico opening towards the centre of the court. Otherwise, the complex uses local materials. The main body of assembly is built out of 15-by-15-by-30-centimetre hand-pressed blocks made of stabilized earth mixed with a small quantity of cement, while the roof tiles were also made on site along with traditional mats of woven wooden lathes that form the ceilings of the accommodation. All ventilation is natural and passes through the roof and, although the farm is well supplied with water, electricity and sewerage, there is no telephone connection. This affords a dramatic idea of how remote and primitive this institution really is—it stands there implanted like the emblem of a future hybrid civilization in the middle of the bush.

[. . .]

Our progressive reaction to the modernization process seems to assume a critically topographic, place-oriented character the closer one moves to the centre of 'universal civilization', to coin Paul Ricoeur's felicitous term.[7] This is surely evident in the compensatory form of the Olbia Social Centre at the Akdeniz Üniversitesi on the outskirts of Antalya. Typologically speaking, the introverted spine of the centre suggests nineteenth-century galleria. This has both positive and negative connotations. Positive to the extent that the double-sided covered walkway connects to transport facilities, student accommodation and faculty buildings. Negative to the degree that an introspective 'galleria', when not inserted into existing urban fabric, always produces on its outer perimeter an alien 'backstage' space to which one cannot relate in a meaningful way (see the residential student union designed by Diamond and Myers and built in the campus of the University of Alberta, Edmonton, Canada in 1969). However, Cergiz Bektas provides a countervailing component to this 'backstage' effect, in an open-air amphitheatre with its *scena* facing into the campus.

---

[7] Paul Ricoeur, 'Universal Civilization and National Cultures', 1961 in *History and Truth* (Evanston, Northwest University Press, 1965).

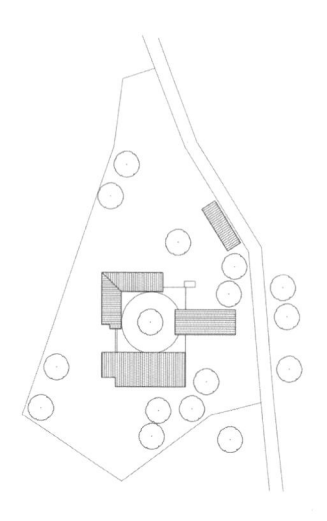

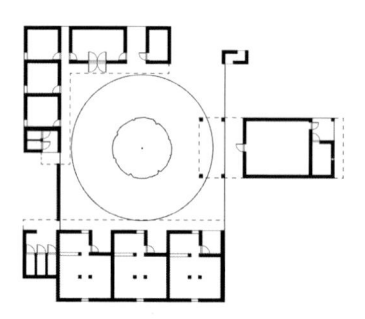

FIGURES 50 AND 51 Kahere Eila Poultry Farming School, Koliagbe, Guinea. Heikkinen-Komonen Architects, 1997–2000. Site plan (top) and the plan of the school complex (below).

The inner spine (galleria) is lined from end to end with cafeterias, restaurants, student clubs, multi-purpose auditoria, galleries and an array of shops. It is just this commercial continuum that enabled the university, with its limited funds, to take advantage of the BOT method (Build, Operate and Transfer), by which private investors glean the profit from the complex for nine years before transferring the ownership back to the university. Does not this ambiguous status—part shopping centre, part student forum—account for the mixed iconography of the syntax employed? Thus, on the one hand, stone-faced, anti-seismic, concrete-framed construction with mono-pitched, red-tiled roofs, having agrarian connotations, while on the other a wide ornamental watercourse, lined on both sides by an all but neoclassical timber pergola carried on precast concrete columns. This combination suggests a promenade through a discrete mall, rather than the traditional dense urban fabric that was the original inspiration. Be that as it may, there seems to be little doubt as to the popular reception of this work or as to its role in compensating for the absent 'space of public appearance' in a late-modern campus.

Finally realized in 1997, the Nubian Museum at Aswan, Egypt, exists as a consequence of modernization in the most direct sense imaginable. Had not a vast section of the Nile Valley been totally inundated in 1971 to provide hydropower for the new High Dam at Aswan, thereby creating Lake Nasser, there would have been no need to house the priceless remains of the twenty-two Egyptian monuments covered by the man-made flood.

Dr Mahmoud El-Hakim originally conceived the building as an internal topography, served by pedestrian ramps, surrounding a large statue of Rameses II in the centre, lit from above. The statue still occupies this position, although the elimination of the ramps and the skylight from the scheme means that it is now neither readily visible nor naturally illuminated. El-Hakim had intended that the flow of objects and visitors would culminate at the lowest level of the museum, at its eastern portico, where it would divulge into an external exhibition court. According to the landscape architects, Werkmeister and Heimer, this sequence was then to have been amplified by a stepped rock formation conducting visitors back onto the roof of the building, from which a stream of water would have descended as a metaphor for the Nile. Subsequent modification of El-Hakim's design weakened the didactic and cultural intentions of the initial concept, despite successful remedial efforts on the part of Dr Leila Masri to rescue something of Werkmeister's original landscape.

From the point of view of the never-ending conflict between modernization and cultural form, the initial brief seems to have been compromised by the modern curatorial tendency to maximize air-conditioning and artificial illumination, often at the expense of the relationship between users and exhibits. However, the building is well detailed and well constructed, its architecture seems successfully to represent the rich legacy of Nubian culture and it asserts itself on the site in such an authoritative manner as to counter the popular prejudice that Nubia is a backward part of the country.

I have elected to view the works premiated for the eighth cycle of the Award as responses, at distinctly different cultural levels, to the impact of modernization. This seems to be the one factor linking architecture with a capital A as we find, say, in the Nubian Museum, to what we might more generally characterize as local environmental culture, as this appears in the Aït Iktel development, the work of the Barefoot Architects, the SOS Children's Village and the Kahere Poultry Farming School. In each of these instances, the common denominator seems to have been a concerted effort to improve local living standards in the face of largely indifferent forms of modernization, operating at a globalized distance at ever-increasing speeds. What would appear to be intrinsically Islamic about all these works is the assumption of responsibility for the basic wellbeing of the society on the part of a relatively small number of enlightened individuals.

However, with the exception of the Jordanian orphanage, we can hardly speak of architecture in professional terms in these four projects, particularly with regard to sites as remote as the plains of Rajasthan, the High Atlas Mountains and the interior of Guinea, where the societies in question have been confronted with the challenge of improving the conditions of everyday survival and the maintenance of health. This goal has been achieved in part by revitalizing traditional forms of habitation and construction pertinent to the region and its climate, and in part by providing new water, power and sewerage infrastructures through sustainable forms of eco-technology. This, in turn, has led to additional benefits at the socio-cultural level, particularly with regard to the emancipation and education of women and, in the case of the Barefoot Architects, with respect to the categorical repudiation of the persistent legacy of the Indian caste system.

These four realizations, all of which display an ecological dimension in one way or another, serve to remind us of the way in which bolding culture, broadly understood, is ultimately inseparable from culture as such, in both a political and an artistic sense. It is a sign of the times that, as with the Olbia Social Centre, all four works were achieved without any significant input on the part of the state—at either a local or a national level—as opposed to those premiated works realized in Iran, Egypt and Malaysia. In these other, possibly more professional undertakings either the local government or the nation state played a key role in initiating the project. Under this sponsorship, architecture tends to assume a more broadly instrumental character, subtly linked, even in the case of Iran, to pressures deriving from modernization and to the processes of cultural disruption and displacement: for example, the obsolescence, from a universal middle-class standpoint, of the traditional Iranian courtyard house, not to mention the brutal autoroute incisions cut into the traditional labyrinthine urban fabric as long ago as the early 1930s. No doubt, the impact of modernization in the case of the Datai Hotel takes a somewhat different form, although even here, the indisputable quality of its eco-sensitive, quasi-vernacular architecture has ultimately been achieved in the name of exotic tourism, devised, all but exclusively, for the entertainment and enjoyment of a global, jet-setting elite. In sum, we are still some way from the authentic contemporary cultural response to which Serageldin aspires [. . .]

22 The Predicament of the Place-Form: Notes from New York (1997)

[...]

In India, signs of a consumer and advertising economy are on the increase. No one begrudges a good car, refrigerator, television or whatever but the tendency to treat things and even people as commodities is growing. Land itself enters the cycle of profit and one sees the inflation of prices in cities like Delhi and Mumbai. There will be the tendency to build upwards, and to use skyscrapers as billboards for commerce as has happened already in the USA. At a later stage tradition itself becomes a "consumable" of a kind – a device for lending allure and atmosphere to "products," including buildings. Inevitably there is a turning outwards and an embracing of foreign, imported fashions rather than an investigation of what is valuable in the indigenous. The new Indian middle class seems out of touch with the masses of the countryside, and even more so with the decimated masses who live a stone's throw away in the squatter settlements. The old socialist worldview crumbled under the weight of its own bureaucracies, but a "new right" market strategy will not deal with India's deeper structural problems, even if it does lead to more coloured Marutis on the road.

Balkrishna Doshi, *The Future of Indian Architecture*, 1988

Today the categoric, post-colonial distinctions between the First and Third Worlds begin to lose validity. The new situation seems to be shaped by paradoxical displacements in which microcosmic so-called First Worlds emerge as luxurious enclaves within the body of the Third World while former First Worlds, America *par excellence*, begin to disaggregate into a set of microcosmic Third Worlds in one sector after another. We need only to look at childbirth mortality statistics in the USA or the mass illiteracy rate, not to mention its chronic uneven

Source: Kenneth Frampton, "The Predicament of the Place-Form: Notes from New York," in *Contemporary Architecture and City Form: The South Asian Paradigm*, ed. Farooq Ameen (Mumbai: Marg Publications, 1997), 101–9.

distribution of wealth, or the fact that today millions of children in the USA are living in poverty, to find in North America all the tell-tale symptoms of a Third World country in the making. And that which is demographically evident at the level of health, education, and social welfare, also manifests itself in American architecture and urbanism in equally paradoxical ways.

One well-known indicator in this regard is the wasteful and profligate system of low-density, speculative residential land subdivision that prevails in the US and has done so continuously, since the end of the Second World War. We may set against this, at the conceptual level, Serge Chermayeff and Christopher Alexander's canonical text *Community and Privacy* dating from 1963, in which they argued for a categoric change in American suburban land-settlement procedure. They opted, as we know, for low-rise, high-density courtyard housing as a way of achieving a new and more economical method of residential settlement in relation to the escalating urbanization that was then emerging in megalopolitan regions all over the United States. The proposition was by no means anti-motopian but the simple canonical pattern of their generic courtyard housing would not have allowed for cars to be housed within the actual body of the dwelling, as in the typical American suburban house and garage. Instead, the parking was grouped and the general access to the housing would have involved a short, covered walk from parking place to dwelling. While such a proposition was completely opposed to the "market norm" and was thus equally incompatible with the extant local zoning codes and building by-laws, it was in no way opposed to the main lines of the prevailing neo-capitalist economy. It was however totally antithetical to the drive towards conspicuous consumption and it was this perhaps, as much as anything else, that limited its potential influence on the emergent forms of regional urbanization. It is a regrettable fact that as an alternative mode of land settlement, it would exercise no influence whatsoever on the practice of land subdivision in North America. It was "still born", because, among other things, it failed to provide a sufficiently marketable middle-class image of the "received" suburban house. Of course, one may also claim that it did not afford all the other amenities that are normally provided by the typical suburban dwelling; above all the largely fictitious image of individual sovereignty and "largesse"; the infamous "keeping up with the Jones's". Either way round, the influence of the Chermayeff/Alexander model in the US was virtually negligible and as far as current generic patterns of American land settlement are concerned, it might never have been proposed.

It is one of the ironies of the interrelationship between the so-called First and Third Worlds that Indian architects categorically demonstrated very comparable alternative land-settlement patterns that could with minor adaptation have been employed equally effectively in both worlds. It is a significant and yet an understandably ironic fact that this remarkable production has also been largely ignored by the Western world. I have in mind of course the quite remarkable forms of aggregate housing and land settlement that have been realized in India over the past forty years; certainly, from around 1953 when Doshi worked for Le Corbusier on Peon housing [Maison des Péons] in Chandigarh and up to the 1990s when the Vastu-Shilpa Foundation published its

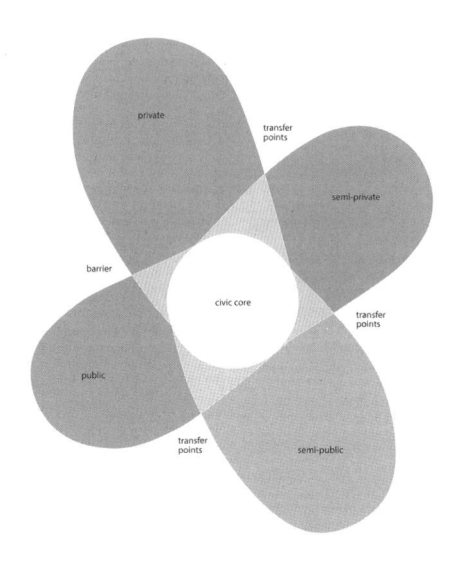

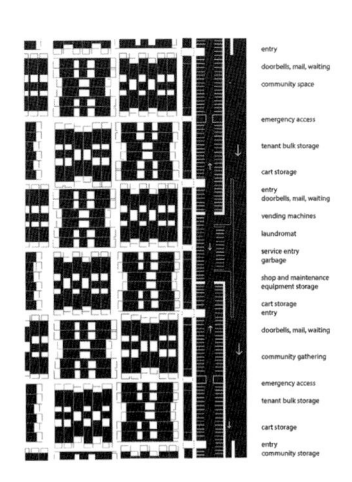

FIGURES 52 AND 53 Serge Chermayeff and Christopher Alexander, *Community and Privacy: Toward a New Architecture of Humanism* (New York: Doubleday, 1963). Anatomy of urban realms: areas of responsibility (top); urban clusters incorporated into a linear superblock (below).

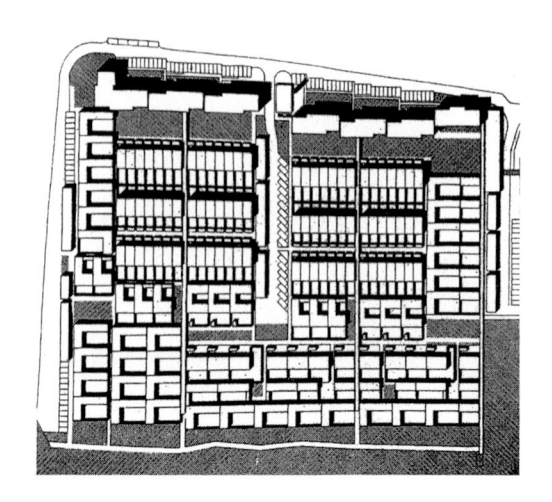

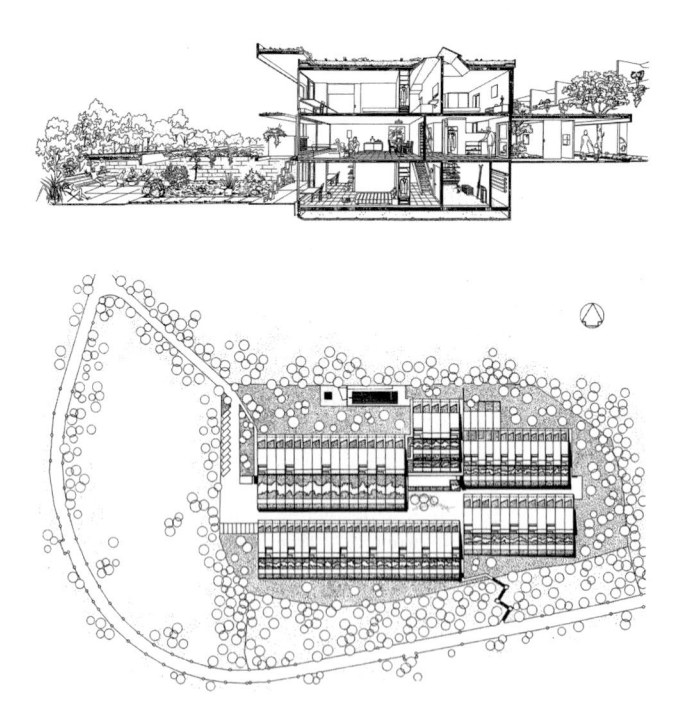

FIGURES 54–56 First phase of the low-rise, high-density housing plan for the Garden City Puchenau, Austria. Roland Reiner, 1965–67 (top). Siedlung Halen, Bern, Switzerland. Atelier 5, 1955–1961. Section through the terraced housing (middle) and site plan (below).

FIGURES 57 AND 58 Belapur Incremental Housing scheme, Navi Mumbai, India. Charles Correa, 1983-1986. Schematic diagrams of the basic housing configuration composed of nine units with a courtyard (9×9 meters), is grouped into a larger housing configuration (21×21 meters) with a shared space at the heart of this artist village (top); The Asian Games Village, New Delhi, India. Raj Rewal Associates, 1980–82 (below).

exhaustive study for the development of the Aranya Township situated on the Bombay-Delhi highway close to the city of Indore.

Departing from low-rise, high-density housing studies made by Le Corbusier for North Africa, the Côte d'Azur, and India, a number of Indian architects elaborated a series of interlocking unit types thereby proliferating a set of urban place-forms that were close to those that had been first projected by the Team X faction of CIAM; by such figures as Aldo van Eyck, Jan van Stigt, Piet Blom, and Georges Candilis with Alexis Josic and Shadrach Woods. This Indian production first emerges fully in Ranjit Sabikhi's YMCA Staff Quarters (1963) and in Kuldip Singh's Usha Niketan housing complex finished in New Delhi in the following year. This line is picked up by Raj Rewal in his French Embassy staff housing (1969) and in his Sheikh Sarai housing of 1982. The approach was further developed in Rewal's Asian Games Housing, New Delhi, completed in the same year. It is perhaps important to note that this project was equipped with courts for the parking of automobiles in groups. A similar trajectory may be traced through Doshi's career, starting with his tentative PRL Housing for Ahmedabad of 1960 and going on to his Gujarat State Township (1969), his Electronic Corporation Township, Hyderabad (1971), his Kata Township (1976), his US Embassy Residences (1978), and his Vidyadhar Nagar Satellite City Plan projected for Jaipur in 1986. Charles Correa's career follows a similar course even if his carpet-housing realizations have been less extensive. One thinks none the less of his so-called Tube Housing for Ahmedabad (1962), his Jeevan Bima Nagar Township (1972), his three-storey terraces for the Gujarat Housing Board of the same year, his Calvetty housing (1980, unbuilt), his L&T Township (1982), and his Incremental Housing realized in Belapur, New Bombay.

From this thirty-year experience of building aggregate low-rise housing in India the following provisional observations may be made. Outside of the remarkable practice of Atelier 5 in Switzerland (1960-96) and the equally heroic achievements of Roland Rainer, over the same period in Vienna, Linz, and above all Puchenau, plus the exceptional work realized by Kamran Diba in his Shustar New Town in Iran, the most extensive demonstrations of the "place-form" potential of low-rise, high-density housing have surely been made in India. So far this momentous achievement has been insufficiently appraised not only within but also without the South Asian continent and this stricture surely applies as much to China, Japan, and South-East Asia as it does to the critical apparatus of the West. It is a significant and a somewhat sobering fact, that most of this work was realized in the service of industrial corporations, life insurance companies, or under the auspices of quasi-governmental bodies. One senses that this form of patronage may be losing its power due to regrettable changes in the prevailing socio-economic and political climate. Despite the fact that Doshi's Aranya settlement near Indore is now in the process of being realized (for rich and poor alike, with the rich, in effect, subsidizing the poor), large building corporations are now beginning to take over the construction of townships and/or walled-in enclaves for an upwardly mobile middle class. At the same time, one knows only too well that all those generic models of low-rise, high-density developments cannot be made available to the poorest sectors of the population. As we are aware, in order to ameliorate the most impoverished levels of spontaneous urbanization one has to abandon the professional practice of architecture as we know it and to adopt instead strategies that are oriented primarily towards the post-facto provision of the basic infrastructure, namely water, sewage, power, and transport, not to mention the ubiquitous demand for modern telecommunications. Charles Correa was to confront this issue head-on in his 1970 proposal for decanting the continually imploding population of Bombay into an area to be established as New Bombay across the water. Over the last twenty-five years this settlement has reluctantly come into existence under the auspices of the Maharashtra government although unfortunately it has not been equipped with inter-city rapid transit and so far it has not attained anything like the two million it was scheduled to accommodate. In the meantime, the population continues to implode and now around half of Mumbai's population of nearly ten million are squatters. As Correa notes in his book *The New Landscape* (1985) it is just such implosions that will fulfil the projection that by the year 2000 there will be some fifty cities in the world with populations of around fifteen million.

SOURCES

Serge Chermayeff and Christopher Alexander, *Community and Privacy: Toward a New Architecture of Humanism* (New York: Doubleday, 1963).

Charles Correa, *The New Landscape* (London: RIBA Enterprises, 1985).

Balkrishna Doshi, "Postscript: The Future of Indian Architecture," in ed. Curtis, W.J.R. *Balkrishna Doshi: An Architecture for India* (Random House Incorporated and Rizzoli, 1988), 170–94.

23 Plan Form and Topography in the Work of Kashef Chowdhury (2016)

It is one of the redeeming characteristics of our pluralistic age that despite the mediatic triumph of spectacular star architects, a subtly differentiated culture of building still prevails here and there throughout the world, as much in Bangladesh as anywhere else in South Asia. Much of this is due to the legacy of Louis Kahn in Bengal, that is to say his monumental National Assembly at Sher-e-Bangla Nagar in Dhaka, finally completed posthumously in 1979, five years after his death. Kahn received this commission in part through the auspices of the distinguished Bangladeshi architect Muzharul Islam, a politically committed and talented designer to whom every contemporary Bangladeshi architect of stature is inevitably indebted, Kashef Mahboob Chowdhury no less than any other member of his generation.

However, what distinguishes Chowdhury from both Kahn and Islam is his particularly sensitive feeling for the rain-swept plains and inundations of the Bengal delta. As he put it in the Commonwealth Association of Architects Conference, held in Dhaka in 2013:

> This is Bengal, a geo-cultural region woven out of an intricate network of rivers and canals and to which all art forms respond—from the emotionally rendered Bhawaiya songs, and the colors of the stitched Nakshi-Kantha textiles, to the living and lost architecture of the delta. Much of my childhood was spent by the side of the river Padma, which draws its waters from the Ganges. It is difficult to put into words my memories with those waters, of the clouds—both above and soaked in reflection. And the finest and softest of all soils: the alluvial layers where the ground was still moist from receding waters.[1]

Source: Kenneth Frampton, "Plan Form and Topography in the Work of Kashef Chowdhury," in Kenneth Frampton and Robert Wilson, *Kashef Chowdhury: The Friendship Centre, Gaibandha, Bangladesh* (Zürich: Park Books, 2016), 8–12.

[1] Chowdhury, Kashef. "Silence and Chaos." *The Architectural Review*, December 2013, 26–27.

Perhaps no other work to date by Chowdhury comes closer to this sensibility than his so-called Friendship Centre, constructed between 2010 and 2012 in Gaibandha, in the remote northern region of the country. Built of carefully selected bricks from a local brickwork, this single-story structure is subtly integrated into its low-lying site in such a way as to make it seem inseparable from the flood plains which surround it on every side. This seemingly limitless, low-lying plain is seasonally flooded by the Brahmaputra-Jamuna river—a vulnerability that led Chowdhury to provide the Friendship Centre with a wide orthogonal berm, which runs around the temenos of its rectangular site on all four sides. As a result, access to this quasi-sacrosanct compound has entailed the further provision of two raised walkways, one serving as a monumental gate and one comprising a narrow auxiliary staircase access rising to the same datum above the top of the berm. The paradoxical hermeticism of the Friendship Centre is announced by a monumental approach consisting of a single-story porter's lodge and a broad ramp, which ultimately give onto a brick causeway situated on top of the berm.

From this elevated datum, an equally broad flight of steps descends at a 45-degree angle into the orthogonal labyrinth of the centre itself. The latter is divided at once into two zones of exactly equal size. The first of these to be encountered after the initial descent is, in essence, a pedagogical-cum-administrative sector comprising offices, training pavilions, a tea-room, a prayer hall, and classrooms accommodating some thirty-six students respectively and situated back-to-back. This arrangement enables the classrooms to be combined into a larger volume on the occasion of lectures or festive activities through the removal of a lightweight, demountable partition. The second "private" zone is connected to, and yet symbolically separated from, the relatively "public" domain by three deep, arcuated brick tunnels. This zone serves essentially as a dormitory and refuge, where members of the local community receiving training or attending workshops may stay for limited periods of time. To this end, some twenty-seven virtually cubic bedrooms are provided, usually accommodating two beds per room and interspersed with toilets and washing facilities. Both public and private zones feature rain-harvesting tanks as part and parcel of the labyrinthic "townscape" that makes up the undesignated open space. The overall "mat building" of the centre comprises a trabeated brick structure, built in accordance with standard brick sizes, thereby eliminating, as much as possible, the use of cut bricks. This trabeated system consists of loadbearing brick piers and brick lintels of short and wide spans these last being integrated into the continuous reinforced concrete slab that covers the occupiable space—and sustains a turf roof which, given the aquatic climate, is as green as the attendant flood plain. As the architect has remarked, this work has a somewhat Piranesian aura, in part due to its quasi-subterranean character and in part stemming from its fragmentary brick syntax. This austere, all but archaeological aesthetic is augmented by the absence of air conditioning, which has been omitted as much for ideological reasons as for restrictions on the budget.

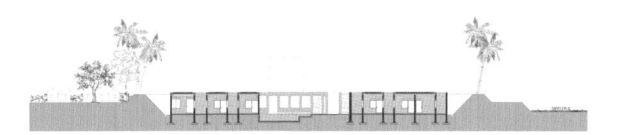

FIGURE 59 AND 60 The Friendship Centre, Gaibandha, Bangladesh. Kashef Mahboob Chowdhury, 2012. Section (top); panoramic view of the complex (below).

As Kazi Ashraf reminds us, this topographic mat building arises as much out of the collective Bengal memory of ancient Buddhist monasteries as out of the increased threat of inundation due to escalating climate change. Moreover, the "prohibitive costs for landfill, as well as seismic activity and the low weight bearing capacity of the silty soil, discouraged adopting the usual response of raising the whole site above the high flood level."[2]

Chowdhury would largely repeat this exercise in his two-story Friendship Hospital at Satkhira in the remote south of the country. Here the strategy was quite different in that a decision was made to address the question of inundation through a unifying aqueous spine consisting of a cranked canal plus a large rainwater harvesting tank, freshwater being "a valuable resource where saline ground water is unusable for most practical purposes."[3] Water and topography are both crucial elements in Chowdhury's architecture. We encounter them as latent presences in his Chandgaon Mosque located in a village on the northern periphery of Chittagong, Bangladesh's second largest city. This dualistic reinterpretation of the traditional mosque in Bengal, divided between a main prayer hall and a semi-covered entrance court, assumes a particularly powerful "yin-yang" abstract form in concrete, naturally illuminated pure circular cut-out in the second. Such abstract clarity, referential to traditional typologies, will reappear in other works by Chowdhury, for example in his proposal for the new Institute of Architects Bangladesh in Dhaka, ostensibly harking back in its form to the Etakholamura Temple in Comilla, dating from between the eighth and the twelfth century. Thus, for Chowdhury, abstract form may be brought to imply the sacred in and of itself, as in the three-story pyramidal house around a central court projected for Alipore in Kolkata. As he puts it:

> I'm tired of efficient buildings. Buildings that offer you not a moment to pause, to ponder, to wish, to recollect. Buildings that work well, better than you'd wished for and give you nothing else. In an office or railway station—yes; but in a home or in front of art in an art gallery, I look for a loss of time. Absence of time.[4]

This temporal depletion prompts one to conclude that today the Modern Movement has little choice but to retrace its steps, turning back to tradition in order to arrive at viable new hybrid models for the development of our urban future.

---

[2] Ashraf, Kazi. "Modern Ruin." *The Architectural Review*, December 2013, 23.

[3] "Friendship Hospital, Satkhira." *The Architectural Review*, December 2013, 36–37.

[4] Chowdhury, Kashef. "Silence and Chaos." *The Architectural Review*, December 2013, 26–27.

24 2018 Society of Architectural Historians Plenary Talk (2018)

The double honor of being made a Fellow of the Society of Architectural Historians and being asked to give this year's plenary address, leaves me with a great deal of uncertainty as to what would be an appropriate topic. This dilemma arises in large measure out my being somewhat manque, since, despite my formal education as an architect at the AA School of Architecture in London, I am neither an architect nor strictly speaking an historian. I prefer to think of myself as a teacher of architecture, having spent most of my adult life in this activity, although even this is somewhat questionable since it is by no means clear that the art of architecture can be taught; witness all the great architects of the 20th century who never set foot inside an architectural school; among them Frank Lloyd Wright, Henry van de Velde, Mies van der Rohe, Le Corbusier and Tadao Ando. Further proof of this, if any more were needed, is the fact that I have spent consciously or unconsciously a great deal of my time trying to ascertain the grounds upon which a significant culture of modern architecture may still be effectively cultivated. My first move in this direction was the book *Modern Architecture: A Critical History*, which aside from being an operative history of the rise and fall of the Modern Movement, was also the agency with which I first observed the inroads made into architecture by the advent of high-speed film and the impact that this invention had on both our reception and conception of architecture. I am alluding to the all but prophetic last paragraph that ended the first edition of this book dating from 1980:

> The veil that photo-lithography draws over architecture is not neutral. High-speed photographic and reproductive processes are surely not only the political economy of the sign but also an insidious filter through which our

Source: Kenneth Frampton, Plenary Talk at the 71st Annual International Conference of the Society of Architectural Historians, 20 April 2018, Saint Paul, MN.

tactile environment tends to lose its responsiveness. When much of modern building is experienced in actuality, its photogenic quality is denied by the poverty and the brutality of its detailing. Time and again an ostentatious display of either structure or form results in the impoverishment of intimacy; in that which Heidegger recognized as the 'loss of nearness'. How rarely do we encounter a modern work where the inflection of a chosen tectonic penetrates into the innermost recesses of a structure, not as a totalizing force but as a declension of an articulate sensibility. That modern society still possesses a capacity for such an inflection finds its confirmation in the finest work of Aalto.

What I had in mind when I wrote this text was the way in which both high-speed film and the reflex camera had facilitated a proliferation of images at a lower level of resolution than what had previously been achieved by the plate camera with its capacity to reveal the tactile grain of the diverse materials from which a building may be composed. For me the proof of this lay in my experience as the technical editor of the British magazine *Architectural Design* when we published Stirling and Gowan's Leicester Engineering Building in 1961 with the remarkable photographs of this work taken by Richard Einzig with a plate camera. I realized then that these changes in representational technique affected not only our perception of built form but also our conception of the relationships obtaining between constructional form and the organization of space. With this I already became preoccupied as I would be for the rest of my career with trying to determine the basis upon which a rationally responsible culture of architecture could still be pursued.

It is ironic and always somewhat surprising to me that my account of the Modern Movement would be published in the very same year as the first Architectural Biennale staged in Venice in 1980 by Paolo Portoghesi as a postmodern *mise-en-scène* centered about the axis of the Arsenale in the form of a so-called *Strada Novissima*, comprising a series of scenographic facades, designed by the emerging architects of the moment, and built by the operatives of the Italian film industry. This new street was, in effect, a seemingly spontaneous reification of Robert Venturi's postmodern, populist concept of the 'decorated shed' as this had appeared in 1963 in his MoMA paper entitled *Complexity and Contradiction in Architecture*. My resignation from the commissioning body of the Biennale came well before the opening and eventually led to my essay "Towards a Critical Regionalism: Six Points for an Architecture of Resistance" which was first published in 1983 in Hal Foster's anthology *The Anti-Aesthetic: Essays in Postmodern Culture*. Apart from its attempt to save architecture from its reduction to scenography, this essay was inspired by two quite independent intellectual reflections; in the first instance by Paul Ricoeur's 1961 essay, "Civilizations and National Cultures" in which he discriminated between civilization as universal technology and culture as "the ethical and mythical nucleus of mankind," and in the second, by Alexander Tzonis and Liane Lefaivre's first coinage of the term 'critical regionalism' in their 1981 essay "The Grid and the Pathway" featuring what could surely be recognized as regionalist mannerisms in the work of the leading Greek architects of the 1950s, namely, Dimitris Pikionis and Aris Konstantinidis.

I should perhaps add that I was already moving towards a kind of regional awareness as a result of noticing in the 1960s, while working on *Architectural Design*, the rapport that seemed to emerge in Europe in the late 1950s and early 1960s between local architects and the city-states in which they happened to be working. I had in mind at the time the relationship between, say, Oswald Mathias Ungers and Cologne, Gino Valle and Udine, and Ernst Gisel and the city of Zürich. But the final syndrome which gave my elaboration of the Critical Regionalist thesis its manifesto form was unquestionably Ricoeur's recognition that culture as a mythical spiritual sense of belonging was no match for the cold instrumentality of universal technology. Ricoeur's essay seemed to me to hold the key as to the potential accessibility of architectural form in relation to the ordinary members of society. This opposition between culture and civilization was for me the dialectic which I gave substance to in my "Six Points for an Architecture of Resistance." Namely, the avant-garde versus the rear-garde of our late Modernity, *place* versus *space* after Heidegger's concept of space-endlessness versus the idea of bounded domain. In Greek, *peras*, as he puts it, is not that point at which something ends but rather the boundary at which something begins its presensing.

In my view no one has understood what I intended by Critical Regionalism more sensitively than the Marxist critic Fredric Jameson, who in his 1994 book, *The Seeds of Time*, wrote:

> [p. 190 . . .] while it can be said that Critical Regionalism shares with them [stylistic postmodernist architects] a systematic repudiation of certain essential traits of high modernism, it distinguishes itself by attempting at one and the same time to negate a whole series of postmodern negations of modernism as well, and can in some respects be seen as anti-modern and anti-postmodern simultaneously, in a "negation of the negation" . . . the universal standardization of commodities and "life styles" are precisely what Critical Regionalism seeks to resist. Yet its slogan of an *arrière-garde* would also seem incompatible with a postmodern "end of history."

Jameson continues:

> [. . .] the current slogans of marginality and resistance, as they are evoked by Frampton, would also appear to carry rather different connotations than those deployed in, say, current evocations of multi-culturalism.

Jameson went on to relate my emphasis on the tectonic joint to my equally salient notion of the dis-joint, that is to say, an articulate junction which precisely expresses the point at which one formal, tectonic system ends and another begins. The one area of my regionalist thesis which Jameson understandably resisted was the implication that a region could consolidate itself in such a way as to establish a cantonal sense of political sovereignty. This he saw as a totally fragile proposition in the face of the worldwide neoliberal hegemony which today is now more extensive than it was in the mid-1990s.

I have dwelt on Critical Regionalism because somehow it still remains as a cultural reference even after three decades, particularly in Latin America and South East Asia. While I have since moved on to the idea of tectonic form as the resistant stratagem within the long evolution of the Modern Movement, as this may be found in the poetry of construction in the work of such figures as Frank Lloyd Wright, Auguste Perret, Mies van der Rohe, Louis Kahn, Jørn Utzon, and Carlo Scarpa, as these architects are critically interpreted in my *Studies in Tectonic Culture: The Poetics of Construction in Nineteenth and Twentieth Century Architecture* of 1995.

However, we cannot surely conclude that a poetic of construction is in and of itself sufficient ground from which to cultivate a critical practice of architecture, and at this point I find that I have no choice but to re-assert the time-honored need for a hierarchization of space, and to argue that this must come as much from the society as from the relatively autonomous tradition of architecture as an end in itself.

This discourse returns me to the one book that has effectively determined my entire outlook on architecture, namely Hannah Arendt's *The Human Condition* of 1958, above all for the socio-cultural and political emphasis that she places on 'the space of appearance' as the one value to be unequivocally articulated in development of environmental form. At the same time, it is clear that we are more inundated with images today than ever before which is surely reflected in the fact that part of this convocation has been devoted to the challenge posed by the digital and its impact not only on the design and realization of architecture but also on historical research and on the writing of the architectural history, and above all on the management of archives and the retrieval and general accessibility of archival material.

And while I continue to argue for the cultivation of a critically resistant architecture not only in terms of maintaining the Arendtian 'space of public appearance' but also by virtue of integrating built form into its attendant landscape, I am compelled to admit that today, we are ever more exposed to spectacularly irrational works, often of a gargantuan size, that are proliferated across the surface of the globe by one star architect after another. Thus whether we like it or not, we are all enmeshed in Guy Debord's *Society of the Spectacle* as first identified by him as a syndrome in 1967.

One is reminded in this context of Karl Marx's prescient prophecy made some 130 years ago, the immortal words, "All that is solid melts into air." Today we witness on a daily basis the proliferation of ever higher, more meaningless high-rise structures, invariably curtain-walled and clustered, cheek by jowl, around the financial capitals of the world irrespective of whether this happens to be Manhattan, London, Dubai, Jakarta or elsewhere in Asia and the Far East. Meanwhile, the world continues to be overwhelmed by burgeoning refugee populations and extreme changes in the earth's climate. This is surely among the more recent consequences of the *Society of the Spectacle* of which Guy Debord wrote in 1988:

> It is indeed unfortunate that human society should encounter such burning problems just when it has become materially impossible to make heard the least objection to the language of the commodity; just when power—quite rightly because it is shielded by the spectacle from any response to its piecemeal and delirious decisions and justifications—believes that it no longer needs to think; and indeed can no longer think.
> Guy Debord, *Comments on the Society of the Spectacle*, 1988: 38.

SOURCES

Arendt, Hannah. *The Human Condition* (Chicago: University of Chicago Press, 1958).

Debord, Guy. *Society of the Spectacle*, trans. Freddy Perlman and Jon Supak (New York: Black & Red, 1967, rev. ed. 1977).

Debord, Guy. *Comments on the Society of the Spectacle*, trans. Malcolm Imrie (London: Verso, 1988).

Frampton, Kenneth. *Modern Architecture: A Critical History* (London: Thames & Hudson, 1980).

Frampton, Kenneth. "Towards a Critical Regionalism: Six Points for an Architecture of Resistance," in *The Anti-Aesthetic: Essays in Postmodern Culture*, ed. Hal Foster (Port Townsend, Washington: Bay Press, 1983), 16–30.

Frampton, Kenneth. *Studies in Tectonic Culture: The Poetics of Construction in Nineteenth and Twentieth Century Architecture* (Cambridge, MA: MIT Press, 1995).

Jameson, Fredric. *The Seeds of Time* (New York: Columbia University Press, 1994).

Ricoeur, Paul. "Universal Civilization and National Cultures," (1961) in *History and Truth* (Evanston, IL: Northwest University Press, 1965), 276–67.

Tzonis A. and Lefaivre, L. "The Grid and the Pathway: An Introduction to the Work of Dimitris and Susana Antonakakis," *Architecture in Greece*, n.15 (Athens, 981).

Venturi, Robert. *Complexity and Contradiction in Architecture* (New York: The Museum of Modern Art, 1963).

SECTION 4
The Predicament of Architecture in the New Millennium

25 Introduction to Section 4

The theme of "predicament" has been a recurring feature of Frampton's critical discourse. To many critics, it rendered his outlook *a priori* "negative" and "pessimistic," a charge Frampton has repeatedly denounced as absurd. As Frampton has often indicated, his work has constantly attempted "to determine limits in order to do work of quality," and predicament in that sense serves as a rhetorical vehicle through which such limits can be identified and transgressed. Likewise, Frampton often returns to Gramsci's slogan "Pessimism of the intellect, optimism of the will"[1] in expressing his commitment to an ongoing critical analysis of the social, cultural, and political urgencies of the present time (i.e., the critical present), while suggesting effective strategies of transformation through architecture. This last section of the book addresses, on one hand, Frampton's conviction that the unfinished project of modernity still carries unique emancipatory potential capable of improving the lives of ordinary people through modern design, and on the other, his recognition that in the new millennium we face contemporary, unfamiliar, and wicked challenges. In facing them, we can no longer employ courses of action prescribed by the avant-garde modernism of the twentieth century. Hence, as Frampton suggests, we need new political and cultural imagination(s).

In 1991, Kenneth Frampton was awarded the highest national honor for architectural education in the United States,[2] and in his talk—here reprinted as "Architecture, Philosophy, and the Education of Architects"—Frampton addressed the issue of architecture's autonomy vis-à-vis the public realm, by

---

[1] See Antonio Gramsci, *Prison Notebooks*, trans. Joseph A. Buttigieg (New York: Columbia University Press, 2011).

[2] The Topaz Medallion for Architectural Education, jointly awarded by the American Institute of Architects (AIA) and the Association of Collegiate Schools of Architecture (ACSA), is the highest national honor awarded to educators who had an outstanding impact not only on architectural education, but on the discipline and practice of architecture and on society at large. Frampton delivered his award address at the 79th Annual Meeting of the ACSA in Washington, DC.

discussing the role of theory and philosophy in contemporary architectural education. He argued that the introduction of philosophy into the architecture curriculum would afford the evaluative ground on which to construct a truly public realm and a meaningful public discourse; both are necessary to guarantee "the worldliness of the world." In warning against the dangers of theory divorced from practice (such as the metatheory, Frampton suggests, emerging in schools of architecture across the United States), he reminds us (after Gianni Vattimo) that contemporary architecture and philosophy are analogous in their quest "to edify": to configure the public realm in such a way as to render (public) life ethical.[3]

In the essay that follows—"Reflections on the Autonomy of Architecture: A Critique of Contemporary Production,"[4] a work produced in the same year—Frampton returns to the idea of relative autonomy of architecture as a contingent practice. He revisits the distinction between architecture and building, through Hannah Arendt's conceptual labor-work-action triad, and employs Edmund Husserl's concept of the "lifeworld" in arguing that architecture is both "a cultural discourse and a frame for life." In an increasingly privatized society where the existence of the public realm is never certain and the lifeworld is no longer a permanent repository of cultural values, Frampton argues, architecture has lost its fundamental links to institutional forms and thus its ability to produce true spaces of public appearance. In this essay, Frampton reexamines arguments he made just a year prior in another seminal text, "Rappel à L'ordre: The Case for the Tectonic"[5] (not reprinted in this volume), and revisits distinctions between the Vitruvian classical triad (*utilitas, firmitas,* and *venustas*)[6] and Gottfried Semper's quadripartite theory.[7] Frampton thereby argues that the root of architectural autonomy lies in the triad of earthwork (topography), construction (tectonic), and hearth (typology) as the embodiment of institutional form, and thus returns architecture to its ur *métier*, the tectonic of the realized form. As Frampton notes, although there is no absolute autonomy in practice (architecture "belongs as much to society as to ourselves"[8]), the relative autonomy of architecture hinges on the fact that it is constructed. This

---

[3] Gianni Vattimo, "Project and Legitimization I," *Lotus International*, no. 48/49 (1986): 125.

[4] Kenneth Frampton, "Reflections on the Autonomy of Architecture: A Critique of Contemporary Production," in *Out of Site: Social Criticism of Architecture*, ed. Diane Ghirardo (Washington, DC: Bay Press, 1991), 17–26.

[5] Kenneth Frampton, "Rappel à L'ordre: The Case for the Tectonic," *Architectural Design* 60, no. 3–4 (1990): 19–25.

[6] Vitruvius, *Ten Books on Architecture*, trans. Morgan Morris Hicky (Cambridge, MA: Harvard University Press, 1914). This is the first unabridged English translation.

[7] Gottfried Semper, *The Four Elements of Architecture and Other Writings*, trans. Harry F. Mallgrave and Wolfgang Herrmann (Cambridge, UK: Cambridge University Press, 1989). Originally published in 1851 as *Die vier Elemente der Baukunst*.

[8] By "ourselves," Frampton here means architects.

autonomy is therefore bound to architecture's dual relationality: to its own *métier* and to the lifeworld.

In 1999, Frampton was invited to deliver a keynote address at the 20th Congress of the International Union of Architects (UIA). In this talk, titled "Seven Points for the Millennium: An Untimely Manifesto,"[9] Frampton asserts that "we are coming to the close of a century in which contemporary architecture has often been inseparable from the writing of manifestos." Indeed, he takes this opportunity to rework his 1983 six-point manifesto "Towards a Critical Regionalism" into this new seven-point manifesto, recognizing that architecture faces different challenges while attempting to define its scope and role at the dawn of the new millennium. Frampton makes a strong argument for bringing architectural practice closer to the social and cultural needs and aspirations of the new century, and suggests that what we lack is the political and ideological will to bring existing, promising "models" to realization in order to afford some degree of control over the meaning and significance of the urban fabric. Going a step further, Frampton insists that the cultivation of landscape ought to become a priority for architecture and planning education, replacing the traditional obsession with designing free-standing objects. In closing, he discusses the predicament of the environment and the state of the profession vis-à-vis the "unavoidable interplay between reason and power," arguing that the parallel forces of modernity and democracy tend to undermine regional cultures and to condemn society to techno-scientific rationality whose *raison d'être* is always in the perpetuation of existing power relations. To break out of this destructive impasse, Frampton advises, we need new forms of political and cultural imagination—a new social contract.

In only one text does Frampton discuss citizen participation in the process of co-designing and making architecture in the West[10]—"Typology and Participation: The Architecture of Álvaro Siza" (2016).[11] This essay focuses on Siza's São Victor and Bouça housing settlements in Porto (1974–1977), and on the more recent design for the Quinta da Malagueira barrio near Évora (1977–2006), in Portugal. Beyond his foreseeable interest in the way Siza has realized collective forms and spaces of collectivization in these settlements, Frampton also

---

[9] Kenneth Frampton, "Seven Points for the Millennium: An Untimely Manifesto," *The Journal of Architecture* 5 (Spring 2000): 21–33.

[10] Prior to this essay, Frampton had not written extensively about advocacy planning and other participatory design and planning practices; where he did address them, it was typically with a dose of skepticism while clearly indicating that such undertakings often move beyond "architecture as an autonomous discipline . . . as it is commonly understood." In the second edition of *Modern Architecture*, Frampton briefly mentions Giancarlo de Carlo's Nuovo Villaggio Matteotti in Terni, Italy (1969–1977), a low-rise housing settlement designed with and for the workers' union in Italy's largest steel company, Ilva S.p.A and contemporary with the São Victor and Bouça housing schemes in Porto. For reference, see K. Frampton, *Modern Architecture: A Critical History*, 2nd ed. (London: Thames & Hudson, 1985), 289–90.

[11] Kenneth Frampton, "Typology and Participation: The Architecture of Álvaro Siza." *Art Forum* 54, no. 7 (March 2016).

emphasizes how "collective architecture" is achieved not only through architectural design but through the active participation of future residents. As proof, he offers SAAL—*Serviço Ambulatório de Apoio Local* (Local Ambulatory Support Service)—a socialist organization that emerged in the aftermath of Portugal's 1974 Carnation Revolution. Nuno Portas, an architect, urban planner, and critic who became the country's secretary of state for housing after the revolution,[12] initiated SAAL as an architectural and political experiment intended to address extreme housing shortages and poor living conditions in Portuguese cities. SAAL insisted on a different process of designing and building facilities: the architect co-designed new housing settlements with SAAL members, who would then take part in the construction of the buildings. Even though the process of what Frampton calls "collective design" is always complex and difficult, it coaxes both architect and community toward unforeseen outcomes, and thus Frampton highlights it here as another significant domain of practice for architecture in the new millennium.

In 2013's "Towards an Agonistic Architecture,"[13] an opinion essay for *Domus*, Frampton employs Chantal Mouffe's concept of agonistic pluralism.[14] Two months later, in October 2013, he delivered a lecture with the same title at SCI-Arc, where he elaborated on his use of Mouffe's concept in architecture.[15] In the essay, which arguably contains only a hint of the relevance of Mouffe's work, Frampton introduces analogies between his theory of resistant architecture and Mouffe's theory of agonistic politics. While in his view architecture "cannot act politically" (as in *politics*), indeed it can configure and articulate spaces of public appearance and the public realm, where *the political* has the capacity to emerge. Most important for Frampton, architecture acting agonistically is a pluralist architecture, conceived in sharp contrast and in resistance to the scenographic and spectacular architecture of the neoliberal generation. What distinguishes architecture acting agonistically, Frampton concludes, is the mandate to articulate space of public appearance "in a culturally significant manner."

The concluding essay, *The Unfinished Project at the End of Modernity: Tectonic Form and the Space of Public Appearance*,[16] in many ways brings everything together in a true retrospective of Frampton's life-long concerns

---

[12] In a personal note to the editor dated 22 September 2021, Frampton indicates that he met with Nuno Portas in New York prior to Portas' appointment to this position in 1974. For an interview with Portas where he discusses SAAL, see "The SAAL Process: Nuno Grande interviews Nuno Portas," Canadian Centre for Architecture, https://www.cca.qc.ca/en/articles/issues/12/what-you-can-do-with-the-city/2239/the-saal-process.

[13] Kenneth Frampton, "Towards an Agonistic Architecture," *Domus* 972 (September 2013), https://www.domusweb.it/en/opinion/2013/10/03/_towards_an_agonistic_architecture.html.

[14] Chantal Mouffe, *Agonistics: Thinking the World Politically* (London: Verso, 2013).

[15] Kenneth Frampton, "Towards an Agonistic Architecture," SCI-Arc Media Archive, 4 December 2013, YouTube video, https://www.youtube.com/watch?v=92xYjPAVJfI.

[16] Kenneth Frampton, *The Unfinished Project at the End of Modernity: Tectonic Form and the Space of Public Appearance* (London: Sir John Soane's Museum, 2019).

and arguments. It was first given as a public address on 11 November 2019 on the occasion of being awarded the Soane Medal by Sir John Soane Museum in London.[17] Frampton opens this highly evocative essay in the following way:

> The title of this lecture points to the self-imposed difficulty of combining an excursus into the ontology of building with an appraisal of some of the most significant architectural works of the last half-century, with the implication that one is the vindication of the other and *vice versa*. Looking back, it now seems that this juxtaposition of theory and practice was already latent in the three essays that I wrote during the first two decades of my academic career in the United States. Each of these essays was somehow motivated by my nostalgia for the Modern Movement in architecture that had flourished in Europe and Southern California between the World Wars.[18]

Frampton concludes the essay in the following way:

> In all of these examples I have attempted to show how, despite our political incapacity to confront the environmental nemesis of our time, architecture can still be pursued as the cultivation of a poetics of construction dedicated whenever possible to the realisation of a "space of public appearance" within which society may still realise some measure of its potential sovereignty . . . [I]f we are to cultivate an architecture of resistance to our compulsive commodification of the environment, it is to the *earthwork* that we must look as the means of achieving significant transformation of a given site so that a "space of public appearance" might spontaneously emerge.

---

[17] The Soane Medal's mission is to promote a broad understanding of the importance of architecture in society. It recognizes architects, educators and critics who have made a major contribution through practice, history, and/or theory, and have enriched the public understanding of architecture. In awarding Kenneth Frampton, the committee chaired by Sir David Chipperfield wrote: "Kenneth Frampton occupies a unique position in architectural culture of the last half century. His work as an architect, writer, critic, educator and academic has shaped and informed the outlook of countless students and architects." https://www.soane.org/soane-medal.

[18] Frampton, *The Unfinished Project at the End of Modernity*, 3.

Truth, as Le Corbusier wrote, does not now lie in extremes; it lies, as he put it with self-deprecating irony, in a constant struggle to maintain a state of equilibrium whatever one's *métier*. Hence the wider ideological implications of his beautiful metaphor of the architect as acrobat. "Nobody asked him to do this. Nobody owes him any thanks. He lives in the extraordinary world of the acrobat."

But are we not all in the last analysis acrobats, that is to say, is not the species as a whole caught on its technological high wire from which if it finally falls it will be impossible to recover? In the meantime the culture of the tectonic still persists as a testament to the spirit: the poetics of construction. All the rest, including our much-vaunted manipulation of space, is mixed up with the lifeworld, and in this it belongs as much to society as to ourselves.

Kenneth Frampton, *Studies in Tectonic Culture: The Poetics of Construction in Nineteenth and Twentieth Century Architecture* (Cambridge, MA: MIT Press, 1995), 387.

26 Architecture, Philosophy, and the Education of Architects (1991)

The laws of chance are supposedly divided equally between heads and tails, between success and disappointment, between the many and the elect. Finding myself on this occasion to fall in the latter category, that is to say, to be chosen to represent a field of practice, my mind turns not only to those distinguished teachers who have preceded me but also to those unacknowledged figures who were certainly as gifted and surely as dedicated. I have in mind such luminaries as Jerzy Soltan of Harvard and the late Harwell Hamilton Harris, but of course once one starts in this vein, the list becomes endless. "Remember to remember," wrote Henry Miller, reminding one that honoring is largely a matter of recalling not only those figures who have influenced one for good or ill—in my case I think of Hannah Arendt and the aphoristic Tomás Maldonado—but also of recognizing those more intimate colleagues who have aided one's development in various ways.

In the first instance, then, I would like to acknowledge Peter Eisenman, with whom I disagree on almost everything, but who has nonetheless always been the most loyal of friends, a figure of vital spirit, despite or even because of all the pyrotechnics that constantly emanate from his magician's crucible. It was Peter after all who got me into this game in the first place, for it was he who invited me to Princeton a quarter of a century ago for a profligate, transatlantic weekend in the Lowrie House in Princeton with the somewhat over determined presupposition that I could, or rather should, become the Sigfried Giedion of the group, notwithstanding that the group barely existed or that then as now I was hardly of Giedion's stature. This was the Princeton in which I would teach and

Source: Kenneth Frampton, "Topaz Laureate Address at the ACSA Annual Meeting," in *Journal of Architectural Education* 45, no.4 (July 1992), 195–6. Also published in John E. Hancock, and William C. Miller, eds., *Architecture, Back to Life: Proceeding of the 79th Annual Meeting of the Association of Collegiate Schools of Architecture* (Washington, DC.: ACSA, 1991). This title was modified from the original 1991 title.

in which I would be educated, and it was there in this idyllic university, with its White Russian emigres and languid squirrels, that I would meet but a year later the young Paul Segal who played a major role in endorsing me for this honor. I also have to thank all those many ex-students who served to enrich my life; those whose names I can remember as well as those even more numerous whose names I can no longer recall.

Being unable to honor adequately this apostolic debt, I turn to acknowledge the Association of the Collegiate Schools of Architecture, which over the last decade seems to have become all too inadvertently the cultural arm of the AIA. The last quarter of a century has seen the ACSA transform itself from a somewhat disjointed syndicate into a national body of ever-widening prestige and influence. This has been due in no small measure to the upgrading of the *Journal of Architectural Education*, which, under a series of distinguished editors and equally able editorial boards, has evolved from a parochial news sheet into an intellectual magazine of national, if not international, standing. It says much of the current stature of this publication that I recently structured a short graduate seminar about the issues raised in its pages over the last few years.

This brings one, however precipitously, to touch on the place of theory in contemporary architectural education and to treat in passing 'the uses and abuses of history and theory' in current teaching practice. Among the more striking changes in education over the past decade has been the informal entry of philosophy into the average curriculum, for there are surely few faculties today that are not infiltrated by autodidactic philosophers who have helped to augment and correct the long since mandatory lectures in architectural history. Naturally, someone of my persuasion can only regard this spontaneous development in a favorable light however much it may irritate the die-hard pragmatist. Indeed, I would go further and advocate that all graduate students ought to receive some instruction in philosophy during their architectural education. Anglo-American pragmatism notwithstanding, it is philosophy that affords the evaluative ground on which to construct a truly public realm and discourse, without which no architecture worthy of the name can come into being. Whether by implication or otherwise, architecture is civic by definition; that is, it is the physical substance of the *res publica* that even in the private arena guarantees the worldliness of the world.

Furthermore, one has sufficient reason to claim after Gottfried Semper that, aside from music, dance, and the weaving of textiles, architecture has more in common with philosophy than any other poetic discourse. Irreducibly integrated with that which Edmund Husserl called the "life-world" and formulated inevitably as a frame for culture rather than as culture itself, architecture has more to share with a subject that reflects on the nature of things—on what I have called "the status of man and the status of his objects"[1]—than with those ultimately

---

[1] Frampton, K. (1979) "The Status of Man and the Status of his Objects: A Reading of *The Human Condition*," in Hill, M. (Ed) (1979) *Hannah Arendt: The Recovery of the Public World*. New York: St. Martin's Press. pp. 101–30.

representational disciplines of painting and sculpture that, notwithstanding the triumphs of modern abstraction, remain essentially figurative.

Having said this, I cannot but remark today on the conjunctions and disjunctions obtaining between architecture, art, philosophy, and politics and on what we may identify as strategies for evasion, distraction, and legitimization: strategies that, however un-consciously, either attempt to compensate for our failure to realize a collectively significant architecture or alternatively seek to legitimize this failure in the name of another more dominant discipline. I have in mind, of course, the tendency to occlude architecture as the ground of an ethical practice and also the subtle and at times obvious displacement of architecture by various simulations or compensatory ploys. We need only recall the sixties and the early seventies to remind ourselves of the infamous era of design methods and all the multifarious attempts to reduce the generation of architectural form and space to logarithmic manipulations of various kinds. Even that very intelligent craftsman Konrad Wachsmann published a book in the late sixties that, in the name of some kind of Archimedean idealism, tended to reduce architecture to nothing but the elements and processes of fabrication and assembly.[2] In this instance, one might say that production itself became the displaced locus of the sublime. [...]

Indeed, such is the universal domination of technoscience, the never-ending cycle of maximized production and consumption, and the privatization of the late modern world, that architecture as a unique form of craft-based knowledge and, more importantly, as the constitution of the world itself is constantly to be found wanting in terms of technoscientific or socioeconomic criteria, as though such maximized rationality was the be-all and the end-all of human existence. I am well aware of the reactionary tendency of my argument, but nonetheless we would be foolhardy to overlook the ideological prejudices that have accompanied the introduction of computer-aided design into the general system of architectural production and the way in which CAD tends to favor, however surreptitiously, the monopolization of the profession and the reduction of both design and production to the relatively simple modular coordinates that are optimum from the point of view of the staff hours spent programming.

If we pass from what I would like to characterize as *science envy* in contemporary architecture to the surprisingly parallel manifestation of *art envy* as an even more subtle ploy with which to evade authentic architectural creation, then we enter into a realm of surrogate creativity, one that promises more immediate rewards in terms of artistic satisfaction, libidinal pleasure, and notoriety. Along the fragile frontier separating the academy from the profession and the media, there seems to be much to be gained from fusing and confusing the boundary that serves to distinguish architecture from art. To these evasive reaction formations we now have to add a third digression, namely the production of theory as an end in itself, as an elaborate discourse with which to advance one's

---

[2] Wachsmann, K. (1961) *The Turning Point of Building*, New York: Reinhold.

status within the university system, as Jim Mayo has reminded us in a recent issue of the *JAE*.[3]

To the information explosion, then, we now have to add the theory explosion, and as a result we are once more brought to concede the imminence of that state of barbarism against which Lewis Mumford warned, namely of that state of affairs in which one will be so engulfed with information as to be incapable of assimilating it, that is to say, one will be unable to discriminate between the pertinent and the impertinent or, even more tragically at the level of critical thought, between critique on the one hand and complicity on the other. This tendency becomes chronic at the point at which theory divorced from practice becomes a kind of metatheory, a regressive theory of theory. I have in mind that ever-imminent risk of a subtle *trahison des clercs* in which we collectively rationalize as normative the irredeemable brutality of our everyday environment.

"Architects don't invent anything; they transform reality."[4] These are the words of Álvaro Siza, which in my view should be inscribed over the doors of every architectural school if only to remind us that all theory should be ultimately oriented toward effecting transformation. With this of course we are returned to Karl Marx and to the fact that the political must of necessity transcend the profession and the various vested interests that support its particular division of labor, along with the state of disinformation in which we are maintained both as architects and as citizens. Architecture is ultimately a rationalized craft rather than a profession, and for this one needs a theory of fabrication treating critically ends and means, the what and the how, the real and the potential, rather than a pre- or post-facto theory of legitimization, which may be as negative at the level of substance as it is effective at the level of rhetoric.

We are caught in a time when the new is no longer new and the old cannot be restored; we are constrained by a curiously emptying moment in which, to quote Hans Magnus Enzensberger, "the avant-garde has become its opposite: anachronism. A moment in which, with the designation of *experiment*, the avant-garde excuses its results, takes back, as it were, its action and unloads all responsibility on the receiver."[5]

In such times, I feel we have no choice but to rescind the myth of progress and to return to the time-bound timelessness of the intrinsic rather than the extrinsic; that is, we need to concern ourselves *primarily* with the inner substance of things rather than with their superficial imagery.

The role of theory in such a time is to protect the culture from oversimplification but at the same time to maintain the clarity of its critically constructive

---

[3] Mayo, J., Littman, E. and Burgess, P. (1981) "Political Knowledge and the Architectural Studio," in *Social Science in the Design Studio, Journal of Architectural Education*, 34/3, Spring 1981, pp. 24–28.

[4] Siza, Á.V., Van Toorn, R. and Bouman, O. (1994) "Desperately Seeking Siza: A Conversation with Álvaro Siza Vieira," in Van Toorn, R. and Bouman, O. (Eds.) (1994) *The Invisible in Architecture*. London: Academy Editions. pp. 204–13.

[5] Enzensberger, H.M. (1974) *The Consciousness Industry: On Literature, Politics and the Media*. New York: Seabury Press. pp. 36–41.

aim. As Gianni Vattimo has suggested, philosophy and architecture can perhaps only be united today under the sign of edification wherein, as he puts it; "the only possibility of edifying in the sense of building is to edify in the sense of rendering ethical, that is to encourage an ethical life, to work with the recollections of traditions, with the traces of the past, with the expectations of meaning for the future, since these can no longer be absolute rational deductions."[6]

From this it follows, as he goes on to say, that an ethical practice must by definition lead to an architecture that is determined by its parts rather than by the whole, that is, we are returned to an architecture of microepisodes rather than to a global, overreaching totalization. This then is an ethic of the marginal rather than the mainstream, of the small rather than the big, of the significant, resistant fragment rather than yet another fashionable conformity.

---

[6] Vattimo, G. (1986) "Project and Legitimization I," *Lotus International*, No. 48/49 (1986), p. 125.

27 Reflections on the Autonomy of Architecture: A Critique of Contemporary Production (1991)

Save for the axiom that nothing can be regarded as autonomous in an absolute sense, it is difficult to know how to initiate a discourse on the topic of *architectural autonomy*. Among the many aspects of the cultural enterprise, it may be claimed that architecture is, in fact, the least autonomous, compelling us to admit to the contingent nature of architecture as a practice.

It is one of the paradoxes of everyday life that although reality presses in on us from every side, we tend to overlook its effects, particularly when they do not happen to suit our ideological prejudices. Few architects care to remind themselves that only 20 percent of the total built output in developed societies is subject to the advice of the profession, so that the greater part of the man-made environment escapes our creative intervention. This disturbing fact means that we have to acknowledge the limited domain in which we are asked to operate, and in so doing we should recognize that there is a world of difference between architecture as a critical act and building as a banal, almost metabolic activity.

As is well known, the emergence of architecture as a self-conscious individual practice is inseparable from the rise of the burgher class in the last half of the fifteenth century. Our notion of architectural design as a specifically modern, innovative, nontraditional procedure cannot be traced back beyond this moment in history, when the first signs of divided labor and the dissolution of preliterate guild culture are discernible in the methods by which Brunelleschi erected the

Source: Kenneth Frampton, "Reflections on the Autonomy of Architecture: A Critique of Contemporary Production," in *Out of Site: Social Criticism of Architecture*, ed. Diane Ghirardo (Washington, DC: Bay Press, 1991), 17–26.

dome over Santa Maria del Fiore in Florence. We are indebted to Giulio Carlo Argan for his observation that this is precisely the moment when the so-called *artes liberales* gain their ascendancy over the *artes mechanicae* and when the rise of the individual architect/artist, as a protoprofessional, brings about a corresponding fall in the stature of the *maestri* or the master-craftsmen.[1] This condition is reflected in the fact that although the generic cathedral and the everyday shed were markedly different undertakings within guild culture, there seems to have been a symbiotic continuity in the medieval worldview that served to unify the entire production an agrarian-based civilization. This continuity is evident in the fact that the barn and the temple emerged from the same genre of craft production.

It is hardly an accident that the two schisms that concern us here should occur at the same time, that is to say that labor should become divided at precisely the moment in which it becomes possible to distinguish between architecture and building and when it becomes necessary to discriminate between the architect, on the one hand, and the master mason on the other. It is important to note that this schism is accompanied by the process of secularization. This seems to have been one of the preconditions, so to speak, for the emergence of empirical science and for the rise of the new technocratic-cum-mercantile class. The nineteenth-century Gothic revivalist A.W.N. Pugin was surely justified in his polemical view that the Renaissance represented exactly the point at which exclusively economic and productive values began to usurp the place of the spirit; the moment, that is, when *homo economicus* replaces *homo religioso*. Self-conscious and schizophrenic, the Renaissance barely believed in its own ideology. It is already historicist in its dependency on the spiritual authenticity of the antique world.

The hypothetical autonomy of any given practice is relatively delimited by the sociocultural context in which this practice unfolds. That this societal limitation is apparently greater in architecture than in any other art suggests that we should distinguish precisely between the province of architecture and the province of art. It is necessary to note that, unlike all other forms of so-called fine art, architecture mixes with that which the phenomenologist Edmund Husserl identified as the "life-world," and it is this irreducible condition that sets obvious limits on the autonomy of the field.[2] That is to say, architecture is both a cultural discourse and a frame for life. One might say, to stretch the Marxist terminology, that it is both superstructure and infrastructure. This last means that architecture is appropriated by the society in a way that is categorically different from that of art. In its appreciation of art, society seeks to preserve the intrinsic, inalienable essence of the artwork in its mint condition. Moreover, after the medieval period, society covets the individual signature. (It is an interesting coincidence that the terms for business [firm] and signature [*firma*]

---

[1] Argan, G.C., *The Renaissance City*, New York: George Braziller, 1970.

[2] Husserl, E., *The Crisis of European Sciences and Transcendental Phenomenology: An Introduction to Phenomenological Philosophy*, Evanston: Northwestern University Press, 1989.

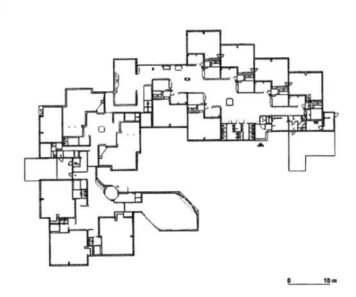

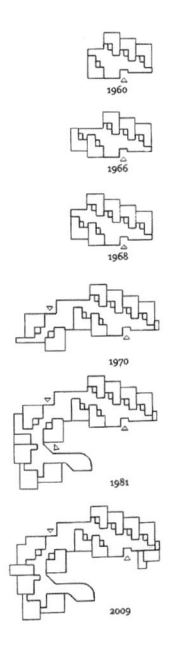

FIGURES 61–63 Montessori School Delft, The Netherlands. Herman Hertzberger, 1960–1966. Overall plan (top left); planned extensions between 1960–2009 (below left); and exterior view (top right).

come from the same root.) In architecture, on the other hand, society tends to transform the subjective originality of the work through the process of appropriation. Architecture in any event does not have the same iconic or fetishistic status as art, nor despite the emergence of the star architect, is it possible to give comparable artistic status to the "signature building."

The idea of appropriation returns us to the unfashionable doctrine of functionalism, although it is removed from the idea of a perfect ergonomic fit or any notion that there is a directly causal relationship between form and behavior or that a building will accommodate only one absolutely fixed pattern of use. The Dutch architect Herman Hertzberger does not intend such a fit. His idea of what is appropriate and open to appropriation is generic and institutional rather than reductively functional.

Aside from the disturbing schism that obtains in all postguild culture between the projection and the realization of built form, architectural practice has been slowly and surreptitiously undermined in the course of this century by the increasing privatization of society. Architecture has been hard-pressed to sustain its proper discourse in a society in which the public realm hardly exists and in which the continuity of the life-world as a repository of values becomes increasingly unstable. It is obviously difficult to sustain the legitimacy of architecture in a society that is constantly being overwhelmed by the innovations of technoscience, by demographic change, and by the ever-escalating cycles of production and consumption that constant modernization serves to sustain.

Lacking a collective *raison d'être*, architecture has turned first this way and then that in an effort to legitimate itself and to bring its practice into line with the dominant discourse, be it applied science as the reality principle or applied art as a psychosocial compensation. The first of these impulses no doubt partially accounts for the rise of ergonomic-cum-logarithmic design methods in the early 1960s and for the rather drastic attempts to convert architecture itself into a form of technoscientific practice. I am referring, of course, to the way in which leading British and American schools of architecture—the Bartlett School at London University, in the first instance, and the faculty of architecture at the University of California at Berkeley, in the second—changed their respective names in the sixties from schools of architecture to schools of environmental design, thereby implicitly abandoning the old bourgeois, elitist, hierarchical connotations of architecture and pretending instead to the wider scope of addressing the supposedly scientific design of the environment as a whole. It says much about the pendulum of ideological fashion and the intrinsic resistance of architecture as a craft that the Bartlett School has since reassumed its former denomination as a School of Architecture.

Anxiety and envy have accompanied such pendulum swings as architects have attempted to justify their *modus operandi* by appearing to be scientists or, alternatively, by representing architecture as though it were fine art, writ large. One may speak, perhaps, of "science envy" in the first instance and of "art envy" in the second. We may regard the late Buckminster Fuller as a characteristic case of science envy, and any number of contemporary architects, from Frank

Gehry to Peter Eisenman, seem only too happy to have their work classified as art. Indeed both of these legitimating ploys may be detected in Eisenman's career, in which there is a noticeable shift from the science envy of the early theory, with its dependency on structural linguistics, to the art envy of the later work, where the justifying critique has recourse to literature and philosophy. It should also be noted that there is a semiotic thread that unifies Eisenman's career, although this hardly changes the nature of his attempt to justify his idiosyncratic practice through extra-architectural references, be they scientific categories such as fractal geometry or the supposedly subversive aims of late avant-gardism. Either way, the possibility of architecture being an essentially tectonic or institutional discourse is largely denied.

One may claim that, unlike either science or art, architectural practice favors stasis rather than process and that it tends, however weakly, to resist the fungibility of the industrialized world. In this regard, latter-day appeals to science and art may be seen as subtle efforts to accommodate architecture to the dominant categories of a totally privatized and process-oriented world.

This state of affairs has produced strange convergences. For a latter-day radical like Daniel Libeskind, the institutions of the contemporary life-world are to be eschewed on the grounds that they are contaminated by a totally destitute political and ethical reality. A similar sentiment may be detected in the stance of Leon Krier, even if Krier's recent flirtations with practice seem to deny the total negativity of his earlier claim that, "I do not build because I am an architect: I am an architect therefore I do not build." Today, while Libeskind projects neo-avant-gardist works as though they are nothing more than colossal pieces of sculpture, Krier invites us to return to a petrified neo-Biedermeier manner, as though only such a low-key, classical order still embodies the essence of a strictly architectural culture.

It is symptomatic of the times that both architects owe their ascendance in some way to the revival of drawn representation, for although drawing has always played a fundamental role in architectural practice, there is convergence today between the revival of drawing and the assertion of architecture as though it were a branch of fine art. The socioeconomic crisis attending architecture in the seventies was overcome in part by the proposition that quality architecture could still be pursued as drawn representations that would be readily appreciated and consumed by the art market. The salon mannerism that attended all this is very revealing. One is reminded, by the way of our example, of the Institute for Architecture and Urban Studies exhibition entitled *The Idea as Model* [1976],[3] for which Eisenman produced a three-dimensional, isomorphic, axonometric model of one of his houses in which the axonometric, like the skull in Holbein's painting *The Ambassadors*, could be perceived only from a particular viewpoint. These subtly interrelated gestures, stimulated by the pervasive rise

---

[3] Pommer, R., Frampton, K. and Kolbowski, S. (Eds.), *Idea as Model*, New York: Institute for Architecture and Urban Studies and Rizzoli, 1981.

of the media, evade, in my view, the issue of architectural autonomy in a more fundamental sense: that is to say, the question as to what belongs intrinsically to architecture and not to the other arts.

Clearly architecture cannot be reduced to architectural representation at any level, nor can it be passed off as large-scale sculpture. In attempting to advance a hypothetical model of architectural practice that lies beyond the idiosyncrasies of any specific style, one may say that the autonomy of architecture is determined by three interrelated vectors: typology (the institution), topography (the context), and tectonics (the mode of construction). It should be noted that neither the typological nor the tectonic are neutral choices in this regard and that what can be achieved with one format and expression can hardly be realized with another.

On balance, the formal *parti* is of greater import than the tectonic, for obviously the selection of the type as the basic spatial order has a decisive impact on the result, however much the constructional syntax may be elaborated in the course of development. The primacy of the type perhaps makes itself most evident in the basic difference between building and architecture: for where building tends to be organic, asymmetrical, and agglutinative, architecture tends to be orthogonal, symmetrical, and complete. These distinctions would not be so crucial were it not for the fact that building and architecture tend to favor the accommodation of different kinds of institutional form.

The organic architecture pursued in various ways by such architects as Frank Lloyd Wright, Richard Neutra, R.M. Schindler, Erich Mendelsohn, Eileen Gray, and Alvar Aalto affords us sufficient evidence as to the potential of what Neutra termed the *biorealist* culture of building. By a similar token, a modern architecture largely inspired by the classical can be found in the work of Ludwig Mies van der Rohe, Giuseppe Terragni, and Le Corbusier. It is obvious that our traditional institutions of power have been so frequently embodied in classical form that only with difficulty can classicism be brought to represent and embody more informal and hypothetically more democratic, kinds of civic agencies. In this regard Aalto's town hall in Säynätsalo, Finland may be seen as housing a seat of government in a particularly informal way, so that it presents and represents the institution in an intimate and accessible manner.

Architecture is fundamentally linked to institutional form in ways that are little understood today because contemporary society has become so privatized. From the micro to the macro scale, we have become poorly skilled as a society at discriminating between private, public, and semipublic space, and this lack of a common perception in hierarchical terms has had a brutalizing effect on contemporary architecture. The aestheticization of late modernism as a compensatory strategy becomes patently evident at this point, since irrespective of whether the stylistic affinities are neotraditionalist or neo-avant-gardist, the outcome tends to be the same, namely that architecture is increasingly reduced to a matter of superficial appearance: that is to say, it is valued solely as a convenient situation-setting rather than as a cultural value in itself. In other words, late modern building seems often to be totally divested of any articulated sociosymbolic substance, even if all the necessary functions are provided for. The fact that the civic institution has become a fragile entity in the late twentieth century is made all too clear at the level of architecture, particularly when the museum emerges as the last public building of our time. As surrogate temple or simulated *res publica*, the museum has become the compensatory realm of our totally secular, suburbanized spirit; the last depoliticized vestige, so to speak, of that which Hannah Arendt once called "the space of public appearance."[4]

It is a sign of our times that aesthetic display has come to be used as a form of packaging to such an extent that architecture is often called upon to provide nothing more than a set of seductive images with which to "sell" both the building and its product. And while the aesthetic may well be regarded as the abstract, autonomous, self-referential quantum of late modern form, the vernacular returns us to the anthropological origins of building and to that moment in the mid-nineteenth century when the German architect Gottfried Semper formulated a new theoretical basis for architecture on the grounds of its anthropological origins. Through his transcultural worldview, Semper sought to construct a theoretical framework that would be capable of transcending the idealistic impasse of eclecticism.

Semper's quadripartite theory as contained in his essay *The Four Elements of Architecture* (1852)[5] still constitutes a valid model with which to adumbrate the relative autonomy of architecture today. To the extent that Semper's four elements constitute a categoric break with the classically humanist Vitruvian triad of "firmness, commodity, and delight," his categories may be used as means for delineating the scope of contemporary practice. I am alluding, of course, to his reworking of the paradigm of the primitive hut, in the terms of an anthropological exhibit that he saw at the Great Exhibition of 1851. Semper was prescient in realizing that the generic hut comprised the following components: (1) an earthwork, (2) a hearth, (3) a framework and roof, and (4) a screen wall. He was particularly susceptible to the last component because of the etymological connotations of the word *wall* in German, wherein a light, basketlike wall, known by the term *die Wand* is to be distinguished from a heavy, masonry wall, indicated by the term *das Mauer*. Semper's four elements give rise to a whole discourse that may be said to express itself in terms of heavy versus light. Thus the framework, roof, and enclosing screen are light structural elements tending toward the immaterial, whereas the earthwork and hearth together encapsulate the rudimentary institutional nexus of the work.

In the Greek *megaron*, consisting of a single cellular space with a door at one end, the earthwork may be seen as raising itself up in the form of *heavy*, load-bearing masonry, wherein the *light* correspondingly withdraws, as it were, to form the beams spanning the walls, supporting a flat or low-pitched roof. The hearth is contained within the *cella* of the megaron. Meanwhile the outriding

---

[4] Arendt, H. *The Human Condition*, University of Chicago Press, 1958.

[5] Semper, G., *The Four Elements of Architecture and Other Writings*, trans. Mallgrave, H.F. and Herrmann, W., Cambridge: Cambridge University Press, 1989.

walls establish the place form of the dwelling; where this *temenos* contains a temple, the boundary serves to separate the *cella* from the profane world beyond the walls.

The interaction of nature with culture in architecture manifests itself first and foremost through the effects of gravity and light. The structure both resists and reveals the impact of gravity on its form, wherein light discloses, as it were, the intrinsic nature of the structure. Even more important, from an institutional point of view, light may assume a hierarchical significance, in which darkness is associated with the privacy of the megaron and light comes to be associated with the space of public appearance—the *agora*. Both temenos and agora depend primarily upon the topographical context that is, on the "marking of the ground" that for Italian architect Vittorio Gregotti is the first world-creating act, coextensive, so to speak, with Semper's primordial knot as the first tectonic joint. The deepest roots of architectural autonomy lie here, one might say: not in the Vitruvian triad of classical lore but in the far deeper and more archaic triad of earthwork (topography), construction (tectonic), and hearth (type) as the embodiment of institutional form. These three aspects permit the structured articulation of the work as it passes from public to private and from sacred to profane, or of nature as it is mediated by light, gravity, and climate within the tectonic of the realized form.

Since around 1750, the species has been overwhelmed by the all too rapid transformation of basic material and ethical conditions and by the ever-escalating impact of technoscientific technique. These two interrelated processes have shaped the modern myth of progress. Since the turn of the century, the juggernaut of technology has been mediated if not mitigated in a number of ways. From the sculpture of Brancusi to the theater of Appia, from the philosophy of Heidegger to the architecture of Barragán, the archaic came to be reasserted as a foil to the idea of progress. This critical qualification does not depend however upon a categoric rejection of technology or on the acceptance of any particular expression. However, unlike futurism, the self-consciously archaic refuses to see advanced technology as transcendental in itself. Perhaps this complex double qualification has never been more succinctly expressed than by Aldo van Eyck when he wrote that that which antiquarians and technocrats have in common is a sentimental attitude toward time, the antiquarian being sentimental about the past, and the technocrat sentimental about the future. Van Eyck's insistence on the priority of the present does not entail some fictitious return to the past or presuppose a categoric repudiation of modern technique. It amounts instead to a critical view in which both modern and archaic technologies may be accepted and mixed together without being fetishized.

Such an attitude does not necessarily entail a reactionary cultural stance, for it seeks an appropriate elaboration of present conditions in a way that is capable of sustaining the life-world in all its richness, without wishing to preempt the significance of this world through the maximization of either technology or aesthetics. Such an attitude challenges all our received ideas of creativity to such an extent that we will be compelled to acknowledge that much that passes for originality in our time comes into being not so much out of poetic exuberance as out of competitiveness.

Behind our preoccupation with the autonomy of architecture lies an anxiety that derives in large measure from the fact that nothing could be less autonomous than architecture, particularly today when because of the domination of the media we find it increasingly difficult to arrive at what we want. Under such skeptical circumstances, architects often feel constrained to perform acrobatic feats in order to assure attention. In so doing, they tend to follow a succession of stylistic tropes that leave no image unconsumed, so that the entire field becomes flooded with an endless proliferation of images. This is a situation in which buildings tend to be increasingly designed for their photogenic effect rather than their experiential potential. Plastic stimuli abound in a frenzy of iteration that echoes the information explosion. We drift toward that entropic state that Lewis Mumford once described as a new form of barbarism. In the meantime, the ideology of modernity and progress disintegrates before our eyes and the imminent ecological disaster of late industrial production is manifest everywhere. There is no logical imperative, however, that these conditions demand an artistically fragmented, over-aestheticized expression in the field of architecture. On the contrary, one may argue that such a level of disjunction needs, even demands, an architecture of tranquility, an architecture that lies beyond the agitations of the present moment, an architecture that returns us, through the experience of the subject, to that brief illusive moment touched on by Baudelaire, to that instant evoked by the words *luxe, calme, et volupté*.[6]

---

[6] Baudelaire, C., *Flowers of Evil/Les fleurs du Mal* (1857), New York: Bantam Books, 1964.

28 Seven Points for the Millennium: An Untimely Manifesto (1999)

The expectations that attend a keynote address are invariably out of proportion to the presumed capacities of the speaker. In one way or another one finds that all one can do is to recapitulate in a different way the concerns with which one has been preoccupied in the past. I am alluding, as some of you may recognise, to an essay I wrote in 1983, bearing the title "Towards a Critical Regionalism: Six Points for an Architecture of Resistance",[1] in which I reflected on a series of topics to which I shall partially return today in a somewhat different form. These themes vary from practical strategies to be applied within the limitations of our epoch to wider critical forays that can only be exercised and thus fulfilled over a much longer term.

Since we are coming to the close of a century in which contemporary architecture has often been inseparable from the writing of manifestos, I thought that one might indulge once more, on the occasion of the Twentieth UIA Congress, in an untimely manifesto, treating successively with the following seven themes: first with the issue of environmental education, not only as this concerns the profession but also in relation to the way this affects the society as a whole; then with the question of the relative autonomy of architecture as this has had and continues to have an impact on both the profession and the society. The third point will attempt to treat the socio-ecological implications of our current patterns of land settlement, while the fourth point will turn to the need for architects to maintain their leadership role in the building team, retaining as

Source: Kenneth Frampton, "Seven Points for the Millennium: An Untimely Manifesto," *The Journal of Architecture* 5 (Spring 2000): 21–33. This essay is the transcription of the keynote address given at the 20th Congress of the International Union of Architects (UIA), Beijing, China in June 1999.

[1] K. Frampton, Towards a critical regionalism: Six points for an architecture of resistance," in Foster, H., ed., *The Anti-Aesthetic: Essays in Postmodern Culture* (Port Townsend, Washington, Bay Press, 1983), pp. 16–30.

much as possible their mastery over the craft of building in the widest sense. The fifth point will try to argue that the design of landscape is of greater critical consequence than architecture on its own, thereby suggesting that we give as much priority to the greening of the world as to building with bricks and mortar. Point six highlights the need for an incremental urban strategy, while point seven deals with the inevitable conflict between power and reason as the ultimate dialectic in the field of environmental design.

ARCHITECTURE AND SOCIETY: ENVIRONMENTAL EDUCATION AND THE FUTURE OF THE PROFESSION

With the demise of the socialist project with which modern architecture was once so intimately involved, the profession is faced with the challenge of trying to determine the scope of its role in the next century. This is an issue that cannot be coherently addressed without involving the relationship of architecture to society as a whole. It is well known that the intentions of the client are absolutely seminal to the successful outcome of any architectural endeavour and that without a sensitive, intelligent and responsible client, the aspirational range of a project becomes extremely limited. Good clients do not necessarily guarantee architecture of quality, since the architect may not be of comparable calibre, but there is little doubt that the reductive client, born of bureaucratic rigidity or speculative ruthlessness assures a mediocre result well before pencil has been set to paper. To cultivate an adequate client base, the education of the society in the field of environmental design should be given the highest priority, beginning at the high school level as many have advocated over the past twenty years.[2] It should be obvious that one cannot raise the general level of environmental culture without enlightening society as a whole with regard to certain cultural and ecological issues. It is no longer possible to evade these factors since they will prove fundamental to the character of architectural practice in the next century.

At the same time the profession should adjust its own pedagogical goals, particularly when it comes to maintaining a balance between professional training and the responsibility of giving its aspirants a sufficiently broad education. It is essential to admit that the practice of architecture is still ultimately a craft, however much its processes may be qualified by techno-scientific methods and applications. This irreducible fact should help us to understand why architecture as a discipline has always been situated rather uncomfortably within the confines of the university. As the Portuguese architect Álvaro Siza has put it:

> We developed the idea that the architect is a specialist in nonspecialization. Building involves so many elements, so many techniques, and such

---

[2] See the five-volume high-school course in design by Leonardo Benevolo, *Corso di disegno per i licei scientifici* (Laturza, 1976).

different kinds of problems, that it is impossible to command all the requisite knowledge. What is required is an ability to interrelate diverse elements and disciplines. Because architects have a broad overview and are not constrained by concrete knowledge, they are able to connect various factors and maintain the synthesizing capacity of nonspecialization. In this sense the architect is ignorant, but he is able to work with many people and coordinate the integration of a vast number of particulars. These are skills one can acquire only through experience. With them, we are able to face the new situations that accompany each project.[3]

As to an appropriate curriculum for maintaining this synthesising capacity at the turn of the century, one may suggest a number of areas that still seem to be essential to the formation of the architect. Among them one may emphasise the following:

(a) **History:** Ideally architectural history should be taught as cultural history which is a challenge since architects and architectural historians are not generally trained to approach the topic in this way. It is important that curricula be developed to include within their overview three important subsets: the history of landscape, technology and industrial design. It is certain that different subsets will have to be emphasised in different cultural situations depending on the part of the world in which the architect is being trained.

(b) **Design:** Training in building design as a tripartite procedure involving three different media at the same time; that is to say (i) the hand drafting of initial concepts before passing to other modes of representation, (ii) the continual building of models at all scales in order to assess the concepts under consideration and (iii) computer-aided design to be used for drafting and modelling in relation to the two other modes. Obviously one needs to oscillate constantly between all three modes in the generation of a design.

(c) **Technique:** At the end of the century, it seems that the teaching of technology may be best approached through two strategies; (i) the teaching of current technique through analytical case-studies of contemporary building culture and (ii) the teaching of technology through simplified comprehensive design projects in order to expose the student to the task of synthesising different techniques.

The crisis of the architectural academy is at least in some measure a reflection of the crisis facing the profession. In this context we may posit the thesis that the more the practice of architecture becomes removed from the needs of the society as a whole, the more it tends to become an overly aestheticised discourse that addresses itself exclusively to the spectacular preoccupations of an *arriviste* class. Inside architectural schools this discourse is often served by a mystifying theoretical eclecticism, drawn largely from other disciplines,

---

[3] See discussion between Álvaro Siza and Peéra Goldman in *Technology, Place & Architecture* (New York, Rizzoli, 1998), p. 155.

and removed from the basic conditions and needs of environmental design. As Vittorio Gregotti pointed out some time ago, architectural practice requires for its realisation societal need, technological mediation and constraint in order to exist at all, even if the 'rules' for the development of the discipline at an intrinsic level can only be found within architecture itself.[4]

[...]

THE CRISES OF LAND SETTLEMENT IN THE AGE OF THE MEGALOPOLIS

Half a century ago the dialectical interplay between civilisation and culture still afforded the possibility of maintaining some control over the shape and significance of the urban fabric. The past thirty years have radically transformed the metropolitan centres of the developed world. What were still essentially nineteenth century cities in the early 1960s (e.g. Glasgow, Sydney, San Francisco and Shanghai) have since become overlaid by the matrices of megalopolitan development, the free-standing high-rise and the serpentine freeway. The former has come into its own as the instrument for capitalising on the increased land values brought into being by the latter. The typical city centre which, up to thirty years ago, still presented a mixture of residential stock with secondary industry has now become little more than a 'motopian' landscape dominated by tertiary industry.

By a similar token the unremitting suburbanisation of North America and the simultaneous dissolution of the nineteenth century provincial city structured about the railroad has been brought about by the deliberate maximisation of private transport, sponsored by the oil and automobile lobbies and by the corresponding contrived decline of public transport in all its aspects. While these symbiotic consumerist processes are at their most extreme in the United States, it is clear that this tendency is to be found throughout the developed world, so much so that one is tempted to assert that if there is a single apocalyptic invention in the twentieth century it is the automobile rather than the atomic bomb.

Meanwhile, by a reciprocal and similar process, there is a corresponding implosion of urban populations in the vast hinterland surrounding capital cities, particularly in the Third World where such growth has been exponential. The population of Bombay virtually doubled between 1900 and 1950 when it topped out at two million. In the next half century it would increase almost eightfold to a figure over fifteen million. As in Latin America where the phenomenon was first fully acknowledged, most of this expansion occurs in the form of so-called spontaneous housing: barriadas, fervillas, etc., where land is appropriated *en masse* and shacks come into being overnight without any of the normative infrastructures considered to be essential to health, above all water, sewage disposal, power and public transport. If the projections of a decade and a half

---

[4] V. Gregotti, Editorial, *Casabella* (March 1982). Gregotti writes: "... it is architecture itself that needs, for its very production, social relations. Architecture cannot live simply by mirroring its own problems ... even though the professional tools required for architecture as a discipline can be found only within that tradition."

ago are correct, by the year 2000, as Charles Correa remarks in his prophetic book *The New Urban Landscape*,[5] there will be fifty cities in the world with populations of fifteen million or more, of which more than forty will be in the Third World. Dhaka, Jakarta, Bombay, Canton are among the cities he specifically mentions.

This spontaneous global urbanisation produces urbanised regions comparable to the megalopoli of the developed world, first given this name by the French geographer Jean Gottmann in 1961. I have in mind such well-known conglomerations as the Boston–Washington corridor, the Greater Los Angeles region that by now runs into San Diego without a break, the so-called Randstad in North-Western Europe, the Hokkaido to Osaka megalopolis in Japan that is now fed by the bullet train for the entire length of the island system. With the singular exception of these megalopoli that are relatively well served by public transport, the exploding megalopoli in the United States tend, both socially and economically, towards becoming Third Worlds encapsulated within so-called First Worlds.

It is demagogic to object that we lack appropriate strategies to deal with such apocalyptic developments. One generic way to treat such implosions was posited by Charles Correa, Pravina Mehta and Shirish Patel in their 1964 plan for New Bombay, through which at least two million of Bombay's burgeoning population would have been decanted eastward to the other side of the bay.[6] The hard fact is of course that the necessary investment in public transport has not been made and that today, after nearly forty years, this plan has yet to be fulfilled since the necessary infrastructure has still to be completed.

Without lamenting about the loss of the traditional city as this was generally available as an essential and comprehensible part of human civilisation from the Middle Ages to the beginning of the twentieth century, we may nonetheless claim two essential factors that must be seriously addressed if we are ever to come to terms in a socio-ecological sense with the current rate of urbanisation. These are (i) the provision of adequate public transport systems of varying interlocking speeds, from high velocity inter-city trains to local light-rail, tram and bus systems and (ii) the general establishment of more collective, ecological patterns of land settlement in both the First and Third Worlds.

[...] We are surely familiar with the paradigms that could be applied to the general dilemma that we confront at the scale of the urbanised region. What we generally lack, however, is painfully obvious; namely the political and ideological will to bring these models into being. Sufficient and successful demonstrations of low-rise, high-density housing have been made throughout the world over the past thirty years, but for such land-settlement patterns to become normative we would have to introduce draconian legislation that would severely restrict not only high-rise development but almost all forms of low-density suburban

---

[5] C. Correa, *The New Urban Landscape* (Bombay, India, The Book Society of India, 1980), p. 10.

[6] C. Correa, P. Mehta and S. Patel, *The New Urban Landscape*, op cit., pp. 67–78.

settlement. The current patterns of speculative suburban subdivision would have to be outlawed and the consumerist illusion attending our exaggerated individuality would have to be relinquished.

[...]

LANDSCAPE FORM AS A REDEMPTIVE STRATEGY

Since megalopolitan development now takes place at a global scale, it is obvious that few options are available that are capable of improving in any significant way the socio-cultural and ecological character of the average urbanised region. Other than the insertion of new systems of public transport only one possible strategy seems to be universally available, namely the blanket application of landscape interventions, in one form or another, as a way of ameliorating the environmental harshness of large tracts of our urbanised regions. The ubiquitous black-top parking lots of the North American continent are a case in point for clearly all such lots could be transformed into shaded parking areas through the subsidised application of tree planting as a coordinated public programme. Given the present escalation of global warming, the ecological long-term benefit accruing from such a provision would be considerable. The related enclosure of such spaces by planted berms would lead to further benefits of a more cultural nature, together with the enactment of legislation prohibiting the use of asphalt for the surfacing of parking areas, in order to reduce the destructive distribution of water run-off produced by the automotive system. It is well known that one may easily construct parking bays out of perforated, prefabricated concrete paving elements. These may be filled with earth and seeded with grass, so that the entire parking network throughout a megalopolis could be transformed into a landscape. The ecological and cultural benefits of such provisions ought to be self-evident.

This general 'greening' strategy possesses other pastoral benefits that we have so far not addressed; *first* that the current tendency to reduce the built environment to an endless proliferation of free-standing objects (of a more or less aesthetic quality depending on the circumstances) would be overcome by a landscape provision which would integrate all such objects into the surface of the ground and second, landscape would have the advantage of being much more culturally accessible to 'the average' person, than the contemporary built environment with all the seemingly unavoidable harshness of its instrumentality. This may also go some way towards explaining why landscape architects may be more readily allowed to treat the reorganisation of large tracts of land where planners and urban designers run into different forms of obstruction and resistance.

It is for these reasons among others that I am convinced that architectural and planning schools throughout the world should give much greater emphasis to the cultivation of landscape as an overarching system rather than concentrating exclusively, as they have tended to do up to now, on the design of buildings as free-standing objects.

[...]

RATIONALITY AND POWER

When we address ourselves at the end of the century to the entire predicament of the environment and the state of the profession in respect of the next century, we would do well to bear in mind the unavoidable interplay between reason and power in almost every design and policy decision both large and small. As the Danish planner Bent Flyvbjerg puts it in his book *Rationality and Power: Democracy and Practice* of 1998: "Power concerns itself with defining reality rather than discovering what reality really is"[7] [...] I have opted for the theme of 'rationality and power' as my last point for much the same reason that I chose to end my book *Studies in Tectonic Culture* (1995) with a quotation from Guy Debord's *Commentary on the Society of Spectacle* of 1988, particularly for his contention that the spectacle (the media) has allowed power to assume that it no longer has to take responsibility for its decisions, just as it encouraged science to enter into the service of 'spectacular domination.'[8]

Whether this indictment is justifiable or not, there is surely no doubt as to the perennial play of power and reason with regard to the application of technology. The irony is that while power under democracy ostensibly comes into being as the mandate of the electorate, we also know that it often acts against the electorate's self-interest, due, amongst other factors, to the influence of the media, the rise of global marketing and the corresponding decline of the nation state. As a result of this the natural and the human environment become ever more degraded, from the phenomenon of global warming to oceanic pollution, from wholesale deforestation to the destruction of the landscape through tourism.

Accompanying the misinformation of the media, there is also mediatic information of a more positive kind, with the paradoxical result that while the environment as a whole becomes increasingly barbaric, an incidental architecture of richness and subtlety now may be found all over the world. And while there is also a great deal of unauthentic, acritical and insensitive building, there are also many works of exceptional stature. Thanks to the universal distribution of information, these may just as easily be found in the so-called provinces as they are still occasionally to be found in the so-called centres of civilisation.

[...] Flyvbjerg's conclusion is that while power sets out the ground rules for reason, it deliberately blurs the lines between rationality and rationalisation, so that power and rationality are essentially opposed. Flyvbjerg argues that power always prevails in any showdown between power and reason and that the greater the power the less it is accessible to reason. Moreover, as he puts it,

---

[7] B. Flyvbjerg, *Rationality and Power: Democracy and Practice* (Chicago and London, University of Chicago, 1998), p. 2.

[8] K. Frampton, *Studies in Tectonic Culture: The Poetics of Construction in Nineteenth and Twentieth Century Architecture* (Cambridge, MA, MIT, 1995), p. 377.

contemporary planning is as much marked by pre-modern tribal power relations as it is by rationality and democracy. Thus the ideals of a liberative democracy cannot be realised once and for all, and in fact have never been achieved in this sense. As he states, to register a government as democratic is always in some sense a piece of propaganda. Finally, Flyvbjerg concludes, after Michel Foucault, that in undermining tradition and religion, modernity and democracy condemn the species being to the unending arduous task of producing itself. Architecture, it should by now be clear, is in some specific sense inseparable from this relentless procedure.

29 Typology and Participation: The Architecture of Álvaro Siza (2016)

At the age of eighty-two, the Portuguese architect Álvaro Siza is possibly the only modern master who, after having realized some four hundred works in a diverse range of scales and programs, remains as firmly committed as ever to the unfinished socialist project that galvanized the European avant-garde throughout the interwar era. Siza began as a housing architect, and while the first decade of his career was largely devoted to the design of private houses, he soon forayed into the quintessentially modernist typology of social housing during the intense optimism of the so-called Portuguese Spring of April 1974 and the total collapse of António Salazar's forty-year-old totalitarian regime, the Estado Novo. Siza's projects were built in Porto under the auspices of SAAL, the Serviço Ambulatório de Apoio Local (Local Ambulatory Support Service), an organization created in the immediate aftermath of the 1974 revolution with the support of the interim socialist government. Its goal was to improve living conditions in Portuguese cities and remedy the nation's severe housing shortage through nothing less than a radical reimagining of architecture's social role. Following SAAL's experimental model—which the art historian Suzanne Cotter, who helped to organize an encyclopedic exhibition on the organization's history at Porto's Museu de Arte Contemporânea de Serralves in 2014, has described as "one of the most compelling processes in twentieth-century architecture"—architects would design housing projects in dialogue with local communities. The buildings would be constructed with the participation of the users themselves, in a marked departure from the

Source: Kenneth Frampton, "Typology and Participation: The Architecture of Álvaro Siza." *Art Forum* 54, no. 7 (March 2016).

top-down, rigidly hierarchical processes that defined much of postwar urban design and architecture.

The first fruits of this participatory program were the São Victor and Bouça housing settlements, the remarkable low-rise residential structures designed by Siza and built between 1974 and 1977. However, designing by committee was by no means an easy process, as Siza would make clear when he remarked of the workers' groups collaborating with the SAAL architects:

> Their attitude was sometimes authoritarian, they denied all awareness of the architect's problems, they imposed their way of seeing and conceiving things. The dialogue was very contentious . . . To enter the real process of participation meant to accept the conflicts and not to hide them, but on the contrary to elaborate them. These exchanges then become very rich, although hard and often difficult.[1]

The São Victor terrace housing compound was a two-story settlement, built in the midst of derelict terrace housing that had been partially demolished. Siza seems to have imagined the development as if it were a reclamation of an ancient ruin—establishing his habitual approach of reading a site as a palimpsest, incorporating into his design not only the texture of the ground but its history and erstwhile culture.

The second SAAL development, the Bouça housing quarter, was built on a trapezoidal site that had been cleared of existing buildings. It is enclosed on its longest side by a four-story brick wall, which served as a necessary acoustic shield to mediate the noise of an adjacent railway. The scheme comprised four parallel four-story blocks made up of different combinations of duplex units. In some instances, the topmost duplex was connected to the ground by freestanding external stairs, rising dramatically out of the forecourt between the blocks. In others, the lower duplexes were accessed via a horizontal gallery that was cantilevered in front of the block. Within each apartment, internal stairs were organized so that residents could choose which spaces would be most convenient for living and which for sleeping; the alternatives arose out of the ongoing exchange between the architect and the future residents. The terraces were of varying length due to the shape of the site, and while at one end they conclude in the acoustic wall, at the other end each was to have terminated in a diminutive corner building, or *bâtiment d'angle*, dedicated to a communal facility such as a launderette, a library, or a convenience store. These proposed facilities testify to Siza's commitment to the social scope of the project as a whole; the fact that they were never realized seems, in retrospect, indicative of the limits of the SAAL system. Indeed, after the right-wing coup of November 1975, the power of the SAAL organization was

---

[1] France Vanlaethem, "*Pour une Architecture Épurée et Rigoureuse*," *ARQ: Architecture/Québec*, No. 14 (August 1983), 18.

already diminished, and the whole participatory enterprise was effectively dissolved the following year.

Although Siza's next housing project proceeded without the support of SAAL, he continued to integrate certain aspects of the participatory process. Immediately after Bouça, Siza began work on a low-rise, high-density housing scheme for a district known as the Quinta da Malagueira, situated immediately outside the Alentejo city of Évora. Siza's mandate was to design and build twelve hundred residential units within a domain already occupied by squatter settlements and midrise social housing dating from the 1960s. As in Bouça, he took the interwar social housing of the Weimar Republic as a distant model for the project's massing and organization, although the individual unit he designed was very different. Here, he opted for a two-story dwelling, with an L-shaped plan flanking the contiguous sides of a square patio walled off from the street. Developed consistently by the architect over a twenty-year period under the patronage of the city government, the Malagueira housing complex was, in effect, a reworking of the white-washed low-rise homes that have long been the native form of Mediterranean cities. In fact, one may argue that the only thing that distinguishes Siza's design from the vernacular fabric is the rhythmic placement and proportion of door and window openings throughout, a format that seems to have been taken from the absolute abstraction favored by Adolf Loos, which was perhaps most didactically articulated in his Alexander Moissi house, projected for the Venice Lido in 1923.

One of the more unusual devices Siza employed in his scheme is an elevated service duct, raised on concrete piers and rendered in unplastered concrete block, which produced a pseudo-viaduct that meanders through Malagueira's episodic housing terraces like a relic from another time. Justified on the grounds of increasing the accessibility of gas, electricity, and other utilities for the purposes of maintenance and repair, this collective form, which links the disparate units both literally and compositionally, may be seen as a surreal compensation for the unfortunate absence of communal amenities. Here, too, Siza envisioned community buildings that were never completed, a failure he attributed to the tension between the Communist municipal administration of Évora and the reactionary conservative government in Lisbon: "From the outset, there was conflict. It was a latent conflict between central and local governments . . . The funding was only and exclusively granted for the construction of the dwellings, but never for the collective facility. Still today, there are hardly any community facilities in the neighborhood."[2] Despite all these limitations, Malagueira has stood the test of time—particularly with regard to its capacity to absorb street parking, a provision that was not considered necessary at the outset of the project—suggesting that the

---

[2] Juan Rodriguez and Carlos Seoane, Eds., *Siza by Siza* (Póvoa de Varzim, Portugal: AMAG, 2015), 179.

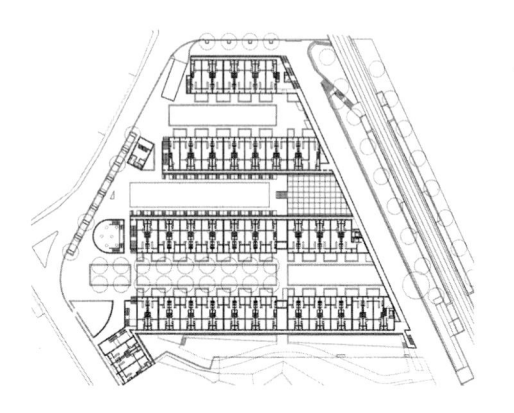

FIGURES 64 AND 65 Bouça housing settlement, Porto, Portugal. Álvaro Siza, 1974–1977. Site plan (top); Forecourt between the housing blocks (below).

design of explicitly designated communal spaces is not the only means of producing a collective architecture.

[...]

I have characterized Siza as the last modern housing architect, inasmuch as housing itself would progressively disappear from the welfare-state agenda of European governments from the mid-'80s onward. Siza would go on to propose extensive medium-rise urban residential developments for Milan and Naples in 1986, but by then the politics of neoliberalism were gaining traction all over the world; the grand postwar experiment in democratic socialism was over. Recently, however, the worldwide refugee crisis and the astonishingly rapid urbanization of developing nations has, once again, rendered the shortfall of affordable housing a crisis of unmanageable proportions. And the urgent need for solutions—both social and architectural—has made Siza's pioneering experiments in collective design more relevant than ever.

30 Towards an Agonistic Architecture (2013)

1. THE STATE OF THINGS

Das Spiel ist aus ("The game is over")[1] is the title of a poem by the Austrian poet Ingeborg Bachmann, by which I believe she meant the project of the European Enlightenment, the vision of Schiller, Goethe, Hegel, Schinkel, Marx and Freud, in a word, Jürgen Habermas's "unfinished modern project," which, it now seems, will never be realised, not even partially; not because we lack the resources and the technique to do so, but because we are unable to muster the necessary political will to effect a decisive change, for we are totally deluded by 'the society of spectacle'[2] and thereby rendered impotent as a body politic, and by the repression of alternative modes of being, by which we might still be able to save ourselves.

Le Corbusier's elegiac vision of *une ville radieuse* of 1934, his erotic project of Baudelaire's *Luxe, calme et volupté*, will never materialize, not because we lack the essential wherewithal, as the oil-rich, instant city of Dubai makes abundantly clear, but because the "species-being" has been unable (so far) to make the ethical and political leap necessary to engender a society capable of living within an ecological domain of homeostasis. Instead, we seem to be transfixed by the auto-destructive task of laying the world to waste and ourselves with

---

Source: Kenneth Frampton, "Towards an Agonistic Architecture," *Domus* 972 (September 2013), https://www.domusweb.it/en/opinion/2013/10/03/_towards_an_agoni..ic_architecture.html.

[1] Cited by Anselm Kiefer in his speech on the occasion of receiving German Book Trade Peace Prize in Frankfurt, 2008.

[2] Guy Debord, *Comments on the Society of the Spectacle*, Verso, New York 1998, p. 39.

it, as rapidly as possible. The hegemonic power of the "universal" West is such that there seems to be no other model than the profligate project of Americanising the entire world, the limitless consumerist dream by which all are equally mesmerised – the symbol and instrument of which is the automobile. It is this device surely that has proven to be the primary apocalyptical invention of the 20th century, with result that the world now consumes in a few weeks the amount of petroleum it used to burn in the course of a year in the middle of the last century.

This is the heart of the Pandora's box from which much else, equally deleterious, patently stems, even if we hesitate to acknowledge the cumulative evidence. Thus one may readily claim that the mass ownership of the automobile is the one agency from which much else follows: the advent of global warming; the melting of the ice cap; the phenomenon of extreme weather; the elevation of the sea (now projected as becoming as much as one metre by the end of the century); the pollution of the oceans and the destruction of the rainforests in our reckless pursuit of oil reserves; the suburbanisation of the planet, surely to be followed by its eventual abandonment and desertification; the insupportable air pollution of our megalopolitan centres; the subtle corruption of democratic processes in terms of both governance and the prosecution of justice – these aporias occurring equally at both an international and national level. Much of this is surely due to the overwhelming power of global mega-corporations, accompanying worldwide electronic surveillance and concomitant restraint on the exercise of investigative journalism. Needless to say, I have in mind the global oil, chemical and pharmaceutical corporations, the industrialisation of agriculture,[3] the genetic modification of food[4] and the maximisation of the supermarket system – the latter effectively inducing the demise of main street and with it the provincial city as a still remaining potential for local culture and direct democracy. In short, the globalised maximisation of profit as an end in itself, at no matter what cost to biodiversity,[5] or even to the survival of Homo sapiens, the extinction of which is now, for the first time, distinctly foreseeable. Perhaps no one has written more succinctly about our current paradoxical state of hyperactive paralysis than Jean Baudrillard, who, at a symposium entitled "Looking Back on the End of the World," staged at Columbia University, New York in 1986, remarked:

> We are no longer in a state of growth; we are in a state of excess. We are living in a society of excrescence, meaning that which incessantly develops without being measurable against its own objectives. The boil is growing out

[3] See Wendell Berry, *The Unsettling of America: Culture and Agriculture*, Aron, New York 1978, pp. 39–95.

[4] The corporate tyranny of genetically modified seed as evident in the ongoing struggle between the Indian environmentalist Vandana Shiva and Monsanto chemical to preserve the rights of Indian farmers to keep their seed for re sowing.

[5] It is estimated that some 30,000 animals and plants are becoming extinct every year. Among the threatened species are pollinating honey bees. It is obvious that their extinction would have disastrous consequences.

of control, recklessly at cross purposes with itself, its impacts multiplying as the causes disintegrate. [. . .] This satiation has nothing to do with the excess of which Bataille spoke, which all societies have managed to produce and destroy in useless and wasteful exhaustion. [. . .] We no longer know how we can possibly use up all these accumulated things; we no longer even know what they are for. Every factor of acceleration and concentration brings us closer to the point of inertia.[6]

Two current news items merit our attention in this regard. The first of these is the decision taken by the Chinese technocratic elite to forcibly move, over the next decade, 250 million rural people from the agrarian hinterland into dense, high-rise urban fabric. This ironic reversal of the precepts of the Communist Manifesto of 1848 has the ostensible purpose of creating a consumerist base upon which to expand an internal Chinese economy comparable to the current production/consumption cycle obtained in the US. The second item concerns the equally draconian decision by the Ecuadorian president, Rafael Correa, to abandon, for lack of international commitment, his attempt, via a UN-backed trust fund, to raise 3.6 billion dollars, in order to preserve 4000 square miles of virgin rain forest from the ravages of oil drilling. These seemingly unrelated incidents are symbiotically linked by a recent commitment on the part of the Chinese Republic to consume some 40,000 barrels a day of Ecuadorian oil.[7]

2. WHAT ARE ARCHITECTS FOR IN A DESTITUTE TIME?

This paraphrase of Hölderlin's question can be applied to contemporary architecture, since the bulk of contemporary practice is global rather than local, with star architects travelling incessantly all over the world in pursuit of the equally dynamic flow of capital. Herein we are witness the vox populi's susceptibility to the mediagenic impact of spectacular form which is as much due to the capacity of "superstar architects" to come up with sensational, novel images as to their organisational competence and technical ability. Hence, the advent of the so-called Bilbao effect, where cities and institutions compete with each other in order to sponsor a building designed by a recognisable brand name. In recent years this has been nowhere more evident than in Beijing, where diverse architecture stars rival each other to design one spectacular building after another. Hence Herzog & de Meuron's sensational National Olympic Stadium of 2008, which was followed by Rem Koolhaas's equally sensational 230-metre-high CCTV tower of virtually the same date. We are informed that the latter is destined to programme some 250 "spectacular" TV channels a day to an audience of one billion people. Given the sensational aestheticism sought

---

[6] See *Looking Back on the End of the World*, edited by Dietmar Kamper and Christoph Wolf, Semiotext(e), Columbia University, New York 1989, p. 29.

[7] Clifford Krauss, *Plan to Ban Oil Drilling in the Amazon is Dropped*, in *The New York Times*, August 17, 2013, pp. B1 and B3.

in both these works, it is surely no accident that they would each make a totally irrational and structurally uneconomic use of steel.

Koolhaas's "catatonic" atypical skyscraper is symptomatic of a world in which cities rival each other for the dubious honour of sponsoring the highest building in the world, the title being held as of now by Dubai which, while barely a city at all, has nonetheless to its renown the 160-storey Burj Tower. In this vein the Manhattanisation of the world proceeds without redress, in which each successive high-rise (no matter where) is little more than another free-standing, abstract cipher testifying to the presence of global speculation. As Tadao Ando put it some time ago: "I think over a certain height, architecture is no longer possible."

In the meantime, any kind of ecologically coherent, rational pattern of land settlement continues to elude us, despite all the efforts made in the 1960s and '70s[8] to arrive at low-to-medium-rise densities as alternatives with which to resist the unending expansion of commodified urban sprawl, which is still being sustained by subsidised motorways serving such low densities as to make any kind of public transit economically unfeasible.

Here and there, there are exceptions to this pattern: the designated bus lanes of Curitiba, Brazil; the high-speed trains of Japan and the European continent; and the technological lyricism of the Zurich tram system. But in the main, the automobile prevails. Moreover, after the spectacular travesties of Milton Keynes and Marne-la-Vallée – the non-place urban realm *par excellence* – in both instances, we have virtually abandoned the idea of projecting new cities. As Mies van der Rohe put it in the early 1950s: "There are no cities, in fact, anymore. It goes on like a forest. That is the reason why we cannot have old cities anymore; that is gone forever, planned city and so on. We should think about the means we have for living in the jungle and maybe do well by that." Such resignation would not be shared by the distinguished Portuguese architect Álvaro Siza, who remarked to me some 20 years ago: "Yes, I have many projects, but I am not happy. How can one be happy when Europe has no project?"

In 1983, following Alex Tzonis and Liane Lefaivre's essay *The Grid and the Pathway*[9] (1981), which was inspired by Paul Ricœur's post-colonial thesis distinguishing between *Universal Civilization and National Cultures*,[10] I elaborated the Tzonis/Lefaivre concept of Critical Regionalism in my *Six Points for an Architecture of Resistance*. This text appeared in Hal Foster's anthology of essays on postmodern culture, published under the title *The Anti-Aesthetic*.[11]

---

[8] See Roland Rainer, *Livable Environments*, Verlag für Architektur Artemis, Zurich 1972; also Serge Chermayeff and Christopher Alexander, *Community and Privacy: Toward a New Architecture of Humanism*, Anchor Books, New York 1965.

[9] See Alex Tzonis Liliane Lefaivre, "The Grid and the Pathway: An Introduction to the Work of Dimitris and Susana Antonakakis", *Architecture in Greece*, 15, 1981, pp. 164–78.

[10] See Paul Ricœur, *Universal Civilization and National Cultures*, in *History and Truth*, Northwestern University Press, Evanston 1965.

[11] See Kenneth Frampton, *Towards a Critical Regionalism: Six Points for an Architecture of Resistance*, in *The Anti-Aesthetic*, edited by Hal Foster, Bay Press, Seattle 1983.

Eight years later Fredric Jameson, in a brilliantly critical overview of various postmodern architectural stratagems entitled *The Seeds of Time*, put paid to any illusions that we might still entertain as to the geopolitical possibility of a regionally resistant culture, despite the fact that it was precisely this mythical promise that exercised an influence on many peripheral architects. In his comprehensive critique of my naïve proposition of 30 years ago, he wrote:

> Frampton's conceptual proposal, however, is not an internal but rather a geopolitical one: it seeks to mobilize a pluralism of 'regional' styles (a term selected, no doubt, in order to forestall the unwanted connotations of the terms national and international alike) with a view towards resisting the standardizations of a henceforth global late capitalism and corporatism, whose 'vernacular' is as omnipresent as its power over local decisions (and indeed after the end of the Cold War, over local governments and individual nation states as well).
>
> It is thus politically important, returning to the problem of parts or components, to emphasize the degree to which the concept of Critical Regionalism is necessarily allegorical. The individual building here belongs no longer to a unique vision of city planning (such as the Baroque) nor a specific city fabric (like Las Vegas) but rather to a distinctive regional culture as a whole, for which the distinctive individual building becomes a metonym.[12]

Despite Jameson's sensitive appraisal of my interpretation of the Critical Regionalist thesis, he nonetheless arrives at the precipitous Marxist conclusion that any vestige of regional otherness and identity has preciously little capacity to resist the subtle spectacular domination of corporate power. However, the fact remains that regional differences continue to be cultivated, above all, at the level of regional cuisine and viticulture, even though such cultural differences have always remained open to subtle forms of hybridisation throughout history. Even if we have no choice but to forego any naïve assumptions as to local sovereignty, regionally counter-hegemonic tectonic form surely still retains at the grass roots level the capacity to resist the variously reductive forms of stylistic postmodernism with which the hegemonic power of the centre prefers to surround itself.[13]

Thus, for me, a liberative promise for the future resides in an agonistic architecture of the periphery as opposed to the subtle nonjudgmental conformism of ruling taste emanating from the centre. I attempted to suggest exactly this in my marginal participation in last year's Venice Biennale. My anthology *Five North American Architects*, displayed in the Arsenale, asserted the presence

---

[12] See Fredric Jameson, *The Seed of Time*, Columbia University Press, New York 1994, pp. 202–03.

[13] See Kenneth Frampton, *Rappel à L'Ordre, the Case for the Tectonic*, in *Architectural Design*, 50, no. 3/4, 1991.

in North America of a counter-hegemonic "otherness" cultivated mainly on the periphery of a vast continent, as opposed to the pluralistic, aesthetically reductive false differences patronised in subtle ways by hegemonic power.[14]

One of the most surprising and gratifying aspects of contemporary practice over the past two decades has been the way in which accomplished architects from the so-called "first world" have found themselves building from time to time in the equally eponymous "third world". This, in itself, may not be that unusual, but what has been unique of recent times is the exceptionally refined sensibility and rigour that has invariably been applied to the regional and, at times, aboriginal situation, so that one has the uncanny sense that the outcome could not have been more practically and poetically achieved if it had been handled by locally rooted architects rather than outsiders. One of the first instances of a work of this order is John and Patricia Patkau's Seabird Island School, built for a Northwest-Pacific Indian band in Agassiz, British Columbia over the years 1988–91 (Figures 66 and 67).

A number of things are notable about this work. First, it was commissioned by an exceptionally enlightened civil servant from the Canadian Ministry of Education; second, the architects realised that for the band to be able to construct this school by themselves, a model would have to be prepared since it was evident that they were not able to read drawings, particularly for a work of such extreme geometrical complexity. Finally, there are striking topographic and cultural aspects to this work: above all, the humpback form of its shingled roof, which echoes the profile of a nearby mountain, and the canted outriggered timber spans of its portico, which overhang the southern front of the school. The latter makes a subtle reference to the fish-drying racks that used to feature prominently in front of the Indian houses in wood that line the coastline.

A comparable, reciprocal work for a prominent member of an aboriginal Australian tribe was built in Yirrkala in Northern Territory of Australia in 1994 to the designs of Glenn Murcutt. I have in mind the Marika-Alderton House, built for Banduk Marika who was then a tribal representative in the Australian parliament in Canberra. This two-storey, virtually all-timber house stands elevated one metre off the ground in order to avoid flooding and provide a clear view of the horizon – a traditional defensive feature of importance in the native culture. Situated 12½ degrees south of the Equator, where humidity reaches 80 percent, the house had to be capable of being completely opened up so as to facilitate cross ventilation. This is the primary reason behind the storey-height, hinged timber shutters which, when raised, also provide sun shields for the veranda of the house. Since the house is located on sand dunes close to the ocean, it is provided with a slatted timber floor to allow sand to fall through.

The main volume of the house was made equally permeable by virtue of pivoting metal roof vents, oriented by weather vanes, so as to align their vents with the prevailing airflow. These devices were installed so as to equalise the pressure within and without whenever the house is subject to winds of cyclone

---

[14]See Kenneth Frampton, *Five North American Architects*, Lars Müller Publishers and Columbia University, New York and Zurich 2012.

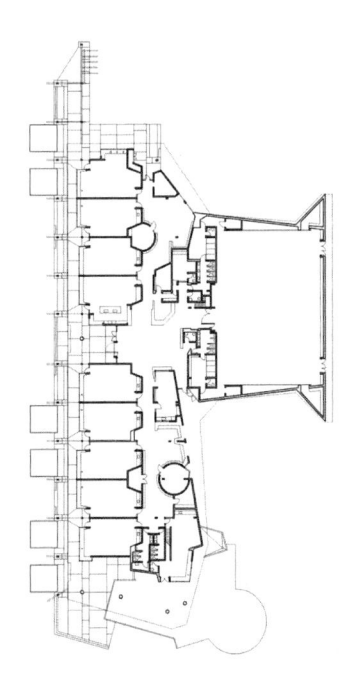

FIGURES 66 AND 67 Seabird Island School, Agassiz, British Columbia, Canada. John and Patricia Patkau, 1988–1991. Plan and section (top); east exterior view (below).

force, which raises the risk that internal pressure will blow the house apart. As in the case of Seabird Island School, this house makes an allusion to the native domestic tradition without the slightest attempt to replicate it. With its metal standing-seam roof, metal roof vents and metal structural frame and tubular uprights to stiffen the timber frame and its cladding, it is an unequivocal translation of the traditional hut into modern form. In this regard, one should note that the building was prefabricated in Sydney, and trucked overland to its site in the north. In effect this building established a totally new standard for Australian aboriginal housing in the region. Prior to this, the native populations of the area had been settled by the government bureaucracy in inadequately ventilated concrete blockhouses.

Another remarkable contribution to aboriginal culture in the post-colonial era was made in the mid-'80s by the remarkable Finnish figure of Eila Kivekäs who became involved with the Finnish reception of the Guinean intellectual Alpha Diallo, who rather remarkably had elected to translate the Finnish national epic, *The Kalevala*, into Fula, his native language.

After Diallo unexpectedly died in Finland, Kivekäs arranged for the return of his remains to Guinea and soon after went to Guinea herself to establish a local craft centre which had the aim of improving the status of women in the country, along with the overall health of the society. To this end, Kivekäs founded the Development Association Indigo in Mali, a small town of 1000 people in Guinea, the name of the institution being derived from the traditional indigo-blue cloth produced by women in the region. Eventually Kivekäs would commission the Finnish architects Heikkinen-Komonen to build three works for her in Guinea; her own house in Mali (1989), the Poultry Farming School in Kindia (1990) and a local health centre nearby. One should note that the school came into being largely because of Diallo's conviction that the most important priority for the future well-being of Guinea society was to increase the amount of protein in the daily diet. In all three buildings Heikkinen-Komonen used inexpensive materials, which were readily available, such as bamboo screens, concrete blocks, large bricks made of stabilised earth and roof tiles made of cement, reinforced by glass fibre.

From the point of view of the poetics of light and the regional aura, the single-storey Villa Eila in Mali is perhaps the most "aboriginal" building of the three. Here a continuous monopitch tiled roof and a long woven bamboo screen wall covering the southern face serve to enclose four volumes under a single roof. By contrast, the Poultry Farming School is almost classical in its minimalist composition, assembled about a square courtyard. This square is enclosed by two single-storey volumes situated to the south and the northwest corner of the court.

The buildings are made out of blocks. The first is the permanent dwelling for the instructor/caretaker, while the second consists of three separate, four-person dormitories for students. The dominant element situated on axis to the east of the square is the double-height lecture hall with its monumental timber portico. The latter is a tectonic *tour de force* in lightweight timber construction built out of transverse beams, elegantly and economically stiffened by wire cables. Finland was also involved in the realisation of a women's centre in Senegal in 1995, located just outside the city of Rufisque. This single-storey building, made out of concrete blocks dyed bright red, consists of a simple U-shaped enclosure. It is fitting that this women's centre was designed by three young Finnish women, trained as architects in Helsinki, namely Saija Hollmén, Jenni Reuter and Helena Sandman. Here the powerfully expressive image stems from the theatrical form of the protective enclosure, from the red colour and the subtle perforations here and there in the perimeter's block work.

I would like to include in this essay on the potential scope of agonistic architecture a comment on the extraordinary work of Studio Mumbai in Bombay, founded in 1995, under the direction of the architect Bijoy Jain. Studio Mumbai seems to be on a Kropotkinian approach to building culture, harking back to the workshops of William Morris and even further back in time to the carpenter as the first architect. In many respects, Jain, although trained as an architect, has become a kind of latter-day master-builder whereby he serves as a coordinator of carpenters. Through a kind of transgressive creativity, Studio Mumbai has demonstrated its mastery not only over carpentry and joinery but also over ceramics, coloured plasterwork, masonry and milled stonework.

All the same, one has to acknowledge that the beautiful houses that Studio Mumbai has built in the state of Maharashtra are, in the last analysis, rather expensive, bourgeois residences that could hardly be more removed from the more modest works I have touched on here. Nevertheless this is still a kind of reciprocal, "other" architecture, wherein, by definition, Jain has chosen to distance himself from the brand architecture of our society in all its aesthetic guises.

By the term "agonistic" I wish to evoke the idea of an architecture which continues to place emphasis on the particular brief and on the specific nature of the topography and climate in which it is situated, while still giving high priority to the expressivity and the physical attributes of the material out of which the work is made. I have taken the term itself from the political theory of Chantal Mouffe, recently published under the title *Agonistics. Thinking the World Politically* (2013). While architecture, obviously, cannot act politically, by appropriating the term I wish to evoke a pluralist architecture that is categorically opposed to the stylistic, hegemonic spectacularity of the neo-liberal worldview, that is to say the falsely sensational and superficial aestheticism of our time. In my view, it is precisely this ever-changing fashionable emphasis on the decorative or minimalist envelope that has effectively robbed architecture of one of its most fundamental attributes, namely, the time-honoured mandate to organise and orchestrate the space of public appearance in a culturally significant manner. Mouffe's agonistic political theory also mentions a reappraisal of the region as a counter-hegemonic entity capable of countering to an equal degree both the faltering nation state and the overarching force of an indifferent globalised economy.[15]

---

[15] See Chantal Mouffe, *Agonistics: Thinking the World Politically*, Verso, London 2013, p. 57. As she put it after Massimo Cacciari, "The modern state is torn from the inside under the pressure of regionalist movements, and from the outside as a consequence of the growth of supranational powers and institutions and of the increasing power of world finance and transnational corporations."

31 The Unfinished Project at the End of Modernity: Tectonic Form and the Space of Public Appearance (2019)

The title of this lecture points to the self-imposed difficulty of combining an excursus into the ontology of building with an appraisal of some of the most significant architectural works of the last half-century, with the implication that one is the vindication of the other and *vice versa*. Looking back, it now seems that this juxtaposition of theory and practice was already latent in the three essays that I wrote during the first two decades of my academic career in the United States. Each of these essays was somehow motivated by my nostalgia for a Modern Movement in architecture that had flourished in Europe and Southern California between the World Wars. This was a movement that can now no longer be pursued with the same conviction as during the time when the modern project was oriented, not only towards the creation of a liberative architecture, but also towards the modernisation of society as a whole, and in particular to realise the welfare state as a normative condition. This social democratic vision, perhaps first fully articulated in Gunnar Asplund's Stockholm Exhibition of 1930, has since been totally undermined by the commodifying drive of neoliberalism.

The first of these three essays, entitled "Labor, Work & Architecture" was published in 1968 in Charles Jencks and George Baird's semiotic anthology, *Meaning in Architecture*. With a passing reference to Sigfried Giedion's *Space, Time and Architecture* of 1941, the title of the essay was derived from Hannah

Source: Kenneth Frampton, *The Unfinished Project at the End of Modernity: Tectonic Form and the Space of Public Appearance* (London: Sir John Soane's Museum, 2019). Originally delivered as the 2019 Soane Medal Lecture.

Arendt's unusual distinctions between 'labour' and 'work' as they appear in her masterwork *The Human Condition* of 1958.[1]

[...]

"Labor, Work & Architecture" coincided with the 1968 student revolt, epitomised in Europe by the *les évenements de mai* that took place in Paris in that year. The second essay of 1983—"Towards a Critical Regionalism: Six Points for an Architecture of Resistance"—virtually coincided with the first formulation of postmodernism via Jean-François Lyotard's book *The Postmodern Condition*, published in French in 1979, and written, one should note, by a former associate of Louis Althusser's radical faction, *Socialisme ou Barbarie*. In my view it is disturbing that Lyotard's thesis, predicated, in part, on the divided nature of our specialised language games, should bring him to pronounce the domination of the future by the instrumentality of techno-science. This advent of the 'Postmodern Condition' would find its cultural echo in the stylistic postmodernism of the first full architectural biennale, staged in Venice in 1980 [...] It was this scenographic provocation that prompted "Towards a Critical Regionalism", which was first published in Hal Foster's anthology *The Anti-Aesthetic: Essays in Postmodern Culture*. Apart from the influence of Arendt and the contradictory discourse of the Frankfurt School, as in Herbert Marcuse's *Eros and Civilization* of 1955, the main inspiration behind my polemic was Paul Ricoeur's essay, "Universal Civilisation and National Cultures" of 1961, in which he identified universal civilisation as the wholesale implementation of Western technology, while he envisaged culture as the ethical and mythical nucleus of mankind. Ricoeur was of the opinion that techno-scientific instrumentality often demands nothing less than the total abandonment of the past. He concluded his essay stating that "It is a fact every culture cannot sustain and absorb the shock of modern civilization. There is the paradox how to become modern and return to the sources".[2]

I took the term 'critical regionalism' from Alexander Tzonis and Liliane Lefaivre's 1981 text *The Grid and the Pathway*, in which they made a comparative critique of the two most prominent Greek architects of the 1950s, comparing the trabeated forms of Aris Konstantinidis to the tactile topographic approach of Dimitris Pikionis, particularly the latter's undulating landscape on the Philopappos Hill, built adjacent to the Athenian Acropolis in 1959. Influenced by Tzonis and Lefaivre, I developed my critically regionalist manifesto as a stratagem

---

[1] Hannah Arendt, *The Human Condition* (Chicago: University of Chicago Press,1958) [For the detailed discussion of Arendt's distinction between *labor* and *work*, and between *animal laborans* and *homo faber*, and for Frampton's argument supporting the implications of Arendt's work on the distinctions between "architecture" and "building" vis-à-vis "spaces of public appearance," see "The Status of Man and the Status of His Objects: A Reading of *The Human Condition*" in Section 1 of this volume. Footnote inserted by the editor.]

[2] Paul Ricoeur, "Universal Civilization and National Cultures" (1961) in *History and Truth*, trans. Chas. A. Kelbley (Evanston: Northwestern University Press, 1965), 276–7.

with which to offset the impact of universal civilisation by stressing the crucial importance of the place-form as a 'space of public appearance'[3] [...]

The fifth resistant point of my polemic, given under the heading 'Culture Versus Nature', emphasised the inflection of architectural form by topography, climate, light, and, finally, by the tectonic of the building itself, designed not only to resist gravity but also the passage of time.

My third essay, entitled, "Rappel a l'Ordre: The Case for the Tectonic" and published in 1990, amplified the concept of the tectonic by alluding to the initial coinage of the term in both Gottfried Semper's *Four Elements of Architecture* (1851) and Karl Bötticher's *Tektonik der Hellenen* (1844-52). Bötticher regarded the joint as the primary architectural element, which not only embodied the building's material presence but also enabled it to be perceived as a symbolic form. The most felicitous aspect of Bötticher's version of the tectonic was his idea of the core form (*Kernform*) versus the art form (*Kunstform*). This distinction can be understood via his analysis of the Doric order whereby the column itself, which is initially merely the superimposition of tapered, cylindrical, stone blocks, comes to be perceptible as a column via the art form of the flutes. This idea is related to the Semperian concept of the *Bekleidung* in that the cladding of a building may simultaneously both reveal and conceal its basic structure. In his essay, Semper identified the 'Four Elements of Architecture' as (1) the earthwork elevating the hut above the ground, (2) the hearth recessed into the earthwork, (3) the framework and roof and (4) the 'woven' infill wall providing the basic enclosure. All of these elements were present in the Caribbean hut that Semper first witnessed in the Crystal Palace exhibition of 1851. With regard to my appraisal of canonical architectonic works of the last half century, we may condense Semper's four elements into the *earthwork* and the *roofwork*.

[...]

In my view the *earthwork* and its extension into the landscape, embodying a cosmogonic transformation of the site, has the potential today of constituting the core of a resistant architecture. This is an architecture that is capable of mediating our compulsive commodification of the environment by virtue of integrating a building into its site rather than merely proliferating yet another free-standing aesthetic object unrelated to either its site or to other objects in its vicinity.

Perhaps the first intimation of the tectonic in the modern tradition is to be found in the work of Le Corbusier, where the *earthwork-roofwork* dialectic appears in his Maison de week-end at La Celle-Saint-Cloud, France of 1935, where the earth is mounded up over the house thus covering its vaulted, shell-concrete roof with turf. Le Corbusier's ingenious synthesis of vernacular form with modern, industrialised materials and techniques is evident in both the exterior and interior: rubble stone walling combined with concrete shell vaults

---

[3] Arendt, op. cit., 204.

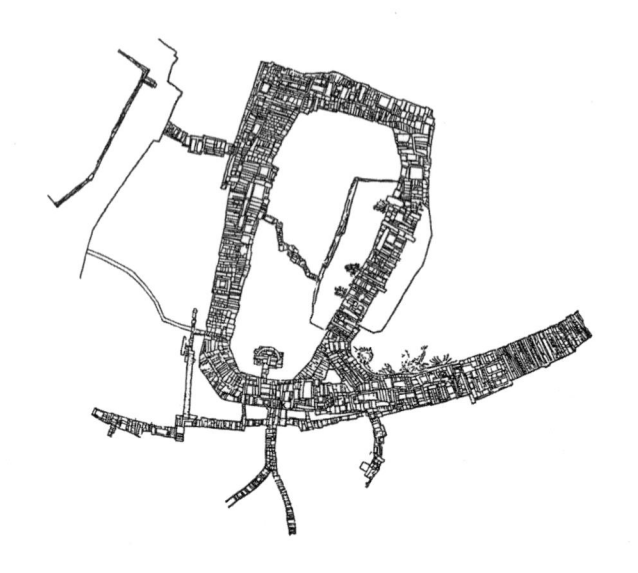

FIGURES 68 AND 69 Philopappou Hill, Acropolis, Athens, Greece. Dimitris Pikionis, 1954–1957. Site plan (top); Pathways approaching the Acropolis (below).

with glass lenses, steel-framed plate glass, the precision tilework, bent plywood soffits and the thick irregular mortar joints to the coursing of the brick chimney.

Le Corbusier followed this project with his Pavillon des Temps Nouveaux of 1937, which was inspired by a reconstruction of the Hebrew temple in the wilderness. This daring *roofwork* comprised an inverted tent held in place by a wire-cable, suspension structure. This was yet another hybrid, demonstrating the poetic potential of combining vernacular form with modern technology.

The *earthwork-roofwork* emerges after the Second World War as a topographic *tour de force* in Jørn Utzon and Tobias Faber's 1947 competition entry for the London Crystal Palace site. This project was an early manifestation of Utzon's life-long preoccupation with his transcultural pagoda/podium paradigm which attained its ultimate expression in his 1957 winning entry for the Sydney Opera House, a duality which he returned to more modestly in his Bagsværd Church, completed outside Copenhagen in 1976.

An *earthwork-roofwork* dialectic combined with a 'space of public appearance' is also evident in Alvar Aalto's Säynätsalo's Town Hall of 1948. Here, the earthwork is piled up to form a diminutive public place in the heart of the composition. Meanwhile, the *roofwork* is a brick-faced, concrete structure, culminating in the mono-pitch roof of the council chamber, the honorific status of which is represented within by the two timber-trusses supporting a timber-framed roof.

Surely one of the most monumental expressions of the *earthwork-roofwork* syndrome is the suspended wire-cable roofs of the gymnasia that Kenzo Tange designed for the Yoyogi National Gymnasium, built for the Tokyo Olympic Games of 1964. Here, the major and minor *roofworks* are accompanied by an elaborately terraced and ramped staging ground which extends well outside the footprint of the stadia.

At almost the same time, a more modest interplay of *earthwork* and *roofwork* is manifest in the first work of the Portuguese architect, Álvaro Siza: the Boa Nova Teahouse at Leça da Palmeira of 1963, where a restaurant is cradled under a pitched roof and poised on top of a stepped earthwork built on top of a natural rock-outcrop. Siza immediately followed this notable project with his Leça Swimming Facility (1961–66) in which one descends from the datum of a coastal road into a rocky esplanade set before the sea with two pools, one being allocated to children and the other to adults. The *earthwork-roofwork* interplay is dramatised in this instance by a narrow threshold accompanied by a mono-pitched roof over adjacent changing rooms.

[...]

Another European architect whose work is equally as topographic is Rafael Moneo. One of the Spanish architect's most compelling early works was his National Museum of Roman Art in Mérida, Spain, where he inserted a reinforced concrete superstructure, clad in brick tiles of Roman proportions, with matching brickwork, into the archaeological substrate of a Roman city, in such a way that it evoked not only the antique past but also the lost past of the medieval city that was built over its ruins. This more recent past is alluded to in the top-lit, brick-faced warehouse that houses the collection, which is reinforced by brick buttresses, suggestive of Gothic architecture.

The internal, brick-tiled, arcuated concrete cross walls then descend via brick-faced concrete piers into the sacrosanct remains of the subterranean Roman city. Here, immersed in an antique undercroft, visitors pick their way through Roman footings to exit via a tunnel into the nearby open-air remains of a Roman stadium and theatre.

Moneo would further demonstrate his feeling for the urban grain in two subsequent works of comparable power. The first example is his 800-metre-long, brick-faced, L'Illa block of 1992, designed for Barcelona in collaboration with the Catalan urbanist, Manuel de Solà-Morales. In this work, his intervention comprises a stepped, mega-structural office block paralleled by a 'space of public appearance' in the form of a top-lit galleria running beside the Avenida Diagonal.
[. . .]

Moneo is hardly alone in Spain for his feeling for the topographic integration of a building into its site as is evident from the best of Spanish architecture over the past fifty years: from the Vall d'Hebron velodrome, designed by Bonell and Rius and set down in 1984 amid the chaotic inner suburbs of Barcelona, to the necropolis of the Igualada Cemetery fashioned out of a disused quarry in 1994 by Enric Miralles and Carme Pinós.

Moving across the Atlantic, the heroic Brazilian tectonic tradition in reinforced concrete was inaugurated in 1955 by the Museum of Modern Art in Rio de Janeiro, designed by Affonso Reidy. It is this work more than any other that exerts a decisive influence on the emerging tectonic form of the Paulista School of which João Vilanova Artigas and Paulo Mendes da Rocha were the leading figures. One may readily detect the influence of Reidy's museum on Artigas' FAU School, São Paulo of 1961, with its monumental top-lit atrium which may be seen as the ultimate 'space of public appearance', with its zero bending-hinged supports just above grade, as in Reidy's museum. Something similar can also be found in Mendes da Rocha's Paulistano Athletic Club in São Paulo of 1958, which combines a suspended wire-cable *roofwork* with a cantilevered reinforced concrete *earthwork*. In this example, we have a typically Brazilian 'space of public appearance', located in downtown São Paulo, and open on its perimeter so as to encourage the infiltration of passers-by. As the academic and educator Maria Isabel Villac has remarked, this building aspires to a wider political significance, transcending its dynamic form. At the same time, one is struck not only by the elegant ingenuity and clarity of the structure but also by its inherent economy.
[. . .]

More modest but equally arresting megastructures were realised by Mendes da Rocha in São Paulo in the late 1990s and early 2000s. These include the 2002 Patriarca Square regeneration project, the 300-metre galleria of the Poupatempo complex (1998) adjacent to the Itaquera metro stop, designed to accommodate everyday transactions between the municipality and its citizenry; and the Dom Pedro II Park bus station (2001). It is typical of Mendes da Rocha's technological flexibility that all three of these interventions would be built in part of welded steel rather than concrete.

FIGURES 70 AND 71 Madrid-Barajas Airport Terminal 4, Madrid, Spain. Rogers Stirk Harbour + Partners with Estudio Lamela, 2005 (top); Luigi Bocconi University, Milan, Italy. Grafton Architects, 2008. View of the auditorium under the new public square (below).

The rhetorical *roofwork* may also be found in the work of the Anglo/Italian 'Hi-Tech' architects, namely, Richard Rogers, Renzo Piano and Norman Foster, and in particular in their design of airport terminals. In the case of Rogers, the most notable example is his Barajas Terminal completed outside Madrid in 2006, a work which, in my view, is the masterwork of the office. For Piano, it is his terminal at the mega-airport of Kansai in Japan dating from 1989, where the *earthwork* consists of an audaciously created artificial island. In this instance the bearing of the tubular steel supports of the *roofwork* have to be constantly adjusted by jacks, due to continual land settlement. Finally, there is the brilliant example of Stansted Airport (1991) designed by Foster Associates as the third London airport and inspired by the invention of mobile departure lounges as pioneered by Eero Saarinen in his Dulles Airport, Washington, DC of 1958. Stansted Airport was conceived as a *roofwork* mat-building built on top of an *earthwork* within which was incorporated a rail-head with a direct link by train to the capital city. The simplicity and horizontal gestalt of the welded, tubular steel, umbrella *roofwork* at Stansted was crucial to Foster's ambition of creating a monumental "space of public appearance", comparable to the great rail termini of the nineteenth century, in which departing and arriving passengers would pass through the same honorific volume. Unfortunately, this ambition would be thwarted by the paranoid, security-obsessed bureaucrats of our late-modern era who, while accepting the spatial continuity of the design, insisted on separating the two classes of passengers by a partition wall. Nevertheless, the horizontal panoramic grandeur of the modular umbrella roof at Stansted is poised above an *earthwork* and a broader landscape like a classical villa with its tubular steel peristyle, overlooking a parterre of parking.

[. . .]

Fretton's arguably most emotionally affecting work is his Fuglsang Art Museum, built at Lolland in southern Denmark in 2008, which encompasses within its galleries the panoramic backdrop of an unspoiled agrarian landscape. Fretton has written of this work in a way that captures the full range of the cultural and political ramifications of this 'space of public appearance':

> I am an advocate of social democratic society in a time when less well meaning ideologies have the upper hand. Consequently, I seek to create conditions for productive sociability and social awareness in the buildings that I design. When designing I look for configurations that are surprising and have a wide appeal in the basic ranges of pleasure, political dimensions that can be experienced bodily and the capacity to allow artistic exploration and the development of ideas. I find many of these qualities in buildings that already exist, in the physical changes that people make to them and the meaning they acquire through word of mouth, film, TV, and literature. In the Fuglsang Art Museum the entrance sequence brings strangers temporarily into contact before they disperse into the spaces for art. Among the galleries they find a room where they can come together again to appreciate the views

of the surrounding agricultural landscape, which like the collection of art in the museum is an artefact but made anonymously by successive generations of local people.[4]

In terms of architectural culture, Dublin has recently risen to the fore, having been influenced over the last half century by such luminaries as Mies van der Rohe, Louis Kahn, Alvar Aalto and James Stirling and by the teaching in the 1970s of Ed Jones, Su Rogers and John Miller at the Royal College of Art. This heritage which was independently cultivated within the architectural faculty of University College Dublin under the charismatic leadership of Shane de Blacam, led to the emergence of Group 91 which worked on the restoration of the Temple Bar district in Dublin in the early 1990s. The two most fertile practices to emerge from this experience are, firstly, that of Sheila O'Donnell and John Tuomey and, secondly, Grafton Architects, founded by Shelley McNamara and Yvonne Farrell. The latter practice first came to international prominence after winning a limited competition for the expansion of the leading Italian business school, the Luigi Bocconi University in Milan. Their entry was successful in part because theirs was the only design that was able to meet the requirement of providing an *aula magna* that was positioned so as to be equally accessible to both the university and the city. Completed in 2008, this 'space of public appearance' marked the beginning of their penchant for using wide-span, cantilevered reinforced concrete construction, which has seen them work closely with engineers.

After the Milan project, Grafton were able to build on their reputation of expertise in the design of business schools and this led over the years first to the design and realisation of a brick-faced business school in Toulouse, France (on-site) and now their Marshall Building for the London School of Economics, situated on a prominent site on the south-west corner of Lincoln's Inn Fields. It is surely symptomatic of the current prowess of Irish architecture that this is the second work to be commissioned by the LSE from the Group 91 generation, the first being a student centre built to the designs of O'Donnell and Tuomey on a tight site near the northern end of the campus. Currently under construction, the Marshall Building is, surely, the most major expansion to be undertaken by the LSE in its entire history and as such could hardly be a more appropriate vehicle for Arendt's 'space of public appearance'. Subject to the influence of the Paulista School, Grafton Architects have opted here, as they have elsewhere in recent years, for a tectonic *tour de force* in the form of a cantilevered reinforced concrete construction, combined in this example with a three-storey honorific public threshold for the LSE with an ingenious layer of teaching offices and lecture halls stacked above. Grafton are following the Marshall Building by an even more unequivocal 'space of public appearance', this time in their native Ireland. Their project for the Dublin City Library, to be built behind a Georgian

---

[4] Tony Fretton, *AEIOU: Articles, Essays, Interviews and Out-Takes* (Heijningen: Jap Sam Books, 2018), 125.

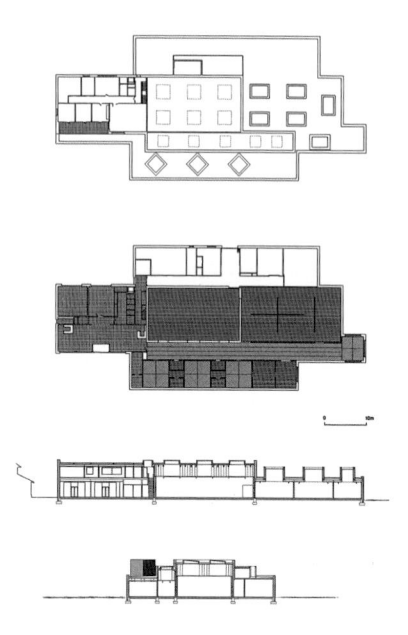

FIGURE 72 AND 73 Fuglsang Art Museum, Lolland, Denmark. Tony Fretton Architects, 2008. Building plans and sections (top); east-facing panoramic window (below).

terrace facing onto Parnell Square in the centre of Dublin, will see a heroically cantilevered reinforced concrete structure soaring above the reading room in recognition of the one art, above all others, that embodies the essential cultural spirit of the Irish nation.

In all of these examples I have attempted to show how, despite our political incapacity to confront the environmental nemesis of our time, architecture can still be pursued as the cultivation of a poetics of construction dedicated whenever possible to the realisation of a 'space of public appearance' within which society may still realise some measure of its potential sovereignty. My perhaps vain attempt to posit a viable theory of architecture, not only in terms of an ontology of building, but also with regard to what tectonic expressiveness has been able to achieve over the past half century, brings to my mind Sir John Summerson. Apart from being the illustrious Curator of Sir John Soane's Museum and an exceptionally erudite and eloquent scholar, Summerson took upon himself, in the late 1950s, the unenviable task of attempting a theory of modern architecture for the post-war period in a memorable lecture that he gave to the RIBA in 1957, under the title "The Case for a Theory of 'Modern' Architecture", in which he argued that either programmatic functionalism or the syntactical legacy of classicism had to be the source of unity. In his exclusion of any hybrid discourse he seems not only to have revealed his disdain for the Arts and Crafts tradition, with its roots in the vernacular, but also for the erstwhile cosmopolitanism of the British Modern Movement between the wars. With the possible exception of Le Corbusier and Viollet-le-Duc, Summerson appears to have been largely disinterested in anything that lay beyond the confines of his island nation.

In today's inter-connected, globalised world, such provincialism is no longer viable, even if, as we have seen it has led to some of the country's most talented architects completing their best work abroad. Yet if we are to cultivate an architecture of resistance to our compulsive commodification of the environment, it is to the *earthwork* that we must look as the means of achieving significant transformation of a given site so that a 'space of public appearance' might spontaneously emerge.

Postscript. What I wanted to acknowledge from you is not what you said at all [. . .] but the way that you said it [. . .] Not too many people have stood up there and talked about 'ethical.' I can think of ten years of lectures, that's the first time I heard that word mentioned in that context [. . .] There's something that you bring to the content of the discussion, and I think people who were listening to it can sense it, which is a conviction about the intrinsic value of the subject matter. Whether it is its merits or its demerits, and you feel that in that discussion, and you communicate that, which is that [. . .] this is something which has a kind of content, and kind of meaning, and a kind of integrity that comes out in the sensibility of the discourse, whether one would want to contest the discourse point by point or not. Which wouldn't be your argument, that the emotive content supersedes the intellectual content— strangely coming from you. That's where a lot of its power comes from, from its conviction. It's not so much that we are persuaded, you are persuaded. It's an unusual quality, you know. I wanted to acknowledge it, and I wanted you to know that the audience, whether it articulates it or not, feels it and feels the conviction. It has a certain amount of potency, and I want it to acknowledge it and to thank you for that.

Eric Owen Moss, closing remarks at Kenneth Frampton's lecture
"Towards an Agonistic Architecture" held at SCI-Arc, 4 December 2013,
https://channel.sciarc.edu/browse/kenneth-frampton-towards-an-agonistic-architecture-december-4-2013.

Afterword

"The Criticism of Architecture is Worth More Than Architecture"

Clive Dilnot

I

From both within and without there is perhaps a natural tendency to see Kenneth Frampton's work as a variant of architectural criticism *per se*. This is so even if, at the same time, for all that is affirmed and praised there is also a recognition that in the underlying thrust of the arguments there is nonetheless *something* which exceeds the norms of architectural practice and criticism and that this exceeding disquiets, even embarrasses architecture in the same moment as the work, in its moments and considered as a project as whole, enhances.

'Disquiets' here means the sense that at once in the breadth and depth of its comprehension of the architectural project—the manner of how within it buildings and projects are approached and analyzed, of how it takes up the history of the modern movement, in its voice, its stance—in short, by all that it encompasses (this being one of its salient qualities)—Frampton's work is asking of architecture something that in the generality it can scarcely deliver; that the work offers a challenge which both practice and criticism find difficult to contend with, even if, at the same time, it is heard and in varying degrees valued.

Something of this ambiguity is caught by Eric Owen Moss in his closing remarks to a lecture ("Towards an Agonistic Architecture")[1] that Frampton gave at SCI-Arc in Los Angeles, in 2013:

> What I wanted to acknowledge from you is not what you said at all [...] but the way that you said it [...] Not too many people have stood up there and talked about 'ethical.' I can think of ten years of lectures, that's the first time I heard that word mentioned in that context [...] There's something that you bring to the content of the discussion, and I think people who were listening to it can sense it, which is a conviction about the intrinsic value of the subject matter, whether it is its merits or its demerits [the listener] feels that and you communicate that [...] this is something which has a kind of content, and kind of meaning, and a kind of integrity that comes out in the sensibility of the discourse. That's where a lot of its power comes from, from its conviction. It's not so much that we are persuaded, *you are* persuaded. It's an unusual quality, you know. I wanted to acknowledge it, and I wanted you to know that the audience, whether it articulates it or not, feels it and feels the conviction. It has a certain amount of potency, and I want to thank you for that.[2]

Owen Moss's comments capture two things of utmost importance to Frampton's criticism. The first is the reference to "ethics," which in Frampton's case means also intrinsically and inescapably to politics seen from an emancipatory perspective—or as he says it in the closing lines of the interview which opens this volume: "Irrespective of these ideological affinities and associations, one thing is for sure—namely, everything I have written has been written with the mind of an architect, one who has been obsessed with the vision of a liberative future that now seems unattainably utopian". Given that, conventionally at least, these belong to distinct realms, the passage in Frampton's work from the project of emancipatory politics through architectural practice and into the continuing development of the modes of historical criticism which have become his essential gift to the field, is more seamless, it flows with more continuity, than might be supposed. The point is emphasized when, earlier in the same interview as the lines quoted above, he notes:

> This question [of the relation of practice, thought and politics] compels me to acknowledge in retrospect what is the one significant architectural achievement of my life, namely, the design and realization of an eight-storey block of duplex apartments in the center of London in 1962, at the age of thirty-two. This work was obviously influenced by the ethical/aesthetic vision of

---

[1] Reproduced in this volume, Section 4. From here on in, uncited page numbers are to quotations taken from this volume.

[2] Eric Owen Moss, closing remarks at Frampton's lecture "Towards an Agonistic Architecture" held at SCI-Arc, 4 December 2013. I have slightly adapted Owen Moss's remarks for this context. The quotation is given on p. 316 of this volume.

the Russian Constructivists, and in the end, it was naïvely inspired by their slogan, 'Down with religion, religion is a lie; down with art, art is a lie; long live the constructivist technician.' This vision was the ethos inspiring this work, and in the last analysis this also accounts for the overall character and substance of the first edition of *Modern Architecture: A Critical History* of 1980 and hence its "operative" manifesto-like character (25).

The flow between these moments is not arbitrary. It stems from the deep conviction that in the end the political—thought in the wide sense as the space of "the public world"[3]—is the *only* ground on which objectively architecture can found itself. Or, as Frampton puts it in an early essay, following a quotation from Arendt:

> In this passage [. . .] Architecture is revealed [. . .] as being fully contingent on the preservation of a truly political realm at an effective scale, since rationality itself, i.e., rational truth or as Habermas has characterized it, *purposeful rational action*, in no way guarantees the appearance of the human world upon which architecture reflexively depends. For lacking an ultimate end, lacking the metaphysical unity of antiquity or of Christendom, lacking above all even the possibility of a scientific determination of needs, architecture can only be predicated ultimately on the political arena. In this respect it becomes increasingly apparent that the only way in which our self-consuming ideology of waste will be overcome, and architecture redeemed, is through the participatory democratic determination of the nature of our environment. The alternative is to remain subject to that which Arendt has described as the most tyrannical government of all [. . .] the totalitarianism of technique.[4]

The second crucial point that Owen Moss captures is his sense of Frampton's "conviction about the intrinsic value of the subject matter"; this is the sense that for Frampton there are things that *only* architecture can give the world, by means specific to it and these things *matter*, at once to architecture but also—and this extension is significant—to the world. The converse of this is that the world *matters* to architecture; that architecture, as much as it may on

---

[3] "Public world" has to be understood here literally and not merely figuratively. The term is not confined to Arendt. It refers to a wider scope of the world. The public world refers to that space in which and through which the "basic aims" of politics can be brought into being, namely, to borrow a sentence from Badiou, "to ensure that humanity is capable of determining its own destiny, in a fundamentally peaceful, egalitarian configuration" because politics is the indexical truth "of a human community's ability to take control of its own destiny and form of organization." Architecture is the moment of constructing the physical and symbolic thresholds which model, enact and make emblematic these moments. The quotations are from Alain Badiou, *In Praise of Politics* (Cambridge, UK: Polity Press, 2019) p. 90, 7.

[4] The quotation is from the concluding paragraph of "Industrialization and the Crises of Architecture" (1974). See p. 65 in this volume.

occasion wish to, cannot dispense with the world. The elision of this relation is a Faustian bargain which necessarily extracts its price from architecture. It is his conviction on these points (verging on the absolute in respect of both moments), that empowers the critical project—at once in its attempt to delineate affirmatively the nature and character of this mattering, and in the necessary counter to this affirmation, the critical scourge of all that denies and blocks architecture's taking-place. It is to this *doubled* sense of architecture and its possibilities that Frampton has the utmost fidelity.[5] What underpins it are two moments.

The first is the sense that, as a configurative and constructional discipline, a practice of fabrication and the installation of place, architecture is constituted by and itself constitutes (embodies, enacts) the movement of a unique circulation of thinking and practice. This circulation has no precise or exact counterpart in any other field. It is related to, and in necessary relation with, what subtends it and with what in turn it indissolubly depends upon—and to which it, in turn, necessarily addresses, relates to and reciprocally engages. "Uniqueness" does not mean autonomy. It is uniqueness in the pattern of relations that it engages (that it practices and thinks) and in the manner of how it stands in the world. In turn it is this pattern of relations which opens the potential virtues (values, qualities, particularities) of architecture and architectural configuration. "Potential" because these virtues, while existent, emphatic and defensible are fragile, continually under threat, undermined from within as much as from without.

The second moment or conviction arises directly from this understanding, but it builds on the point made earlier that the public world constitutes the *only* ground on which architecture can found itself. This is the conviction that this relation to the world is at once the inescapable determination of architecture—which "may only be legitimized through the activation of the public sphere—a political realm that, in its turn, is reciprocally dependent on the representational and physical embodiment of the collective," and the source of its *work*, its value: "Its sole legitimacy stems, as it must, from the social constituency it accommodates and represents. Place, at this juncture, irrespective of its scale, takes on its archetypal aspect, its ancient attribute which is as much political as it is ontological" (195). If architecture depends on this, both in the generality and the specificity,[6] the world in turn depends upon building for the articulation of

---

[5] "Taking-Place" means architecture's coming-into-being in its possibilities. "Fidelity" therefore is not simply and unabashedly to architecture as-is in its professional manifestations, but to its achievable possibilities. Conversely, what must therefore be opposed, what demands the strongest possible critique, is all that delimits, blocks, undermines, betrays, the possibility of this taking-place of architecture, in itself and in its public world.

[6] "Architecture is a microcosmogonic art form that is unable to create Arendt's 'space of human appearance' without the wish and the will of the society. In the last analysis [. . .] practice [. . .] is unable to transcend rudimentary functionalism without the desire of the client for creating an environment that is infused with deeper values" (p. 17).

those necessary thresholds between material, emblematic and lived—in the widest sense the political—possibilities.

This is of the very essence of Frampton's stance. Put slightly differently, it is the thesis that architecture matters to the world because it is a mediation of *and to* the public world: that in the thresholds it creates it acts as the anticipatory configuration and modelling of relations between persons and their worlds and does so at once in space and in time, and at once materially and symbolically.[7] Architecture in this sense is a configurative practice of technical material culture whose existential moment is focused on the accommodation of the human subject in the world.[8]

But what is also key in this relation is that this practice occurs through (and this is perhaps the only point, in the end, that distinguishes architecture from building) the *discovery* of moments of realizable public human existence; of the mediation between what is "real" and what is immanently possible in the material, spatial and lived conditions of finite existence.[9] Or, as Frampton puts it at one point, the "appropriate elaboration of present conditions in a way that is capable of sustaining the life-world in all its richness, without wishing to preempt the significance of this world through the maximization of either technology or aesthetics"[10] (278).

---

[7] "Threshold" is an important concept in Frampton's work. It appears numerously in its cultural or chronological sense of that which anticipates a break in the pattern of things, but it appears architecturally in the sense of that which in building mediates—or fails to mediate—between persons, public institutions and social forces. The fullest instances of this are given on page 47 in this volume; the first as critique of lack, the second as the affirmation of what is possible (both passages are reproduced below in this essay).

[8] Hence Frampton's insistence that "Architecture, unlike the other arts, is as much a presentation as it is a representation, and *vice versa*, whereby the [subject] 'body-being' encounters both aspects simultaneously" (86). If we take Frampton's proposition literally rather than "merely" poetically, it forces the question of what, precisely, in its instantiation in the world, architecture "does"; what *work*, objective and subjective, in relation to the modes of our being and acting in the world, it performs.

[9] "Real" does not mean simply "what is." It refers rather to actuality, to that condition of the real which always contains within its immanent possibilities. Architecture is a perception of these possibilities in respect of our being in the world.

[10] Which means here also economics, or market forces, or private interest. Architecture's role against such one-sidedness (which always means the one-sidedness of power) is mediatory, a point Frampton captures if somewhat too gently, given the weight of what is contained here, in the opening line of the Jerusalem seminar: "Since the emergence of the profession, a salient, often undeclared aspect of architectural practice has been the reconciliation of conflicting values through the creation of inflected form." The entire work of designing, including but beyond architecture, is the negotiation of incommensurable requirements and demands. It in the space of this negotiation—which can only happen within the configurative act because this is the only point in which these irreconcilable demands are compelled to meet—and in the consecutive creation and organization of "inflected form" that the possibility of creating critical distance on the circumstances of

This is what constitutes architecture's "taking place" in world. This matters today both as-such and because (and this constitutes the third driving force of Frampton's work) architecture in its generality is in grave danger.[11] Neither in its practice nor in its thought does it possess the axioms and critical norms with which it can contest the erosions of the conditions and capacities that the world daily makes in respect of its taking place.[12] They do not give it (essentially, they do not allow it)[13] the means to contest these forces and therefore to "sustain that desire that is proper to it."[14] In removing from architecture its ability to comprehend its context, to maintain a basis of decision, and to keep in force a sufficient program, these forces render architecture incapable of maintaining itself in the generality other than in an essentially subaltern role.

force arises. On the question of power/force see the section "Rationality and Power" in the essay "Seven Points for the Millennium: An Untimely Manifesto" (1999), this volume, pages 281–7.

[11] The very real brilliance of *moments* of architecture and building today occurring by no means only in the traditional centers of wealth and power, may appear to belie this fear. But this is only the paradox that Architecture globally lives off. Its shadow, as Frampton's line makes clear, is the exponential growth of the crudity and destitution of the dwelt world as a whole. To be sure, the exceptions of course are real, and not to be gainsaid. Their value is that they demonstrate *as fact* the possibility of making building, of doing architecture, of designing, that stands at once within what-is ("the rules of the situation") and without (in extension of these rules and limits), and in at least defiance of the forces that would erode their possibility. They are then "in spite of." Their affirmation is that the given limits of what-is, the normally unthought and hence presupposed limits of circumstance and condition, can be transcended. Their recognition is that this affirmation as a possibility that could not entirely be deduced from given circumstances. The problem, explored below, is that recognition is *not* comprehension. The exception stays the exception in that in fundamental ways it is *not* understood.

[12] Manfredo Tafuri's point from 50 years ago still applies: "What is of interest here is the precise identification of those tasks which capitalist development has taken away from architecture [. . .] what it has taken away in general from ideological pre-figuration." The conclusions Tafuri draws from this, that "Architecture is therefore obliged to return to pure architecture, to form without utopia [. . .] to 'sublime uselessness'." See *Architecture and Utopia: Design and Capitalist Development* (Cambridge, MA: MIT press, 1972) p. ix. Section IV of this paper below takes up this question.

[13] "Allow" means here that, acting as an ideology, as all institutionalized models of criticism and practice will tend to, criticism disallows (even in part without knowing it is doing so) or more likely it fails to comprehend, the thought that might allow it to escape from these dangers.

[14] Alain Badiou, *Infinite Thought* (Cambridge, UK: Polity Press, 2009) p. 35. Badiou uses the phrase in relation to philosophy. It has no less resonance to architecture. Its value, of course, is to ask the *question* as to what that "desire proper" to architecture consists in and should be. One could see all Frampton's work as, in part, an attempt to answer to this question.

The danger therefore is real.[15] This gives to criticism a special urgency. Its task becomes, in the first moment, the perception and articulation of this danger, in the second the attempt to apprehend—identify, name, give substance to—those immanent capabilities by which such "danger" might at least be resisted and engaged.[16]

Owen Moss is therefore right to have put his finger on these two points. It is precisely these that characterize Frampton's criticism. But at the same time, they are also what makes this criticism so difficult to place. This problem comes back to the opening line of these notes and the point that there is an inevitable desire in architecture at once to identify what is distinctive in Frampton's criticism (the manner of its forcefulness, its compulsion, how it acts in spite of, meaning in spite of the conditions that act to make criticism of this sort extraordinarily difficult to sustain) and yet also to assimilate it, to hold this criticism to the limits of what-is (and in respect of practice no less than of criticism). Prefaced by predicates (no matter how affirmative)[17] or associated with emblems that distract as much as inform ("Critical Regionalism") the desire remains to identify the work within the norms and limits of existing critical practice.

II

In many ways this is to be expected. For no matter how much we wish to see it as secondary, an irritant to practice, as necessarily "less-than," deficient in

---

[15] To the point where, to quote a now often over-used but still resonant and essential phrase from Walter Benjamin, "Even the dead will not be safe if the enemy wins." The full sentence from Benjamin has even more force for Frampton's practice: "Only that historian will have the gift of fanning hope in the past who is firmly convinced that even the dead will not be safe if the enemy wins. And this enemy has not ceased to be victorious." Frampton's entire historical aim of "saving" the project of the modern movement (and with it the possibilities for an architecture adequate to our times) is captured in this line. Walter Benjamin, "Theses on History" in *Illuminations* (New York, NY: Harcourt, 1968), p. 255.

[16] The reference here is to the line from Hölderlin made famous by Heidegger's deployment of it in the essay "The Question Concerning Technology": "But where the danger is, grows/The saving power also" applies. The question is: can the "saving power" be apprehended? See: *The Question Concerning Technology and Other Essays* (New York, NY: Harper, 1977) p. 28. It is worth noting here Heidegger's point in the concluding lines of this essay (p. 35): "Because the essay of technology is nothing technological, essential reflection on it and decisive confrontation with it must happen in a realm that is, on the one hand, akin to the essence of technology and, on the other fundamentally different from it." Such a realm, Heidegger says, is art: "But [. . .] only if reflection on art, for its part, does not shut its eyes to the constellation of truth after which we are questioning." The lines are suggestive. But the realm in which these questions and the "constellation of truth" involved here can be addressed is not art but design. It is designing that spans this relation and which, in the artificial, is the agency of mediation not only of praxis but history.

[17] See for example the citation for Frampton's award of the Golden Lion for Lifetime Achievement by La Biennale di Venezia in 2018. Reproduced in this volume on p. 2.

what it offers ("cruelly, it does seem to be the case that aesthetic criticism is worth having only, or principally, where it is of answering form comparable to its object"[18]) criticism is for us—and as much so for practice as for reflection and far more than we wish to acknowledge—inescapable. "Sculpted into the very structure of modern sensibility," our dependence, Giorgio Agamben insists, is such that "when we are before a work of art we no longer attempt to penetrate its innermost vitality, identifying ourselves with it, but rather [only] attempt to represent it to ourselves according to the critical framework furnished by the aesthetic judgment."[19] Despite therefore the obloquy that it daily brings upon its head (for criticism as we experience it is perpetually a disappointment, and particularly so for the practitioner)[20] it is not a question of "if" criticism. However much we might on occasion wish it, criticism cannot be slung off as easily as some desire. Necessary, for there is no alternative mode of reflection,[21] institutionalized,[22] it is for us an inescapable moment of the production and reception of works.[23]

It is this last point that raises the sharpest concerns. The implications of criticism in terms of the relation—and lack of relation—between works and understanding are all the more so because it has become, in effect, for us, not only the "essential organ of sensibility"[24] before a work, but, far more dangerously, the central medium of our understanding of what it is that works are what

---

[18] George Steiner, *Real Presences* (Chicago, IL: University of Chicago Press, 1989) p. 15.

[19] Giorgio Agamben, *The Man Without Content* (Stanford, CA: Stanford University Press, 1999) p. 40. The quotations from Agamben that follow come from the chapter in his short book on aesthetics which he devotes to Lautréamont's (in)famous aphorism of 1870, "*Les jugements sur la poésie ont plus de valeur que la poésie*" ("Judgements on poetry are worth more than poetry") from which the title of this Afterword is obviously borrowed.

[20] Not least because, as will be noted below, the Kantian framework privileges the spectator. To anticipate a point to come, Kant acknowledges a faculty of judgment, he does not acknowledge a faculty of configuration.

[21] Lacking any conception of configurative work—because it is unable to see mediation as a ground of truth concerning our condition—philosophy offers no *direct*ly useful reflection on architecture. As a resource for thought its value is indirect although not, as Frampton shows in his use most obviously of Arendt, without consequence or necessity. On Frampton's disposition towards the use of philosophy in architectural reflection see for example, in this volume, the essays "Towards an Ontological Architecture: A Philosophical Excursus" pages 85–90, and "Architecture, Philosophy, and the Education of Architects," pages 265–70.

[22] In the modern world "criticism" now means the entire institutional apparatus by which a profession represents itself to the world and to its practitioners (including of course its pedagogies) but extending into every form of public representation: professional societies, journals, exhibitions, the entire apparatus of architectural publication. It now even constitutes a profession. On this theme it is useful to consider the section on the institutionalization of science in Martin Heidegger's essay "The Age of the World Picture." See *The Question Concerning Technology and Other Essays* (New York, NY: Harper, 1972), pp. 124–26.

[23] See Agamben's summary paragraph on this, *ibid.*, p. 46.

[24] *Ibid.*

they do; of the nature of the work they perform and not least of the contexts and circumstances (the "settings" in every sense the word) within which they are constituted and in relation to which they act. As Agamben again chides us, this problem is all the more intensified because even though "criticism has become such spontaneous and familiar experience to us [. . .] we do not yet think seriously enough about it."[25] We especially, he says, do not think sufficiently about the meaning and the mechanisms of aesthetic judgement, above all about the manner in which the norms and the *limits* that underlie aesthetic judgement enter the conception of the work and above all into the comprehension of what the work does, its *work*, of all that it achieves—or fails to achieve. These understandings pass far more deeply into everyday practice than is acknowledged.

In any case, opened out beyond aesthetic judgement to the wider question of the norms that underlie practice, the point is echoed more broadly: "Every professional practice takes place in front of theoretical background; this holds even for practices that vehemently deny any theoretical involvement."[26] So, the designer Gui Bonsiepe, adamant in reminding those who think that practice has a dispensation from theoretical and critical influence, that this posited freedom is illusory.[27]

This last point has implications for architecture for it suggests that it incurs a double critical determination. In so far as it sees itself, as at least in part, as art—if architecture is not an art, if it does not possess a poetic, on what then does its claim to distinction from building lie?—it must necessarily subject itself to aesthetic judgement, even if it does so in forms (the ideal of autonomy) that it engineers to be consonant with its practices. But in so for as it is *necessarily* also a practice in the world—"a building is at the same time an object, an investment and a cultural and personal expression"[28]—then it is subject to norms and premises in the second sense, that is, it is subject to the variety of seemingly external concepts, models, categories, expectations, practices, and forces[29] ("theory" in this sense never takes a singular form)[30] that largely unconsciously, and in almost every case without sufficient reflection, set the norms for and limits and possibilities to practice. Detailing sometimes minutely, sometimes broadly, what is and what is not possible, what is and what is not acceptable,

---

[25] *Ibid.*, p. 41.

[26] Gui Bonsiepe, *The Disobedience of Design* (London, UK: Bloomsbury, 2022), p. 102.

[27] About economics, Keynes famously said much the same thing: "Practical men, who believe themselves to be quite exempt from any intellectual influences, are usually the slaves of some defunct economist." See John Maynard Keynes, *The General Theory of Employment, Interest and Money* (1936). The sentences come from the final paragraphs of the book.

[28] Frampton quoting Cecil D. Elliot in his introduction to *Technology, Place and Architecture: The Jerusalem Seminar*, see page 124 in this volume.

[29] Constructional, technological, above all economic.

[30] In relation to any field, "theory" cannot finally be distinguished from the variety of moments, both "practical" and "intellectual" that constitute the unique circulation of thinking that constitutes it.

what "can" and "cannot" be done—and crucially, and by no means least, what can and cannot be *thought* regarding that practice—these "exogenous" forces are, naturally enough, incompletely assimilated into architectural thought.[31]

This double determination is significant. It is sometimes thought that criticism (or theory and ideas in the Bonsiepe/Keynes instances) is all but innocent (or ineffectual) in its influence on practice—that the latter overrides the former, which of course on occasion it does, configuration having precisely the capacity to permit the configurer to do so. This is in fact perhaps the key value of configurative practice: that configuration is capable of re-drawing relations and hence of acting *against* critical limits; this is what constitutes the exceptional and exemplary moments of work. The tragedy of configurative practice, however, is that while such re-drawing may be recognized, we have very little critical capacity to comprehend and articulate the nature of the decision/s and the re-drawing offered. Judgement remains essentially silent as to what is re-worked. Description and analysis have to work against its tenets: it is always in spite of, not because.

But the more basic impulse, that criticism in the wide sense has no real part in the visceral immediacy of practice comes from the view, with its origins in Kant, that, *as judgement*, criticism is essentially after-the-fact; a process of post- (sometimes pre-) facto legitimization, of judgement in the sense of assessing conformity to model.[32] This is to mistake the ways in which critical thought and the norms of practice and force enter the understanding—and equally and crucially into the *failure* to understand—what is made. It is to underplay how the critical, in the threefold form of the norms of aesthetic judgement—theoretical concepts, categories and models—and the force of pressure of axiomatic limits to practice, determines, in any situation, the *a priori* limits to the comprehension of possibility—and at a deeper level determines the conceptions, instinctual as well as rational, of what it is that works do, of how they are constituted and how in turn they constitute.

In architecture, these tensions are evident on all sides. The attempted elision of architecture and art already contains an ambiguity that cannot easily be

---

[31] As noted below, the concept of autonomy effectively banishes them, but we are also dealing here with two centuries of the modern split between "aesthetics," "ethics," and "technics"—the latter of which today includes economics. Broken in this way, architecture lies in-between these more determinant moments. Since in its mediatory configurative realm architecture is not accorded the status or a condition of "truth" it lingers in an intellectual no-man's land. This explains perhaps the compensatory strategies that it resorts to.

[32] The gap between this view of criticism and what is necessitated for architecture is caught by Frampton in the following sentence: "Architecture is ultimately a rationalized craft rather than a profession, and for this one needs a theory of fabrication treating critically ends and means, the what and the how, the real and the potential, rather than a pre- or post-facto theory of legitimization, which may be as negative at the level of substance as it is effective at the level of rhetoric" (268).

dissimulated. Objectively, the identification can never be complete. Frampton supplies a succinct summary:

> Architecture is appropriated by the society in a way that is categorically different from that of art. In its appreciation of art, society seeks to preserve the intrinsic, inalienable essence of the artwork [. . .] In architecture, on the other hand, society tends to transform the subjective originality of the work through the process of appropriation. Architecture in any event does not have the same iconic or fetishistic status as art, nor despite the emergence of the star architect, is it possible to give comparable artistic status to the 'signature building' (274).[33]

The metaphoric identification of architecture-as-art can therefore never entirely succeed at the practical level. The intellectual difficulty is no less. If the identification of architecture as art forces the point that what critically stands for the work of art stands also (though sometimes as if through a distorting lens) for it, still, even if architecture adapts the norms of aesthetic judgement to its own practices—by focusing it for example on the quest for autonomy—then as Frampton never tires of pointing out, this has profound consequences, both for practice and understanding.

The problem is endemic to the model. When Agamben releases his sharpest criticism of the limits of aesthetic judgement it has two parts. It confronts us, he says, "with the embarrassing paradox of an instrument that is indispensable to us in knowing the work of art, but that not only does not allow us to penetrate its reality but at the same time points us towards something other than art."[34] The first point refuses the idea that a purely aesthetic judgement is adequate to comprehension: when the work is offered for "aesthetic enjoyment" and thus taken and thought of primarily in its formal aspects, "this remains far from attaining the essential structure of the work": such criticism is unable to think of the work "in its proper stature"; is unable to comprehend what "gives itself

---

[33] Note here also Frampton's point, developed more extensively in the essay from which this line comes ("Towards an Ontological Architecture: A Philosophical Excursus," pages 85–90) that, in his view, "Architecture is consummated by the 'body-being' at both a sensuous and a referential level, rather than as an aesthetic manifestation that is exclusively visual and abstract" (85). The concluding line to the essay augments the point that, "What is intended [by the concept of ontological architecture] is an architecture in which the corporeal potential of the subject is envisaged as being realized both individually and collectively through the referential experience and articulation of the built-form" (90). While such an architecture does not in the slightest stand outside the poetic it cannot be identified with an architecture conceived through the metaphor of "art."

[34] Agamben, *ibid.*, p. 43.

in the work." "So long as man is prisoner of an aesthetic perspective," Agamben concludes, "the essence of art remains closed to him."[35]

The second indicates that the problem with judgement is that it essentially defines the work not by what it *does* but by what, in terms of its nominal *identity*, it is, or more precisely—and this is the thrust of Agamben's argument—by what it is *not*. The paradox of aesthetic judgement is that while it is devoted to developing a concept of the object (for the purposes of judging—as in ice-skating for example—the attainment that instances of this object or act reach) it derives this concept not from the analysis of the work it *does* but only from reflection on what, supposedly, it essentially "is." But the only way that judgement can pursue the goal of forming such a concept is by differentiating it from all that it is not.[36] Aesthetic judgement begins therefore—and Agamben insists, it does not in the end escape from—negation.[37] It is for this reason that (paradoxically in light of its stated desire for an object of identity) judgement finds enormous difficulty in saying, *affirmatively*, what art, or architecture, actually is—meaning, in what consists its *work*, what it *does*.[38]

Applied now in terms of the form—the quest for autonomy—in which this search for what it is that architecture "is" is pursued, it means that architecture in this mode becomes defined primarily *not* in terms of its complex taking-place

---

[35] Agamben, *ibid.*, p. 102. The paragraph that follows distills the essence of the danger that the aesthetic as such, or valued entirely in itself, poses: "This original structure of the work of art—as that which in the poetic act discloses 'a more original temporal being and reveals us as historical beings, "for whom [. . .] at every instant our past and future are at stake—is now obscured. At the extreme point of its metaphysical destiny, art, now a nihilistic power [. . .] points to the alienation of nothing less than man's original historical space. In the work of art man risks losing not simply a piece of cultural wealth, however precious, not even the privileged space of his creative energy; it is the very space of his world, in which and only in which can he find himself as man and as being capable of action and knowledge."

[36] On this see Agamben, *ibid.*, pp. 42–45, particularly his immediate dissection of the negation involved in Kant's definition of the "four essential characteristics" of aesthetic judgment (p. 42) and the quotation from Kant pp. 44–45 and Agamben's gloss. The chapter as a whole is useful for articulating a number of key issues concerning the limits of Kantian aesthetic judgement (which is precisely why I have drawn on it here). It is noticeable that by its end, Agamben is describing criticism as aesthetic judgment as "that irritating but [as yet] irreplaceable instrument of our apprehension" (p. 49). For another telling, but far too little referenced, critique of Kant (here as the critique of "subjective aesthetics") see the first part of Hans George Gadamer's *Truth and Method Truth and Method* (London, UK: Sheed & Ward, 1989). The sections "Transformation into structure and total mediation" and "The ontological foundation of the occasional and the decorative" are especially germane. See also Frampton's quotation from Gadamer, p. 85 of this volume.

[37] A determination that in Agamben's view is bringing about a crisis in judgement, one that requires, as he puts it, the development of a "more original, that is more initial, way to think art" (Agamben, p. 51). This is a project that Agamben begins in the later chapters of his book *The Man Without Content*, though it remains unfulfilled in his later work—a task however that has only grown in necessity in the three decades since Agamben drafted these notes.

[38] To put it in a slogan: What *exactly* is the work of the work of architecture?

in relation to that to which it must *necessarily* relate (that which it draws from as it reciprocates to) but only, or essentially, in terms of what it is *not* and from what (if ambiguously) it differentiates itself.[39] The result is the attempt to define architecture *not* principally through thinking affirmatively concerning the particular form of circulation between the inseparable complex elements and relations of practice and theory—relations that constitute the character and movement of its unique activity—but only *first*, by negation, by differentiating architecture from building, construction, setting, place, ground, land, society, technology, economic forces; from, in short, all that to which in practice, to borrow a phrase, "it owes at least its phenomenal existence."[40]

Architecture, however, cannot thrive in such estrangement. Vittorio Gregotti's injunction applies: "Architecture cannot live simply by mirroring its own problems [. . .] Even though the professional tools required for architecture as a discipline can be found only within that tradition, it is architecture itself that needs, for its very production, social relations." As Frampton puts it even more strongly:

> Even if the 'rules' for the development of the discipline at an intrinsic level can only be found within architecture itself [. . .] architectural practice requires for its realization societal need, technological mediation and constraint in order to exist at all [. . .] While all the arts are in some degree limited by the means of their production and reproduction, this is doubly so in the case of architecture, which is conditioned not only by its own technical methods but also by productive forces lying outside itself.[41]

Autonomy is hence won at considerable cost. Frampton characterized some of these in 1991:

> Behind our preoccupation with the autonomy of architecture lies an anxiety that derives in large measure from the fact that nothing could be less autonomous than architecture, particularly today when because of the domination of the media we find it increasingly difficult to arrive at what we want. Under such skeptical circumstances, architects often feel constrained to perform acrobatic feats in order to assure attention. In so doing, they tend to follow a succession of stylistic tropes that leave no image unconsumed, so that the entire field becomes flooded with an endless proliferation of images. This

---

[39] What historically drives this attempted affirmation-by-negation is anxiety—the threat of dissolution into commercial negation (of architecture into mere construction and building) and the urge to differentiate it from all that it might be confused with; to give to architecture a distinct formal identity (in imitation of its rival professions and sciences as they draw their division of labor and constitute their identity).

[40] The phrase is from Roland Barthes. See *Image/Music/Text* (London, UK: Fontana, 1977), p. 111.

[41] For the Gregotti quote and Frampton's gloss see page 284 in this volume. Even more succinct is Frampton's line that "Among the many aspects of the cultural enterprise [. . .] architecture is, in fact, the least autonomous, compelling us to admit to the contingent nature of architecture as a practice" (271).

is a situation in which buildings tend to be increasingly designed for their photogenic effect rather than their experiential potential. Plastic stimuli abound in a frenzy of iteration that echoes the information explosion. We drift toward that entropic state that Lewis Mumford once described as a new form of barbarism. In the meantime, the ideology of modernity and progress disintegrates before our eyes and the imminent ecological disaster of late industrial production is manifest everywhere (279).[42]

Autonomy weakens architecture, most obviously in practice, for it weakens "the process[es] by which decisive priorities are established" (195) and hence the capacity for effective decision. But what is weak in practice is necessarily weak in concept. The anxiety of autonomy does not lead to the depth interrogation of the complex multiplicity of what architecture should necessarily deal with. The requisite questioning as to what truly belongs to architecture (its "taking-place") is evaded, but this evasion does not salve the anxiety.

Hence what sets limits to practice sets also, perhaps deeper, certainly more difficult to access, limits to understanding. It does so in ways already suggested, in terms of the comprehension of what is and what is not possible, even of the comprehension of what constitutes the "taking-place" of architecture and, crucially, of what prevents or obstructs or makes difficult that taking place. One consequence is that, lacking a sufficient basis of thought—and therefore a sufficient collective *raison d'être* in its own actions and contexts of operation—architecture seemingly has little choice but to adopt a *reduced*[43] conception of itself, an alignment of practice, limits and self-conception brought into conjunction not just with shifting dominant fashions and discourses, but at a more fundamental level with the core "categories of a totally privatized and process-oriented world" (275).

III

This double loss, at once of willed reduction of architecture and the *consequent* capitulation to the assigned limits of the given reduces, considerably, the critical potential of architectural practice. It no less reduces understanding. If we now wanted to summarize the implications for criticism (and therefore for architectural thought as a whole) of what has been discussed above, it would be as follows. That having lost the "natural" comprehension of the work, "criticism" becomes *not* understanding, but its *substitute*.[44] That, especially in the form of

---

[42] The quotation comes from the essay that most extensively deals with this problem: "Reflections on the Autonomy of Architecture: A Critique of Contemporary Production." See pages 271–80.

[43] "Reduced" is a key term in Frampton's work. The critical anger is repeatedly directed at what erodes and at the consequences of this reduction.

[44] On grounds of length, an entire section has had to be taken out of this essay that dealt with the historical loss of the comprehension of work. The point derived from a line from

aesthetic judgement, "criticism" it is not the understanding of work but only its substitutive *representation*. It is what *stands in for* what is essentially missing in the understanding of work. It follows that a "criticism"—a thought and a practice—capable of (to quote Agamben once again) "penetrating the innermost vitality of the work" is the project of trying to recover, in the circumstances of now, the "full satisfaction" (i.e., the comprehension) of the work—the understanding of the taking-place of the work and what blocks, empties, reduces that taking place.

The difficulty—but also the possibility—of this task is given in a crucial line from Hegel: "To judge a thing that has substance and solid worth is quite easy, to comprehend it much harder, and to blend judgement and comprehension in a definitive description is the hardest thing of all."[45] The import of this line in the context of Frampton's criticism is that if we wished to identify a single sentence that could at once delineate, encompass and indicate the achievement of Frampton's work as criticism it is this. And in two senses. First, in the wide, historical, sense because in asking for a *combination* of requirements—comprehension, definitive description, judgement—that Kantian judgement can never attain,

---

Hegel, quoted by Agamben, in which Hegel gives Kant's critical project a crucial historical twist: "The philosophy of art is therefore of a greater need in our day than it was in the days when art by itself as art yielded full satisfaction." "Full satisfaction" means here more than the "pleasure" of the work, it means informed instinctive apprehension. In losing the moment of full satisfaction, we lose the experience of self-understanding, i.e., the innate comprehension of the work in its world: an understanding which included, as of right as it were and in the same moment, the processes by which the work came to be, the aspirations to which it was addressed, and the norms by which it stood and found received legitimacy in the world. These moments in turn constituted a layered apprehension, not broken up or individuated between the elements but, on the contrary, where the moments reinforce one another in a unifying apprehension of the work as a totality. Today, by contrast, not only do we not "take in," do not identify with the work in the same way, we *can no longer do so*. It is not even *that* we no longer attempt to penetrate the work, it is that for reasons very largely connected with the rise of the structures of modern thought and consciousness we are no longer *capable* of doing so. This is an issue that Frampton explores in the essay "Industrialization and the Crisis of Architecture" reprinted in this volume. An implication of this is that we are thereby inherently disconnected from the deepest moments of work. Unable to grasp it, to make it ours in the manner we once did, in a fundamental sense we do not *know* it. We remain, in crucial respects, blind to our own objects. We do not know—or at least we do not *adequately* know—their "taking-place," what they achieve: configuratively (in their organization, their disposition, in the extraordinary act of translation of complex and incommensurable necessity and possibility into form); and, constitutively, in terms of the worlds they make, the manner in which they give "look" and "outlook," how they constitute a polity, an economy, a mentality. See G.W.F. Hegel, *Aesthetics: Lectures on Fine Art*, trans. T.M. Knox, Vol. 1 (Oxford, UK: Clarendon Press, 1975), pp. 11. Quoted in Agamben, *ibid.*, p. 41.

[45] G.W.F Hegel, *Phenomenology of Spirit*, trans. A.V. Miller (Oxford, UK: Oxford University Press, 1977), p. 3.

Hegel's line stands as a refutation of Kant's critical model. The sentence is therefore historical in consequence. In effect it both describes the limit points of "modern" criticism as we have historically known it, and it sketches the possibilities of another task for critical thought, the rudiments (one should not overestimate its schematic) of a "method" or a way of approaching the work that might allow us to begin to overcome the loss of self-understanding of works that Kantian criticism both accepted and then enacted as the structure of "judgement." In this sense, Hegel points towards the hope of at last gathering work in adequate comprehension *of the truths that it contains*.[46]

Second, because although Hegel does not appear to any extent in Frampton's work, what his sentence points to as the necessary tri-partite, interactive and *combinatory* structure of adequate critical method—"definitive description, comprehension, judgment"—is in effect manifest in Frampton's work across the entirety of his writings. Beginning from the crucial essays of the 1970s (which, more than is at the moment perhaps realized, set the base for what is to come)[47] through the sequence of *Modern Architecture: A Critical History* (a book which is, in a strict sense, without end; which is in fact a continuous text spanning more than four decades) through the definitive critical volumes of the 1990s and through again to his most recent work, *The Other Modern Movement: Architecture 1920–1970*[48]—the combination of description, analysis, comprehension and judgement concerning the architects and buildings which he studies (and significantly their conditions of production) constitute, in effect, instances of Hegel's precept, with the whole amounting to a colossal series of such moments. Taken together, this work is a definitive refutation of

---

[46] Nothing can be done in criticism, in critical thought or in historical criticism without a notion that the critical work is an *exploration* of the truths lying at the core of all that is being considered—which are in the end truths of the possible and its limits. Objectively, this exploration can never be final—since the artificial, of which architecture is obviously a moment, cannot be determined in advance of its realization But, without the impulse towards truth, criticism is merely opinion. It is worth adding here that modern thought has extreme difficulty in considering the work of architecture as a condition of truth concerning mediation. In an epoch of the artificial this is one of the sources of our unhappiness. It means that we do not value the act that has the most importance for us. Architecture loses here on all sides.

[47] It was the effective "disappearance" of the availability of these essays for the general reader that was one of the original motivations in making this book. A more exhaustive treatment of Frampton's critical thought in the 1960s and 1970s is necessitated, including a fuller reproduction of his writings from these years.

[48] New Haven, CT: Yale University Press, 2021. It will strike anyone who reads this volume with the Corringham block in mind (see p. 44) that the latter could—perhaps should—have been one of the last case studies in the book. To my mind, this book contains perhaps the strongest realization of Hegel's precept that Frampton achieves. Perhaps because these studies are absent a *single* overarching concept, i.e., they are absent a single defining predicate. Methodologically, the buildings analyzed are approached in the manner through which and in which they reveal themselves. They are described and analyzed in terms of how they are engendered and realized from the manner of their coming-into-being, both conceptually and practically, as complex works.

the limits of Kantian criticism.[49] Whereas the latter refuses comprehension, declares it on grounds of its ineffability impossible ("This faculty whose sources are hidden from us; it can be made no further intelligible") and constructs instead a substitutive representational model of architecture to stand in for missing "understanding," the entire aim of Frampton's work is *understanding*, comprehension obtained through the double capacity of "beholding" (and the "originality and range" of the apprehensive reflection which that induces)[50] and "definitive description" (calibration).[51]

The implications of these bodies of work are of course not confined to the individual works. To repeat the point made in the opening lines of these notes: there remains a tendency to see what Frampton does, critically, as a variant of criticism *per se*, criticism as-is; to focus on moments or aspects of the work. If understandable, what is missed in so doing is the degree to which Frampton's *oeuvre*, taken as a whole, is a project of a far more profound and original kind: that it constitutes nothing less than a proposal for a new direction and a new set of tasks—a new basis—for architectural criticism. But since, in the terms of his own criticism, Frampton is also proposing and enacting new ways of comprehending, valuing and of *practicing* architecture, then it constitutes—and it seeks to effect—a re-setting of the basis of architectural thought and practice as a whole. In that this project—and again by necessity—does not stop at the given limits of architecture but extends outwards to the entire realm of what is

---

[49] Kant does not figure explicitly in Frampton's work. The single reference in this volume to Kant or "Kantian"—it comes from the "Critical Regionalism" essay of 1983—is however telling (p. 192): "Not least among these reactions is the reassertion of Neo-Kantian aesthetics as a *substitute* for the culturally liberative modern project" (p. 201, my emphasis). The passage continues in a way that situates the necessary break with Kant/Neo-Kantianism in terms of the latter's connection to passivity and the refusal of an active operationalism: "Confused by the political and cultural politics of Stalinism, former left-wing protagonists of socio-cultural modernization now recommend a strategic withdrawal from the project of totally transforming the existing reality. This renunciation is predicated on the belief that as long as the struggle between socialism and capitalism persists (with the manipulative mass-culture politics that this conflict necessarily entails), the modern world cannot continue to entertain the prospect of evolving a marginal, liberative, avant-gardist culture which would break (or speak of the break) with the history of bourgeois repression."

[50] The phrase is Heidegger's. See "Age of the World Picture," *ibid.*, Appendix 1, p. 138. The context in which the phrase arrives is significant: "The modern age requires [. . .] in order to be withstood in the future, in its essence and on the very strength of its essence, an originality and range of reflection for which we are preparing somewhat but over which we can never gain mastery."

[51] The two terms "beholding" and "calibration" are Frampton's, as when he says in response to a question in a lecture at the Harvard Graduate School of Design in 2013: "If one is going to teach, or engage in teaching activities closely, I think it is quite important to try to—I'm going to use the word *calibrate*—present production, to try to find a way of *beholding it*, which is productive, enlightening." Some acute observations on "beholding" in contrast to representing and representation (and the objectification built into the latter) can be found in Martin Heidegger, "Age of the World Picture", *ibid.*, pp. 130–32.

constituted through how we build, act and are in the world. It therefore constitutes a work of critical thinking in the deepest sense of the term.

IV

The Question of Project, or What Remains Unfinished

The original schema for this Afterword included a section on the "grammar" of Frampton's criticism, those concepts, categories, propositions, approaches which effectively distinguish the character of the criticism that Frampton's work advances from what I have been calling here "aesthetic judgement."[52] Since this would however have required a considerably extended essay I will end the afterword with my notes for just one of these, the question of what is unfinished, what remains to be done, and just as importantly, thought. Moreover, the question of *project* is crucial. For if one hopes that the methodological moments of Frampton's criticism can sustain in the future the critical practice of others, "project" is *structurally* that which today demands to be taken up architecturally, and in the deepest sense. There is some sense too in concluding with reflections on project because the essay with which this book concludes ("The Unfinished Project at the End of Modernity")—which directly deals with this issue—is also chronologically the most contemporary essay in the book, and in its timing parallels *The Other Modernism: Architecture 1920–1970*. Both the essay and the book are focused, in effect, on this question of *project*, a question which is "unfinished" in a very profound sense, and which is not at all, pace Frampton's own apology, of merely "nostalgic" interest.

*

This poses the question of how we understand the *necessity* of project, and hence the *manner* (a crucial term, since it relates to the question of the forms things take) in which there is still an "unfinished project."

To do this it is necessary to go back to the origins of Frampton's criticism. These can be traced back to the point in the 1960s and early 1970s, where, faced

---

[52] Beginning with the question, "what does criticism today require of itself?" and without being in any manner definitive (and necessarily omitting much of what is vital), the grammar was to have dealt (if in the end only indicatively) with ten moments: comprehension, or the taking place of architecture; stance, or the necessary attitude; encompassing, or increasing the reach of criticism; critique, or opposition without end (to that which refutes or blocks the taking-place of architecture); ontology, or possibility; periphery, or location; resistance, or telling it like it is; method, or voice (beholding); theory (or history); project, or what is unfinished.

with the erosion of the modern project, architecture in his view, begins to lose an effective sense of its critical mission. As Frampton says in a personal reflection:

> I am a member of that generation of so-called modern architects, who first came of age as active practitioners in the early sixties and whose concept of modernity [. . .] was already historically mediated; that is to say, unlike the pioneers of the inter-war period (1918–39) we did not conceive of ourselves as trying to engender an architecture whose form was totally unprecedented. Instead, we already saw our task as a qualified restoration of the creative vigor of a movement which had become formally and programmatically compromised in the intervening years. It was, of course, quite impossible to recapture the energy and the optimistic belief systems of this previous epoch, but none the less we could still conceive of ourselves as returning to a modern line in architecture, irrespective of the different forms that this might assume. It is hard to say exactly when this mediated but still modern *modus operandi* began to falter.[53]

It came perhaps with the realization "that we had been, in any event, the last generation of students capable of entertaining the projection of utopian urban schemes in *both a programmatic and a formal sense.*"[54] Frampton continues, "Thereafter, the emerging Megalopolitan reality instantly transformed such projections into historical *non sequiturs*, with regard to which one could no longer suspend even a modicum of disbelief." In any event, "there is little doubt that by the mid-sixties, we were increasingly bereft of a *realistic* theoretical basis on which to work. Without the radical cultural and political programs of the revolutionary modern movement we had no alternative theory," to counter the various reductive developments that came in its wake: developments which had as their common denominator the fact that they represented a decisive "political and symbolic move away from the institutional and residential fabric of the society, towards the productive imperatives of neo-capitalism. Pragmatically and ideologically [they] responded to the new levels of productive and communicational efficiency then being demanded by the expansion of the tertiary economy."[55]

If at first sight it had appeared as if the loss of the modern project could be overcome without effort, that the new conditions opened new possibilities for construction beyond those envisaged in the modern movement,[56] the price paid was that economic and semiotic reality intervened; or, as Guy Debord captured it in a telling sentence, once reduced to the provision of a marketable image, the architect's task becomes little more than a moment of service to

---

[53] See "Place-Form and Cultural Identity" essay included in this volume, Section 3.

[54] *Ibid.*, emphasis in the original. The importance of this double moment cannot be overstressed. See below.

[55] *Ibid.*, composite quotation from pages 220–21. Quotation slightly altered for this purpose.

[56] Frampton surveys these in some depth in the same essay.

capitalism's desire "to refashion the totality of space into *its own particular décor.*"⁵⁷ In a footnote to his paper on Arendt in 1979 Frampton pulled out some of the implications of this shift:

> Innumerable examples exist of the specific displacement of the public realm in contemporary building. Among the more recent instances, one might cite the following: The Ford Foundation Building, New York, for its provision of a false "public" foyer which is programmed in such a way as to assure that no public realm may be allowed to come into existence. The Centre Pompidou, Paris, for its reduction of its "users" to the same status as the "services" – the users being piped-in, so to speak, on one side, and the services fed into the structure on the other. In short, the reduction of a museum to the status and the model expressiveness of an oil refinery. The Richards Laboratories at the University of Pennsylvania where service towers are rendered as monumental elements and where the whole structure is pervaded by a sense of "religiosity" inappropriate to the processal nature of a laboratory building. In this last example a misplaced monumentality fails to transcend the manifest absence of an appropriately "representative" or "commemorative" program, whereas in the first case the presence of a "representative" program is rendered null and void by the rhetoric of the machine. Consciously designed as a cultural supermarket, art in the name of populism is reduced to a commodity. (49)

The consequences for the built environment as a whole were no less deleterious. Again, in the language of 1979 (the cusp of the "neo-liberal" world we now live in should not be forgotten):

> Elevated on freeways or pedestrian decks or alternatively sequestered behind security fences, we are caused to traverse large areas of abstract, inaccessible urban space that can be neither appropriated nor adequately maintained. In a similar way we are confronted by piazzas whose hypothetical public status is vitiated by the vacuousness of the context or alternatively we

---

⁵⁷ *The Society of the Spectacle* [orig. 1967] (Berkeley, CA: Bureau of Public Secrets, 2014) p. 91 (emphasis in the original). It should not be thought that this reference to Debord is gratuitous. Debord was important to Frampton, most obviously for his critique of the dominance of representation and hence of spectacle in contemporary capitalist societies but more widely for his critique of the ideological work that the spectacle performs. See for example the quotation from Debord on page 255 in this volume: "It is indeed unfortunate that human society should encounter such burning problems just when it has become materially impossible to make heard the least objection to the language of the commodity; just when power—quite rightly because it is shielded by the spectacle from any response to its piecemeal and delirious decisions and justifications—believes that it no longer needs to think; and indeed can no longer think." Given Frampton's continuing concern over the baleful consequences of the over-dominance of representation in architecture and its connection to an architecture of spectacle, Debord has a highly pertinent line: "Wherever representation becomes independent, the spectacle regenerates itself" (Debord, *ibid.*, p. 6).

are conducted down streets evacuated of all public life by the circulatory demands of traffic. We pass across thresholds whose public-representative nature has been suppressed or we enter foyers which have been arranged or lit in such a manner as to defeat the act of public promenade. Alternatively, we are caused to depart from airports whose processal function defies the ritual of leave-taking. In each instance our value-free commodity culture engenders an equivalency wherein museums are rendered as oil refineries and laboratories acquire a monumental form. By a similar token public restaurants come to be rudely incarcerated in basements, while schools find themselves arbitrarily encased within the perimeters of windowless warehouses. In each case a ruthless cultural reduction masks itself by the rhetoric of *kitsch* or by the celebration of technique as an end in itself (47, 49).

It is important to remind ourselves of these conditions. Even as history their moments are eclipsed by spectacle. But what both paragraphs reveal is that the vital question that now arose: "Why Architecture?"—meaning what, in this context, can its role and purpose be?—empties out even as it becomes increasingly acute. Despite significant individual efforts, nothing in the intervening period that has arisen from these "decisive shifts in focus" in architectural development has construed a satisfactory *general* answer to this question. On the contrary, the problems that were implied in Frampton's reflections on his own trajectory, and made evident in the quotations above, have in fact only intensified the force of the question, so that in many ways we are merely living in repetition of this earlier moment. Now as then, sundered in its programmatic and formal moments, architecture in the generality does not possess an affirmative model of the *work* of architecture (of what it is that architecture does, what its capabilities are) capable of withstanding either the wider pressures exerted by the world (economic, technological, communicative) or the weaknesses of the essentially reductive models (no matter whether "aesthetic," "methodological" or "technological") offered as the substitutes for this gap.

But a second question then arises: how is this loss, this gap or void to be thought? Is its source—and this brings us back to the question of project—perhaps to be found less in these developments in themselves (which in the end are symptomatic rather than causative, the product of the inability to think through circumstance rather than their becoming, except as moments of spectacle, truly generative in themselves) than, not exactly in the demise of the modern movement *per se*, but rather, in the loss of the deeper *structure*, the pattern of relations that were constitutive of that project?

Frampton captures a sense of this when, in the summary of the project of modern movement that he gives in the opening lines of the "The Unfinished Project of Modernity" (2019),[58] he describes it as a project "oriented, not only

---

[58] See pages 305–15.

towards the creation of a liberative architecture, but also towards the modernization of society as a whole, and in particular to realize the welfare state as a normative condition. This social democratic vision, perhaps first fully articulated in Gunnar Asplund's Stockholm Exhibition of 1930, has since been totally undermined by the commodifying drive of neoliberalism" (305).

There are two moments of importance in these lines. The first and most important lies in the patterning and linkage, the sequence of overlapping contexts described here: the project of the modern movement oriented, *not only* "towards the creation of a liberative architecture" *but also* "towards the modernization of society as a whole," *and this modernization conceived of not passively in its economic and technological generality but actively in the specific political, ethical and social context of the wider project to* "realize the welfare state as a normative condition," *the whole taking place within and at once empowered, legitimated and motivated by an egalitarian* "social democratic vision." What is crucial here then are not only the terms but the linkages. What undermines the *project* of the modern project is the erosion and destruction, the disarticulation, of these linkages. It is all that undoes context and connection, and which architecturally has the consequence which Frampton referred to earlier when he said his were "the last generation of students capable of entertaining the projection of [. . .] schemes in *both a programmatic and a formal sense.*" We land, in other words—and this is a territory we are still in—in a situation where there is a split between program and form, reserving the first to interests, permitting only the second and in the process emptying "project" of force.

"Programmatic," we can see now, does not mean merely the program of the built instance, it means both this specific loss (program now determined by economic force and, what comes to the same thing, technological expediency) and, crucially the loss or the unavailability of the nesting within which the "programmatic" made sense and in that making sense had the weight to force or enable its realization. Frampton noted (in 2000) what we have lost in this separation:

> In contrast [to the loss of program] we may evoke the kind of delicately nuanced programmatic design that used to make itself regularly manifest in the heyday of the modern movement, let us say between 1925 and 1975, especially in the design of such public amenities as high schools and hospitals. In these instances, particular attention was paid not only to aesthetic and representational values but also to the threshold or interface between the institution and society. Within these micro-spaces there was an adequate hierarchical articulation of the relationship of the public domain to the private, culture to nature, and so forth.[59] We may perhaps exonerate the degeneration of this system of values in contemporary architectural

---

[59] These lines anticipate the studies collected in *The Other Modern Movement: Architecture 1920–1970.*

practice by arguing that our current *modus* is nothing more than a direct reflection of the depoliticization of society as a whole. Indeed, the fact that one can hardly think of an exemplary school or hospital built in the United States in the last thirty years (let alone affordable housing) speaks to the fundamental *malaise* that lies at the base of all this: that is to say, our society's current incapacity to guarantee the fundamental civilized rights of education and health to all (180).

This is the real force of the phrase "undermined by the commodifying drive of neoliberalism." The usual way of understanding this comment is to see the drive of the commodity form as an almost objective (and subjective) force that *in itself* removed the possibility of the continuity of the modern project. Without in any way weakening this obviously correct understanding of the processes at work here, there is a second way of reading this development which gives a slightly different stress and opens another set of questions. This revolves as much around ideology as the direct effect of commodification per se. Arguably, what became the overpowering work of political ideology after 1945—and increasingly so after 1980 and into our own moment—has been the necessity, not only to present Capital as fact and as objective necessity, but also (and all the more emphatically the closer it has got to our time) to *refuse* qualitatively different possibilities, above all in terms of the economy and especially in terms of the trajectory of development we are set on; but also politically, socially and psychologically, in so far as these moments raise the possibility of "doing things otherwise." Today this reaches the quasi-pathological state not only of denying the deepest social problems we face but even more emphatically of refusing possible answers to these problems if these are felt to in any way compromise Capital.

This general opposition to what is other than the commodity becomes all the more apparent in that what has distinguished the last several decades, especially after 1980 or so and intensifying as we get closer to our own times, is the opposition to the public sector. What we have seen, what we experience, is not only the acute intensification of consumption but (in direct line with this) the unravelling, in favor of private ownership, of all that had been established in the last century under the heading of the public realm—this term being used now in the literal sense of all that which "belonged to" the public and was therefore held, at least in part, outside the realm of pure private interest. Against this, today, the very notion of a significant "public project," or of a project at scale orientated towards the public which does not have monetary gain as its object, has become all but impossible.[60] What is vetoed in short—today absolutely

---

[60] To put this slightly differently, the logic of the commodity, in which the latter constitutes as both the objective and the *subjective*, the medium of existence has come to pass as an only marginally incomplete totality, a totality in which the entirety of what-is is essentially subsumed to its limits.

vetoed—is any sense of a human project *beyond* what is commensurate with private interest and gain.

We are perhaps only now beginning to realize the extent to which Capital demands that we live and act *without* project. As Alain Badiou puts it, with some necessary brutality:

> It is certain today that neither Europe nor, more generally the West, is the site of any project whatsoever. They are sites of maintenance [. . .] the great garages of globalized capitalism. They exert their power by ensuring, across the world, whatever the political forms or religious or national ideology [. . .] that the principle of the free market is not questioned, and the zones of pillage remain free zones for commercial competition. Capitalist globalization prescribes no other objective for human life than to integrate into this globalization. Today all subjectivities are convoked in relation to this situation. In reality, this amounts to a violent subjective injunction, the real content of which is: "Live without Idea."[61]

In the essay "Towards an Agonistic Architecture"[62] drafted only a few years before Badiou, Frampton had both widened and focused this loss:

> *Das Spiel ist aus* ("The game is over") is the title of a poem by the Austrian poet Ingeborg Bachmann, by which I believe she meant the project of the European Enlightenment, the vision of Schiller, Goethe, Hegel, Schinkel, Marx and Freud, in a word, Jürgen Habermas's 'unfinished modern project,' which, it now seems, will never be realized, not even partially; not because we lack the resources and the technique to do so, but because we are unable to muster the necessary political will to effect a decisive change, for we are totally deluded by 'the society of spectacle' and thereby rendered impotent as a body politic, and by *the repression of alternative modes of being*, by which we might still be able to save ourselves.[63] Le Corbusier's elegiac vision of *une ville radieuse* of 1934, his erotic project of Baudelaire's *Luxe, calme et volupté*, will never materialize, not because we lack the essential wherewithal . . . but because the "species-being" has been unable (so far) to make the ethical and political leap necessary to engender a society capable

---

[61] Alain Badiou and Giovanbattista Tusa, *The End* (Cambridge, UK: Polity Press, 2019), composite quotation: pp. 101, 80–81, 78, 82. On the logic that in the absence of project decision reverts to force an additional sentence from Badiou is pertinent: "Since there is no project, or as long as there is no project, everyone knows there is only one answer to the question, what is to be done? Profit will tell us what to do." Alain Badiou, *The Century* (Cambridge, UK: Polity Press, 2007), p. 9.

[62] Reproduced in this volume pp. 295–304.

[63] The key evocation in both Badiou and Frampton is the closure of the subject. Frampton's "repression of alternative modes of being" essays seamlessly into Badiou's "subjectivities convoked in relation" to the nihilism of what now is. The converse for both is that, going forward, "Subjectivity [. . .] must root itself in the possibility that there is something other than this." Badiou, *ibid.*, p. 82.

of living within an ecological domain of homeostasis. Instead, we seem to be transfixed by the auto-destructive task of laying the world to waste and ourselves with it, as rapidly as possible. The hegemonic power of the "universal" West is such that there seems to be no other model than the profligate project of Americanizing the entire world, the limitless consumerist dream by which all are equally mesmerized (295–296).[64]

The erosion of project implicates—erodes—the capacity for action, in architecture as in any other field: "As Álvaro Siza once put it to me, in reply to a letter congratulating him on his many new commissions, 'Yes, I have many projects, but I am not happy. How can one be happy when Europe has no project?'" (17). Siza's lament has to be taken here in its full double force. "How can one be happy when Europe has no project?" means, pace Badiou, precisely this. But it clearly means also—and this follows from, but also helps encapsulate the larger absence—lack of a sufficient project whereby architecture finds motive and purpose in acting. "Sufficient project" means here that "project" becomes both a locus or possibility of resistance (if not to commodification *per se*, for that is scarcely achievable in this moment, at least to its *entire* victory) *and* that which enables, which provides sufficient energy for—sufficient *cover* we almost might say—the realization of an architecture *and a thought of architecture*, capable of an adequate answer to the question, "Why Architecture today?"

This is where we come back to the question of the "unfinished *project* of modernity" but *not* now as historical project in the sense usually attributed to it, rather in terms of examining what is possible for now, and for the future with respect to architecture. And, with this question now being thought of not internally as it were—as if it could be generated from within an already denuded architecture—but structurally and relationally, in terms of the pattern of linkages and relations between the "architectural project" ("liberative" architecture, meaning today an architecture capable in some manner of assisting in the diversion of the disastrous trajectory we are now set on) and those wider projects, of society, of social policy, of a politics that is not destined to authoritarianism which can provide the former with the *equivalent* today, of what the projects of "the modernization of society"/the realization of "the norms of the welfare state"/of the politics of "social democracy" provided for the modern movement.

Let us re-cap the structure of what is involved here.

The essence of "project" is that it is more than mode (in the devalued sense of this term). This is why "project" in this sense is not an "ideology" (Tafuri) nor is it a set of principles (Vitruvius) nor is it even a set of elements (Semper). Project, in the wide the sense I am using it here, *is the network of relational conditions that engenders*. "Engenders" means here that it sets a potential world in motion towards its realization. What enables this realization, what gives it

---

[64] The paragraph that follows on p. 296 is equally important.

the possibility, the motivation, the *courage* to engender another world, is the network of relational conditions that reinforce key moments of this coming into being. Without this network nothing can occur. The moments in separation (without relation) lack the capacity to engender world. They can only engender moments, but these moments lack relation. In isolation they cannot engender "world." "Project," in the sense that the modern movement is caught, and which is now again necessitated, is the schema of realizing world through relational engendering—a world that "is" through its *modes* (now using "modes" in the strong sense of manner) of coming-into-being where these moments, the multiple conditions of world making, are not distinct but are in relation. Architecture is obviously a part of this nexus. Precisely so is Frampton's entire point.[65]

All of this means that despite even his own protestations, the evocation of the modern movement that Frampton offers is by no means *simply* nostalgic. It is in fact, to repeat the point, *structural* in its implications. But it is also contemporary. If it is commonplace to deny the purchase of the modern *movement* today, that denial ignores the degree to which the larger project that the modern movement addressed itself to, and which in turn was the basis of its actions, still remains. It does so objectively, in that we remain irredeemably modern even as we transition into another epoch.[66] It does so architecturally in that the twin problems (which are also possibilities) of the "typological formulation of entirely unprecedented modernizing programs" and the necessity of an inventiveness in regard to making "approach to the organization of a new way of life"[67] that is not merely gestural or rhetorical, *remain no less necessary today*.

To put this another way, if commodification undermined the ethos of the modern movement, there remains, beneath commodification, the social world: a world that politically there is a necessity to recover if we are to avoid varieties of incompetent and therefore brutal authoritarianisms. Neither the project of a "liberative architecture" nor that of the "modernization" of society as a whole thought through a social economy, nor that the prospect of a normative basis of action arising from the aspirations of the social (welfare) state, has been *wholly*

---

[65] "Engendering the world from its own manner of rising-forth" is a summary of Agamben's position here. In relation to both architecture and the question of how moments conceived in isolation cannot work to engender a world consider Frampton's references to Bogdanov and *Protokult* in the USSR of the 1920s (See especially pages 61–2 in this volume). The thesis that Marxism/the USSR lacked a theory of culture (i.e., a theory of active and engendering relations)—and that its tragedy stems in part from this lack—is explored sociologically in Zygmunt Bauman, *Socialism as Culture* (London, UK: George Allen & Unwin, 1976) and in the concluding section "Culture and Fate in Marxism" to Gillian Rose, *Hegel Contra Sociology* (London, UK: Athlone, 1981), pp. 214–220.

[66] On the relation between modernity as we have known it and the emerging world of the artificial *per se*, see: "The Artificial and What It Opens Towards" in Tony Fry, Clive Dilnot and Susan C. Stewart, *Design and the Question of History* (London, UK: Bloomsbury, 2015), pp. 165–204; Clive Dilnot, "Designing in the World of the Naturalized Artificial" in *Design in Crisis: New Worlds, Philosophies and Practices*, edited by Tony Fry and Adam Nocek (London, UK: Routledge, 2020), pp. 93–112.

[67] The quotations in this paragraph and the next come from *The Other Modern Movement*, *ibid.*, p. vii, viii.

eclipsed by the banalities and crudities of the wholly economic world—a world, we should remember, even as we accord it the status an inevitable event, that however much it is ideologically occluded and devalued, is wholly supported by, and is essentially parasitical on, the deeper social and natural economy. The "recouping" of the modern project is therefore perhaps less nostalgia and more the determination, first to think the "enduring challenge of the unfinished modern project" and second, to think out the conditions of how architecture in *this* moment, organized through a movement and therefore capable of acting at scale, can "contribute to the evolution of society in a critically liberative manner."[68]

This brings us back to the notion of the project now thought in the light of Badiou–Frampton–Siza, *i.e.* in terms of the (acute) conditions of now but also thought connectively in the sense of the way the *project* of the modern movement, in the interlinking, the sequencing, of its moments and relations constructed a project recognizing both infrastructural and superstructural moments—and the significance (meaning the significance to the public, to persons) of *threshold passages* between them. The consequence of these relations—as Frampton's work on Aalto for example makes clear[69]—was the empowering of the architectural project. Today, we need a *structurally* equivalent project. Commodification as the erosion of it causes architecture too to forget the *structure* of the modern project. It especially causes architecture to forget that this structure of relations and enclosing two-way hierarchies are for architecture—this is the entire point of Frampton's criticism—*necessary* to its taking place. They are what every exemplary work of architecture which is not a case of "false plenitude" in one way or another, re-creates. This is why "project"—in the structural sense of the "unfinished project of modernity"—becomes the central category of a re-constituted critical project. *Project* is in the end the *only* answer to the question "Why architecture?" That is, either one has "Project" or one is left with the question "Why Architecture?" and with projecting answers to it that are merely substitutes papering over the void. Looked at it this way, we can say that what Frampton has worked towards, across five decades, is the *attempt to make a place, once again, for project* and *therefore* for the taking place of architecture. What is left for those to come in these benighted times is the question of how this is constituted, not least out of the sites for practice and thought that Frampton has constructed.

---

[68] *Ibid.*
[69] See the essay "The Legacy of Alvar Aalto" in this volume.

Bibliographic Sources (Per Section)

SECTION 1

The Status of Man and the Status of His Objects: A Reading of *The Human Condition*
Source: Kenneth Frampton, "The Status of Man and the Status of his Objects: A Reading of *The Human Condition*," in *Hannah Arendt: The Recovery of the Public World*, ed. Melvin Hill (New York: St. Martin's Press, 1979), 101–30.

Industrialization and the Crises in Architecture
Source: Kenneth Frampton, "Industrialization and the Crises in Architecture," *Oppositions*, no. 1 (1973): 57–82.

Apropos Ulm: Curriculum and Critical Theory
Source: Kenneth Frampton, "Apropos Ulm: Curriculum and Critical Theory," *Oppositions*. no. 3 (May 1974): 17–36.

***Modern Architecture: A Critical History*, Introduction to the 1st Edition**
Source: Kenneth Frampton, "Introduction," in *Modern Architecture: A Critical History* (Thames & Hudson, 1980, first edition), 8–10.

Towards an Ontological Architecture: A Philosophical Excursus
Source: Kenneth Frampton, "Towards an Ontological Architecture: A Philosophical Excursus," in *A Genealogy of Modern Architecture: Comparative Critical Analysis of Built Form*, ed. Ashley Simone (Zürich: Lars Müller Publishers, 2015), 8–27.

SECTION 2

America 1960–1970: Notes on Urban Images and Theory
Source: Kenneth Frampton, "America 1960–1970: Notes on Urban Images and Theory," *Casabella*, no. 359–360 (1971): 25–40.

The Generic Street as a Continuous Built Form
Source: Kenneth Frampton, "The Generic Street as a Continuous Built Form," in *On Streets*, ed. Stanford Anderson (Cambridge, MA: MIT Press, 1978), 309–37.

Technology, Place & Architecture
Source: Kenneth Frampton, "Introduction" and "Public Building, Form and Influence: The Atrium as Surrogate Public Form," in Kenneth Frampton, Arthur Spector, and Lynne Reed Rosman, eds., *Technology, Place & Architecture: The Jerusalem Seminar in Architecture* (New York: Rizzoli, 1998), 12–15, 272–73.

Civic Form
Source: Kenneth Frampton, "Afterword: Architecture in the Age of Globalization," in *Modern Architecture: A Critical History* (Thames & Hudson, 2020, fifth edition), 636–42 (excerpt).

The Legacy of Alvar Aalto: Evolution and Influence
Source: Kenneth Frampton, "The Legacy of Alvar Aalto: Evolution and Influence," in *Alvar Aalto: Between Humanism and Materialism*, ed. Peter Reed (New York: Museum of Modern Art, 1998), 118–39.

Toward an Urban Landscape
Source: Kenneth Frampton, "Toward an Urban Landscape," *D: Columbia Documents of Architecture and Theory*, no. 4 (1995): 83–93.

Megaform as Urban Landscape
Source: Kenneth Frampton, *Megaform as Urban Landscape: 1999 Raoul Wallenberg Lecture* (Ann Arbor, MI: The University of Michigan A. Alfred Taubman College of Architecture and Urban Planning, 1999).

Land Settlement, Architecture, and the Eclipse of the Public Realm
Source: Kenneth Frampton, "Land Settlement, Architecture, and the Eclipse of the Public Realm" in *The Pragmatist Imagination: Thinking About "Things in the Making,"* ed. Joan Ockman (New York: Princeton Architectural Press, 2000), 104–11.

SECTION 3

On Reading Heidegger
Source: Kenneth Frampton, "On Reading Heidegger," *Oppositions*, no. 4 (October 1974): Editorial Statement.

Towards a Critical Regionalism: Six Points for an Architecture of Resistance
Source: Kenneth Frampton, "Towards a Critical Regionalism: Six Points for an Architecture of Resistance," in *The Anti-Aesthetic: Essays in Postmodern Culture*, ed. Hal Foster (Port Townsend, Washington: Bay Press, 1983), 16–30.

Tadao Ando's Critical Modernism
Source: Kenneth Frampton, "Tadao Ando's Critical Modernism," in *Tadao Ando: Buildings, Projects, Writings*, ed. Kenneth Frampton (New York: Rizzoli, 1984), 6–9.

Place-Form and Cultural Identity
Source: Kenneth Frampton, "Place-Form and Cultural Identity," in *Design After Modernism: Beyond the Object*, ed. John Thackara (London: Thames & Hudson, 1988), 51–66.

Modernization and Local Culture
Source: Kenneth Frampton, "Modernization and Local Culture," in Kenneth Frampton, Charles Correa, and David Robson, eds., *Modernity and Community: Architecture in the Islamic World* (London: Thames & Hudson and The Aga Khan Award for Architecture, 2002), 9–16.

The Predicament of the Place-Form: Notes from New York
Source: Kenneth Frampton, "The Predicament of the Place-Form: Notes from New York," in *Contemporary Architecture and City Form: The South Asian Paradigm*, ed. Farooq Ameen (Mumbai: Marg Publications, 1997), 101–9.

Plan Form and Topography in the Work of Kashef Chowdhury
Source: Kenneth Frampton, "Plan Form and Topography in the Work of Kashef Chowdhury," in Kenneth Frampton and Robert Wilson, *Kashef Chowdhury: The Friendship Centre, Gaibandha, Bangladesh* (Zürich: Park Books, 2016), 8–12.

2018 Society of Architectural Historians Plenary Talk
Source: Kenneth Frampton, Plenary Talk at the 71st Annual International Conference of the Society of Architectural Historians, 20 April 2018, Saint Paul, MN. Transcript by the Society of Architectural Historians.

SECTION 4

Architecture, Philosophy, and the Education of Architects
Source: Kenneth Frampton, "Topaz Laureate Address at the ACSA Annual Meeting," in *Journal of Architectural Education* 45, no.4 (July 1992), 195–96. Also published in John E. Hancock, and William C. Miller, eds., *Architecture, Back to Life: Proceeding of the 79th Annual Meeting of the Association of Collegiate Schools of Architecture* (Washington, DC.: ACSA, 1991).

Reflections on the Autonomy of Architecture: A Critique of Contemporary Production
Source: Kenneth Frampton, "Reflections on the Autonomy of Architecture: A Critique of Contemporary Production," in *Out of Site: Social Criticism of Architecture*, ed. Diane Ghirardo (Washington, DC: Bay Press, 1991), 17–26.

Seven Points for the Millennium: An Untimely Manifesto
Source: Kenneth Frampton, "Seven Points for the Millennium: An Untimely Manifesto," *The Journal of Architecture* 5 (Spring 2000): 21–33.

Typology and Participation: The Architecture of Álvaro Siza
Source: Kenneth Frampton, "Typology and Participation: The Architecture of Álvaro Siza." *Art Forum* 54, no. 7 (March 2016).

Towards an Agonistic Architecture
Source: Kenneth Frampton, "Towards an Agonistic Architecture," *Domus* 972 (September 2013), https://www.domusweb.it/en/opinion/2013/10/03/_towards_an_agonistic_architecture.html.

The Unfinished Project at the End of Modernity: Tectonic Form and the Space of Public Appearance
Source: Kenneth Frampton, *The Unfinished Project at the End of Modernity: Tectonic Form and the Space of Public Appearance* (London: Sir John Soane's Museum, 2019).

Biographies

Kenneth Frampton is an architect, critic, historian, and was the Ware Professor of Architecture at the Graduate School of Architecture, Planning and Preservation at Columbia University, where he taught between 1972 and 2021. During his tenure at Columbia, he directed the PhD program in history and theory of architecture from 1993 to 2006. He previously taught at the Royal College of Art in London, the ETH in Zurich, the Berlage Institute in The Netherlands, EPFL in Lausanne, and the Accademia di Architettura in Mendrisio. He has written extensively on modern architecture, with some of his most important works including *Modern Architecture: A Critical History* (Thames & Hudson, 1980; fifth edition 2020), *Modern Architecture and the Critical Present* (Architectural Design, 1982), *Studies in Tectonic Culture: The Poetics of Construction in Nineteenth and Twentieth Century Architecture* (MIT Press, 1995), *Labour, Work & Architecture* (Phaidon, 2002), *Genealogy of Modern Architecture: Comparative Critical Analysis of Built Form* (Lars Mueller, 2015) and *The Other Modern Movement* (Yale University Press, 2021). Frampton is a founding editor of *Oppositions* (1973–1984) and the author of several hundred essays, seminars, and lectures, with critical writings spanning almost 60 years. Amongst other honors he was presented with a Lifetime Achievement Award by the Society of Architectural Historians in 2018, and the Golden Lion for Lifetime Achievement of the 16th International Architecture Exhibition of La Biennale di Venezia in 2018.

Miodrag Mitrašinović (Editor) is a Professor of Architecture and Urbanism at Parsons School of Design, a division of the New School university. His professional and scholarly work has been published internationally, and he has served in a variety of scholarly, professional, and editorial roles. Miodrag is the co-editor of *The Emerging Public Realm of the Greater Bay Area: Approaches to Public Space in a Chinese Megaregion* (Routledge 2021); *The Public Space Reader* (Routledge 2021); *Cooperative Cities* (*Journal of Design Strategies* Vol. 8,

2018); editor of *Concurrent Urbanities: Designing Infrastructures of Inclusion* (Routledge 2016); co-editor of *Travel, Space, Architecture* (Routledge 2009); and author of *Total Landscape, Theme Parks, Public Space* (Routledge 2006). Two of his books received grants from the Graham Foundation for Advanced Studies in the Fine Arts.

Index

Aalto, Alvar 14, 97, 106, 134, 138, 151, 171, 220, 276, 313, 343
   heterotopic syntax 140, 154, 155
   legacy of 139–55
   at the millennium 154–5
   structural map of General Town Plan, Imatra (Finland) 151, 152*f*
   see also Säynätsalo Town Hall, Finland
abstract idealism 121
Academie Royale d'Architecture 45
Adorno, Theodor 5
aesthetic judgement, paradox of 328, 331
Aga Khan Award for Architecture (AKAA) 188, 231, 232
Agamben, Giorgio 324, 331
agonistic architecture 19, 303
   of the periphery 18, 191
   see also "Towards an Agonistic Architecture" (Frampton)
agonistic pluralism 262
agricultural production 123
Aicher, Otl 35, 72, 77
Aicher, Otto 23, 35
airports 136
   Barajas Airport, Madrid 136, 311*f*, 312
   Dulles Airport, Washington 312
   Kansai mega-airport, Japan 312
   Kennedy Airport, New York 13, 166
   Newark, New Jersey 13, 166
   processal function of 47, 337
   Stansted Airport, London 312
   terminals, design of 312
Aït Iktel village, Morocco 232, 233
Alberti, Franco 94
Alexander, Christopher 22
   Community and Privacy 12, 97, 159, 178, 240, 241*f*

Alexander Moissi house, Venice Lido 291
Alexanderplatz, Berlin 171
Ali Qapu palace, Isfahan 134
alienation 56, 76, 179, 195
   self-alienation 55, 109n23, 195
Alipore, Kolkata 250
Althusser, Louis 306
Ambasz, Emilio 23
ambiguity of architecture 38, 44–5
"America 1960–1970: on Urban Images and Theory" (Frampton) 7, 93, 101–9
American Institute of Architects (AIA) 259n2
Ancient Greece
   Miletus, Greek Hippodamia city 42*f*
Anderson, Stanford 94, 95
Ando, Tadao 7, 187, 211–17
   on nature 213, 216, 217
   "From Self-Enclosed Modern Architecture Towards Universality" 212
animal laborans 46–7, 49, 50, 87
Antonioni, Michelangelo 109n23
appearance, space of *see* space of appearance
Appleyard, Donald 94
   A View from the Road 102
applied science 75, 97, 157, 227, 228, 274
"Apropos Ulm: Curriculum and Critical Theory" (Frampton) 6, 34–5, 67–79
Aranya Township, Bombay-Delhi highway 244
arcades
   linear 115, 119
   open-sided 127
   Parisian 127
Archaeological Museum, Arles 132
architects 8n22, 15, 16*f*, 18, 25, 46, 56, 57, 78, 81, 82, 116n10, 134, 161, 162, 168, 175, 186, 189, 192, 194

350

INDEX

American 12, 93, 190
Anglo/Ital-'Hi-Tech' 312
British 171
Catalan 173
ethical role for 96
European 19, 96, 191
Expressionist 170–1
Finnish national romantic 146
Germany 132–3, 143n8, 171
Indian 190
Japanese 211
postmodern 202
post-World War II 32, 187
purpose of 297–300, 302–3
radical 211
responsibilities of 114
Scandinavian 171
"star architects" 24
architectural criticism (Frampton) 8, 317–43
grammar of 334
origins of criticism 334–5
purpose of 343
what remains unfinished (project issue) 334–43
Architectural Design 12, 19
architectural education 180, 265–9
contemporary 260, 266
curriculum *see* curriculum
Frampton's honor for 259
mediatic malaise 24
mediatization 24
philosophy, place in 22
architectural production 187, 267
The Architectural Review 1, 102
architecture
agonistic *see* agonistic architecture
ambiguity of 38, 44–5
as art 274, 275, 325, 327
autonomy of 260, 271–9
quest for 238–9
and building *see* building
civic 98
compared with art 267, 272, 274, 325, 326, 327
future of 282–4
Japanese 211–17
and law 32n7
liberative 342
as material culture 17, 22, 90
modern *see* modern architecture
ontological 36, 90, 327n33
and place 123–9
architecture–place–culture–public realm configuration 2, 185
and the public world 4–6

resistant architecture theory *see* resistance, architecture of
sign architecture 102–3
and society 282–4
world architecture 18, 189–90, 321n8
architektōn 38
Arendt, Hannah 3, 17, 40, 43, 44, 51, 57, 62–3, 65, 94, 103, 131, 185, 201, 207, 265, 336
action, concept of 15, 33
conception of "public" 32–3
Frampton's reading of 4–6, 11, 31–3, 36, 191, 324n21
on freedom 5, 6
labor-work-action triad 6, 32, 34, 37–8, 260, 306
lecture at The New School 11
masculine nouns and pronouns, use of 6n20
political philosophy/participatory democracy xix, 11, 19, 31
works of
The Human Condition see The Human Condition (Arendt)
"Introduction into Politics" 5
see also common public world (Arendtian); public realm; space of appearance; space of public appearance
Argan, Giulio Argan 45, 272
Ariza, Wanderley 16*f*
Arnahan, Ali 232
art 25, 45, 49n25, 50, 56, 62n7, 64, 154, 163, 209, 247, 312, 323n16
applied 61, 274
appreciation of 272, 327
of architecture 232, 251
architecture as 274, 275, 325, 327
art envy 267, 274, 275
art form versus core form 307
art galleries/museums 250, 313
autonomous 194, 197
compared with architecture 267, 272, 274, 325, 326, 327
and design 323n16
fine art 272, 274, 275
high 107
microcosmogonic 17, 320n6
modern 58n6
and non-art 144n10
permanence of 45n17
Pop Art 103
and science 61, 104, 275
social 15, 43, 57
Soviet revolutionary art and architecture 4, 33n7

"street" 61
  Ulm School on 70n4
  works of 23, 44, 50n29, 61, 85, 324
Art Nouveau 58
artifice versus instrumentality 46
Artigas, João Vilanova 310
Arts and Craft movement, England 56, 143
Ashraf, Kazi 250
Asian Games Housing, New Delhi 244
Asplund, Gunnar 23
  Stockholm Exhibition (1930) 23, 338
Association Aït Iktel de Développement 232, 238
Association of Collegiate Schools of Architecture (ACSA) 259n2, 266
Atelier 5, Switzerland 12, 18, 242f, 244
Atlanta Peachtree Center, Georgia 129
atrium, as surrogate public form 126–7, 129
Australia, Marika-Alderton House 300
Austria
  Garden City Puchenau 242f
  Ringstrasse plan, Vienna 39f, 41, 46
  Vogelweidplatz Sports Center, Vienna 171
autonomy of architecture 260, 271–9
  concept 326n31
  cost 329–30
  quest for autonomy 328–9
avant-garde 111–15, 253, 268
  cinema 109n23
  European 289
  German 34
  historical founders 201
  ideology 226
  late avant-gardism 275
  modernism 8, 208, 259
  and modernization 201
  neo-avant-garde 162
  postmodernist 202
  progressive 201
  rise and fall of 201–3
  Russian 34
  Soviet 142
  twentieth-century 171
  utopia 83

Badiou, Alain 340
  Infinite Thought 322n14
Bagsværd Church, Denmark 204–5, 205f
Baird, George
  Meaning in Architecture 11, 305
Bakema, Jacob 171
Baker Dormitory, Cambridge (Massachusetts) 171
Bangladesh 8
  Chandgaon Mosque, Chittagong 250

Friendship Centre, Gaibandha 190, 247, 249f
Friendship Hospital, Satkhira 250
Banham, Reyner
  Theory & Design in the First Machine Age 25
Barajas Airport, Madrid 136, 311f, 312
Barefoot Architects, India 233, 234, 238
Barefoot College campus, Tilonia, Rajasthan 189, 233
Baroque style 55
Barre à Marne (Noissy I complex) 170
Barthes, Roland 58n6, 188n19, 329n40
Bartlett School at London University 274
Bashō, Matsuo 25
Baudrillard, Jean 296
Bauhaus (Staatliches Bauhaus), German art school 70–3, 77
  Dessau Bauhaus 70
  and Hochschule für Gestaltung school 70
  newspaper 70n3
  program (1919) 59f
  Weimar Bauhaus 75
  workshops 62n8
Baukunst (the "art of building") 193, 195
Bauman, Zygmunt 89
Bektas, Cergiz 235
Belapur Incremental Housing scheme, Navi Mumbai, 243f
Bell, Daniel 194
Benevolo, Leonardo
  History of Modern Architecture 74
Benjamin, Walter 220–1
  "Paris, Capital of the Nineteenth Century" 127
Benôit, Georges 123
Bense, Max
  Aesthetica 73
Bentham, Jeremy 56
Berlin Philharmonic, Germany 14, 172f
Berlin U-Bahn megastructures 114
Berlin Wall, fall of (1989) 134
Bibliothèque Nationale, France 134
Bill, Max 35, 70, 71, 72
Billington, James 64
Blom, Piet 244
Boa Nova Teahouse, Leça da Palmeira 309
Bochum University, Germany 117f, 119, 171
body being/body image 89
Bogdanov see Malinovsky, Alexander (Bogdanov)
Bonsiepe, Gui 12, 35, 325
  "Über Formale und Informale Sprachanalyse: Carnap und Ryle" 74

Bos–Wash corridor, United States 178
Botta, Mario 208
Bötticher, Karl
  Die Tektonik der Hellenen 209, 307
Bouça housing settlement, Porto 14–15, 261,
    290–1, 292*f*
  duplex units 290
  four-story blocks 290
bounded domain, Heideggerian notion of 35,
    187, 207
bourgeois utilitarianism 60
Brahmaputra-Jamuna river 248
Braudel, Fernand 200n4
Brazil
  Museum of Modern Art in Rio de Janeiro
      310
  Paulistano Athletic Club in São Paulo 310
  tectonic form 310
  volcanic topography, of Rio de Janeiro 168
Brinkman, M.A. 115
British Library, London 133*f*, 134
British Productivist school 221
Broch, Herman 55–6
Brunelleschi, Filippo 45, 271–2
Brunswick Center, London 118*f*, 120
Brussels World Fair (1958) 72
Bryggman, Erik 142
Buckminster Fuller, Richard 25, 234, 274
Build, Operate and Transfer (BOT) method
    237
building 5, 44, 53, 57, 83
  action and process of 38
  and architecture 4, 52
  biorealistic evidence 276
  contemporary 49n25
  critical theory of 7, 15
  degree zero of building culture 8, 188n19
  emancipatory public character 34
  function of 2
  house-building 41n10, 76n20
  industrialized 76, 76n20
  ontology of 263, 305, 315
  in the Renaissance 45
  signature 274
  see also buildings; housing
buildings 2, 49n26
  airports *see* airports
  cultural 171
  designing *see* design
  laboratory, processual nature of 49n25,
      336
  libraries *see* libraries
  office 129, 138
  public 40, 100, 107, 126, 277
  representational 179
  see also building community; community
      centers
bureaucratic socialism 76
Byker Wall housing complex, Newcastle 171

Cacciari, Massimo 19
Cambridge University School of Architecture
    19
Canada
  Robson Square, Vancouver 169*f*
  Seabird Island School, Agassiz, British
      Columbia 301*f*, 302
  University of Alberta, Edmonton 115, 117*f*,
      129, 235
Candilis, George 117*f*, 118*f*, 119, 244
Cannery Building, San Francisco 107n15
capitalism 5, 7
  late 98
  neo-capitalism 73, 104
Carnation Revolution (1974), Portugal 262
Carr, Edward H. 35, 192
Casa dei Paria (Maison des Péons),
    Chandigarh, India, 1951 240
Casabella 93–4
CASE *see* Committee of Architects for the
    Study of the Environment (CASE)
center versus periphery 18
Centraal Beheergebouw insurance company
    office building, the Netherlands
    128*f*, 129
Central Library, The Hague 129
Centre Pompidou, Paris 49n25, 336
Chandgaon Mosque, Chittagong 250
Chapanis, Alphonse 75
Chermayeff, Serge
  Community and Privacy 12, 97, 159, 178,
      240, 241*f*
Chilehaus, Hamburg 171
Chowdhury, Kashef Mahboob 247–50
Ciriani, Henri 131–2, 170
cities 33, 40, 103n7, 111n2, 175, 206, 213, 239,
    245, 285, 297
  capital 284
  city-in-miniature 120, 126, 129, 132, 179
  European 76n20
  examples
    Miletus, Greek Hippodamia city, 5th
        Century BC 42*f*
    typical walled medieval city 42*f*
  foundation of 131, 178, 207n17
  medieval 153
  Mediterranean 291
  new 298
  nineteenth-century 284
  populations 284, 285

Portuguese 262, 289
walk-around 161
see also generic streets; Lynch, Kevin; *polis* (city); street; urban design; urban landscape; urban planning; urban populations, capital cities; urban schemes, utopian; urban sprawl; urbanization
citizen participation 261–2
city crown concept 170, 173
City Hall, The Hague 129
city-states 18–19, 40, 178–9, 191, 207
civic architecture 96
"Civic Form" (Frampton) 96, 131–8
civic forms 7, 96, 98, 131, 175
civic institutions 96, 132, 134, 136, 177, 277
civilization
  agrarian-based 272
  bourgeois 49, 55
  and culture 200–1, 224, 225, 253
  hybrid 189, 235
  and instrumental reason 201
  mediocre 199
  modern 199, 306
  technological 5, 185
  universal 7, 18, 33, 199, 200, 201, 204, 208, 224, 226, 227, 235, 252
  urban 107
  world 199
Classical architecture 83
Colegios di Arquitectos, Spain 19
Coleridge, Samuel Taylor
  On the Constitution of Church and State 200n4
collective architecture 262
Colquhoun, Alan 11, 22
  "Typology and Design Method" 22
Columbia University 13
Committee of Architects for the Study of the Environment (CASE) 13
commodification 23, 131, 339, 341–3
  compulsive 263, 307, 315
  destructive 7, 98, 164
  technocratic 96, 98, 181
  total 162
  universal 227
  wholesale 34, 93, 96
common public world (Arendtian) 3, 5, 15
Commonwealth Association of Architects Conference, Dhaka 247
community 15, 35, 76n20, 108n20, 159, 163, 262, 319n3
  buildings 291
  centers *see* community centers
  collective core 189
  design 19
  ideological conceptions of 41
  industrial 151
  local 248
  logic of 339n60
  self-reliant 233
  social costs borne by 78, 79
  Utopian 234
  viable 57
  without propinquity *see* community without propinquity
  see also Community and Privacy (Alexander and Chermayeff)
Community and Privacy (Alexander and Chermayeff) 12, 97, 159, 178, 240, 241*f*
community centers 14, 16*f*, 291
community without propinquity 41, 94, 111n1, 194, 207n18
compulsive commodification 263, 307, 315
Comte de Lautréamont 8
conformism 3, 18, 191, 299
Congrès Internationaux d'Architecture Moderne (CIAM) 17, 143, 244
constructivism 25, 142–6, 149–50, 201
consumerism 23, 179, 211, 216, 221
  consumer goods 47, 51
  First-World 233
  kitsch 64
  universal 134
consumption 47, 51, 87, 90
  culture of 55
  democratization of 104
  energy 108
  fabrication of goods for 44
  identity of 49–50
  industrial 51, 58
  instant 62
  intensification of 339
  limitless 65
  mass consumption 46, 49, 58
  processes of 53
  and production 60, 72, 84, 101, 195, 224, 225, 267, 274
  resistance to 212
Cooper Square Housing, New York 115
Correa, Charles 190, 243*f*, 244, 285
  The New Landscape 245
  The New Urban Landscape 285
Correa, Rafael 297
Corringham Building, Bayswater (London) 20*f*, 21*f*
cost-benefit analyses 19
Cotter, Suzanne 289
courtyard housing model 190, 240
  Marcus Garvey Park Village, Brooklyn 27*f*
craft production 71, 196, 234, 272

critical culture 226–9
critical history 3, 6
critical intentionality 22
critical modernism 187
critical present, concept of 3, 36, 259
critical rationalism 98
Critical Regionalism 186, 187, 188, 188n16, 191, 206, 210, 224, 225
    fundamental strategy 204
    and world culture 203–4, 206
    see also resistance, architecture of
critical theory 3, 7, 36, 69
    of architecture of resistance 33, 188
    of building 7, 15
    development of 74–9
    Frankfurt School 35, 50, 69
    and Hochschule für Gestaltung (German design school) 77, 79
    and *The Human Condition* 50–2
    phenomenological–hermeneutical basis for 185
    see also Hochschule für Gestaltung (German design school, Ulm)
Crosby, Theo 12
    Uppercase 74
Crystal Palace, London 53, 54*f*, 61
    Great Exhibition of 1851 34, 55, 56, 277, 307
cultural identity 188, 225, 227
    see also "Place-Form and Cultural Identity" (Frampton)
culture
    architectural 211
        architecture as material culture 17, 22, 90
        architecture–place–culture–public realm configuration 2, 185
    bourgeois 201
    and civilization 200–1, 224, 225, 253
    of consumption 55
    critical 226–9
    design 6, 23
    elitist 194
    mass culture 7, 202, 333n49
    material culture 17, 22, 90, 144, 321
    and nature 208–9, 286
    world culture and Critical Regionalism 203–4, 206
    see also *Studies in Tectonic Culture* (Frampton)
Cumming, Roger A. 115
curriculum
    architectural 22
    design 283
    history 283
    ideology of 69–74
    technique 283
    see also "Apropos Ulm: Curriculum and Critical Theory" (Frampton); architectural education
cycle of production 58, 60, 62, 65, 195, 225, 274

The Damned (film) 209
de Blacam, Shane 313
de Carlo, Giancarlo 195, 261, 261n10
de Saint-Exupéry, Antoine 219
de Solà-Morales, Manuel 17, 170, 310
Debord, Guy
    Commentary on the Society of the Spectacle 24, 254, 255, 287, 336n57
Delijaicov, Alexandre 16*f*
democracy 5, 7
    citizen participation 261–2
    continual enactment of 33
    dependence on spaces of public appearance 178
    direct 296
    future of 96
    liberative 288
    and modernity 261
    participatory 8, 19
        participatory social 14
        suppression of 3
    popular 179
    power under 287
    and rationality 288
    social 19, 341
    and spaces of public appearance 99
democratization of consumption 104
Denmark
    Bagsværd Church 204–5, 205*f*
    Fuglsang Art Museum, Lolland 312, 314*f*
design xviii, 11
    airport terminals 312
    of buildings 2
    challenge of 23
    civic 17–18
    collective 262
    community 19
    deactivation of profession 104–5
    design culture 6, 23
    Design Methods approach 19
    dogmatic 104
    of environment 24
    and ethics 9
    graphic 12
    housing 26
    industrial 22, 23
    "mathematization" of 22
    modern 8
    participatory 15

public forms 8
resistance through 5
transformation through 15
"Typology and Design Method"
    (Colquhoun) 22
urban 93, 94, 98, 102, 104, 164, 170, 200,
    206, 286
    postwar 290
Design Methods approach 19
designing-based perspective 3
Desmoulins, Camille 127
destructive commodification 7, 98, 164
Deutsche Werkbund, Germany 56
Development Association Indigo, Mali 302
Dewey, John 73
Diallo, Alpha 302
Diallo, Bachir 234
Diamond, A.J. 115
Diba, Kamran 190, 244
Dilnot, Clive 8
Domus (Frampton) 191
Doric order 307
Doshi, Balkrishna 190, 240
    The Future of Indian Architecture 239
drawing 26, 141*f*, 143, 300
    in architectural practice 275
    as "instrument of intuition" 25
    re-drawing 326
    revival of 275
Drexler, Arthur 222
Drop City, Arizona 234
Dublin City Library, Ireland 313, 315
Ducasse, Isidore Lucien 8
Duchess Street house, London ("The Aurora
    Room") 39*f*
Duiker, Johannes 101
Dulles Airport, Washington 312

early modern movement 146
earthwork-roofwork dialectic 307, 309, 310,
    312, 315
École Nationale des Ponts et Chaussées 34, 45
Economist Building, London 114
education, architectural *see* architectural
    education
Egypt
    Nubian Museum, Aswan 237, 238
Einstein Tower, Potsdam 171
Eisenman, Peter 12–13, 26, 94, 265, 275
Electronic Corporation Township, Hyderabad
    244
El-Hakim, Mahmoud 237
elitism 194
Elliot, Cecil D. 124–5
    Technics and Architecture 124

Engineers Union building 138
Enlightenment 45, 193, 201, 202n7, 228, 295, 340
    conditioning perspectives of 84
    dark side 35, 82–3
    development of modern architecture after
        83
    French 177
    history 226
    ideal 228
    legacy of 79
    progress, myth of 35, 187, 203
    tabula rasa fantasies of 195
    utopian legacy of 226
environmental education 282–4
Enzensberger, Hans Magnus 268
Erskine, Ralph 171
Esberick, Joseph 107n15
Escobar, Arturo 191
Estado Novo (Portuguese totalitarian regime)
    289
European Union (EU)
    market-driven policies 19

Faber, Tobias 309
Fanon, Frantz 231
Farrell, Yvonne 1–2, 8–9, 313
Fathy, Hassan
    Architecture for the Poor 231
Feininger, Lyonel 59*f*
feminism 221
Finland
    The Kalevala 302
    Munkkiniemi suburb, Helsinki 142
    National Pensions Institute, Helsinki 138,
        141*f*, 171
    nature 153
    Säynätsalo Town Hall 14, 209, 276, 309
    Southwestern Finland Agricultural
        Cooperative Building, Turku 142
    structural map of General Town Plan,
        Imatra 152*f*
    Tooloo area, Helsinki 171
    Turku 700th Anniversary Exhibition and
        Trade Fair (1929) 142
    Turun Sanomat Building, Turku 142
    Viipuri City Library 142, 143
Fitts, Paul M. 75
Flyvbjerg, Bent 287–8
    Rationality and Power 286, 287
Ford Foundation Building, New York 49n25,
    336
formalism 76, 176
    rhetorical 95, 107
Foster, Hal 187
    The Anti-Aesthetic 306

Foster, Norman 129, 221, 312
  The Anti-Aesthetic 186
Fourier, Charles 234
Fox, Charles 53
Frampton, Kenneth 2–3, 4, 7
  ACSA/AIA award address (1991) 11
  architectural criticism 8, 317–43
    grammar of 334
    origins of criticism 334–5
    purpose of 343
    what remains unfinished (project issue) 334–43
  chronological concepts 6n19
  critical historical method 3, 6
  Golden Lion for Lifetime Achievement award (2018) 1
  interview with Mitrašinović 11–26
  meaning of architecture for 2, 5
  reading of Arendt 4–6, 11, 31–3, 36, 191, 324n21
  works of
    "America 1960–1970: on Urban Images and Theory" 7, 93, 101–9
    "Apropos Ulm: Curriculum and Critical Theory" 6, 34–5, 67–79
    "Civic Form" 96, 131–8
    Domus 191
    A Genealogy of Modern Architecture 36, 95
    "The Generic Street as a Continuous Built Form" 95, 96, 111–21
    "Industrialization and the Crises in Architecture" 31, 33–4, 53–65
    "Labour Work & Architecture" 11
    "The Legacy of Alvar Aalto" 96
    "Megaform as Urban Landscape" 17–18, 98, 166, 167–76
    Modern Architecture: A Critical History see *Modern Architecture: A Critical History* (Frampton)
    Modernity and Community 188
    "Modernization and Local Culture" 188, 231–8
    The Other Modern Movement: Architecture 1920–1970 332, 334
    "A Philosophical Excursus" 6
    "Place-Form and Cultural Identity" 7, 187, 224–5, 227
    "Plan Form and Topography in the Work of Kashef Chowdhury" 190, 247–50
    "The Predicament of the Place-Form: Notes from New York" 190, 239–45
    "Rappel à L'ordre: The Case for the Tectonic" 260
    "On Reading Heidegger," 185, 185n1, 193–7
    "Reflections on the Autonomy of Architecture: A Critique of Contemporary Production" 260
    "Seven Points for the Millennium: An Untimely Manifesto 261
    "The Status of Man and the Status of His Objects" 31
    Studies in Tectonic Culture xx 1, 2n6, 14, 17, 254, 264, 287
    Tadao Ando: Buildings, Projects, Writings 187
    "Tadao Ando's Critical Modernism" 187
    "Toward an Urban Landscape" 97
    "Towards a Critical Regionalism" 1, 188, 199–210, 224, 261, 281, 306
    "Towards an Agonistic Architecture" 33n7, 191n29, 262, 295–303, 316, 318, 340–1
    "Towards an Ontological Architecture" 327n33
    "2018 Society of Architectural Historians Plenary Talk" 4n15, 8, 251–5
    "Typology and Participation" 14–15, 261, 289–93
    "The Unfinished Project at the End of Modernity" 262–3, 305–16, 334, 337–8
    "What is Architecture?" 100
    see also *individual texts*
France 232, 313
  Archaeological Museum, Arles 132
  Barre à Marne (Noissy I complex) 170
  Bibliothèque Nationale 134
  Centre Pompidou, Paris 49n25, 336
  civic building 131
  Galerie d'Orléans, Paris 127
  La Celle-Saint Cloud, Maison de week-end (Le Corbusier) 307, 309
  Museum of the Great War, Péronne 132
  Palais Royale, Paris 127
  Paris exhibition (1900) 57
  Paris opera house 127
  Parisian arcades 127
  and philosophy 86
  Toulouse business school 313
Frank, Charlotte 132–3
Frankfurt School 4, 5, 227
  critical dialectic method 7
  critical theory 35, 50, 69
  ontological and phenomenological philosophy 36
  phenomenology 36

social and critical theory 34–5
socio-cultural analyses 51
succession of 51
Frankfurt-Römerberg Center, Germany 115, 118*f*, 120
Free University, Berlin 120
freedom 5, 6, 50, 111n2, 195, 325
Fretton, Tony 312
   AEIOU: Articles, Essays, Interviews and Out-Takes 313n4
Friendship Centre, Gaibandha, Bangladesh 190, 247, 249*f*
Friendship Hospital, Satkhira 250
Fuglsang Art Museum, Lolland, Denmark 312, 314*f*
functionalism 64
fungibility 87, 275
Futurism 25, 201, 278

Gadamer, Hans-Georg 22, 36
   Truth and Method 89–90
Galerie d'Orléans, Paris 127
Galleria Vittorio Emmanuele, Milan 129
garden cities 151, 178
   pioneers 123
   suburbs 143
   see also Garden City Puchenau, Austria
Garden City Puchenau, Austria 242*f*
Garnier, Charles 127
Gehry, Frank 274–5
"The Generic Street as a Continuous Built Form" (Frampton) 95, 96, 111–21
generic streets 7, 95, 115, 120
   comparative survey
      applicability and variation 115–16, 119–20
      linear arcade 115, 119–20
      multilevel megastructure 115, 120
      perimeter block 115–16, 119, 207
   concept/definition 112, 121
   criteria for categories and examples 115
   rationale and potential 120–1
   see also cities
Germany
   Alexanderplatz, Berlin 171
   Bauhaus (Staatliches Bauhaus) *see* Bauhaus (Staatliches Bauhaus), German art school
   Berlin Philharmonic 14, 172*f*
   Berlin U-Bahn megastructures 114
   Berlin Wall, fall of (1989) 134
   Bochum University 117*f*, 119, 171
   Chilehaus, Hamburg 171
   Deutsche Werkbund, 56
   Einstein Tower, Potsdam 171
   Frankfurt-Römerberg Center 115, 118*f*, 120
   Free University, Berlin 120
   German Applied Art School reform movement 70
   Hamburg-Steilshoop proposal (1966) 116
   Haupstadt Berlin competition entry (1958) 113
   Hochschule für Gestaltung school *see* Hochschule für Gestaltung (German design school, Ulm)
   Karlsruhe project (1971) 116, 119
   Nazi Germany 69
   Sparticist Revolt (1919) 60
   Spreebogen competition entry (1993) 132, 134
   Weimar Republic 70n2, 70n4, 143, 143n9, 170, 291
   see also Frankfurt School; Ulm city, Baden-Württemberg, Germany
Geschwister-Scholl Foundation, Germany 69, 70
Getty Center, Los Angeles 132
Giamarelos, Stylianos 188n16
Giedion, Sigfried 265
   Space, Time and Architecture 305–6
Gisel, Ernst 19
Glickman, Michael 13
Goethe, Johann Wolfgang 18
Golden Lane Housing (1952) 112
Gothic Revival 134, 272, 309
Gottmann, Jean 178, 206
Gowan, James 13
Grafton Architects 313
Gramsci, Antonio 3, 15, 73, 259
Grand Ducal School of Arts and Crafts, Germany 70n2
Gray, Eileen 276
Greece
   Greek National Library 136
   Philopappou Hill, Acropolis, Athens 306, 308*f*
   Stavros Niarchos Foundation Cultural Center, Athens 135*f*, 136
   see also Ancient Greece
Greenberg, Clement 94
   "Avant-Garde and Kitsch" 202
   "Modernist Painting" 202
Greenhill, Nigel 115
Gregotti, Vittorio 98, 170, 278, 284, 329
Gropius, Walter 70
   Zukunftskathedrale 60
Group 91, Dublin 313
Gruber, Karl 42*f*
Guggenheim Museum, New York 127
Guinea 8

INDEX

Kahere Eila Poultry Farming School,
   Koliagbe 189, 234, 235, 236f
Villa Eila 235
Gujarat Housing Board
   three-storey terraces for 244
Gujarat State Township 244
Gut Garkau farm complex, Ostholstein
   (Schleswig-Holstein) 140, 170

Habermas, Jürgen 22, 51, 65, 186n7, 188, 195,
      227, 228, 295
   'condition-situation' 229
   'Technology and Science as Ideology'
      226–7
Hadassah Hospital, Mount Scorpus 171
Hague City Hall, the Netherlands 129, 132
Hamburg-Steilshoop proposal (1966) 116
Hara, Hiroshi 211
Häring, Hugo 140, 170
Harris, Harwell Hamilton 265
Haupstadt Berlin competition entry (1958) 113
Hays, K. Michael 185, 186
"head-hand" connection 266
Hegel, G.W.F. 331, 332
hegemonic power 7, 224, 227, 296, 299, 300,
      341
Heideggar, Martin 7, 35, 36, 140, 206–7, 228
   on art 323n16
   bounded domain concept 35, 187, 207
   "Building, Dwelling, Thinking" 193, 206
   on "loss of nearness" 210
   paradoxical thesis 193
   reading 193–7
   see also "On Reading Heidegger"
      (Frampton)
Heikkinen, Mikko 189, 234, 302
Hertzberger, Herman 129, 274
HfG Ulm 19, 23
High Dam, Aswan 237
high-rise construction, micro-scaled
      environmental undesirability 196
High-Tech School 221
history and theory 23, 26, 266
Hochschule für Gestaltung (German design
      school, Ulm) 12, 34, 67, 68f, 69,
      72–5, 77
   creating 69
   and critical theory 77, 79
   and German Applied Art School reform
      movement 70
   raison d'être of 78
Hodges, Craig 26
Höger, Fritz 170
Hölderlin, Johann Christian Friedrich 297,
      323n16

Hollmén, Saija 303
Holyoke Center, Cambridge, Massachusetts 120
homeostatic plateau 196
homo faber 60, 87, 177, 306n1
   artifice versus instrumentality 46
   duality of 44–6
Hope, Thomas 39f
House of Friendship, Istanbul 170
housing
   aboriginal 302
   affordable 180, 293, 339
   aggregate housing 240
   assisted suburban housing 178
   basic stock 233
   Belapur Incremental Housing scheme,
      Navi Mumbai, 243f
   complexes 171
   Cooper Square Housing, New York 115
   cost of 76n20
   courtyard housing model 27f, 190, 240
   defining 41n10
   design 26, 289
   developments 151
   ecologically responsible production 146
   episodic terraces, Malagueira housing
      project 291
   estates 76n20
   extreme shortages 262, 289
   generic housing prototype 115
   high-density 18
   "housing question" 145
   London bye-law housing 112
   low-rise, high-density 26, 116, 151, 176,
      178, 190, 242f, 244, 285, 291
   mass housing 113
   Muslim communities 232
   public programs 177
   Royal Mint Square Housing, London 115, 119
   social 95, 289, 291
   socialist 116
   Spangen housing 115, 119
   spontaneous 284
   stereometric high-rise flat slab
      construction 196
   student housing 119
   terraced 242f, 290, 291
   Third World housing deficit 160
   unrealized projects 149n15
   see also Bouça housing settlement, Porto;
      Quinta da Malagueira housing
      project, Évora.; Royal Mint Square
      Housing, London 115, 119; São
      Victor housing settlement, Porto;
      Serviço de Apoio Ambulatório
      Local (SAAL)

Housing for Ahmedabad 244
Howard, Ebenezer 123
human artifice and public realm 40–1
The Human Condition (Arendt) 4–5, 6, 11, 12, 31, 32, 37–52, 131, 178
  and critical theory 50–2
  ontological implications 88
  relevance of 52
  see also Arendt, Hannah
Husserl, Edmund 36, 260, 266, 272
Huxtable, Ada Louise 106
Huyssens, Andreas 202

ideology
  Anglo-American perspective 219–23
  avant-garde 226
  and commodification 339
  of the curriculum 69, 72
  end of 194
  green-city 151
  mediatory 73
  of modernity 279, 330
  of the motopian open city 111n1
  national 340
  political 339
  postmodern 186
  and "project" 341
  Renaissance 272
  of waste 12, 65, 319
Incremental Housing, New Bombay 244
India 8
  Aranya Township, Bombay-Delhi highway 244
  Asian Games Housing, New Delhi 244
  Barefoot Architects 233, 234, 238
  Barefoot College campus, Tilonia, Rajasthan 189, 233
  Belapur Incremental Housing scheme, Navi Mumbai, 243*f*
  Casa dei Paria (Maison des Péons), Chandigarh 240
  Electronic Corporation Township, Hyderabad 244
  Gujarat State Township 244
  Incremental Housing, New Bombay 244
  Jeevan Bima Nagar Township 244
  Plan for New Bombay (1964) 285
  population 284, 285
  Santiniketan College 234
  social-work 233
  Studio Mumbai, Bombay 303
  Tube Housing for Ahmedabad 244
  Usha Niketan housing complex, New Delhi 244
  YMCA Staff Quarters 244

industrial design 22, 23, 71n5, 72, 74, 75, 84, 283
industrial production 34, 49, 56, 58, 72, 75, 76n20, 83, 108, 140, 158, 175, 279, 330
industrialization 6, 34, 58, 78, 109n23, 123, 196, 211
  advanced 75
  of agriculture 18
  future of 76n20
  "Industrialization and the Crises in Architecture" (Frampton) 31, 33–4, 53–65
  and crisis of 1851 53, 55–7
  and crisis of 1918 57–8, 60–2, 64–5
information theory 74
Institute for Architecture and Urban Studies (IAUS), New York 24, 26, 93, 95
  The Idea as Model 275
Institute of Architects Bangladesh, Dhaka 250
institutionalization 32, 324n22
intellect, pessimism of 3, 259
International Architecture Exhibition (16th) 2
International Union of Architects (UIA) 260
  Twentieth Congress 281
interstitial architecture 227
Iran, White Revolution 179
Ireland
  Dublin City Library 313, 315
  Parnell Square, Dublin 315
  University College Dublin 313
Italy 140
  Alexander Moissi house, Venice Lido 291
  Galleria Vittorio Emmanuele, Milan 129
  Luigi Bocconi University, Milan 311*f*, 313
  Nuovo Villaggio Matteotti, Terni 261n10
  Venice Biennale exhibition (1980) 222
Ito, Toyo 211

Jahn, Helmut 222
Jain, Bijoy 303
James, J.R. 105*f*
Jameson, Fredric 187, 190, 191
Japan
  architecture 211–17
  Hokkaido to Osaka megalopolis 285
  Koshino House, Ashiya, Kobe 214*f*, 217
  Shinjuku area, Tokyo 114, 173
  timber construction 211
  Tokyo Bay Project 173
  Tokyo Metropolitan Gymnasium 173
  Yoyogi National Gymnasium 309
Jeevan Bima Nagar Township, India 244
Jellicoe, Geoffrey 18
Jencks, Charles 187, 202, 222

INDEX 361

The Language of Post-Modern Architecture 221, 222
Meaning in Architecture 11, 305
Jenner, John 115
Johns, Jasper 222
Josic, Alexis 115, 117f, 118f, 119, 244
Journal of Architectural Education 266
Jugendstijl 58

Kahere Eila Poultry Farming School, Koliagbe, Guinea 189, 234, 235, 236f
Kahn, Louis 77, 106, 107n15, 220, 247, 254, 313
    monumentality, sense of 134
    "neo-Kahnian layout" 189, 234
    Philadelphia proposal (1953) 113
Kansai mega-airport, Japan 312
Kant, Immanuel 326, 331, 332, 333
Karlsruhe project (1971) 116, 119
Kennedy Airport, New York 13, 166
Kesting, Hanno 35, 72
Khan, Louis 247
kitsch 7, 49, 50, 56, 57, 65, 195
    Las Vegas 12, 94
Kivekäs, Eila 234, 235, 302
Klaus, Georg
    Cybernetics in the Light of Philosophy 74
Knowles, Ralph 197
Komonen, Markku 189, 234, 302
Koolhaas, Rem 17
Koshino House, Ashiya, Kobe (Japan) 214f, 217
Krier, Leon 170, 187, 220, 275
Kundera, Milan 18, 189

labor and work
    architectural corollaries of 37–8, 40
land settlement 97, 177–81, 240
    crises in age of megalopolis 284–6
landscape
    form 286
    remedial 7
    urban 157–64
    see also "Megaform as Urban Landscape" (Frampton)
language 58n6, 83, 100, 193, 195
    of 1979 336
    architectural 144n10
    of architecture 2n6
    of Classical architecture 83
    of the commodity 255
    of construction 2n6
    games 90, 306
    language-games 228
    "pattern language" concept 22
    twisting of 199

Larkin Building, Buffalo 127, 129
Las Vegas, United States 101–3, 107, 299
    kitsch 12, 94
    Las Vegas Strip 109n23, 222
law 158, 179
    and architecture 32n7
    bye-law housing 112
    of ecology 150n18
Le Corbusier 77, 111–12, 131, 168, 244, 251, 264, 276, 295–6, 309, 315
    Casa dei Paria (Maison des Péons), Chandigarh 240
    earthwork-roofwork dialectic 307
    La Celle-Saint Cloud, Maison de week-end 307, 309
    "Musée à Croissance Illimitée," proposal for 132
    Plan Obus 170
Leça Swimming Facility, Portugal 309
Lefaivre, Liliane 203
    The Grid and the Pathway 306
"The Legacy of Alvar Aalto: Evolution and Influence" (Frampton) 96
Lenin, Vladimir 58, 60
lgualada Cemetery, Barcelona 174f, 310
libertinage 55, 56
Libeskind, Daniel 275
libraries
    British Library, London 133f, 134
    Dublin City Library, Ireland 313, 315
    Greek National Library 136
    Viipuri City Library, Finland 142, 143
lifeworld 260, 266, 272
light and climate control 208
L'Illa Block, Barcelona 170, 310
linear arcade, generic street 115, 119–20
Lloyds Building, London 129
London Roads Study (1960) 114
London School of Economics, Marshall Building 313
Loos, Adolf 38, 40, 52, 197, 216, 291
    "Architecture 1910" 38
Los Angeles, United States 103, 109n23, 194, 318
    Brentwood area 132
    General Motors in 157
    Greater Los Angeles 285
    ground surfaces 105f
    "instant utopia" of 104
Lowrie House, Princeton 13
Luigi Bocconi University, Milan 311f, 313
Lynch, Kevin 94, 95, 106
    The Image of the City 102
Lyotard, Jean-François 188, 227
    The Postmodern Condition 228, 306

McCloy, John J. 69
machine production 49, 83, 225
McLeod, Mary 186
McNamara, Shelley 1–2, 8–9, 313
Madrid-Barajas Airport Terminal 4, Spain 311*f*
Makahari Convention Center, Chiba 173
Maki, Fumihiko
    Fujisawa Gymnasium 173
    "Some Thoughts on Collective Form" 171, 173
Malagueira housing project *see* Quinta da Malagueira housing project, Évora.
Maldonado, Tomás 12, 71, 73, 75–7, 265
    "Communication and Semiotics" 74
    Design, Nature and Revolution (Princeton lectures) (1967–1970) 11, 35
Malinovsky, Alexander (Bogdanov) 60–1, 64
Mander, Jerry 202
Manifesto of Futurist Architecture 46
mannerism 3, 252–3, 275
    elite 106
Marcuse, Herbert 5, 36, 51, 108, 203n11
    Eros & Civilization 11
Marika, Banduk 300
Marika-Alderton House, Australia 300
Martin, Leslie 220
Marx, Karl 49, 50, 64, 226, 268, 295, 340
Marxism 4, 50, 109n23, 191, 221
Masri, Leila 237
mass consumption 46, 49, 58
mass culture 7, 202, 333n49
mass production 18, 46, 58, 71n5
material culture 144, 321
    architecture as 17, 22, 90
materialism 65
Mayo, Jim 268
megaform 7, 17–18, 95, 98, 132, 134, 136, 168, 170–5
    concept 170, 173
    horizontal megaforms 176
    versus megastructure 171–2
    origin of 170–1
    see also "Megaform as Urban Landscape" (Frampton)
"Megaform as Urban Landscape" (Frampton) 17–18, 98, 166, 167–76
megalopolis 17, 50, 78, 153, 154, 160–3, 167, 212
    development 284, 286
    dystopia of 161
    ever-expanding 160, 176
    flux of 187, 207
    global 98
    land settlement crises in age of 284–6

    late modern 175
    modern 175
    Osaka 285
    processual function 187, 207
    random 18, 175
    regions 240
    "space-endlessness" of 170
    terminology 167, 178
    Tokaido 212
    type forms 114
    ubiquitous 158
    universal 179
megalopolitan conditions 7
megalopolitan ecology 150–1, 153
megaron 43
megastructures 168, 170, 208
    Berlin U-Bahn megastructures 114
    versus megaform 171–2
    multilevel 115, 120
Mehta, Pravina 285
Meier, Richard L. 95, 107–8, 129, 132
    A Communications Theory of Urban Growth 94, 107
Mendelsohn, Erich 171, 276
Mendes da Rocha, Paulo 310
Mengoni, Giuseppe 129
Mercuse, Herbert
    Eros and Civilization 306
Merleau-Ponty, Maurice 36
    The Phenomenology of Perception 89
Meyer, Hannes 107n15
Middleton, Robin 35
Mies van der Rohe, Ludwig 276
Miletus, Greek Hippodamia city, 5th Century BC 42*f*
Miliutin, N.A. 197
Miller, Henry 265
Miller, John 313
Miralles, Enric 173
Mishan, E.J. 108
    The Costs of Economic Growth 107
Mitrašinović, Miodrag 27*f*
    interview with Frampton 11–26
modern architecture 101, 140, 186, 212, 222, 282
    acceptance of 77
    conditions for 81–2
    development 83
    emergence of 82
    Eurocentric focus, perceived (Frampton) 3
    evolving of 82
    genealogy 3, 7
    history 36, 81, 82
    legacy 189
    modern architects 335
    new goals and limits for 213

role of 213
study of "on the periphery" 18
success and failure of 83
theory 38, 315
tropes of 190
Modern Architecture: A Critical History (Frampton) xiii, xxi, 1, 6, 17, 18, 23–5, 35, 36, 80*f*, 81–4, 96n11, 186, 251, 332
modern movement 18, 82, 216, 232n4, 250, 252, 263, 305, 335, 341
  British Modern Movement 315
  demise of 337
  early 146
  ethos of 342
  evolution of 254
  history 170, 317
  humanizing 102
  pre-war 223
  project of 323n15, 337, 338, 343
  rationality of 112–13
  revolutionary 187, 221, 335
  rise and fall of 251
  and tectonic form 254, 307
modernity
  concept 220, 335
  and democracy 261
  generic 71n5
  ideology of 279, 330
  and modern movement 342
  origin of 81
  and phenomenology 23
  "pluralizing modernity" 191
  unfinished project of 8, 227–8, 259, 295, 341, 343
  universal 213
  see also "The Unfinished Project at the End of Modernity" (Frampton)
Modernity and Community (Frampton) 188
modernization 199, 200, 202–3, 215, 237, 274
  and avant-garde 201
  and consumerism 232–3
  cultural 201
  forms of 238
  global 185, 187, 189, 210
  instrumental 5
  liberative role of 224
  and local culture 232
  process of 201, 213, 223, 232, 233, 235
  of society 338, 341, 342
  socio-cultural 201, 333n49
  of Swedish middle-class society 23
  technology-driven 188
  "utilitarian instrumentalism" 33
  and vernacular culture 235

"Modernization and Local Culture" (Frampton) 188, 231–8
Mohammed, Rafeek 234
Moneo, Rafael 17, 170, 309, 310
Montessori School Delft, The Netherlands 273*f*
monumentality 106, 134
  misplaced 49n25, 336
Morris, Charles 73–4
Morris, William 56, 303
  "The Revival of Architecture" 56n3
Morris Gift Shop, San Francisco 127
Moss, Eric Owen 318, 319, 323
Motopia 40, 103, 194
Mouffe, Chantal 19, 262
  Agonistics. Thinking the World Politically 303
Muller, Walter 74
multilevel megastructure, generic street 115, 120
Mumford, Lewis 268, 279, 330
Munkkiniemi suburb, Helsinki 142
Murcutt, Glenn 300
Museum for the First World War, Peronne 132
Museum of Modern Art, New York 23, 26, 41n9, 103n7, 132, 222, 310
Museum of Modern Art, Rio de Janeiro 310
Museum of the Great War, Péronne 132
Muthesius, Herman 56
Myer, John R.
  A View from the Road 102

Narodnik reformism 60
National Assembly, Sher-e-Bangla Nagar 247
National Pensions Institute, Helsinki 138, 141*f*, 171
nature 84, 195, 215
  action of 217
  Ando's concept of 213, 216, 217
  beauty of 153
  and climate 3, 303
  contingent, of architecture 271
  and culture 208–9, 286
  dynamic 229
  ecological 197
  erosions of 44
  Finnish 153
  man's metabolism with 51, 65, 134
  new 124, 161, 162
  processual, of a laboratory building 49n25, 336
  rapport with 195
  reconnection with 35
  relationship with 84, 196, 208, 228
Nazi Germany 69

neo-capitalism 73, 104, 240
neo-Classicism 106n15
neo-Conservatism 226
neo-Historicists 226
neo-Kantian aesthetics 201
neo-liberalism 293, 336, 339
neo-Marxism 12
neoplasticism 201
neo-Rationalism 170
neo-Situationists 226
The Netherlands
    Centraal Beheergebouw insurance company office building 128*f*
    Central Library, The Hague 129
    Hague City Hall 129, 132
    Montessori School Delft, The Netherlands 273*f*
    Pampas Plan, Rotterdam 171
    rebuilding of Rotterdam post-war 206
    Spangen Housing, Rotterdam 115, 119
Neues Bauen movement 140
Neutra, Richard 276
New Utopians 104
Newark Airport, New Jersey 13, 166
Nietzsche, Friedrich 228
Nieuwenhuys, Constant
    "New Babylon" 46–7
Nitschke, Oscar 101
Nolli map of Rome 103
nonjudgmental conformism 18, 191, 299
non-place urban realm 12, 41, 94, 111, 157, 176, 194, 195, 207n18, 298
Nordic classical form 142
Norway, traditional shopping streets preserved in 179
Nouvel, Jean 131
Nubian Museum, Aswan 237, 238
Nuovo Villaggio Matteotti, Terni (Italy) 261n10

Ockman, Joan
    The Pragmatist Imagination 98
O'Donnell, Sheila 313
office buildings 129, 138
    Centraal Beheergebouw insurance company office building, the Netherlands 128*f*
Ohtaka, Masato
    "Some Thoughts on Collective Form" 171, 173
Olbia Social Centre, Akdeniz Üniversitesi, nr. Antalya 235, 238
"On Reading Heidegger" (Frampton) 185, 185n1, 193–7
ontology 86, 87, 155, 188, 195, 196, 212, 227, 334n52
    and action 33

ahistorical-ontological future 228
    of building 263, 305, 315
    Human Condition, ontological implications 88
    ontological and phenomenological philosophy 6, 36
    ontological architecture 36, 90, 327n33
operationalism 73
operative criticism 24
opportunist pragmatism 121
Oppositions 34
optimism of the will 3, 259
organicism 24, 142–6, 149–50
The Other Modern Movement: Architecture 1920–1970 (Frampton) 332, 334

Palais Royale, Paris 127
Pampas Plan, Rotterdam 171
Parent, Michel 46
Paris opera house 127
Parisian arcades 127
Parnell Square, Dublin 315
participatory democracy 19
Patel, Shirish 285
Patteeuw, Véronique
    "Critical Regionalism for our Time" 1
Patterns of Association 112
Paulista School 310, 313
Paulistano Athletic Club, São Paulo 310
Paulson, Gregor 23
Paxton, Joseph 34, 53, 54*f*, 55, 61
    see also Crystal Palace, London
pedagogy 22
perimeter block, generic street 115–16, 119, 207
peristyle 149, 312
pessimism of the intellect 3, 259
phalanstère, paradigm of 234
phenomenology 13, 14, 17, 18, 24, 86, 87
    critical 89
    existential traditions 227
    Frankfurt School 36
    of Husserl 86, 272
    interface between infrastructural and superstructural realms of production 197
    leading philosophers 36
    and modernity 23
    phenomenological essence 206
    phenomenological limits 112
    phenomenological-hermeneutical basis for place/production distinction 7
Philopappou Hill, Acropolis, Athens 306, 308*f*
Piano, Renzo 25, 312
picturesque pluralism 94, 102
Pinós, Carme 173

Piven, Francis 108n20
place 41n10, 98, 121, 204, 240
   and architecture 123–9
      architecture–place–culture–public realm configuration 2, 185
   as Aristotelean phenomenon 195–6
   creation 84, 97, 196, 197, 212
   culture of 188, 223
   non-place urban realm 12, 41, 94, 111, 157, 176, 194, 195, 207n18, 298
   permanent 46
   pre-condition for 195
   and production 7, 185, 195, 196
   public 47, 309
   resonance of 196
   sense of 119, 120, 167
   social meaning, conscious signification of 195
   versus space 194, 206, 253
   see also place-form
place-form 95, 125, 126, 187–9, 207–10, 278, 307
   resistance of 206–8
   as a space of public appearance 307
   urban 244
   see also "Place-Form and Cultural Identity" (Frampton)
"Place-Form and Cultural Identity" (Frampton) 7, 187, 224–5, 227
Plan for New Bombay (1964) 285
"Plan Form and Topography in the Work of Kashef Chowdhury" (Frampton) 190, 247–50
planning 158, 160
   Aalto's approach to 151
   advocacy 102, 261n10
   Aicher model 78
   American 102
   city 299
   contemporary 288
   dominant 157
   education 261, 286
   environmental 97, 157
   formalistic 151
   in the nineteenth century 123
   open-city 151
   practices 261n10
   profession 97, 108, 157, 158
   rationalistic 40
   regional 70n4, 71, 96, 150n18
   tabula rasa 121
   town 70n4
   urban 18, 108, 121, 167, 206
plans 146, 161, 189, 222, 223
   apartment 149
   diagrammatic 128*f*
   "doughnut" 129
   forms 129
   housing 242*f*
   infrastructure 206
   layout 149
   master 151, 175, 206
   physical 157
   rational 235
   regional 151, 153
   site 242*f*
   structure 157
Poelzig, Hans 170
polis (city) 7, 32, 35, 40, 57, 191
   see also cities
Pop Art 103, 109
populism 7, 12, 22, 49n25, 94, 106, 194, 336
   admass 76
   communicative or instrumental sign 204
   cultural 222
populist urbanism 102
Portas, Nuno 262
Portman, John 129
Portugal
   Boa Nova Teahouse, Leça da Palmeira 309
   Bouça housing settlement, Porto 14–15, 261, 290–1, 292*f*
   Carnation Revolution (1974) 262
   cities 262, 289
   Estado Novo (Portuguese totalitarian regime) 289
   Leça Swimming Facility 309
   Museu de Arte Contemporânea de Serralves, Porto 289
   São Victor housing settlement, Porto 14–15, 261, 290
Portuguese Spring (1974) 15, 289
Post-Modern Architectures 202
postmodernism
   architecture 202, 220, 335
   postmodern condition 226–9
   reactionary 187
power 40, 228, 336n57, 340
   absolute 64
   agencies of 79n27
   centralization of 227
   communicational 223
   corporate 19, 299
   cultural 223
   decentralization of 227
   devolution of 227
   forms of 79n27
   of global mega-corporations 296
   hegemonic 7, 191, 224, 227, 296, 299, 300, 341
   hydro-power 237
   institutions of 276
   labor-power 49
   legitimate 207

nihilistic 328n35
persuasive 202
political 52
and rationality 287–8
and reason 83, 282, 287
"saving power" 323n16
solar 234
spiritual and temporal 38
tribal power relations 288
world finance 303n15
pragmatic-instrumentalism 73
Pravda newspaper building, Leningrad 63*f*
"praxiology' 73
praxis (radical action) 4, 5, 32, 73, 197, 323n16
predicament 8, 12, 64, 75, 104, 167, 200
    of architecture 76
    capitalist 7
    ecological 158
    environmental 261
    modern 211
    political 108
    theme of 259
    of urbanized region 159–60
    Western 194
"The Predicament of the Place-Form: Notes from New York" (Frampton) 190, 239–45
private realm 52
    and rise of the social 43
PRL Housing for Ahmedabad 244
processual function
    of airports 47, 337
    of labor 37, 87
    laboratory building, processual nature of 49n25, 336
    megalopolis 187, 207
    modern development 206
production 38n4, 44, 50, 51n32, 64, 83, 192, 200, 244
    actual 67
    agricultural 123
    architectural 187, 267
    artistic 197
    arts 329
    asceticism of 55
    building 224
    categories of 87
    conditions of 332
    consumer 196
    and consumption 60, 72, 84, 101, 195, 224, 225, 267, 274
    craft 71, 196, 234, 272
    cycle of 58, 60, 62, 65, 195, 225, 274
    demands of 76
    environmental dialectic of 196
    function of 60

    horticultural 197
    human 197
    industrial 34, 49, 56, 58, 72, 75, 76n20, 83, 108, 140, 158, 175, 279, 330
    levels of 125
    machine 49, 83, 225
    mass production 18, 46, 58, 71n5
    maximized 267
    means of 57, 60
    mechanical 46
    modes of 84
    19th century 57
    optimization of 35, 47, 51, 84, 224
    and place 7, 185, 195, 196
    pre-industrial 55
    primary demands of 76
    primary system of 55
    production art 62n8
    rationalized 47, 125, 225
    serial 144
    stereometric high-rise flat slab construction 196
    sub-categories 196
    of theory 267
    urban 107
Program of the Productivist Group 61–2
Proletkult movement, Soviet Union 61, 62, 64
public buildings 40, 100, 107, 126, 277
    form and influence 126–7, 129
public mode 7, 187, 207
public realm
    decline in 15
    Frampton on 2–3, 5
    perceived erosion of 3
    and human artifice 40–1, 43
    micro public realms 18
    "negative" urban form 52
    public micro-realms 97, 179
    public versus social 15
    recovery of 7
    relationship with architecture 5
    transcendental worldliness of 32
public world 4–6, 319
    common public world 3, 5, 15
Pugin, A.W.N. 56, 272
Purism 201

quadripartite theory (Semper) 260
Quinta da Malagueira housing project, Évora. 14, 15, 261
    unplastered concrete block 291

railway terminals 127, 129
Raina, Neehar 189
Rainer, Roland 18, 244
    Liveable Environments 26

Randstad, North-Western Europe 285
Rapoport, Anatol 73
"Rappel à L'ordre: The Case for the Tectonic" (Frampton) 260
rationalisation 83
  and rationality 287
rationality 65, 98
  abstract 112
  autonomous 51
  and democracy 288
  dialectical 67
  of discourse 83
  internal 203
  maximized 267
  of normative technique 206
  political 199
  and power 287–8
  and rationalisation 287
  techno-scientific 261
rationalized production 47, 125, 225
Ratzel, Friedrich 170
reason
  abstract 206
  instrumental 201, 203
  occidental 229
  and power 83, 282, 287
"Reflections on the Autonomy of Architecture: A Critique of Contemporary Production" (Frampton) 260
Reidy, Affonso 310
Reiner, Roland 242*f*
remedial landscape 7
Renaissance 45, 81, 272
res publica 43, 103, 196, 266, 277
resistance, architecture of 3, 6, 7–8, 18, 109–210, 262
  Critical Regionalism 203–4, 206
  critical theory 33, 188
  culture and nature 208–9
  earthwork 307
  light and climate control 208
  place-form, resistance of 206–8
  topography 208
  visual versus the tactile 209–10
Reuter, Jenni 303
Rewal, Raj
  Asian Games Housing, New Delhi 244
Richards Laboratories, University of Pennsylvania 49n25, 336
Ricoeur, Paul 187–8, 188n15, 200, 235
  History and Truth 199
  "Universal Civilisation and National Cultures" 224, 306
Ringstrasse plan, Vienna 39*f*, 41, 46
Rittel, Horst 19

Robson Square, Vancouver 169*f*
Rockefeller Center, New York 120, 129
Roerich, Nick 23
Rogers, Richard 129, 221, 312
roofwork *see* earthwork-roofwork dialectic
Rossi, Aldo 170
Rowe, Colin 25
Roy, Bunker 233
Royal College of Art
  Lethaby Lecture 77
Royal Mint Square Housing, London 115, 119
Rudofsky, Bernard
  Architecture Without Architects 233
Ruscha, Eduard 106, 109, 109n23
Ruskin, John 53, 56
Russia
  Civil War 60
  Gum Store, Moscow 119
  post-war cultural impact (1918) 62
  Russian Constructivists 25
  Russian Revolution (1917) 14, 60, 64
  see also Soviet Union, former
Rykwert, Joseph 94

Saarinen, Eero 312
Sabikhi, Ranjit 244
Saint-Exupéry, Antoine de 9
Salazar, António 289
Sandman, Helena 303
Sant'Elia, Antonio
  Città Nuova 46, 48*f*
Santiniketan College, India 234
São Victor housing settlement, Porto 14–15, 261, 290
Sartogo, Piero 94
Sartre, Jean-Paul 36
Säynätsalo Town Hall, Finland 14, 209, 276, 309
S.C. Johnson Administration Building, Wisconsin 127
Scharoun, Hans 14, 106, 140, 170
  Breslau Werkbund exhibition building (1929) 171
Schiedhelm, Manfried 115
Schilder, Paul
  Das Körperschema 89
Schindler, R.M. 276
Schnaidt, Claude 12, 35, 74, 75, 76, 77
Scholl, Hans and Sophie 69
Scholl, Inge Aicher 70
Schultes, Axel 132–3
Schumacher, Tom 94
science 50n29, 104, 275, 287
  applied 75, 97, 157, 227, 228, 274
  and art 61, 104, 275
  empirical 45, 272

life-science 221
political 69
science envy 267, 274, 275
science-based instrumentality 22
Spenglerian critics of 75
and technique 51
techno-science 124, 140, 219, 226–8, 267, 306
theory and epistemology 72
value-free 109
Scott Brown, Denise 94, 95, 101, 106
"Learning from Pop" 102–3
"On Pop Art, Permissiveness and Planning" 109
Seabird Island School, Agassiz, British Columbia 301*f*, 302
Segal, Paul 266
Semenov, V. 63*f*
Semper, Gottfried
Four Elements of Architecture 307
Sempter, Gottfried 260, 266–7
The Four Elements of Architecture 277, 307
Sen no Rikyū 213, 215, 216
Senegal
women's centre in 302–3
Serageldin, Ismail 232, 238
serial production 144
Sert, Josep Lluís 120
Serviço de Apoio Ambulatório Local (SAAL)
housing settlements, Porto 14–15, 262, 289
organizational power 290–1
"Seven Points for the Millennium: An Untimely Manifesto" (Frampton) 261
Shinjuku area, Tokyo 114, 173
Shinohara, Kazuo 211
Shustar New Town, Iran 244
Siedlung Halen, Bern, Switzerland 12, 18, 242*f*, 244
sign architecture 102–3
signature building 274
Singh, Kuldip 244
Sir John Soane Museum, London 263
Sitte, Camillo 41–2
City Planning According to Artistic Principles 43
Sittesque "method" of urban design 102
Siza, Álvaro 14, 17, 25, 261, 268, 282–3, 309, 341
architecture of 289–93
Smithson, Alison 112, 113–14, 171
Smithson, Jerzy 18
Smithson, Peter 112, 113–14, 171
social sciences xviii, 107, 108, 109

socialism
bureaucratic 76
Society of Architectural Historians (SAH) 190
Plenary Talk (2018) 4n15, 8, 251–5
Soltan, Jerzy 18, 104, 265
Southwestern Finland Agricultural Cooperative Building, Turku 142
sovereignty 6, 33
individual 240
local 191, 299
political 191, 253
potential 263, 315
Soviet Union, former
avant-garde 142
Pravda newspaper building, Leningrad 63*f*
Proletkult movement 61, 62, 64
revolutionary art 4, 33n7
Winter Palace, St. Petersburg 58
see also Lenin, Vladimir; Russia
space 15, 88, 179, 235, 252, 264, 336
abstract connotations of 194, 206
of arrival 138
of assembly 96, 131
cellular 277
central 129
communal 159
cultural 34
enclosed 119
hierarchical organization of 87, 254
historical 328n35
inaccessible 47
interior/internal 128*f*, 132
limit of 216
metaphysical 84
occupiable 248
open 103n7, 112, 248
passing through 85
phenomenological experience of 14
versus place 194, 206, 253
primitive 212
pseudo-public 129
public 32n6, 52, 97, 114, 115, 178, 319
surrogate 129
top-lit 132
representational 127
semi-public 276
"space-endlessness" 168, 170, 212, 253
space-form 15
street 116, 119, 121
terminology 194, 206
theatrical 189, 234
urban 47, 52, 116, 119, 121, 168, 336
see also space of appearance; space of public appearance
space of appearance 5, 15, 18, 32, 41, 100, 254

human 17, 38, 94, 95, 103, 166, 207, 320
public *see* space of public appearance
  see also Arendt, Hannah
space of public appearance 2, 13, 14, 34, 47, 51, 97, 131, 134, 177, 179, 237, 254, 262, 263, 277, 278, 303, 309, 312, 313, 315
  Brazilian 310
  civic institution as 96
  and crisis 56, 57, 60
  labor and work 38, 40
  new 129
  place-form as 307
  spontaneous 64
  surrogate 127
  see also Arendt, Hannah
Spain
  Barajas Airport, Madrid 136, 311*f*, 312
  Barcelona Olympics (1992) 173
  Igualada Cemetery, Barcelona 174*f*, 310
  L'Illa Block, Barcelona 170, 310
Spangen Housing, Rotterdam 115, 119
Sparticist Revolt (1919), Germany 60
sprawl *see* suburban sprawl; urban sprawl
Spreebogen competition entry, Germany (1993) 132, 134
St. John Wilson, Colin 134, 140
Stansted Airport, London 312
state of things 295–7
Stavros Niarchos Foundation Cultural Center, Athens 135*f*, 136
Stein, Gertrude 127
Stern, Robert 222
Stevens, Thomas 12
Stile Floreale 58
Stirling, James 13
Stockholm Exhibition (1930) 23, 338
streets 124, 134
  active space 121
  "art of the street" 61
  and avant-garde 111–15
  double-sided nature of 112n5
  Norway, traditional shopping streets preserved in 179
  street space 116, 119, 121
  see also "The Generic Street as a Continuous Built Form" (Frampton); generic streets
structuralism, French 221
student protests (1968) 13
Students for a Democratic Society (SDS) 13
Studies in Tectonic Culture (Frampton) xxi, 2n6, 14, 17, 254, 264, 287
Studio Mumbai, Bombay 303
style 57, 84, 154, 221, 224, 225, 226, 276
  International Style 212–13

noble 64
regional 299
Sukiya 213, 215
wabi 215
suburban sprawl 196
suburbanization 178, 179
Summerson, Sir John 315
Suplicy, Marta 14, 16*f*
Svappavaara proposal, Lapland 171
Sweden
  middle-class society 23
  social democracy 19, 23
  Stockholm Exhibition (1930) 23, 338
Switzerland
  Atelier 5, 12, 18, 242*f*, 244
symbolism 106, 234
Szacka, Léa-Catherine
  "Critical Regionalism for our Time" 1

tabula rasa planning 121, 195, 208
Tadao Ando: Buildings, Projects, Writings (Frampton) 187
"Tadao Ando's Critical Modernism" (Frampton) 187
Tafuri, Manfredo
  Architecture and Utopia 322n12
  Theories and History of Architecture 24
Tagore, Rabindranath 234
Takeyama, Kiyoshi 215
Taki, Koji 187
Takyia, André 16*f*
Tange, Kenzo 173, 309
Taniguchi, Yoshio 132
Taut, Bruno 173
  Die Stadtkrone 170
Taylor, Frederick Winslow 75
Team 10 112, 113, 114
technocratic commodification 96, 98, 181
techno-science 124, 140, 219, 226–8, 267, 306
tectonic form 86, 126, 180, 187, 204, 252, 253, 278, 302
  Brazilian tradition 310
  core form versus art form 307
  counter-hegemonic 191, 299
  culture of the tectonic 264
  and institutional discourse 275
  and modern movement 254, 307
  Paulista School 310, 313
  versus purely technical 209
  tectonic value of each component 210
  tectonic versus scenographic 208–9
  tectonic versus topographic 223, 260
  and the typological 276
  see also Studies in Tectonic Culture (Frampton)

Temple Bar district, Dublin 313
Terragni, Giuseppe 276
"time-table war" 57–8
Tokyo Bay Project 173
Tokyo Metropolitan Gymnasium 173
Topaz Medallion for Architectural Education 259n2
topography 170, 208, 223, 260, 276, 278, 307
   and climate 180, 303
   critical importance 208–9
   internal 237
   irregular 208
   natural 178
   topographic syndrome 171
   volcanic, of Rio de Janeiro 168
   and water 250
Toronto Society for the Study of Social and Political Thought 33–4
totalitarianism 228
"Toward an Urban Landscape" (Frampton) 97
"Towards a Critical Regionalism" (Frampton) 1, 188, 199–210, 224, 261, 281, 306
"Towards an Agonistic Architecture" (Frampton) 33n7, 191n29, 262, 295–303, 316, 318, 340–1
   see also agonistic architecture
"Towards an Ontological Architecture" (Frampton) 327n33
Townscape 240
transfiguration, architecture as act of 33
Transformations exhibition (1979) 221–2
Tube Housing for Ahmedabad, India 244
Tuomey, John 313
Turkey
   House of Friendship, Istanbul 170
   Olbia Social Centre, Akdeniz Üniversitesi, nr. Antalya 235
Turku 700th Anniversary Exhibition and Trade Fair (1929) 142
Turner, John
   "Dwelling Resources in South America" 231
Turner, R. Gregory
   Construction Economics and Building Design 124
Turun Sanomat Building, Turku 142
"Typology and Participation" (Frampton) 14–15, 261, 289–93
typology/typologies 129, 143, 170, 175, 235, 260, 276, 342
   and action 15
   building 53
   civic and public 95
   Colquhoun on 22
   modernist 289
   normative 220
   Siza, architecture of 289–93
   traditional 250
Tzonis, Alex 203
   The Grid and the Pathway 306

Ulm (journal) 69
Ulm 2 72
Ulm 5 74
Ulm 10/11 75, 76
Ulm city, Baden-Württemberg, Germany
   "Apropos Ulm: Curriculum and Critical Theory" (Frampton) 6, 34–5, 67–79
   HfG Ulm 19, 23
   Hochschule für Gestaltung school
      see Hochschule für Gestaltung (German design school, Ulm)
   Münster Cathedral 68*f*
   Neo-Marxist circle 12
Ulmer, Gregory L. 25
"The Unfinished Project at the End of Modernity" (Frampton) 262–3, 305–16, 334, 337–8
unfinished project of modernity 8, 227–8, 259, 295, 341, 343
   see also modern movement; modernity; "The Unfinished Project at the End of Modernity" (Frampton)
Ungers, O.M. 19
Unified Education Center, Jambeiro em Guaianases, São Paulo 16*f*
Unified Science 74
United Kingdom
   Arts and Craft movement, England 56, 143
   British Library, London 133*f*, 134
   British Modern Movement 315
   British Productivist school 221
   Brunswick Center, London 118*f*, 120
   Byker Wall housing complex, Newcastle 171
   Crystal Palace, London 34, 53, 54*f*, 55, 56, 61, 277, 307
   Duchess Street house, London ("The Aurora Room") 39*f*
   Economist Building, London 114
   Linear City Proposal for linked townships in Central Lancashire 105*f*
   Lloyds Building, London 129
   London bye-law housing 112
   London Roads Study (1960) 114
   London School of Economics, Marshall Building 313
   Royal Mint Square Housing, London 115, 119
   Sir John Soane Museum, London 263

Stansted Airport, London 312
Townscape (mid-50s) 102
Willis, Faber, Dunmar Building, Ipswich 129
United States
  Anglo-American perspective 219–23
  Atlanta Peachtree Center, Georgia 129
  Baker Dormitory, Cambridge (Massachusetts) 171
  black-top parking lots 286
  Boston–Washington corridor 166, 178, 285
  Cannery Building, San Francisco 107n15
  childhood mortality statistics 239
  Cooper Square Housing, New York 115
  Drop City, Arizona 234
  Dulles Airport, Washington 312
  Ford Foundation Building, New York 49n25, 336
  Getty Center, Los Angeles 132
  Guggenheim Museum, New York 127
  Holyoke Center, Cambridge, Massachusetts 120
  Institute for Architecture and Urban Studies (IAUS), New York 24, 26, 93, 95
  Kennedy Airport, New York 13, 166
  Larkin Building, Buffalo 127, 129
  Las Vegas *see* Las Vegas, United States
  Los Angeles *see* Los Angeles, United States
  mobile-home industry 51
  Morris Gift Shop, San Francisco 127
  Museum of Modern Art, New York 132
  Newark Airport, New Jersey 13, 166
  planning 102
  Richards Laboratories, University of Pennsylvania 49n25, 336
  Rockefeller Center, New York 120, 129
  S.C. Johnson Administration Building, Wisconsin 127
  urbanization 94
universal civilization 5
The Universitas Project (Museum of Modern Art) 23
University College Dublin 313
University of Alberta, Edmonton 115, 117*f*, 129, 235
urban containment, macro-scaled environmental desirability 196
urban design 93, 94, 98, 102, 104, 164, 170, 200, 206, 286
  postwar 290
urban landscape 95, 157–64
  see also "Megaform as Urban Landscape" (Frampton)

urban planning 18, 108, 121, 167, 206
urban populations, capital cities 284
urban schemes, utopian 220, 335
urban sprawl 40, 298
urbanism 17, 47, 95, 160
  and American architecture 240
  fragmentary 164
  populist 102
  theoretical 220
urbanization 41, 196
  American 94
  and the city 7
  continual 150
  degrees of 190
  of developing nations 293
  escalating 240
  global 93
  and industrial production 83
  regional 123, 126, 154, 240
  scale of 123
  split with architecture 35
  spontaneous 245
  unending 7, 17, 93, 166
Usha Niketan housing complex, New Delhi 244
utilitarianism 56, 60, 196
  "utilitarian instrumentalism" 33
utopia/utopianism 3, 25, 46, 56, 194, 203, 318
  anti-utopianism 104, 220
  of avant-garde 83
  community 234
  endemic 113
  Enlightenment 193, 226
  industrialized utopias 83
  instant utopia of Los Angeles 104
  New Utopians 104
  a priori approach 121
  urban schemes 220, 335
Utzon, Jørn 173, 204, 309

Valle, Gino 19
Van der Rohe, Mies 193, 313
Van der Velde, Henry 70n4
Van Eyck, Aldo 177, 244, 278
Van Stigt, Jan 244
Vastu-Shilpa Foundation 240
Vattimo, Gianni 22, 36, 260, 269
Venice Biennale exhibition (1980) 222
Venturi, Robert 94, 101, 187
  "Complexity and Contradiction in Architecture" 41, 95, 106, 222
Venturi, Scott Brown and Associates 12
vernacular 23, 38, 40, 211, 215, 234, 277, 291, 299
  domestic 22

Finnish 145, 146–7
form 146, 307, 309
illusory 194
kitsch 83
loss of 49
lost 204
quasi-vernacular 238
true 106
urban 42*f*
vernacular revival 224
Verne, Michel 127
Verroust, Jacques 46
Vesnin Brothers 101
Vidyadhar Nagar Satellite City Plan, Jaipur 244
Vietnam War 13
Viipuri City Library, Finland 142, 143
Villa Eila, Guinea 235
Villac, Maria Isobel 310
Visconti, Luchino 209
Vogelweidplatz Sports Center, Vienna 171
Von Moltke, Helmuth 57–8

Wachsmann, Konrad 35, 69–70, 267
Webber, Melvin 12, 41, 94, 95, 106, 107, 176, 194
"Comprehensive Planning and Social Responsibility" 108
"The Role of Intelligence Systems in Urban Design" 108
see also non-place urban realm
Weimar Republic, Germany 70n4, 143, 143n9
Bauhaus (Staatliches Bauhaus), art school 75
Grand Ducal School of Arts and Crafts 70n2
interwar social housing 291
Zeilenbau pattern 170
Welfare State 221
Welzenbacher, Lois 171
Werwerka, Stefen 114
"What is Architecture?" (Frampton) 100
The Whole Earth Catalog 234
Wiener, Norbert 74
will, optimism of 3, 259
Willis, Faber, Dunmar Building, Ipswich 129
Winter Palace, St. Petersburg 58
Wittgenstein, Ludwig 216
Wolfe, Tom 106
Woods, Shadrach 115, 117*f*, 118*f*, 119, 120, 244
Hamburg-Steilshoop proposal (1966) 116
Karlsruhe project (1971) 116, 119
What U Can Do 97
workers' councils 14
world architecture 18, 189–90, 321n8
world culture
and Critical Regionalism 203–4, 206
world literature 18
worldlessness 46, 49, 50
Wright, Frank Lloyd 127, 276

Yoyogi National Gymnasium, Japan 309

Zen Buddhism 215
"zero-growth" feedback syndrome 196
Zevi, Bruno 24